Women Warriors in Southeast Asia

This book brings together a wide range of case studies to explore the experiences and significance of women warriors in Southeast Asian history from ancient to contemporary times.

Using a number of sources, including royal chronicles, diaries, memoirs and interviews, the book discusses why women warriors were active in a domain traditionally preserved for men, and how they arguably transgressed peacetime gender boundaries as agents of violence. From multidisciplinary perspectives, the chapters assess what drove women to take on a variety of roles, namely palace guards, guerrillas and war leaders, and to what extent their experiences were different to those of men. The reader is taken on an almost 1,500-year long journey through a crossroads region well-known for the diversity of its peoples and cultures, but also their ability to creatively graft foreign ideas onto existing ones. The book also explores the re-integration of women into post-conflict Southeast Asian societies, including the impact (or lack thereof) of newly established international norms, and the frequent turn towards pre-conflict gender roles in these societies.

Written by an international team of scholars, this book will be of interest to academics working on Southeast Asian Studies, Gender Studies, low-intensity conflicts and revolutions, and War, Conflict, and Peace Studies.

Vina A. Lanzona is Associate Professor of History and the Former Director of the Center for Philippine Studies (2011–2015) at the University of Hawai'i at Mānoa. Author of *Amazons of the Huk Rebellion: Gender, Sex and Revolution in the Philippines* (2009), she is currently working on two book projects: on the participation of Filipinos and Filipino Americans in the Spanish Civil War (1936–1939) and the social history of marriage in the Spanish Philippines.

Frederik Rettig is co-editor of *Colonial Armies in Southeast Asia* (Routledge, 2005) and *Armies and Societies in Southeast Asia* (2020). He has published in the *Journal of Vietnamese Studies* and *in South East Asia Research*, including a special issue in the latter. From 2007 to 2013, he was an Assistant Professor in the School of Social Sciences at Singapore Management University.

Routledge Studies in the Modern History of Asia

140 Conflict, Community, and the State in Late Imperial Sichuan
Making Local Justice
Quinn Javers

141 China in Australasia
Cultural Diplomacy and Chinese Arts since the Cold War
Edited by James Beattie, Richard Bullen and Maria Galikowski

142 Hagi - A Feudal Capital in Tokugawa Japan
Peter Armstrong

143 Lord Salisbury and Nationality in the East
Viewing Imperialism in its Proper Perspective
Shih-tsung Wang

144 Ulysses S Grant and Meiji Japan, 1869–85
Diplomacy, Strategic Thought and the Economic Context of
US-Japan Relations
Ian Patrick Austin

145 Borneo in the Cold War, 1950–1990
Ooi Keat Gin

146 International Rivalry and Secret Diplomacy in East Asia, 1896–1950
Bruce A. Elleman

147 Women Warriors in Southeast Asia
Edited by Vina A. Lanzona and Frederik Rettig

For more information about this series, please visit: https://www.routledge.com

Women Warriors in Southeast Asia

Edited by
Vina A. Lanzona and
Frederik Rettig

LONDON AND NEW YORK

First published 2020
by Routledge
2 Park Square, Milton Park, Abingdon, Oxon OX14 4RN

and by Routledge
605 Third Avenue, New York, NY 10017

First issued in paperback 2022

Routledge is an imprint of the Taylor & Francis Group, an informa business

© 2020 selection and editorial matter, Vina A. Lanzona and Frederik Rettig; individual chapters, the contributors

The right of Vina A. Lanzona and Frederik Rettig to be identified as the authors of the editorial material, and of the authors for their individual chapters, has been asserted in accordance with sections 77 and 78 of the Copyright, Designs and Patents Act 1988.

All rights reserved. No part of this book may be reprinted or reproduced or utilised in any form or by any electronic, mechanical, or other means, now known or hereafter invented, including photocopying and recording, or in any information storage or retrieval system, without permission in writing from the publishers.

Trademark notice: Product or corporate names may be trademarks or registered trademarks, and are used only for identification and explanation without intent to infringe.

Publisher's Note
The publisher has gone to great lengths to ensure the quality of this reprint but points out that some imperfections in the original copies may be apparent.

British Library Cataloguing-in-Publication Data
A catalogue record for this book is available from the British Library

Library of Congress Cataloging-in-Publication Data
Names: Lanzona, Vina A., editor. | Rettig, Tobias, editor.
Title: Women warriors in Southeast Asia / edited by Vina A. Lanzona and Frederik Rettig.
Description: Abingdon, Oxon ; New York, NY : Routledge, 2020. | Series: Routledge studies in the modern history of Asia | Includes bibliographical references and index.
Identifiers: LCCN 2019032590 (print) | LCCN 2019032591 (ebook) | ISBN 9781138829350 (hardback) | ISBN 9781315737829 (ebook) | ISBN 9781317571858 (adobe pdf) | ISBN 9781317571834 (mobi) | ISBN 9781317571841 (epub)
Subjects: LCSH: Women soldiers—Southeast Asia—History. | Women guerrillas—Southeast Asia—History. | Women in war—Southeast Asia—History. | Women in combat—Southeast Asia—History. | Women and the military—Southeast Asia—History.
Classification: LCC UB419.S644 W66 2020 (print) | LCC UB419.S644 (ebook) | DDC 355.0082/0959—dc23
LC record available at https://lccn.loc.gov/2019032590
LC ebook record available at https://lccn.loc.gov/2019032591

ISBN: 978-1-03-240077-8 (pbk)
ISBN: 978-1-138-82935-0 (hbk)
ISBN: 978-1-315-73782-9 (ebk)

DOI: 10.4324/9781315737829

Typeset in Times New Roman
by codeMantra

Contents

List of figures	vii
List of contributors	ix
Preface	xiii
Acknowledgements	xvii
Glossary and abbreviations	xix

PART I
Introduction and background   1

1 **Introduction: women warriors, palace guards, and**
   revolutionaries in Southeast Asian history   3
   VINA A. LANZONA AND FREDERIK RETTIG

PART II
Women warriors in ancient and early modern Southeast Asia   29

2 **'Lady Sinn' (Xian Fu-ren 冼夫人) and the sixth-century**
   Chinese incorporation of a Southeast Asian region   31
   GEOFF WADE

3 **Querulous queens, bellicose *brai*: Cambodian perspectives**
   toward female agency   48
   TRUDE JACOBSEN

4 **The *Regio Femarum* and its warrior women: images and**
   encounters in European sources   64
   CHRISTINA SKOTT

5 **Geisha warriors? The incomparable *prajurit estri* at the court**
   of Mangkunĕgara I   87
   ANN KUMAR

vi *Contents*

PART III
Southeast Asian women warriors and revolutionaries in the modern period

107

6 Heroines and forgotten fighters: insights into women combatants' history in Aceh, 1873–2005

109

ELSA CLAVÉ

7 Women in the early Vietnamese communist movement: sex, lies, and liberation

136

SOPHIE QUINN-JUDGE

8 Recruiting the all-female Rani of Jhansi Regiment: Subhas Chandra Bose and Dr Lakshmi Swaminadhan

158

FREDERIK RETTIG

9 Women guerrillas of the Communist Party of Malaya: Nationalist struggle with an internationalist experience

173

AGNES KHOO

10 Love and sex in times of war and revolution: women warriors in Vietnam and the Philippines

200

VINA A. LANZONA

PART IV
The United Nations, Security Sector Reform (SSR), and the gendering of Disarmament, Demobilisation and Reintegration (DDR)

227

11 The aftermath for women warriors: Cambodia and East Timor

229

SUSAN BLACKBURN

12 Brave warriors, unfinished revolutions: political subjectivities of women combatants in East Timor

246

JACQUELINE A. SIAPNO

PART V
Conclusion

265

13 Rethinking the historical place of 'warrior women' in Southeast Asia

267

BARBARA WATSON ANDAYA

Index

295

Figures

0.1	Paul (Nguyên) Van Thê sculpts the soon to be toppled Trung Sisters Monument, Saigon, early 1960	xiv
1.1	The Dutch capturing of the distressed Tjut Nyak Dhien, Aceh, late 1905	13
1.2	Nguyen Thi Minh Khai honoured as the face of the Southern Uprising, commemorative stamp, issued on 23 November 2012	15
1.3	Captain Lakshmi and Subhas Chandra Bose inspect the Rani of Jhansi Regiment, 22 October 1943, Singapore	16
1.4	At the intersection of oral history and public outreach: Agnes Khoo and Lin Mei	18
2.1	Modern South Chinese representation of Lady Sinn (c. 512–602)	32
3.1	Earth Goddess Neang Dharani standing guard at the Ministry of Water Resources and Meteorology, Phnom Phenh, Cambodia, 2007	52
4.1	Dutch traders served by female guards and staff at the court of Aceh, 1603	73
6.1	Creating controversy online: Tjut Nyak Dhien without jilbab, late 2014	110
7.1	Nguyen Thi Minh Khai as Tovarish (Comrade) Fan-Lan at the Seventh Congress of the Comintern, Moscow, 1935	145
8.1	Rani nurses and soldiers enjoying a slightly less formal moment, early (?) 1944	166
8.2	Captain Lakshmi seated and surrounded by Indian girls and young women, c. 1943	167
9.1	Lin Dong, medical doctor of the dissolved Communist Party of Malaya, and two other women, early 2000s	182
9.2	Cui Hong, CPM sharp shooter and loyal guerrilla fighter, 2002	184
10.1	The solitary sculpture of Dr Dang Thuy Tram at the clinic named after her at Duc Pho, Quang Ngai province, southcentral Vietnam	201

viii *Figures*

10.2 The surrender of Huk Kumanders (commanders)
Linda de Villa (alias Leonora Hipas, aged 16) and
Oscar (alias Emilio Diesta, 21), October 1954   209

10.3 Reintegrating mainstream society: the wedding of
Leonora Hipas and Emilio Diesta, October 1954   211

11.1 Ex-combatant women in Takeo province, southwestern
Cambodia, 2005–2006   232

12.1 Mana Bilesa, in uniform and with assault rifle, East
Timor, 1995   249

13.1 Statue of Thao Suranaree, local heroine of Nakhon
Ratchasima (Korat), Thailand   271

Contributors

Barbara Watson Andaya is a Professor of Asian Studies at the University of Hawai'i at Mānoa and the author of *The Flaming Womb: Repositioning Women in Early Modern Southeast Asia*. She is currently completing a manuscript on gender and sexuality in Southeast Asia from early times to the present.

Susan Blackburn is an Adjunct Associate Professor in the School of Political and Social Inquiry at Monash University in Melbourne. She has taught Southeast Asian Politics, and her research has focused mainly on Indonesia, her best-known book being *Women and the State in Modern Indonesia*.

Elsa Clavé is an Assistant Professor in Southeast Asian Studies at Goethe University, Frankfurt, and an Associate Researcher at the Centre of Southeast Asia in Paris. She works on the cultural history of Southeast Asian sultanates (Indonesia, Malaysia, Southern Philippines) with a specific attention to the political cultures of these polities in the modern and contemporary periods and on the memory of the 1965–66 violence in Indonesia. From 2018 to 2019, she works as a postdoctoral fellow at the Harvard Asia Center.

Trude Jacobsen is an Associate Professor of History and the Former Director of the Center for Southeast Asian Studies at Northern Illinois University, where she teaches Southeast Asian history and thematic courses on global violence and gender issues. She recently published her second monograph, *Sex Trafficking in Southeast Asia: Desire, Duty, and Debt* (2017).

Agnes Khoo is the author of *Life as the River Flows: Women in the Malayan Anti-Colonial Struggle* (2007), a collection of oral histories from women guerrillas of the Communist Party of Malaya. The book's updated e-version was published in January 2018. She is also the translator of the book, *Our Stories: Moving and Labouring, Stories of Migrant Workers in Taiwan* (2011). As an activist and academic, she founded a community-based poultry farm in Ghana, West Africa, with her husband

x *Contributors*

that provides education, training, and employment to youth and women in the community. Agnes lectures at and is the Head of International Relations of Webster University (Ghana). She has a BA degree in Sociology and Social Work (National University of Singapore), MA degree in Development Studies (International Institute of Social Studies, the Netherlands), and a PhD degree in Sociology (Manchester University, UK).

Ann Kumar has held a number of positions at the Australian National University, most recently as the Director of the International Centre for Excellence in Asia-Pacific Studies. Her publications deal with Indonesian history from prehistoric times to the nineteenth century, with a recent book on the prehistory of Japan.

Vina A. Lanzona is an Associate Professor of History and the Former Director of the Center for Philippine Studies (2011–2015) at the University of Hawai'i at Mānoa. Author of *Amazons of the Huk Rebellion: Gender, Sex and Revolution in the Philippines* (2009), she is currently working on two book projects: on the participation of Filipinos and Filipino American in the Spanish Civil War (1936–1939) and the social history of marriage in the Spanish Philippines.

Sophie Quinn-Judge is the author of *Ho Chi Minh: The Missing Years, 1919–1941* and *The Third Force in the Vietnam Wars: The Elusive Search for Peace, 1954–1975.* She is a fellow of the Center for Vietnamese Philosophy, Culture and Society at Temple University, Philadelphia.

Frederik Rettig is a co-editor of *Colonial Armies in Southeast Asia* (Routledge, 2005) and *Armies and Societies in Southeast Asia* (2020). He has published in the *Journal of Vietnamese Studies* and *in South East Asia Research*, including a special issue in the latter. From 2007 to 2013, he was an Assistant Professor in the School of Social Sciences at Singapore Management University.

Jacqueline A. Siapno now resides in California after living in Dili, East Timor, where she had worked in three universities, with government and state agencies, and local and international organisations, and after working as an Associate Professor in the Graduate School of International Studies in Seoul National University. She is the author of *Gender, Islam, Nationalism and the State in Aceh: The Paradox of Power, Co-optation and Resistance*, in addition to numerous articles on Timor-Leste and Aceh, and now lectures at the University of California, Berkeley.

Christina Skott is a Fellow Commoner, a College Lecturer, and the Director of Studies in History at Magdalene College, and an Affiliated Lecturer of the Faculty of History at the University of Cambridge. Her publications have examined various aspects of European knowledge of Southeast Asia in the long early modern era, in particular the ways in which interaction with the region shaped European anthropology. She has also worked on wider scientific exchanges between Europe and Asia with a focus on the role of the Swedish East India Company in the development of European natural history in the eighteenth century. Her present research interests include nineteenth-century economic botany, colonial agriculture, and ecology in the Malay Peninsula.

Geoff Wade researches Sino-Southeast Asian interactions and Chinese foreign policy–historical and contemporary. He has served in various capacities with the Nalanda-Sriwijaya Centre, Institute of Southeast Asian Studies, Singapore (2009–2013); the Southeast Asia-China Interactions cluster of the Asia Research Institute at the National University of Singapore (2002–09); and the China-ASEAN Project at the Centre of Asian Studies at the University of Hong Kong (1996–2002). He is currently employed by the Australian Parliamentary Library in Canberra.

Preface

A few years ago, Glynis Hart wrote with regard to an exhibition on and with female Southeast Asian master weavers that '[i]n traditional Iban culture in the Southeast Asian islands, men gain renown for their skills in war making, and women for their skill at weaving.'[1] Both skills were complementary to the extent that an insufficiently skilled young woman was not regarded worthy of receiving the main prize, whilst 'weaving [in her culture] was known and valued as "women's war".'[2] The usually red-coloured *pua kumbu* would play, among other functions, a key role in the women's reception – from her husband or her unmarried partner – of the thoroughly cleaned and dry-smoked trophy heads.[3] Hence part of the ceremonial sacred cloth would serve as a base cloth for the skull, with the *pua*'s spirit 'believed to envelope and neutralise all negative forces of the enemy's head', which could then bring fertility and abundance to the Iban community.

Our reference to headhunting and sacred blankets, far from essentialising Iban culture or gendering Southeast Asian warfare, rather serves as a metaphor for our engagement with 'women warriors' – in all their historical and geographical variation – in the Southeast Asia region. Our work brings together a wide range of contributors whose patient and measured, but also disciplined and passionate, efforts have allowed for the weaving of the tapestry of war and its aftermath(s) in Southeast Asia by focusing on the active role of women in warring and revolutionary activities: as war leaders, as soldiers, guerrillas, revolutionary and anti-colonial mobilisers, as providers of intelligence, food and supplies, and as court chroniclers and diarists in war zones.

Like more traditional weaving activities, the making of this volume has at times been a collaborative one, at other times more of a solitary one, sometimes a very smooth process, then again disrupted by the exigencies of life and our own shortcomings. It started with Vina (University of Hawai'i at Mānoa) and Tobias (from 2006 to 2013 at the Singapore Management University) organising four successful back-to-back panels at the fifth International Convention of Asian Scholars (ICAS) Conference held in Kuala Lumpur, in August 2007, on the topic of women warriors in Southeast Asia. Opened by Barbara Watson Andaya, a total of thirteen scholars of the region participated in the conference and presented new research on this topic.[4]

xiv *Preface*

An early follow-up project, aiming to be the first stepping stone to this larger and more in-depth book project, was the July 2008 special thematic section published in the IIAS (International Institute for Asian Studies) Newsletter, which featured eight brief essays, mostly revised versions of the conference papers, an introduction, and two specially commissioned contributions.[5]

Based on these earlier efforts, the weaving together of the individual contributions into book form began, bringing together not only our contributors but also their different approaches, time periods, geographies, and events between two covers. While the introduction and conclusion try to identify the overall strings – horizontal and vertical – that are holding this volume together, they also try to work out key nodal points while not forgetting to give a sense of the rich context and contours that makes each chapter unique. Although aided by modern communication technologies and text editing programmes, this process was sometimes as challenging as a potter struggling to give shape to clay, as captured in below illustration that shows Vietnamese sculptor Paul Van Thê moulding a prototype for a monument dedicated to the Trung Sisters.

As suggested by the frame – which depicts graphic artist Marcelino Truong's representation of the making of an early 1960s monument dedicated to Vietnam's most famous heroines, the Trung Sisters, but also aiming to cement the rule of a political regime and its key dynastic figures caught between an increasingly impatient American ally and an implacable communist enemy – catching the essence and the nuances of a subject can be as

Figure 0.1 Paul (Nguyên) Van Thê moulds a small-scale prototype for the Trung Sisters Monument, early 1960s, Saigon. As depicted here by graphic novelist Marcelino Truong, the modelling clearly is demanding not only for the sculptor but also his two models.[6]

Source: Courtesy of Marcelino Truong.

Preface xv

challenging and demanding as taking the right steps from conception of a project towards its completion.

This certainly holds true for the present volume, which was completed over a far longer than expected time period. Thus, the chapters read a little differently now than when they were first conceived a few years back. But far from being outdated, we believe that the chapters still offer fresh insights into the various aspects in the representations, the lives and struggles, and challenges of Southeast Asia's women warriors across different nations and time periods.

Needless to say, this volume would not have come into fruition without the support and collaboration of many people. If it requires a village to raise a child, then a book is certainly more than the effort of the editors and contributors:

We are grateful to Ian Brown, who put the two editors of this volume in touch with each other in mid-2005 when Tobias Rettig broached the subject of women warriors to him and Vina Lanzona was on a sabbatical in London.

We are grateful for the participants of the 2006 International Convention of Asian Scholars (ICAS) panel, who gathered in Kuala Lumpur in July 2006 (and also those who attended one or more of the panels and contributed to the discussions): Barbara Watson Andaya, Susan Blackburn, Pascal Bourdeaux (in absentia), Elsa Clavé-Çelik, Louise Edwards, Christina Granroth, Jean-Marc de Grave, Chie Ikeya, Trude Jacobsen, Vina Lanzona, Vatthana Pholsena, Tobias Rettig, and Jacqueline Siapno.

We are very grateful for Ann Kumar, Geoff Wade, Agnes Khoo, and Sophie Quinn-Judge for coming on board at later stages, and we are very happy that Vatthana's contribution on two Laotian revolutionaries has since been published in chapter form in a book co-edited by Susan Blackburn.[7]

We are grateful to the IIAS Newsletter, and in particular its hands-on editor Anna Yeadell, for providing a forum in July 2008 by dedicating an important section of the newsletter to our topic. It would have been the poorer without the contributions of Vina Lanzona, Geoff Wade, Louise Edwards, Jacqueline Siapno, Tobias Rettig, Elsa Clavé-Çelik, Adrianna Tan, and Susan Blackburn. The special edition, entitled *Women Warriors in Asia*, still is easily accessible online.

As the project took on book form, we are grateful to Gwen Walker of the University of Wisconsin Press and its anonymous referees for their invaluable advice. Your comments made, we hope, this publication a better one, even though we ultimately decided that we should engage with empirical issues first in order to build a solid base before moving on to more theoretical / discursive / conceptual approaches, such as how women, war, and gender are being represented. However, some of the illustrations in this volume are perhaps a nod into the right direction and indicative of the potential of such approaches.

Many thanks to our two referees who opened new doors and facilitated our transition to Routledge, Karen L. Turner and Louise Edwards: many thanks for your trust in the quality of this volume. At Routledge, we owe our thanks to many professional and competent editors and assistants, including Jillian Morrison, Sophie Iddamalgoda, Lily Brown, and now also Alexandra

xvi *Preface*

de Brauw, and especially Senior Asian Studies editor Dorothea Schaefter, who was with us from the start and never gave up on us and the book! Finally, during the final phase, Nazrine Azeez and her codemantra team did a great job proofreading and pagesetting the manuscript for print.

Thanks for all our contributors for sticking with us throughout a long process of preparing the manuscript for publication. Many thanks are due in particular to Barbara Watson Andaya for prodding us on and encouraging us to push the project ahead. From anchoring the opening panel to writing the concluding chapter to this volume, she has been exemplary in her steadfast and steely support of this volume. If this volume was a *Festschrift*, it would be dedicated to her.

Returning to our initial allegory of Iban headhunting and sacred blankets, this volume finally came into being after the creative and painstaking efforts of the individual weavers (and writers), each one contributing their threads and craft to produce a collective work of illumination. We hope that you, the reader, will enjoy this volume and that it will be a fecund source and inspiration to all those interested in the topic and those wishing to make further contributions.

Hawai'i and Singapore, November 2018

Notes

1 Glynis Hart, Southeast Asian Women Weave Life Stories in Fabric, *Ithaca Times*, 20 March 2013 at www.ithaca.com (last accessed 14 December 2018).
2 Robyn Maxwell, *Textiles of Southeast Asia: Trade, Tradition and Transformation* (Hong Kong: Periplus Editions, 2014 [1st ed. 1990; rev. ed. 1994]), p. 107.
3 See, for instance, Vernon Kedit, 'Debunking a Myth', in Peter ten Hoopen, *Ikat Textiles of the Indonesian Archipelago from the Peter ten Hoopen Collection* (Hong Kong: University Museum and Art Gallery, The University of Hong Kong, 2018), p. 97.
4 In addition to the contributors to this volume, Jean-Marc de Grave, Pascal Bourdeaux (in absentia), Louise Edwards, Vatthana Pholsena, and Chie Ikeya presented papers and contributed to the discussions. Four additional papers, namely by Ann Kumar, Geoffrey Wade (both of whom had attended at least parts of the panel), Agnes Khoo, and Sophie Quinn-Judge, were later commissioned.
5 Contributors were as follows: Vina Lanzona, Tobias Rettig, Geoff Wade, Louise Edwards, Jacqueline Siapno, Elsa Clavé-Çelik, SMU alumna turned technological and social entrepreneur Adrianna Tan, and Susan Blackburn.
6 As depicted here by graphic novelist Marcelino Truong, the modelling clearly is demanding not only for the sculptor but also his two models, as rumour would have it, Madam Nhu (1924–2011), the sister-in-law of President Ngo Dinh Diem and first lady of the Republic of Vietnam, and her oldest daughter Lê Thuy (1945–1967). The eventual monument, with the quintessential Vietnamese heroines standing back to back on a giant tripod-like structure would eventually be inaugurated in March 1962 in the Republic of Vietnam's capital. Although Trung Sisters-themed stamps and a first-day-cover would follow one year later, the first Republic of South Vietnam ended in November 1963 with a military coup and the assassination of Ngo Dinh Diem and Madam Nhu's husband. The monument, too closely associated with the regime, was also toppled.
7 Vatthana Pholsena, '"Minority" Women and the Revolution in the Highlands of Laos: Two Narratives', in Susan Blackburn and Helen Ting (eds.), *Women in Southeast Asian Nationalist Movements* (Singapore: National University of Singapore Press, 2013).

Acknowledgements

The authors and publishers would like to thank the following for granting permission to reproduce material in this work:

IP Publishing, and in particular its Director, John Edmondson, for their kind and generous permission to use chapters developed from the following articles, which first appeared in *South East Asia Research*:

Sophie Quinn-Judge, 'Women in the Early Vietnamese Communist Movement: Sex, Lies, and Liberation', *South East Asia Research*, Vol. 9, No. 3 (Nov 2001), pp. 245–269.

Tobias Rettig, 'Recruiting the All-Female Rani of Jhansi Regiment: Subhas Chandra Bose and Dr Lakshmi Swaminadhan', *South East Asia Research*, Vol. 21, No. 4 (Nov 2013), pp. 657–668.

The editor of *Archipel*, Daniel Perret, for his kind and generous permission to use a chapter developed from the following article, which first appeared in *Archipel*:

Elsa Clavé-Çelik, 'Silenced Fighters: An Insight into Women Combatants' History in Aceh (17th-20th c.)', *Archipel* 87 (2014), pp. 273–306.

Harrassowitz Verlag, and in particular Andrea Johari, assistant to the publisher, for their kind permission to publish a revised version of the following chapter that further contains a translation of the extant Chinese records:

Geoff Wade, 'Lady Sinn and the Southward Expansion of China in the Sixth Century', in Shing Müller, Thomas O. Höllmann, and Putao Gui (eds.), *Guangdong: Archaeology and Early Texts / Archäologie und Frühe Texte (Zhou Tang)* (Wiesbaden: Harrassowitz Verlag, 2004), pp. 125–150.

'An image is worth a thousand words', and leads to even more ideas: we are immensely grateful to the following institutions and individuals who granted permission to reproduce illustrations:

The Leiden University Library and its special collection's T. T. Lam Ngo for permission to reproduce a colonial-era photograph from the The Royal Netherlands Institute of Southeast Asian and Caribbean Studies (KITLV).

At 1 Canning Rise, the National Archives of Singapore and Lai Yoke Lan for illustrative materials relating to the Indian National Army's Rani of Jhansi Regiment.

xviii   *Acknowledgements*

Marcelino Truong who generously shared several pre-publication frames from the first volume of his autobiographical graphic novel, first published in French in 2012 as *Une si jolie petite guerre. Saigon 1961–1963*, and four years later in English translation as *Such a Lovely War: Saigon 1961–1963*.

Daniel C. Tsang, Distinguished Librarian Emeritus, University of California, Irvine, for shooting the photo of two Vietnamese 'classics' from the Anti-American War in the bookstore in Ho Chi Minh City.

And many thanks to creative commons, to landscape architect Supanot Arunaprayote for making the splendid photo of Thao Suranari in Korat publicly available, and likewise to user Thai Nhi for sharing a superb photo of the sculpture of Dr Dang Thuy Tram at the clinic named after her in Quang Ngai province.

Every effort has been made to contact copyright holders for their permission to reprint material in this book. The publishers would be grateful to hear from any copyright holder who is not acknowledged here and will undertake to rectify any errors or omissions in future editions of the book.

Glossary and abbreviations

adat	Malay old custom, traditional law
Amazon	female warriors from Greek mythology; by extension a term for female warriors
Anthropophagi	man eaters; cannibals
apsara	the beautiful *apsara* decide on the fate of those engaging in battle and pounce on the souls of dead soldiers
aqua vitae	distilled alcohol
arak	strong [alcoholic] drink prepared on a basis of sugar cane and glutinous rice
asrama	here: all-female camp; more generally: barracks, youth hostel
babad	chronicle; history (e.g. in Java, Bali)
beik tein	in Tetum: illiterate, uneducated, infantile, also 'stupid' – not uncommon comment when East Timorese policewomen raised critical questions
benteng	fort; e.g. benteng inong balèë
bolo	Filipino agricultural tool, similar to the machete and parang; can be used as a weapon
brai	female spirit that steals babies or inhabits female bodies to fulfil her own thwarted maternal instincts (Cambodia)
cadre	term referring to a civilian activist in a communist or other revolutionary organisation
camp followers	male or female train of a traditional army; could serve as cooks, laundresses, housekeepers, porters, nurses
Cbpab Srei	'Code of conduct for women' (Cambodia) going back to the nineteenth century, influenced by Siamese Buddhism
CEDAW	UN Convention on the Elimination of Discrimination against Women (1979)
Comintern	Communist International, also known as the Third International, based in Moscow,

xx   *Glossary and abbreviations*

	Russia, created by Lenin (1919), dissolved by Stalin (1943), of considerable influence in the development of communist movements in Southeast Asia and around the world
commandery	Chinese system of bases to expand power, for instance, among the 'Southern Barbarians'
CPM	Communist Party of Malaya; sometimes also referred to as Malayan Communist Party (MCP)
Cut (also tjoet)	title for Acehnese noblewomen, such as Cut Meutia; also see pocut and cutpo
dayah	Quoranic school
DDR	Disarmament, Demobilisation and Reintegration, as in UN Security Council Resolution 1325 (2000) on women, peace, and security; paradigm put forward to pacify countries torn by civil war
deification	Elevation of humans seen to possess special attributes to the rank of a god/goddess by fellow human beings or the ruler, by the latter often for secular reasons
DRV	Democratic Republic of Vietnam (1954–1975); communist government in North Vietnam that won the war against the independence-minded Republic of Vietnam (RON), declaring the Socialist Republic of Vietnam in 1976
Factory	here: Dutch trading station
FDC	first day (of issue) cover, for instance a letter, post card, or postage stamp franked on the first day of authorised issue
Film / movie	relatively new medium to carry stories, including those of national heroines, such as *Gabriela Silang* (1971), *Tjoet Nja' Dhien* (1988), *The Legend of Suriyothai* (2001)
GAM	Gerakan Aceh Merdeka, or Free Aceh Movement (1976–2005), with a military wing, the TNA
Gerwani	*Gerakan Wanita Indonesia*, or Indonesian Women's Movement (1950/54–1965), women's organisation associated with the KPI, bedevilled as witches after the 30 September 1965 coup attempt, when propaganda claimed they had emasculated the corpses of the six kidnapped generals
generala	female general; honorific title given to Gabriela Silang

Glossary and abbreviations xxi

grasmes	knife used for cutting grass in Aceh; also used as a weapon
hajiah	female haji, who has performed one of the five pillars of Islam, the pilgrimage to Mecca
hikayat	tale, legend, chronicle, such as the Alexander Romance (*Hikayat Iskandar*), the Acehnese chronicle *Hikayat Prang Gompeuni* (History of the War against the [Dutch East India] Company), or the Malay Annals (*Sejarah Melayu*)
HMB	acronym for *Hukbong Mapagpalaya ng Bayan*, or People's Liberation Army, the Communist-led revolutionary organisation that mobilised against the newly independent Republic of the Philippines from 1946 until the mid-1950s
Huk/s	Shortened name for 'Hukbo', meaning Army; refers to the Communist-led guerrillas who fought against the Japanese during World War II in the Philippines and against the Philippine government after the war
Hukbalahap	Shortened name for *Hukbo Laban sa Hapon*, or the People's Anti-Japanese Army, composed of (Huk) guerrillas who fought against the Japanese during World War II in the Philippines
INA	Indian National Army; anti-British army raised by the Japanese with Indian prisoners of war; its second permutation would also include Indian civilians
inong balèë	literally a woman who has been left by her husband; in Aceh, the term can refer to a divorced woman, a widow, and by extension, a female combatant because she would usually have lost her husband in armed conflict
IIL	Indian Independence League, key organisation for Indians in Japanese-occupied Southeast Asia, most notably on the Malay Peninsula and in Singapore
JMBRAS	Journal of the Malaysian Branch of the Royal Asiatic Society
Jataka	tales of the Buddha's lives, influential also in Cambodia
Ka	Shortened for 'Kasama' in Filipino, meaning comrade, such as Ka Teofista
kaphé	also 'kafir', Acehnese term for unbelievers, heathen i.e. for non-Muslim foreigners such as the Dutch

xxii *Glossary and abbreviations*

komportamentu diak	good behaviour (East Timor) to get promotion
kraton	palace, residence of the ratu (ruler)
kris	traditional Malay and Indonesian ornamented dagger, useful for close combat, and often imbued with spiritual significance
kualingking cases	extramarital relations, usually between an older, married, and more powerful male cadre and a younger, female subordinate; pertains to these relations during the Huk rebellion in the Philippines
kumander	Filipino / Tagalog equivalent of a (male or female) commander
luweu tham asèe	dog-chasing trousers in Aceh, also worn by women, to the surprise of the Dutch when searching the corpses
Mahabharata	Hindu epic; in the Javanised version Arjuna's spouse, Srikandi, takes a more active role in warfare than in the Indian original, including the killing of Bisma
mahram	unmarriageable kinsmen, such as brother, father, husband, or any other male relative who could guarantee a Muslim woman's, such as a female GAM member, moral and physical protection
maidan	Persian and South Asian term for a public space that can be used for sports, parades, or displays of power; similar to padang
Mana	term of address that can mean, depending on social context, 'older sister' (Tetum)
Marechaussee	European-led, multi-ethnic and highly mobile policing force used by the Dutch in the 'pacification' of Aceh
MPAJA	Malayan People's Anti-Japanese Army, closely tied to the CPM
netaji	beloved leader, honorific title given to Subhas Chandra Bose
neak ta	ancestor spirits (in Cambodia)
padang	an open green space that can be used for recreational and ceremonial purposes
parental consent	important administrative requirement in the INA that the teenage girls (and boys) had their parents' approval to join
pasukan	troops, team (Malay)
Pasukan Inong Balèë	Inong Balèë Forces, female GAM unit, named after the female unit created by the legendary female admiral Malahayati

Glossary and abbreviations xxiii

Pasukan Tjut Njak Dhien	Tjut Njak Dhien Force – alleged female GAM unit – named after the most famous heroine in the anti-Dutch war of resistance
pateung	intelligence agents (Aceh)
perang	Malay term for war, also written as prang
PKI	Indonesian Communist Party (Partai Komunis Indonesia), founded in 1914, destroyed and banned in 1965–66
PKP	*Partido Komunista ng Pilipinas*, or Communist Party of the Philippines, founded in 1930, and the official name adopted after the merger of the Communist and Socialist Parties in 1938
pocut (potjoet)	title for Acehnese noblewomen; also cut / tjoet, and cutpo / tjoetpo
Politburo	Shortened term for Political Bureau, here the official policy-making organ of the PKP, or the Communist Party of the Philippines
POW	prisoner of war; modern concept applicable to regular, uniformed soldiers
PRC	People's Republic of China, supporter of communist parties and states in Southeast Asia
prajuritan	traditional Javanese fighting costume, also seen to be worn by female warriors
prajurit estri prajurit	means 'soldier' or 'warrior'; *estri* is a *krama* (high Javanese) word for a woman, which because of its polite and respectful character may be translated as 'lady'
PTSD	Post-Traumatic Stress Disorder
pua kumbu	ceremonial cloth traditionally woven by Iban women, important for ceremonial purposes, notably after successful headhunting raids
purdah	from Persian (for curtain); practice in the South Asian context, and among its diaspora, to conceal women; in the RJR, had to be overcome among some girls and women
rani	queen; female equivalent of raja; e.g. Rani of Jhansi Regiment
ratu	ruler, king, queen, sovereign; resides in the kraton
real	Spanish dollar (real = royal), a major currency, due to the high quality of South American silver, in many parts of early modern Southeast Asia until at least 1900
Regio Femarum	kingdom of women (Latin)
rencong	Acehnese knives, forged in the style of *bismillah* (In the Name of Allah)

xxiv *Glossary and abbreviations*

Revolutionary Solution of the Sex Problem	policy put forward by the PKP's secretariat regarding how a married revolutionary could take a forest wife
RJR	female-only Rani of Jhansi Regiment, made up of teenage and adult volunteers, of the Indian National Army
RVN	Republic of Vietnam (1954–1975); government in South Vietnam that existed from partition until take-over ('reunification') by the communist Democratic Republic of Vietnam
sĕlir	concubine and / or second wife, e.g. at the court of a Javanese ruler
Seuramoe Mekkah	Verandah of Mecca, term for Aceh stressing its strong Islamic identity and historical links with Mecca
sites of memory	from French 'lieux de mémoire', concept put forward by Pierre Nora: monuments, street names, museums, names of public buildings that remember significant events and people, often heroes, and sometimes heroines
soe tiha	'get rid of' (Tetum), in this case giving infants born into guerrilla situations to relatives or institutions for fear that they would endanger the entire group
Southern barbarians	term used for people living on, within, or beyond the expanding southern Chinese frontier, including the Nan Yue, usually meaning that these people were still considered uncivilised
Sui shu	standard history of the Sui dynasty (581–618 CE) in China
sultanah	female equivalent of 'sultan', such as the four successive sultanahs who ruled Aceh from 1641 to 1699
SSR	Security Sector Reform, a developing governance tool intended to manage post-conflict societies or transitions towards democracy (e.g. put forward by the OSCE in 1994), through UNSCR 2151 in 2014
testosterone	male sex hormone, named thus in the 1930s, seen to be responsible in the gendering of warfare as small differences can make a big difference
tipu muslihat	smart trick, ruse (Aceh)

Glossary and abbreviations xxv

title(s)	honorific names bestowed by the population or by the ruler on human beings perceived to be exceptional, including 'Sacred Mother' and 'Lady Defender of the Country' for Lady Sinn, 'national heroine' for Tjut Nyak Dhien, and 'generala' and 'Ilocana Joan of Arc' for Gabriela Silang
TNA	Tentera Negara Ache / *Teuntra Neugara Aceh*, or Aceh National Army
trauma	from Greek, literally 'wound'
Ulèëbalang	war leaders turned into hereditary territorial aristocracy in Aceh
UN	United Nations, key international organisation involved in the changing of global gender norms, including in post-conflict societies
UNAMET	UN Mission in East Timor (1999), established by UNSCR 1246 to help in the implementation of the referendum on independence from or integration into Indonesia
UNSC	UN Security Council
UNSC 1325	UN Security Council Resolution 1325 (2000) on women, peace and security; also known as DDR: Disarmament, Demobilisation and Reintegration
UNSC 2151	Security Sector Reform
UNSCR	UNSC Resolution; can call for missions, transitional authorities, and advocate new tools of governance, such as 745 (UNTAC), 1325 (Disarmament, Demobilisation, and Reintegration), 1246 (UNAMET), 1272 (UNTAET), or 2151 (Security Sector Reform)
UNTAC	United Nations Transitional Authority in Cambodia (1992–1993), established by UNSCR 745, to ensure the implementation of the Paris Agreements (1991)
UNTAET	UN Transitional Administration in East Timor (1999–2002), established by UNSCR 1272, tasked with administering the transition from autonomy to independence
Viet Minh	literally the League for the Independence of Vietnam (in full: Viet Nam Doc Lap Dong Minh Hoi), a coalition of pro-independence Vietnamese forces founded and led by Ho Chi Minh in 1941

xxvi *Glossary and abbreviations*

VOC	Verenigde Oost-Indische Compagnie, or (Dutch) United East India Company (1602–1799)
war queen	William Dampier's term for the consort who joined her husband on campaigns
wayang	shadow puppet performance that can also feature heroines such as Srikandi

Part I
Introduction and background

1 Introduction

Women warriors, palace guards, and revolutionaries in Southeast Asian history

Vina A. Lanzona and Frederik Rettig

Why do women choose to court death by fighting against internal or external enemies? What socio-political order do they defend; what foreign or indigenous enemies do they try to conquer? How do they re-integrate into their post-conflict societies? Are societies with relatively egalitarian male-female relations more likely to produce 'women warriors'?

Gaps and puzzles in the literature

Questions such as these can be answered only with the greatest of difficulty. In part, this is because historically recorded participation of women in Southeast Asian warfare, defence, and revolutionary armed struggle is rare if not even elusive. This is surprising because the region has a reputation of having relatively egalitarian male-female relations.[1] This problem is further compounded by the general lack of comparative work on Southeast Asian (and Asian) warfare and revolution.[2] If and when female warriors appear in such publications, they are usually dealt with in a few pages.[3] A good example is Michael Charney's book-length study on Southeast Asian warfare between 1300 and 1900 in which three out of ten chapters deal with elephants, horses, buffaloes, and other animals whereas one finds none on women and warfare.[4] While the overwhelming evidence presented suggests that relative gender equality does not translate to the battlefield, he nevertheless identifies a gendered division of labor with regard to the realms of war and revolution. Following Barbara Watson Andaya's argument about Southeast Asian headhunting societies, Charney argues that women's 'more fundamental participation in warfare was their place in the rituals that attended to it', an 'important role' that was 'not always made clear' by the presumably male chroniclers of battles, perhaps because it remained invisible to them.[5]

Women are generally also absent from comparative and single-country studies on the post-independence armed forces of Southeast Asian states. Leading comparative studies, usually with a focus on military-civil society relations or the role of the military in politics, tend to eschew dealing with 'women' and 'gender' in the armed forces, as indicated by our negative index searches.[6] Even a perceptive author such as Joyce Lebra, who would go on

4 _Vina A. Lanzona and Frederik Rettig_

to publish on the heroine of the Indian Mutiny (1857–1858), the Rani [Queen] of Jhansi, and on a female-only regiment raised in her name in Japanese-occupied Southeast Asia in 1943, fails to make any such index entries in her comparative study of Japanese-trained independence and volunteer forces in Southeast Asia.[7]

Likewise, single-country studies on Southeast Asian states' armed forces are no exception to this. Hence the front cover of a well-known publication on the ideology of the Indonesian armed forces depicts a female sergeant carefully handing the Army Chief of Staff a knife for cutting yellow-coloured festive rice cones on the occasion of the birthday celebrations of Indonesia's most famous (and notorious) military unit but references to gender and women are missing in its index.[8] There are some exceptions to these general omissions, usually in the form of a few dedicated pages,[9] but overall women soldiers are ignored. This could be because their numbers are too insignificant for special mention, or due to problems to access information, or simply because gender is not recognised as a worthy analytical variable or social category.[10] Ironically, the only book-length study that tackles gender in the military head-on focuses on masculinity in the 1940 and 1971 classes of the Philippine Military Academy.[11]

A similar pattern can also be observed among the non-military comparative works on the region, where the emphasis moreover is on a particular time period, such as the early modern era.[12] In these publications, interestingly, one generally finds more references to individual female warriors and even heroines, or institutions such as female palace guards, than are referred to in most of the comparative literature on Southeast Asian warfare and on the region's post-independence armies. Hence Anthony Reid, the scholar most closely identified with putting forward the argument of Southeast Asian women's relatively high social status and autonomy, mentions the existence of female bodyguards or palace guards, and a female corps in various parts of Southeast Asia, but stresses that they did not take 'part in major battles'.[13] In the areas that are now Vietnam, Thailand, and Indonesia, he further identifies 'exceptional women who emerge to save a desperate situation' and who are therefore likely to be 'romanticize(d) and celebrate(d)', but he is careful to use the term 'militant heroines' rather than 'warriors'.[14] As the key proponent of the 'autonomy thesis', Reid wonders 'if such militant heroism played a larger role in Southeast Asia than elsewhere',[15] but overall he stresses that women's involvement in warfare was an exception because 'warfare is normally an exclusively male business'.[16] Even in early modern Southeast Asia, 'violence, the use of arms, and the defense of a touchy sense of honor were fundamentally men's business', thus suggesting a gendered division of labour in the realm or warfare.[17]

Similar to Anthony Reid, Barbara Watson Andaya identifies a gendering of war when she writes that the emphasis by post-independent Southeast Asian states on national history is 'destined to exclude or marginalize women because it focuses on issues such as inter-state diplomacy, political

Intro: Women warriors, palace guards & revolutionaries in SEA 5

leadership and warfare where men play the major role and where the written sources privilege male activities.'[18] To counter this tendency and to include more women, Andaya implicitly uses a wider definition by looking beyond the mere fighting acts on the battlefield. This allows her—we will also see this in her concluding chapter—to write not only about female war leaders and palace guards but about women (and children) as 'camp followers', women (and children) in early modern village societies throwing stones against raiding attackers, and older, menopausal women of high status as peacemakers.[19] The gendering of war is moreover highlighted by Watson Andaya's emphasis on the ritualistic importance of women for successful warfare in headhunting societies.[20] In Southeast Asian societies where actions in the spirit world and in the material world were (and to a considerable extent still are) conceived to be closely connected, the outcome on the battlefield was thus not seen to be uniquely determined by material factors and causes.

The general dearth of comparative studies on Southeast Asian warfare, defence, and revolutionary struggles and the general lack of women in them, as well as a more specialised type of literature that focuses too narrowly on particular countries, regions, organisations, and time periods, thus provide contrast rather than comparison. Hence the last twenty years have seen a considerable output of studies on women in war and revolution, often using oral history, which has provided considerable insight on the previously often ignored female contribution and experience. We thus know a lot more about the Philippine Revolution, the anti-colonial and leftist Huk movement or the communist New People's Army (both in the Philippines), the Rani of Jhansi Regiment in Japanese-occupied Malaya and Burma, women in the Malayan Communist Party, and women fighting in the northern Democratic Republic of Vietnam or serving in the southern Republic of Vietnam.[21] So far, however, these publications have not encouraged comparative studies. This may well be due to hesitations to move beyond disciplinary boundaries and areas of expertise as much as with the only recent surge in studies on women in war and revolution in Southeast Asia.

To complicate matters further, the growing body of specialised studies has not yet filtered into a broader 'global history of women warriors', where 'Southeast Asian' women warriors still receive scant attention. This is not surprising since many of the key publications on women warriors worldwide were published before the 'gender turn' in Southeast Asian studies had gained traction. Among these key publications, anthropologist David E. Jones covers 'Siam' (Thailand) and 'Vietnam' only, whereas the few references to 'Vietnam' in the works of historian Linda Grant De Pauw and international relations scholar Joshua Goldstein eclipse their few other examples from the rest of Southeast Asia, thus suggesting that Vietnam is a case apart.[22] Lack of familiarity with the existing literature can also lead to omissions and even inaccuracies due to outdated and sometimes even inaccurate or outright wrong information. In Jones' *Women Warriors*, for

6   *Vina A. Lanzona and Frederik Rettig*

instance, some of the information on Vietnam is inaccurate, most likely due to his choice of sources and not verifying them.[23] An additional weakness of such global histories, and their encyclopaedic counterparts, is that they frequently narrate or list the exploits of women warriors but fail to provide sufficient and adequate context.[24]

In view of the existing gaps in the various literatures, this volume offers articles and case studies from a considerable range of polities, eras, and disciplines. While warring appears to have been strongly gendered and the participation of women limited, this does not mean that one cannot learn from more case studies. Our book therefore not only seeks to facilitate synchronic and diachronic comparisons, but in combination with the necessary contextualisation, it also intends to provide the interested reader with a better understanding of the wide range of warring and revolutionary activities of Southeast Asian women.

The volume is arranged, as far as possible, chronologically, although we draw a distinction between two major parts, largely due to the kind and quantity of sources available, with the first four case studies largely dealing with ancient and early modern Southeast Asia and the remaining seven studies covering the modern period. Our introductory chapter and Barbara Watson Andaya's conclusion put different articles into thematic conversation with each other in order to lend greater coherence to the volume. In this introduction, we prepare the ground by pairing most of the contributions according to themes that they share. In contrast, Barbara Watson Andaya's concluding chapter emphasises topics that run through several of the contributions.

As a start, it would be wise to define the term 'woman warrior'. While the term 'warrior' is gender-neutral, common definitions, including the one in Merriam-Webster's online dictionary, refer to a warrior as 'a person engaged or experienced in warfare'.[25] It was only recently that the dictionary changed the word 'man' to 'person' to refer to a warrior, although synonyms for this term such as 'man-at-arms', 'serviceman', and 'soldier' remain masculine. These definitions still reflect the general perception of war as gendered, a perception that is supported by the notable research findings of International Relations scholar Joshua Goldstein. His comprehensive and multidisciplinary study suggests that women fighters 'amount to far fewer than one percent of all warriors in history', and in the twentieth century only about three per cent of the combined 'uniformed standing armies' have been female.[26] This leads Goldstein to conclude that the gendering of war is cross-culturally consistent.[27] He attributes this 'universal gendering of war' to a mutually reinforcing combination of nature and nurture, which is due to 'small, innate biological gender differences in average size, strength, and roughness of play' and the 'cultural molding of tough, brave men, who feminize their enemies to encode domination'.[28]

We define the term 'warrior' more broadly, following more recent dictionary definitions, as a 'person' 'engaged or experienced in warfare', including the definitional subcategories of 'a person engaged or experienced in violent

Intro: Women warriors, palace guards & revolutionaries in SEA 7

struggle or conflict' to take account of guerrilla situations, and 'a militarily trained person' in order to cover those who trained for conflict but who never actually see action. This definition includes legendary and historical women warriors, in some cases romanticised, mythologised, or even deified; women who were trained as palatial guards even though most are likely never to have fought in battle; women who participated in dynastic warfare or domestic revolutions, in anti-colonial and independence struggles, in regional, national, transnational, and even international conflicts. More controversially, and outside of our definition, one chapter explores aggressive and malevolent female spirits in Cambodia in order to contrast them with the general absence of such women in the mundane world, and another one touches upon women's ritualistic support in warfare.[29]

Women warriors and palace guards in ancient and early modern Southeast Asia

Researching women warriors in ancient and early modern Southeast Asia presents great challenges, challenges created by the scarcity of evidence about women in the archaeological and archival record, the permeability of borders in what we now call 'Southeast Asia', and the general exclusion of women from the male-dominated realm of politics and war, and their general neglect in historical writings on warfare.

The authors of the four essays in this section, Geoffrey Wade, Trude Jacobsen, Christina Skott, and Ann Kumar, but also the volume's concluding chapter by Barbara Watson Andaya, overcome these challenges by using a variety of sources from within and outside the region, including popular mythology, indigenous beliefs in the spirit realm, ancient inscriptions (epigraphs), diaries, journals, travel literature, and other official and unofficial accounts to investigate how women were involved in warfare, defence, and state making.

Delineating the broad geo-cultural contours of 'Southeast Asia' and widely defining 'women warriors'

Geoffrey Wade's essay focuses on Lady Sinn [Xian fu-ren; c. 512–602 C.E.], the daughter of a prominent Nan Yue family in a geo-political area that is roughly located within today's Guangdong province in southeastern China.[30] Claimed by the Chinese as Ling-nan, it was a frontier area predominantly inhabited by non-Chinese peoples. Lady Sinn's marriage with a key Chinese family in the 530s, in combination with good health and a strong spirit, allowed her to gain unprecedented power and influence. According to Wade, Lady Sinn, through her marriage, 'assumed a power that likely none of her Yue predecessors had possessed.' By participating in the magisterial functions of her husband, whom she survived by more than forty years, she occupied a pivotal position in a network of alliances that connected the Nan Yue with 'the bureaucracy of several successive Chinese states'.

8   *Vina A. Lanzona and Frederik Rettig*

In this role, Lady Sinn served as a regional power-broker and 'strong-woman' who displayed considerable military and diplomatic prowess. She thus played a key role in Chinese state formation and expansion, including the subjugation of neighbouring polities. As Wade argues, however, it was 'her military planning and activities which were to earn her greater accolades' among the Chinese, generating captivating stories of Lady Sinn's military and diplomatic prowess. This also leads him to problematise her role in the subjugation of the neighbouring polities to the more powerful Chinese dynastic state(s): was Lady Sinn a collaborator or an exceptional, independent-minded and politically astute individual who was an excellent mediator between and among political factions?

Wade furthermore puts forward a very strong case in favour of viewing regional categories such as 'Southeast Asia' and 'China' not as static concepts but as geo-cultural spaces that shift across time. Lady Sinn may have been 'Southeast Asian', but her marriage, and her political loyalties, and her military skills make her a major figure in the process of Chinese expansion into the Southeast Asian geo-cultural space.[31] Her political prowess and longevity nevertheless eventually made her part of Chinese national mythology, deified as she was in successive Chinese dynastic states and within increasingly Sinicised local populations. Such incorporation of a Southeast Asian woman—and woman warrior—into the Chinese pantheon is unprecedented and worthy of much greater study.

In contrast to Lady Sinn, Cambodia's pre-modern female leaders are not a source of pride. In fact, as pointed out by Trude Jacobsen, they are largely ignored in royal chronicles and popular memory and thus invisible even though ancient Chinese sources on Funan suggest that this Indianised polity, which predated the Angkorian era, had a female ruler who was also in charge of defence. In contrast, 'bloodthirsty female spirits' remained (and remain) ubiquitous in the spiritual realm. This dichotomy in Cambodian history between the natural and spiritual realms leads Jacobsen to explore female agency in Cambodian history and to stretch her discussion beyond our working definition of a 'woman warrior'. Instead of simply looking at women warriors in the mundane world, she also turns her attention to violent women in the celestial realm and the spirit world.

According to Jacobsen, 'female power in the supernatural world' played an important part in the 'Cambodian collective consciousness', thus contradicting (but also re-affirming) the traditional and still prevalent image of the timid and passive Cambodian woman. Among goddesses, a statue of Preah Neang Dharani, the powerful earth goddess that Buddha had called forth to slay the demon Mara and his armies, presently protects the entrance of the Ministry of Water Resources and Meteorology in Phnom Phenh. Among the celestial spirits, the beautiful *apsara* decide on the fate of those engaging in battle and pounce on the souls of dead soldiers. The potency of less celestial female spirits—among them the bellicose *brai*, who steals babies or inhabits female bodies to fulfil her own thwarted maternal instincts; *ap*, the sorceress; *me sa*, the white lady; and *sreikh mau*, the black

Intro: Women warriors, palace guards & revolutionaries in SEA 9

lady—is astounding considering that Cambodian history generally denies and disregards the influence of female agency and power in the material / mundane world.

But even in the spirit world, many of the violent females are regarded as exceptional and subversive of conservative social norms. Hence, extraordinary circumstances, such as death in childbirth, explain the female violence that is regarded as a transgression in the mundane world. In the worldly realm, however, bellicose behaviour is often attributed to the 'otherness' of women, notably their belonging to specific ethnic or national groups outside the dominant Cambodian identity, such as a Muslim Cham girl who became a 'left-hand queen' and appears to have converted King Ramadhipati I (r.1642–1659), thus leading to his downfall. Unlike warrior women such as Lady Sinn or the Trung sisters in neighbouring Vietnam who were deified, Cambodia's belligerent and aggressive women and leaders have largely been erased in the histories of the mundane world, whereas the spiritual and celestial realms continue to be inhabited by malevolent female spirits.

Highly visible European representations of court amazons, and invisible indigenous female warrior scribes

While Cambodian women's agency and potential for warring and public agency went against elite and popular norms, Christina Skott argues that early modern European visitors to the Southeast Asian islands, notably the sultanate of Aceh at the northern tip of Sumatra but also Javanese courts such as Bantam (today's Banten in western Java) and Mataram (central Java), found the female potential for warring and the carrying of arms so intriguing that they arguably over-represented it. The image of islands of warrior women and women in arms, already prevalent in the late European medieval era prior to the major voyages of discovery, is a persistent theme in the early modern European discovery of 'Southeast Asia'. Using European travel reports, illustrations, and maps, Skott shows that elite European men were fascinated with Southeast Asian customs and the non-European 'other'. In their textual and visual representations of the Acehnese courts, bare-breasted 'amazons' equipped with bows and trained in the martial arts, played an important role, both drawing on and legitimating even earlier ancient Greek myths about 'amazons' and the historical writings of European antiquity.

These early eyewitness reports inspired an entire literature on the world outside of Europe, with later editors, who at the time often happened to be men of the church, inspired to produce similar accounts. Yet Skott observes a historical rupture, roughly beginning by the time of the French Revolution and complete by the mid-nineteenth century, when the travel reports of the early modern era were regarded as too colourful and did not match the findings of adherents of the new school of more systematic and scientific studies. As a result, earlier European claims about Amazon body guards were relegated to the realm of fantasy and popular mythology and consciously erased from the nineteenth-century European corpus of knowledge.

10 Vina A. Lanzona and Frederik Rettig

Was the modern brand of European observers and ethnographers right to assume that the earlier tales of female soldiers were the product of over-heated European imaginations, or had the tradition of using female body guards in some Muslim courts disappeared sometime between the 1600s and the 1800s? The latter in fact is what Skott puts forward in her conclud-ing section, drawing on gender theory, arguing that relatively gender equal societies are negatively influenced if subjected to foreign rule by a more pa-triarchal society.

The idea of women warriors existing mainly in the realm of European imagination is also strongly disputed in Ann Kumar's essay. She shows that early Dutch visitors to the Javanese court of Sultan Agung (r.1613–1645) of Mataram were fascinated by the presence of the *prajurit estri*, or female soldiers and warriors, in the inner circles of Javanese rulers. Hence Rijklof van Goens, who visited the Mataram court a few years after Sultan Agung's demise, estimated them to number 'about 150 young women', of whom most acted as escorts, ten carried the ruler's baggage, while another twenty ac-tually were armed with weapons and guarded the ruler. In the late 1700s, that tradition was still alive at one of the successor polities to Mataram, the court of *Sunan* (prince, king) Mangkunegara I (r.1757–1796) in Surakarta (central Java, today also known as Solo), one of the most important, but also one of the last 'old style' princes in eighteenth-century Java.

Indeed, a 303-double-page page court diary covering the events at the court of Mangkunegara I during the years 1781–1791 was written by a mem-ber of the corps who identified herself as 'a lady scribe and soldier'. Regret-tably, in line with contemporary conventions, she does not reveal anything else about herself. Through a close analysis of this otherwise unidentified soldier scribe, Kumar shows the versatility of at least some of these palace guards. Not only did they possess exceptional military skills, they were also schooled in the refined arts such as dancing, singing, and the playing of in-struments. The writings of the anonymous diarist reveal that at least some of the women warriors of the Javanese courts had a close understanding of religious rituals but also of the workings of politics and the nature of power. Echoing Skott's concluding ideas, the coming of direct colonial power how-ever led to the public 'disappearance' of these women warriors.[32]

Southeast Asian women warriors and revolutionaries in the modern period

The modern period brought about dramatic transformations in the politi-cal, economic, and socio-cultural life of Southeast Asia. Earlier Portuguese, Spanish, and Dutch and British expeditions into the region had generally been content with establishing trading posts and generating commercial profits, although Spanish proselytisation in the Philippines had led to a more territorial-administrative presence, including the eventual replacement of indigenous 'priestesses' by male Spanish friars. By the mid-nineteenth

Intro: Women warriors, palace guards & revolutionaries in SEA   11

century, however, Western powers were pushing for more complete control over territory and populations.

With the exception of the kingdom of Siam (later Thailand), which maintained a semi-colonial independence by acquiescing to Western demands and adapting Western forms of statecraft, the other major states and polities on the mainland soon found their independence gone or much reduced. Britain eventually controlled—through a combination of direct and indirect rule—lower and upper Burma and the sultanates of the Malay Peninsula, but also the strategically located port city of Singapore (but also had imperial interests in the northern parts of Borneo). British rule also brought about considerable migration of Indians and Chinese who would fulfil a wide range of economic roles. Meanwhile, the French asserted protectorate control over the kingdom of Cambodia, established colonial rule in Cochinchina (Southern Vietnam), followed by protectorate rule over Annam (Central Vietnam) and near-colonial rule over the protectorate of Tonkin (Northern Vietnam), later also adding Laos to what the French envisioned to form an Indochinese Union.

In the archipelago, where the Dutch, the Spanish, and also the Portuguese had been present since the early modern period, the Dutch substantially increased their control by bringing together a series of indigenous polities on islands sometimes thousands of kilometres apart, only sparing the Portuguese-controlled half of Timor. Likewise, the Spanish extended their control into the Muslim South, only to be replaced by the Americans following the Spanish-American War of 1898.

What did this mean for women, and in particular the notion of 'women warriors'? As we have seen in the previous section, Skott argued that colonial subjugation generally leads to less visible roles for women and increased gender inequality, although new types of schooling and ideas also provided opportunities for the few who had access to it. Moreover, the failure of more traditional forms of violent anti-colonialism led to interest in modern ideologies, including debates on the role women might play in society and how they could contribute to reformist, or even revolutionary, projects. The short but crucial Japanese interregnum in Southeast Asia, which unseated and humiliated Western colonial administrations during World War II, created favourable conditions for female participation in armed movements and forces that were supported or tolerated by the Japanese, and those that were directed against them. These conditions often extended into the struggle for decolonisation and the creation of (or resistance against) newly independent states.

Islamic and communist ethno-nationalist anti-colonial
resistance: Aceh and Vietnam

Elsa Clavé's essay presents a longitudinal study on Acehnese women who fought for the independence of proudly Islamic Aceh, located on the northern part of Sumatra, during the 1873–2005 period. Her main foci are two

12   Vina A. Lanzona and Frederik Rettig

protracted periods of roughly forty and thirty years, respectively, namely the anti-Dutch War(s) of Independence (c. 1873–c. 1913) and the struggle for independence, or at least more autonomy, by the Gerakan Aceh Merdeka (GAM, Free Aceh Movement) during the 1976–2005 period against a central government perceived to be culturally overbearing and economically exploitative. More limited sources prevent Clavé from dealing more fully with the intervening time period, notably the contribution of an Acehnese women's regiment to the Indonesian War of Independence (1945–1949) against the returning Dutch, and women's role in Aceh's participation in the Darul Islam rebellion (1953–1962) against the new Indonesian Republic's central government.[33]

Clavé first focuses on the two prominent and iconic female leaders in the wars against the Dutch who are highly visible in the local oral tradition, but also nationally, because President Sukarno made them national heroines in the early 1960s.[34] Tjut (or Cut) Nyak Dhien (1848–1908), who belonged to the local nobility by birth and by marriage, supported her first husband against the Dutch right from 1873. She married again shortly after his death at the hands of the Dutch in 1878, but lost her second husband in 1899 only to continue fighting until her capture as a near-blind woman in 1905 (Figure 1.1). In contrast, Tjut Meutia (1870–1910), who belonged to the local ruling class (*ulèëbalang*), died in battle in 1910 shortly after her third husband's death in a Dutch ambush.

Clavé also highlights the role played by less well-known female figures from similar aristocratic (*ulèëbalang*) or religious (*teungku*) elite backgrounds whose names and basic biographical details are known. Drawing on the Dutch war journalist H. C. Zentgraaff, who estimated that 'hundreds and perhaps thousands' of Acehnese women actively participated in the war, Clavé draws attention to the anonymous warriors whose repertoire of action included attacking the Dutch Marechaussee with a *rencong* (Acehnese dagger) but also logistical roles such as the hiding of weapons and ammunition.[35] She argues that these 'foot soldiers' were doubly marginalised because the indigenous sources fail to record their vital role in sustaining the resistance, whereas the Dutch could not conceive of these women as 'enemies' and rather registered them as 'women'.

Briefly touching upon Acehnese women's participation in the Indonesian War of Independence (1945–1949) and the Darul Islam rebellion (1953–1962), Clavé then moves fast forward to the Acehnese's second decades-long struggle. From 1976 to 2005, the GAM (Free Aceh Movement) led an insurgency against a central government it perceived to encroach upon Acehnese identity and siphoning off valuable natural resources. Clavé's juxtaposition with the earlier generations is interesting because the GAM's women can be interviewed and their views cross-checked with the statements of male representatives of the organisation. Thus, a male former GAM leader, for example, who had earlier published a book on Acehnese heroines, denied that the greater number of women joining from the 1990s was due to the GAM's active recruitment efforts. In that context, the apparent failure of new 'heroines' to

Intro: Women warriors, palace guards & revolutionaries in SEA 13

Figure 1.1 A dejected and near blind Tjut Nyak Dhien, her entire body expressing anger and humiliation, ca. late 1905, Aceh, as captured on a photo. Note that the ethnic identity of the photographer remains hidden, whereas that of her four captors suggests that Tjut Nyak Dhien was a rebellious, perhaps even fanatical, Acehnese outcast.

Source: From The Royal Netherlands Institute of Southeast Asian and Caribbean Studies (KITLV) collection, courtesy of Leiden University Library.

emerge from Aceh's thirty-year struggle is interesting. Not only does it raise questions about the extent of social changes that have taken place since the anti-Dutch resistance, but also whether male politicians are eager to revert back to real or imagined pre-conflict peace-time norms or to create new ones by seeking inspiration from the Middle East rather than the Acehnese past.

In contrast to Clavé's longitudinal study that covers more than 140 years, with a focus on four decades of anti-Dutch and three decades of anti-Jakarta resistance in Aceh, Sophie Quinn-Judge's paper zooms in on a roughly fifteen-year period (c. 1925–1941) and focuses on two Vietnamese female communist revolutionaries. Unlike Aceh's heroines who generally already had become wives and mothers when they started fighting against the Dutch, Nguyen Tri Duc (c. 1911–d.n.k.) and Nguyen Thi Minh Khai (1910–1941) began their revolutionary careers in their mid-teens. Even though the Vietnamese proto-communist and communist movements reached out to women and emphasised gender equality, female activists operated in a world still largely dominated by men, Confucian patriarchal values, and sometimes outright chauvinism. Despite the influence of Western ideologies, the young

14   *Vina A. Lanzona and Frederik Rettig*

revolutionaries drew inspiration and strength of purpose from traditional Vietnamese heroines, such as the Trung Sisters (died circa 43 C.E.) and Lady Trieu (c. 225–248), who had led their people against the Chinese nearly two millennia ago. Because of the extent of French control over French Indochina, a considerable part of their revolutionary learning took place in southern China, and even Moscow in the case of Minh Khai.

By drawing on the 'confessions' of Nguyen Tri Duc following her capture and interrogation by the French authorities, and French colonial intelligence and the Communist International's (Comintern) records on Nguyen Thi Minh Khai, Quinn-Judge works out what it meant to be a female Vietnamese revolutionary during the inter-war period. Based on the consulted sources, it appears that Minh Khai (Figure 1.2) was the more self-driven of the two women and better at manoeuvring within a system in which some male revolutionaries behaved like gentlemen and others sought to sexually exploit junior female party members. In fact, Minh Khai managed to gain the attention of Nguyen Ai Quoc (1890–1969, the future Ho Chi Minh), then the most senior Vietnamese nationalist leader and high-ranking Comintern representative for Southeast Asia, whom she apparently married in late 1930 or early 1931.

In contrast to Minh Khai, Nguyen Tri Duc was apparently too young and not astute enough to refuse an arranged marriage with a senior Vietnamese revolutionary, whom she did not love, Le Hong Son (1899–1933), in August 1927. In 1928, her marriage came undone with the imprisonment of her husband and the birth of a short-lived child. One year later, she divorced Le Hong Son and married her true love, Vietnamese communist revolutionary Le Quang Dat. The revolutionary careers of this idealistic communist couple were cut short by arrest at the hands of the French, to whom Le Quang Dat stated his frustration that the party's egalitarian ideals were 'hollow words'. Regrettably, the sources do not reveal what happened to this revolutionary couple following their interrogation by the French.

In contrast, Nguyen Thi Minh Khai had more revolutionary staying power. French policing action soon separated her from Nguyen Ai Quoc, but before long Minh Khai continued with her clandestine activities in China. Politely but firmly she rejected the advances of another party member and arguably profited from her association with Nguyen Ai Quoc, whose aura is likely to have helped her get selected by the Indochinese Communist Party's (ICP) newly formed Overseas Bureau for participation in the Seventh Comintern Congress in Moscow in 1935. While this elevated her to the upper ranks of the ICP and further allowed her to study at the University of the Toilers of the East in Moscow, it was not all plain sailing for her. Vietnamese summaries have thus reduced Nguyen Thi Minh Khai's speech at the Comintern Congress to one focusing on women's issues, even though she primarily addressed wider issues, such as responding to French militarism in the Far East with the mobilisation of a broad popular front. And as late as the end of 1939 or early 1940, she complained in a letter that being a woman 'does not inspire great confidence'.

Intro: Women warriors, palace guards & revolutionaries in SEA 15

Figure 1.2 Although Nguyen Thi Minh Khai had been in French hands roughly four months prior to the premature 'Southern Uprising', which began on 23 November 1940, a stamp commemorating the event and bearing her face was issued exactly 72 years later, on 23 November 2012. It honours her as a 'communist soldier' and, to the right of the hammer and sickle, is featured the monument commemorating the soon repressed uprising. Unlike sites of memory (see the concluding chapter by Barbara Watson Andaya), the nature and the small size of the stamp would allow it to circulate not just within but also beyond the nation.

Source: In the collection of Frederik Rettig.

By this time, she had apparently married Le Hong Phong (1902–1942), a leading party member, and become a mother of a child she soon had to put into the care of her family in order to focus on her revolutionary work. She was arrested by the French in late July 1940 and executed, together with leading male ICP members, in August 1941.

Ethnic minority warriors beyond borders: Southeast Asian Indians and Chinese in the Indian National Army and in the Malayan Communist Party

While the Acehnese women warriors and also the Vietnamese revolutionary activists of the inter-war period were part of a struggle for independence by people who largely shared the same religion, history, ethnic identity, and language, the story of the Indian National Army's (INA) exclusively female Rani of Jhansi Regiment is quite different. Drawing on autobiographies, Frederik Rettig examines the first few months of this unique unit, which brought together women from very disparate Indian communities in Japanese-controlled Southeast Asia in order to liberate British India. Although many of the women had never set foot on the subcontinent, up to several hundred Indian girls and women from very diverse ethnic, class, caste, religious, language, and age backgrounds joined a regiment that was the brainchild of a male Indian politician and former Indian Congress President.

For Subhas Chandra Bose (1897–1945), the regiment was part of his wartime strategy of exploiting the Japanese interregnum in Southeast Asia by mobilising the region's Indian civilians on top of reactivating the Indian prisoners of war in Singapore who had formed a first INA. But it was also part of a political vision of women's capabilities and agency that differed significantly from Gandhi's notion that women were to be loyal supporters of their families. It was therefore only consequent that women's informal networks, and also the more formal ones of the Indian Independence League (IIL), were tapped into for the recruitment of the regiment and that a woman would be in charge of this process.

That woman, who would also serve as Minister of Women's Affairs in Bose's Provisional Government of India, was to be Dr Lakshmi Sehgal (1914–2012), an India-born female obstetrician who had migrated to Singapore for personal and professional reasons only in mid-1940. Unlike the Acehnese independence fighters and the Vietnamese revolutionaries covered in the previous section, she could go about the recruitment publicly and was later also free to narrate her experience in raising the regiment in written autobiographical accounts and in conversation with historians and archivists over the remaining close to seven decades of her long life, thus allowing the historian to zoom in on the first few months of conception and genesis of the regiment.

Figure 1.3 Captain Lakshmi and Subhas Chandra Bose inspect the smartly standing at attention Ranis on Friday 22 October 1943.[40]

Source: Nirvan Thivy Collection, courtesy of National Archives of Singapore.

Intro: Women warriors, palace guards & revolutionaries in SEA   17

Dr Lakshmi Sehgal hence led the first effort at realising Bose's vision by rallying twenty Indian women from all over the island for a female guard of honour that presented their arms to Bose on the occasion of the IIL's women's rally in Singapore on 12 July 1943. Two days later, she accepted Bose's offer to build on that first effort by forming an entire women's regiment. By the end of August, the original nucleus of fifteen women had grown close to a hundred, who were trained by specially selected male instructors. However, roused by Bose's rallies and other outreach activities on the peninsula, teenage girls and women from the Malay Peninsula also wanted to join so that a proper camp had to be set up in Singapore. Moreover, parental consent for teenage volunteers had to be sought too, which Dr Lakshmi achieved in September by travelling to key cities up the Malay Peninsula, including house visits. Bose formally opened the Rani of Jhansi Camp in late October 1943, where young Indian women from various class, caste, religious, and educational backgrounds learned how to train and live together, with the English-speaking girls from educated middle-class households selected early on to form the bulk of the regiment's officers.

Gathered and trained in Singapore and another major centre, Rangoon, Bose intended the Ranis to march into India in the wake of the INA and the Japanese imperial army. Allied aerial superiority prevented this and many of the women ironically served as nurses rather than as combatants. This was due to Bose feeling very protective about them but also because the INA did not have a sufficient number of male nurses to deal with the many casualties. Forced to retreat, the regiment did not survive the end of Japanese rule in the region. While Captain Lakshmi and several of her officers would later become political and social activists in India and Malaya/Malaysia, their regiment has largely been forgotten.

While the Rani of Jhansi Regiment project lasted a mere two years, Agnes Khoo's chapter, which is based on a seven-year oral history project at the turn of the millennium, focuses on the internationalist ideals and personal journeys of three second-generation female cadres and soldiers of the Communist Party of Malaya (CPM; also referred to as Malayan Communist Party, or MCP).[36] Guo Ren Luan (b.1937), later also known by her underground name of Lin Mei, became an activist in the mid-1950s Singapore, while Malaya-born Lin Dong (b.1944) literally grew into the party due to her high-ranking, first-generation parents, whereas Cui Hong (b.1949) from Southern Thailand joined the army with other family members in 1967. They present different cross-sections and roles within a very centralised and hierarchical party that was mostly on the defensive and fighting for its survival from the waning years of the Malayan Emergency (1948–1960).

This led to cross-border revolutionary careers that Khoo calls 'internationalist'. Cui Hong, for instance, the front-line guerrilla and member of the ambush team participated in extremely dangerous excursions from Southern Thailand into Malaysian territory, the first time partially to show her sincerity in the wake of the execution of her older brother during the party's Maoist-style rectification campaign in the early 1970s.

The geographical trajectories of better-educated party members were even more far-reaching. Hence, Guo Ren Luan / Lin Mei twice had to escape anti-communist repression, first by leaving Singapore in 1963 for Indonesia, where she soon found herself on the defensive again following the violent extermination of the Indonesian Communist Party in the wake of right-wing generals' counter-coup against the botched-up communist coup of 30 September 1965. Eventually sent to China in 1977, Lin Mei served as an educator to the children of CPM leaders and cadres who studied in China as guests of the Communist Party of China (CPC).

Lin Dong's trajectory was even more internationalist. Born in the jungle of Selangor state during the Japanese occupation, she joined her parents in China at the age of thirteen to continue her education. At the height of the Vietnam War, she went to the Democratic Republic of Vietnam (North Vietnam) to study medicine for five years, complemented by two further years of studies back again in China, before serving the CPM along the Thai-Malaysian border.

The Tripartite Peace Agreement of December 1989—between the governments of Malaysia and Thailand, respectively, and the CPM—brought these revolutionary careers to a conclusion. All three women accepted an offer by the Thai government to settle down in the 'Peace Villages' in Betong, Southern Thailand. While focusing on these international and internationalist trajectories, Khoo also emphasises how the women struggled not

Figure 1.4 At the intersection of oral history and public outreach: Agnes Khoo and former CPM member and educator, Lin Mei.
Source: Photo in the collection of Agnes Khoo.

Intro: Women warriors, palace guards & revolutionaries in SEA 19

only against colonialism and imperialism, but also against gender oppression, and the extent to which they perceived to have achieved these goals. Throughout her essay, it becomes very clear how much private and public experiences intersect with each other.

Women warriors in the Philippines and in Vietnam: personal desires and collective sacrifices in times of insurrection and war

Indeed, warrior women and revolutionaries often find it difficult to separate personal needs from political convictions. In her essay on the female combatants in communist revolutionary and independence movements in the Philippines and in Vietnam, Vina Lanzona examines what happens if personal relationships and human needs encounter more 'objective' revolutionary and wartime political ideologies against the backdrop of two very different conflicts—low-scale insurgency in the Philippines and full-out war in Vietnam—and in two quite different cultural settings. She examines this through the lives and loves of female activist Teofista Valerio (b.1922) among the Huks in the Philippines, whom she had interviewed in 1993 and 1997, and through her reading of North Vietnamese medical doctor Dang Thuy Tram's (1943–1970) posthumously published diaries. Lanzona discusses how the universal, although often culturally mediated, needs of women for love and family frequently conflicted with the impersonal and explicitly political goals of revolutionary organisations and regular armies. While every armed conflict arguably requires its participants, male and female, to subordinate social ties and personal issues to larger political and economic goals, Lanzona examines the extent to which this was gendered and also subject to culture and context.

In the left-wing Huk guerrilla movement, sexual and familial relationships became a subject of intense debate among the organisation's leadership after the Huks' anti-Japanese impetus had given way to challenging the early post-independent Philippines. So-called 'forest' liaisons—usually involving male leaders—led to resentment among the male rank and file but also threatened Huk support from the conservative, Catholic, countryside. In 1950, a five-strong committee was appointed, including one woman, which came up with 'The Revolutionary Solution of the Sex Problem'. It recommended that extra-marital 'forest liaisons' were permissible provided the male cadre could prove to the party that separation from his wife (or being single) had a negative impact on his revolutionary performance, and provided he had his wife's consent and informed his forest partner about being married.

Unlike in other leftist or communist movements, in which the individual was to subordinate his or her desires to the collective by being 'married to the party', the Huk solution provided scope for individualism (in particular for its male leaders). In contrast to the Huks' 'revolutionary' solution to the sex problem, no such debate is on record in war-time Vietnam. At least for

20 Vina A. Lanzona and Frederik Rettig

highly educated women from northern elite families such as Dr Dang Thuy Tram, the defence of her country against American imperialism took precedence over romantic or even sexual desires, which she captured in her few free moments in diaries that were retrieved by the Americans in 1969 and 1970, respectively.

Whatever the influence of such policies or more implicit norms on the struggle, Lanzona's essay makes it clear that women frequently understood these issues in personal and political terms but frequently found it impossible to separate the two. She also argues that while cultural norms, and perhaps even class norms, have an effect on how women revolutionaries and warriors negotiate the political and the personal, it is important to consider the influence of other variables as well, such as underground activism, low-scale insurgency and full-out war.

Even though modern revolutionaries and women warriors frequently rejected conventional class, ethnic, religious, and gender restrictions as well as traditional societal norms to become effective soldiers, guerrillas, rebels, or committed socialists, they often had to contend with more conservative post-conflict norms and perhaps regrets of having foregone foundation of a family or having served a movement that did not make good on its promises.

Post-conflict lives of Southeast Asian women warriors: Cambodia, East Timor, and the United Nations

If the separation between the political and the personal was so difficult during conflict, how did women warriors and revolutionaries resume their lives after the war? Like the previous essays on women warriors in the modern period, which at least partially drew on interviews, the two essays by Susan Blackburn and Jacqueline Siapno discuss the reintegration of women warriors into their post-conflict societies. Blackburn does so based on consultancies in 2005–2006 for Oxfam Australia, which facilitated encounters and interviews with former combatants in Cambodia and in East Timor, whereas Siapno does so on the basis of years of having lived, taught, and researched in East Timor, often under very difficult circumstances that arguably are reflected in her chapter. Their case studies bring to attention the importance of local circumstance on female combatants' and revolutionaries' post-conflict behaviour, such as having been on the winning or losing side of long-drawn, murderous, and bitter conflicts. Both authors also deal with the emergence of rapidly changing international norms, namely the gendering of international post-conflict governance through a process, first formulated in the 1990s and formalised by the United Nations in 2000 through Security Council Resolution 1325, and known as DDR (Disarmament, Demobilisation and Reintegration).

Susan Blackburn's comparative essay examines the aftermath of war and revolution for female combatants and revolutionaries in two distinctly different conflictual and societal settings, Cambodia and East Timor,

Intro: Women warriors, palace guards & revolutionaries in SEA 21

respectively. She demonstrates the importance of the particular circumstances of armed conflict for the subsequent treatment of combatants and illustrates the consequences of neglecting women in the process of recovery. In post-civil war Cambodia, Khmer Rouge soldiers found themselves on the losing side of a civil war with international dimensions that had reached its peak with the Khmer Rouge's genocidal assertion of power in 1975 followed by Vietnamese occupation beginning in late December 1978. Following the Paris Peace Accords of 1991 and the UN-supervised transition period and elections of 1993, they had little to expect in terms of official recognition or support. Like their male counterparts, Blackburn aptly observes, 'Khmer Rouge female soldiers disappeared back into the obscurity of village life'.

East Timor's women revolutionaries, in contrast, were proud to have won independence against the Republic of Indonesia in a murderous twenty-four-year asymmetric conflict (1975–1999) that cost an estimated 200,000 civilian lives (or about one third of the population). They could thus expect a hero's welcome, but 'many feel that their sacrifices for the nation have gone unrewarded', even though a few 'have indeed received official and social recognition for their role in the conflict'. In line with many other post-conflict societies, including Cambodia, post-conflict East Timor has seen a reversion to more accepted, conservative gender roles.

This resumption of traditional roles in domestic life is also confirmed by Jacqueline Siapno's single-country study based on interviews, in particular with Mana (Sister) Bisoy, the nom de guerre of Maria Rosa de Camara (b.1963). Unlike in Cambodia, some women joined the Armed Forces and the Police of the newly independent East Timorese state, and Mana Bisoy even became a member of parliament. Frequently, however, they found themselves relegated to the lowest ranks of the military and security hierarchy, with their needs and aspirations 'silenced' by their male superiors. According to Siapno, most of the former Falintil women face enormous challenges to social integration, and frequently suffer from physical and mental trauma. In their personal and professional lives, women's needs are often conflated with those of their male counterparts or neglected by indifferent military and government leaders.

Siapno and Blackburn lament a post-conflict 'betrayal' of women. This includes, to differing degrees, the unwillingness or inability of post-conflict governments to re-integrate women into post-conflict society. In the case of Cambodia, Blackburn nevertheless raises the question whether the singling out of former Khmer Rouge members for special assistance would have been perceived fair by the rest of society. Both scholars, however, also draw attention to the 1990s emergence of new international norms such as the DDR and subsequent consolidation through United Nations Security Council Resolution 1325 in 2000, but also to insufficient implementation. Despite the emergence of new international norms and more awareness, therefore, Siapno advocates for a genuine engendering of security reform, including the engendering of 'consultative, inclusive, and participatory' 'democratic spaces'.

22 *Vina A. Lanzona and Frederik Rettig*

For Blackburn, dominant attitudes towards armed conflict and its aftermath can be transformed by recognising the multiple roles women play in wars and by the serious incorporation of gender into post-war decision-making.

Rethinking Southeast Asian women warriors

In her concluding chapter, Barbara Watson Andaya adds to our introduction—in particular with regard to public representations and new technologies—by rethinking the topic of women warriors in Southeast on the basis of this volume's case studies and a rich range of additional examples. One of her key themes relates to official and popular representations of women warriors, notably in the form of street names, monuments, but also shrines and other sites of memory. Andaya raises pertinent questions regarding state elites at the national and sometimes also the regional level investing in public representations for the shaping of official histories, even though many of these frequently semi-legendary warrior heroines often fought for very different polities and goals than today's nation states that appeal to them.

Based on her examples, Vietnam is leading in that regard, followed [in no particular order] by Thailand, Indonesia, and the Philippines. In contrast, the other ASEAN states (and East Timor) appear to have been less inclined to grant historically recorded women such public prominence. At least on the Malay Peninsula, the post-independence governments of Singapore or Malaysia showed little if any interest in the ethnically Indian women of the Rani of Jhansi Regiment. Even more unlikely to be given public recognition are ethnic Chinese or Malay communist women warriors such as Suriani Abdullah (née Eng Ming Ching) or Shamsia Fakeh who do not fit into the new nation states' preferred nationalist narratives.

These more official, elite-driven attempts contrast with popular, bottom-up practices that may well transform a historical woman warrior into a benevolent spirit or even deity whom adherents worship in return of protection or other benefits. What they nevertheless share with the state-supported and frequently at least semi-legendary heroines is their relative plasticity and malleability for present-day official or personal needs. For Andaya, such [posthumous] transformations, although frustrating not only for the historian, nevertheless raise two questions about the past and the future of Southeast Asian women warriors.

Although she is fully aware of the dangers of reading present-day official and popular histories, monuments, and practices backwards into the past, in the frequent absence of historical sources, they may at least provide glimpses about dynamic historical processes, such as the heroisation or even deification of women warriors and the more mundane interests that might drive such 'projects'. Equally prudent about projecting into the future, Watson Andaya also suggests that new techniques and technologies

Intro: Women warriors, palace guards & revolutionaries in SEA   23

of recording, such as photography or digital video and audio recordings, might spell the end of the future creation or transformation (even deification) of warrior heroines. Moreover, twentieth- and twenty-first-century women warriors can leave their own versions of their warring experiences to posterity in the form of autobiographies or interviews with researchers and thus convey not only their experiences in battle but also their attitudes towards issues such as foregone motherhood, separation from children, foregone femininity, the gendering of war, and their possible frustration about inadequate reintegration into post-conflict societies and the frequent return to more conservative gender norms.

The volume: Southeast Asian (un-)exceptionalism?

All the essays in this volume place women at the centre of explorations of warfare, defence, and revolution in Southeast Asia. Instead of treating them as anomalous, ambiguous, and unnatural women, the authors show that since the earliest times to the contemporary period, women in Southeast Asia existed alongside men as they embraced roles as warriors, palace guards, and combatants in war and revolutionary struggles. By using the analytical lens of gender, and by focusing on the lives of women warriors, the essays here show the value of distinguishing the female experience from the masculine understandings of war and revolution. They do so in different ways because of the wide variety of extant sources, from centuries-old observations by foreign visitors to the region to face-to-face interviews with twentieth- and twenty-first-century women warriors and revolutionaries.

The authors here show that women in many parts of the highly diverse Southeast Asian crossroads region have actively participated in a wide variety of conflicts and warring organisations. These included wars of defence against foreign enemies, wars of independence and decolonisation that frequently also took on the character of civil war and revolutionary dimensions aimed at creating a better society, and arguably also wars of aggression. While women served as palace guards in times of peace, they also fought in female-only units, mixed-gender units, as individual fighters, and a few also as leaders in times of war. As such, they risked their lives in a wide range of capacities—often multiple ones—such as in intelligence, logistics, as porters, messengers, as doctors, cooks, nurses, and sometimes even housekeepers, as teachers, organisers, and mobilisers, but also as regular soldiers, commanders, and political officers, and in other capacities. Despite the considerable diversity—ethnic, religious, social, linguistic, but also political and economic differences—of the region, the forms and purposes these warring and defence activities have taken are largely consistent with those of women warriors elsewhere.

Despite the limited number of case studies presented in this volume and a general focus on qualitative rather than quantitative explorations, this volume nevertheless suggests that women's peace-time training in fighting and

24 *Vina A. Lanzona and Frederik Rettig*

their participation in war and revolution has been historically rare. With the exception of some outliers, such as Vietnam during the First and Second Indochina Wars, it is difficult to see how women fighters in Southeast Asia would have beaten the general historical trend noted by Goldstein of constituting 'far fewer than one percent of all warriors in history' or the twentieth-century trend of women not amounting to more than three percent of that century's combined 'uniformed standing armies'.[37]

The Southeast Asian phenomenon of women warriors and revolutionaries hence generally fits historical patterns of the gendering of war as a cross-culturally consistent phenomenon in other world regions.[38] This therefore adds nuance to Anthony Reid's aforementioned assessment of the early modern period that 'warfare is normally male business', and that the alleged relative gender equality in many Southeast Asian societies past and present does not appear to carry over to warring.[39] This present volume complicates this assumption. Despite the limited number of case studies and with the potential exception of Vietnam, the following contributions in this volume have shown that women were almost as visible, present and involved as men, even in areas of warfare and revolution. This volume will hopefully show that there is a lot more to learn about warfare in general and in Southeast Asia in particular by looking at the female experience and participation in it.

Notes

1 See Barbara Watson Andaya, 'Women in Southeast Asia', in Ooi Keat Gin (ed.), *Southeast Asia: A Historical Encyclopedia, from Angkor Wat to East Timor*, Vol. 3 (Santa Barbara. CA: ABC-Clio, 2004), p. 1428.
2 Notable exceptions are H.G. Quaritch Wales, *Ancient South-East Asian Warfare* (London: Bernard Quaritch, 1952); Michael W. Charney, *Southeast Asian Warfare, 1300–1900* (Leiden: Brill, 2004). Volumes on women revolutionaries and nationalists are Mary Ann Tétreault (ed.), *Women and Revolution in Africa, Asia and the New World* (Columbia, SC: University of South Carolina Press, 1994); Susan Blackburn and Helen Ting (eds.), *Women in Southeast Asian Nationalist Movements* (Singapore: NUS Press, 2013). The former features chapters on Indonesia and Vietnam, while the latter's biographical approach features twelve women from seven countries of whom about half a dozen were also engaged in violent conflict.
3 See Quaritch Wales, *Ancient South-East Asian Warfare*.
4 Charney, *Southeast Asian Warfare, 1300–1900*, Chapters 6–8. A little more than a dozen pages feature search terms such as 'women', 'woman', 'amazon'.
5 Ibid., p. 22. Barbara Watson Andaya, 'History, Headhunting and Gender in Monsoon Asia: Comparative and Longitudinal Views', *South East Asia Research*, Vol. 12, No. 1 (March 2004), pp. 13–52.
6 These studies include the following: Zakaria Haji Ahmad and Harold Crouch (eds.), *Military-Civilian Relations in South-East Asia* (Oxford: Oxford University Press, 1985); Viberto Selochan (ed.), *The Military, the State, and Development in Asia and the Pacific* (Boulder, CO: Westview Press, 1991) – no index in this book; Ronald James May and Viberto Selochan (eds.), *The Military and Democracy in Asia and the Pacific* (London: Christopher Hurst, 1998); Muthia Alagappa (ed.),

Intro: Women warriors, palace guards & revolutionaries in SEA 25

Coercion and Governance: The Declining Political Role of the Military in Asia (Stanford, CA: Stanford University Press, 2001); Marcus Mietzner (ed.), *The Political Resurgence of the Military in Southeast Asia: Conflict and Leadership* (London: Routledge, 2011).

7 Joyce Lebra, *Japanese-trained Armies in Southeast Asia: Independence and Volunteer Forces in WWII* (Hong Kong: Heinemann Educational Books, 1977; republished in Singapore by ISEAS in 2010, but without the subheader). The index does not even refer to the Rani of Jhansi Regiment, which is nevertheless covered in a single paragraph on pages 29–30.

8 Leonard C. Sebastian, *Realpolitik Ideology: Indonesia's Use of Military Force* (Singapore: ISEAS, 2006). On the occasion of the fifty-second birthday celebrations in 2004 of the country's *Kopassus*, an acronym that stands for Special Warfare Forces.

9 Tim Huxley, *Defending the Lion City: The Armed Forces of Singapore* (St. Leonards, NSW: Allen & Unwin, 2000), pp. 118–120. The index of Katharine E. McGregor's *History in Uniform: Military Ideology and the Construction of Indonesia's Past* (Singapore: NUS Press, 2007) features 'gender analysis/representations'.

10 Or it could be a bad career choice as International Relations scholar Joshua S. Goldstein writes that he postponed his interest in gender issues to after having gotten tenure for fear that it would 'ruin [his] career'; see his *War and Gender: How Gender Shapes the War System and Vice Versa* (Cambridge: Cambridge University Press, 2001), p. xiii.

11 Alfred W. McCoy, *Closer than Brothers: Manhood at the Philippine Military Academy* (New Haven, CT: Yale University Press, 1999).

12 Anthony Reid, *Southeast Asia in the Age of Commerce, 1450–1680. Vol. 1. The Lands below the Winds* (New Haven, CT: Yale University Press, 1988), pp. 121–129; Barbara Watson Andaya, *The Flaming Womb: Repositioning Women in Early Modern Southeast Asia* (Honolulu, HI: University of Hawaii Press, 2008), see the many pages referred to in the index under 'warfare'.

13 Reid, *The Lands below the Winds*, p. 167.

14 Ibid.

15 Ibid. Antonia Fraser's *The Warrior Queens: Boadicea's Chariot* (London: Weidenfeld & Nicolson, 1988) would be published in the same year, the book's international edition following a year later as *The Warrior Queens: The Legends and the Lives of the Women Who Have Led Their Nations in War* (New York: Vintage, 1989).

16 Reid, *The Lands below the Winds*, pp. 121–129, 167.

17 Ibid.

18 Barbara Watson Andaya, 'Studying Women and Gender in Southeast Asia', *International Journal of Asian Studies*, Vol. 4, No. 1 (2007), p. 115.

19 See Barbara Watson Andaya' concluding chapter in this volume. Also see various index entries under 'warfare' in her *The Flaming Womb*.

20 Andaya, 'History, Headhunting and Gender in Monsoon Asia'.

21 Rafaelita Hilario Soriano, *Women in the Philippine Revolution* (Manila: R.H. Soriano, 1995); Anne-Marie Hilsdon, *Madonnas and Martyrs: Militarism and Violence in the Philippines* (St Leonards, NSW: Allen & Unwin, 1995); several chapters in Florentino Rodao and Felice Noelle Rodriguez (eds.), *The Philippine Revolution of 1896: Ordinary Lives in Extraordinary Times* (Manila: Ateneo de Manila University Press, 2001); Vina Lanzona, *Amazons of the Huk Rebellion: Gender, Sex and Revolution in the Philippines* (Madison, WI: University of Wisconsin Press, 2009); Joyce Chapman Lebra, *Women against the Raj: The Rani of Jhansi Regiment* (Singapore: ISEAS, 2008); Agnes Khoo, *Life as the River Flows:*

26 *Vina A. Lanzona and Frederik Rettig*

Women in the Malayan Anti-Colonial Struggle (Petaling Jaya: SIRD, 2004); Karen Gottschang Turner with Phan Thanh Hao, *Even the Women Must Fight: Memories of War from North Vietnam* (New York: John Wiley, 1998); Sandra Taylor, *Vietnamese Women at War: Fighting for Ho Chi Minh and the Revolution* (Lawrence, KS: University Press of Kansas, 1999). Among academic articles are Sophie-Quinn Judge, 'Women in the Early Vietnamese Communist Movement: Sex, Lies and Liberation', *South East Asia Research*, Vol. 9, No. 3 (November 2001), pp. 245–269; Nathalie Huynh Chau Nguyen, 'South Vietnamese Women in Uniform: Narratives of Wartime and Post War Lives', *Minerva: Journal of Women and War*, Vol. 3, No. 2 (Fall 2009), pp. 8–33; and Mahani Musa, 'Women in the Malayan Communist Party, 1942–89', *Journal of Southeast Asian Studies*, Vol. 44, No. 2 (June 2013), pp. 226–249.

22 David E. Jones, *Women Warriors: A History* (Dulles, VA: Brassey's, 1997), pp. 31–36; Linda Grant De Pauw, *Battle Cries and Lullabies: Women in War, from Prehistory to the Present* (Norman, OK: University of Oklahoma Press, 1998); Goldstein, *War and Gender.*

23 For instance, on page 33 of his *Women Warriors* alone, Jones' accounts of Bui Thi Xuan and Nguyen Thi Minh Khai are not sufficiently precise, and Nguyen Thi Ba's 1907 poisoning 'to death' of 'over two hundred French soldiers' probably refers to the 1908 plot to poison the French garrison in Hanoi, which all of the soldiers survived.

24 Jessica Amanda Salmonson, *The Encyclopedia of Amazons: Women Warriors from Antiquity to the Modern Era* (New York: Paragon House, 1991).

25 See especially Merriam-Webster's online dictionary, www.merriam-webster.com/dictionary/warrior (last accessed 25 November 2018). Anthropologist David E. Jones also refers to an earlier dictionary where the definition of warrior referred to 'man engaged in warfare', in his *Women Warriors: A History*, p. 4.

26 Goldstein, *War and Gender*, p. 10. His study appeared in 2001, but it still remains the most comprehensive study on war and gender.

27 Ibid., pp. 10, 404.

28 Ibid., pp. 34–58, 404–406.

29 The papers in this volume generally do not cover women in Southeast Asia's present-day uniformed armies; this would be worth another publication project where the emphasis would be on regular 'female soldiers' rather than on women warriors, palace guards, and revolutionaries.

30 The Nan Yue were also known to the Chinese as Bai Yue or Southern Yue. Guangdong was previously also known as Canton and Kwangtung.

31 Note that the northern part of what is present-day 'Vietnam' was a Chinese colony for most of the period between 111 B.C.E. and 938 C.E., and again very briefly from 1407 to 1427, not to mention the temporary presence of Chinese nationalists troops from September 1945 to June 1946 to guarantee order in the wake of the Japanese surrender and as part of the allied powers' post-WWII governance.

32 One of the contributors to the 2007 ICAS panel, Jean-Marc de Grave, argued in his unpublished paper entitled 'The *Langenkusuma* Palatial Guard of Female Warriors in Java's Mataram Kingdom and *pencak* Martial Art for Women' that some of the martial arts routines have survived to the present day in a particular dance form.

33 The Darul Islam rebellion started in Western Java in 1949 with the declaration of an Islamic state, with Muslims from South Sulawesi joining in 1951 and those from Aceh in 1953.

34 'Tjut' is the Dutch way of spelling, which was eventually replaced by 'Cut' after independence in a language reform. Tjut / Cut is an honorific title for an Acehnese noblewoman.

Intro: *Women warriors, palace guards & revolutionaries in SEA* 27

35 The Acehnese rencong is forged in the style of Bismillah (In the Name of God). The length of its blade varies from 10 to 50 centimetres.
36 The first generation would be the women who were active from the foundation of the party in April 1930, including guerrilla war in the Malayan Peoples' Anti-Japanese Army (MPAJA), and the immediate post-war period. Among the most famous protagonists joining towards the tail end of this generation are Suriani Abdullah (b. 1924 as Eng Ming Ching, d. 2013) and Shamsiah Fakeh (1924–2008).
37 Goldstein, *War and Gender*, p. 10.
38 Ibid., pp. 10, 404.
39 Reid, *The Lands below the Winds*, pp. 121–129, 167.
40 The high-rise Cathay building is at the back left, the row of shophouses at the top right is where the present-day Hotel Rendezvous is located. The white line drawn on the lawn runs parallel to Bras Basah Road (right) and Stamford Road (left), with the photographer most likely positioned on the now defunct part of Waterloo Street.

Part II

Women warriors in ancient and early modern Southeast Asia

2 'Lady Sinn' (Xian Fu-ren 冼夫人) and the sixth-century Chinese incorporation of a Southeast Asian region

Geoff Wade

'K'uĭ huí pin tô?' ('Where is he/she going?')—This is a modern Cantonese sentence comprising four monosyllabic morphemes, none of which is shared by other variants of Chinese. How is it that a nominally Chinese language should include such a diversity of terms, where even whole sentences can be constructed using non-Chinese elements? The linguistic vestiges of the pre-Chinese language or languages which existed in what is now Guangdong suggest pre-existing cultures which have since been incorporated into a broader 'Chineseness'. The nature of these societies, generally represented in Chinese texts by the names Yue (越), Li (狸/俚) or Liao (獠), remains something of an enigma, due both to the paucity of sources and to the lack of political opportunity among the peoples of Southern China to investigate the non-Chinese elements[1] which gave rise to, and to some degree still exist within their own cultures.[2]

If we are to investigate the ways in which non-China has 'become' China, and Southeast Asian polities and societies have been absorbed in this process, it is necessary to conduct focused research on the peoples and cultures which have been subsumed by China in a series of processes over the last 2,000 or so years by means of which a few states along the Yellow River came to incorporate territory which today extends over half of Asia. So little work has been done on these processes[3] that there exist few constructs to explain the historical expansion of the Chinese borders. Did the expansion occur through military conquests, through cultural incorporation, or through economic integration? Or a combination of these and other elements? In order to build up convincing explanatory frameworks for these processes, it is necessary to pursue individual examples of obvious Chinese expansion within particular temporal and spatial limits, and through these examples build up case studies and later theories of the historical expansion of the Chinese empires.[4]

As a small contribution to this endeavour, in this chapter it is intended to examine the process by which parts of what is today southern Guangdong became subject to Chinese polities. This was something which accelerated during the sixth century of the Common Era and a process in which one of the most important human players was a prominent Nan Yue woman known to Chinese history as Lady Sinn.[5] The name by which she was known within her own society will likely never be known. However, we can state that she

Figure 2.1 Modern South Chinese representation of Lady Sinn (c. 512–602). The drawing exudes a peaceful but still authoritative aura, whereas some sculptures depict her with a feathered crown or mounted on horseback, sword in her belt, and with pestle shaped hair typical of the Lingnan region.

Source: Photo, Geoff Wade's private collection.

was Southeast Asian in that she was a person from a possibly Austroasiatic society located to the south of the Chinese cultural matrixes. She lived on the cusp between Southeast Asia and China, and the story below will suggest how she was complicit in extending the borders of China into Southeast Asian spheres (Figure 2.1).

1. The *Sui shu* account of Lady Sinn

The most detailed account of the life of Lady Sinn is contained within the *Sui shu* (隨書),[6] the standard history of the Sui dynasty (581–618 C.E.). Another biography is included in the *Bei shi* (北 史), the *History of the Northern Dynasties* (compiled in the seventh century), but the essential content overlaps almost entirely with the *Sui shu* account. A brief overview of the standard history account will perhaps be useful before we further analyse the contents.

Lady Sinn & the Chinese incorporation of a SEAn region   33

We read first that Lady Sinn, known also by a later title as Lady Defender of the Country, was from the most prominent of the Nan Yue families, one which exercised control over 100,000 families. She was, from young, an outstanding person and, we are told, she constantly exhorted her clan members, and particularly her elder brother Ting, who presumed on his power to engage in attacks against neighbours, to do right. Thereby, many of the indigenous communities in Lingnan 'came to allegiance'.

In the mid-530s, this woman came to the attention of Feng Rong, a descendant of the Northern Yan rulers who had fled to the south. A marriage was arranged between his son Feng Bao (馮寶), who was the governor of Gaoliang in what is today southern Guangdong, and Lady Sinn. This allowed the Feng family who had been unsuccessfully trying to implement Chinese rule in Lingnan, to use this new marriage alliance to institute Chinese laws and regulations among the huge number of Bai Yue people controlled by the Sinn family. The *Sui shu* suggests that, from this time on, Lady Sinn became a part of the administration of the region by the Feng family, who were agents of the Liang state.

With the rebellion by Hou Ying against the Liang in about 550 C.E., the situation in Lingnan changed, providing the Gaozhou Regional Inspector Li Qianshi with the opportunity to rebel. His attempts to involve Feng Bao in his rebellion were, the account tells us, thwarted by Lady Sinn. The Lady subsequently used a ruse to travel to the rebel's stronghold in an apparent peace gesture, before attacking and capturing the administrative seat.

The death of Lady Sinn's husband Feng Bao occurred in about 558 C.E. in a period of continuing disorder in the Lingnan region. Again, the *Sui shu* informs us, the Lady was involved in 'cherishing' the Bai Yue, suggesting that she remained a powerful figure in the non-Chinese Lingnan firmament. She sent her nine-year-old son Feng Pu, leading their chieftains, to the Chen dynastic capital at Jiankang (modern Nanjing) to seek some recognition. The family was thereby assigned a Chinese title—defenders of the Yangchun Commandery.

Another rebellion, on this occasion by the Guangzhou Regional Inspector Ouyang Ge in 570 C.E., saw a further attempt to involve the Lady's family, but we are told she refused to join them and she and her son subsequently defeated the rebels. This saw the Chen court conferring further titles and rewards on Lady Sinn and her family, suggesting a recognition of their importance in maintaining some sort of Chinese control south of the ranges.

The end of the Chen dynasty in the 580s gave rise to further disruption of people's existence in the Lingnan region. The account informs us that the tribal peoples of Lingnan thus urged the Lady to lead them with the title of 'Sacred Mother'. She is then credited by the Chinese historians, on recognising that the Chen dynasty had fallen, with assisting the incoming Sui general Wei Guang in reaching Guangzhou. Further honours were heaped upon Lady Sinn and her family members by the new Sui court.

34 *Geoff Wade*

We read in 590 C.E. of a further rebellion by one Wang Zhongxuan, a non-Chinese chieftain of Lingnan against the Sui general Wei Guang. The Lady, overcoming a recalcitrant grandson, sent others of her family to destroy those rising against Sui control. Lady Sinn must have been in her late seventies by this time but, the chroniclers advise, she still donned armour to escort the Sui envoy around the various administrations in Lingnan. Yet further titles were assigned to the Lady and her family members, and the *Sui shi* account suggests that she urged her descendants to be loyal to the Chinese/Sui state.

The last major event in which we read of the Lady's involvement was the impeaching of a corrupt Commander-in-Chief in Panzhou (Guangzhou) in 601 C.E. His depredations had reportedly led to many of the tribal people of Lingnan fleeing. The Lady advised the Sui Emperor of the cause of the problems and urged the Commander-in-Chief's dismissal. This was achieved, and the ninety-year-old Lady was imperially commissioned to pacify the region. Travelling to ten *zhou*, we are informed, each was quelled by her arrival with the imperial letter. For this, she and her deceased son Pu were rewarded. She was personally assigned 1,500 households in what was likely Hainan. The Lady, we are told, died in a year equivalent to 602 C.E.

Lady Sinn and her life and times

Who then was this little-known, or at least little-studied, woman whom the Chinese annalists recorded as Lady Sinn? This question, as well as issues of her importance in the historical processes taking place at this time, can be addressed through examining a range of questions.

When did the Lady live?

There is some debate about the exact dates of Lady Sinn, but the details are not really of great importance to the arguments being advanced here. Neither the *Sui shu* nor the *Bei shi* are specific in terms of her birth and death dates. She was certainly born in the second decade of the sixth century, and we are informed in the *Sui shu* that she died at the beginning of the Renshou reign.[7] Zhang Junshao[8] provides his calculations of the major dates in the Lady's life from birth to death. According to his research, the Lady was born in about 512 C.E. and died at ninety-one years old in 602 C.E. Mo Lun and Su Hancai[9] provide a less-detailed chronology.

Lady Sinn's domicile

Both the *Sui shu*[10] and the *Bei shi*[11] note that the Sinn[12] family was from Gaoliang (高涼). This could have referred either to the Gaoliang range or to somewhere else within the Gaoliang Commandery, and modern scholars are divided over where the Sinn family had their domicile. There are some

Lady Sinn & the Chinese incorporation of a SEAn region 35

who claim that she was from the modern coastal area of Yangjiang (陽江), others that she was from Dianbai (電白), and still others that she came from Gaozhou (高州). Those who aver that Lady Sinn's family was based at Yangjiang base the claim on the fact that the Gaoliang Commandery was administered during the sixth century from what is today Yangjiang County. The proponents of the Dianbai claim base it on a reference in the Dianbai County Gazetteer compiled more than 1,000 years after the events. Zhang Junshao,[13] while accepting that the modern Yangjiang was the seat of the Gaoliang Commandery in the period, suggests that Lady Sinn and her family did not necessarily reside at the commandery seat, and likely lived in the Gaoliang Mountain range. Mr Zhang's conclusions, however, are somewhat determined by the fact that he was the head of the Gaozhou Municipal Museum, and his volume promotes Gaozhou as the home of Lady Sinn.

Given the importance of what is today Yangjiang County as both the commandery seat of Gaoliang and a maritime port during the sixth century, it is possible that the major indigenous ruling family of the area could have resided within this city. However, it is also very possible that this was only the Chinese administrative centre and that the indigenes lived in areas away from the Chinese centres. We know very little about the Lingnan urban centres in the sixth century, and there is scant textual evidence to support any statement other than that the Sinn clan lived within the area known to the Chinese as the Gaoliang Commandery.

There is some indication that suggests that the Gaozhou region was the traditional homeland of the Sinn clan, as in the *Xin Tang shu* biography of Feng Ang (馮 盎), Lady Sinn's grandson, it is noted: 'Feng Ang, *zi* Ming-da, was from Liangde (良德) in Gaozhou.' Zhang Junshao proposes that Feng Bao had travelled to live in Lady Sinn's domicile after their marriage, and that their children would have been born in the same place. He thus claims that the Sinn clan would have been based there.[14] He also cites as support for this claim figures showing that in 1984 the modern Changpo Township included sixteen Xian/Sinn surname family villages, comprising over 3,000 persons, and 8 Feng surname family villages, comprising over 2,000 persons.

The nature of the Sinn clan and the ethnic relations of the era

The Sinn clan, which had 'for generations been leaders of the Nan Yue' according to the *Sui shu* and *Bei shi*, was obviously considered to be non-Chinese by the Chinese authors of the texts we are citing. By referring to the family as being Yue, Nan Yue or Bai Yue, the Chinese authors were providing a sign that the people of this family or clan were not considered part of, but were rather outside, Chinese culture.

The people of Gaoliang and other areas to the south of what is now known as the Pearl River Delta had a very distinct place in the perception of the Chinese in the first few centuries of the common era. In the *Nanzhou yiwuzhi* (南州異物志) by Wan Zhen, it was noted of the ethnic groups of what

36   *Geoff Wade*

is now Guangdong: 'To the south of Guangzhou there are bandits called Li (俚). They are centred on the five commanderies of Cangwu, Yulin, Hepu, Ningpu and Gaoliang, and their territory extends for thousands of *li* (里).' Of these Li people, the account went on: 'It is frequently the case that the individual villages have their own commanders, but there is no ruler. They rely on the dangers of the mountains, and do not submit.'[15] In the third-century *Sanguo zhi* (三國志), in *juan* 53 which is entitled 'Biography of Xue Zong', we read: 'While today it is said that Jiaozhou[16] is at least basically pacified, there still exist the Gaoliang bandits of old. The four territories of Nanhai, Cangwu, Yulin and Zhuguan Commandery are still not soothed. Rather, the people rely on banditry, and these places are essentially refuges for fugitives and absconders.' Here then, it appears that Gaoliang had long had a reputation for being a recalcitrant area. Whether the Sinn family was in any way dominant in the society of the third or fourth century C.E. is not indicated by any extant text.

It is worthy of note that in the eighteenth century, Qu Dajun, the author of the *Guangdong xinyu* (廣東信語), tried to push the genealogy of the Xian/ Sinn family back even further by claiming:

> The Xian family are Gaozhou people.... At the end of the Qin,[17] the territory beyond the five ranges (五嶺) was in chaos and the Xian family raised troops to protect the territory. The chieftains thereby did not dare to aggress. When Zhao Tuo (趙佗)[18] declared himself ruler, a member of the Xian family came for an audience carrying 200 poles of valuables and military equipment. Tuo was greatly pleased, and discussed with him administrative issues and military tactics. The member of the Xian family showed himself to be clever and skilled in debate, and there was no-one who could humble him. Tuo appointed him to administer Gaoliang... Now the southern areas all have people surnamed Xian, and they are all descendants of this family....[19]

This however appears to have been part of Qing scholarly efforts to seek out or create longer historical genealogies for areas which were part of Qing China to validate rule over them, and no other extant text provides evidence for Qu Dajun's claims.

The ethnic make-up of the Lingnan region in the sixth century, when the Sinn clan was certainly exercising very widespread control over the people of the area, remains somewhat of an enigma, but we can say with some certainty that Chinese people[20] were in a definite minority. The area remained distinctly non-Chinese throughout the whole of the period we are addressing—from the Han Dynasty to the Tang. Chinese military and political presence seem to have been confined mainly to the commandery seats, and judging by the reports of rebellions, political control was marginal at best during the period prior to the emergence of Lady Sinn. However, there was to be a marked increase in Chinese administrative influence from the middle of the sixth century through to the middle of the seventh century, and I will suggest that Lady Sinn and her marriage alliance with the Feng family was one of the major factors in this expansion.

Under the 'Southern barbarian' (南蠻) chapter of the *Sui shu*, we read: 'The various types of Southern barbarian live mixed together with the Chinese (華人). They are called variously "dan" (蜑), "rang" (獽), "li" (俚), "liao" (獠) and "yi" (夷).[21] They are all without chieftains. They reside in the mountainous *dong*.[22] These are the peoples who in ancient times were called the "Bai Yue". Their custom is to cut their hair and decorate their bodies.' It thus appears that at least by the sixth century, the change of nomenclature from a generic Bai Yue or Nan Yue to more specific ethnonyms was beginning to take place. This might have been related to a greater familiarity by the Chinese with some ethnic distinctions previously ignored. Despite this, Lady Xian and her family were known to the *Sui shu* compilers as Nan Yue.

Lady Sinn and the Feng family

It is quite apparent from the *Sui shu* account that Lady Sinn's husband Feng Bao was from a northern court and was Chinese, and that the Feng family used this marriage to Lady Sinn to exercise greater control over the non-Chinese people of the region. Prior to the marriage, the *Sui shu* tells us, 'as they were people from another place', the Feng's 'orders were not implemented'. The marriage with the dominant family among the Nan Yue was obviously a calculated policy move. In the *Xin Tang shu* biography of his grandson Feng Ang, it is noted: 'Feng Ang, *zi* Mingda, had his origins in Liangde, Gaozhou. He was a descendant of Feng Hong, of the Northern Yan.......[Feng] Bao was betrothed to a woman of the great Yue family surnamed Xian, gradually became a chieftain, and was appointed as regional commander of the commandery. Ang was the third generation.' The marriage seems to have also played a certain role in bringing the Sinn family further into the Chinese world, through the sons and grandsons who could span both Chinese and Yue societies.[23] Feng Ang went on to be a major general under the Tang, and played a great role in helping the Tang establish and subsequently exercise suzerainty over Lingnan.

Through the marriage of the Lady and the Feng family, a cultural blending must have taken place over the following century, an assimilation of the Chinese into the ways of Lingnan and the Sinicisation of the Yue, with the introduction of a written code and the mixing of social, economic, legal, and linguistic systems.

The socio-economic conditions of Lingnan in the sixth century

The Sinn family is said by the *Sui shu* to have controlled over 100,000 tribal families. By comparison, according to statistics from the *Song shu,* during the Song (420–477 C.E.), Gaoliang Commandery had 1,429 households,

38 *Geoff Wade*

Songkang Commandery had 1,513 households, and Haichang Commandery had 1,724 households.[24] Even if these figures are seen as exaggeration and under-statement, respectively, the extent to which Chinese culture was very much a minority culture in parts of the Lingnan region is still obvious. If we take as our general definition that Southeast Asia is 'that which is not China and which is not India' in this region, Lingnan appears to still have been very much part of Southeast Asia during the Sui period.

Some of the imperial histories do provide details of the social life of the non-Chinese people of Lingnan. As noted above, in some texts, the people of Lingnan in this period are referred to as 'Li' (俚). The 'Nanman' section of the *Sui shu* notes: 'The Li people....have the custom of cutting their hair and decorating their bodies. They are also infatuated with attacking each other.' It also speaks of their 'deep-set eyes, high noses, and black curls' and that they went barefoot, used a length of cloth to tie around the body, and in the winter wore robes. The women wore their hair in a pestle shape, and they sat on mats made from coconut palm. The *Account of Geography* in the same work opines of these people: 'The Li people are upright in disposition and value trust…. they also cast bronze into large drums.' 'When they sound these drums, people flood there. The owners of these drums are called "du-lao", and they are selected by popular sentiment.' It also claims that the Li people 'are accustomed to killing each other, and this frequently gives rise to rivalries and feuds.' The sarongs and coconut leaf mats which are described suggest a people with much in common with other Southeast Asian peoples. The bronze drum culture extended over much of what is today southern Guangdong, Guangxi, and northern Vietnam, and there needs to be more research on the cultural systems which existed in this region prior to the large-scale exercise of political control by Chinese regimes and large-scale immigration by Chinese people.

As to the economic activities pursued in Lingnan in this period, agriculture must have been the basis of the economic system. New agricultural techniques and crops would, further, undoubtedly have been introduced from the north. By the middle of the Tang, the Liao people of Lingnan, we are told, were 'living mixed together with the Chinese (華人), intermarrying, planting many fields and building cottages.' There must also have been direct or indirect links with the polities or economies of Southeast Asia, as Lady Sinn presented to the Chen court a rhinoceros horn staff from Funan, the major Khmer polity at that time.

A very notable element in the economic activities of the Lingnan region was slave-trading. According to the *Liang shu* biography of Wang Sengru (王僧孺),[25] 'In the beginning of the Tianjian reign (502–520 C.E.)…. he was promoted to be Regional Inspector of Nanhai. The commandery always had Gaoliang slaves and every year, several ocean-going ships would arrive. The foreign merchants would then exchange goods for these slaves. In earlier times, the region or commandery would purchase them at half their usual price. They would buy them and then immediately sell them on.

Lady Sinn & the Chinese incorporation of a SEAn region   39

Their profits would be several times the cost, and successive administrations considered this to be a normal practice.' It thus appears that at least one of the markets for these slaves who either were derived from Gaoliang or were procured by Gaoliang people was the international trading port of Nanhai/Guangzhou on the Pearl River. This activity certainly extended into the Tang period, as we read in the *Xin Tang shu* biography of Sun Kui, that the Li 'sell people as chattels, and plunder people as slaves.' It appears that slavery was a major element of the economy both domestically and in some of the markets reached by sea.[26]

The Lady's relations with the successive Chinese states

Through her marriage to Feng Bao, Lady Sinn assumed a power that likely none of her Yue predecessors had possessed. By marrying a politically connected Chinese person, and jointly participating in the magisterial functions which her husband had to perform in his official capacity, she became a functionary linking the bureaucracy of several successive Chinese states and her own tribal people. But it was her military planning and activities which were to earn her greater accolades from the Liang, Chen, and Sui polities. Initially it was the Feng family which was recognised as defenders by the Liang, but gradually it became apparent to the Chinese rulers that real power lay with Lady Sinn. The degree to which she assisted these polities in maintaining some nominal control over areas of Lingnan through the second half of the sixth century was reflected in the titles and rewards which were bestowed upon her.

Following her assistance in defeating 'rebellious' forces at the end of the Liang dynasty and sending her son and her chieftains to the Chen capital at Jiankang in 558 C.E., the family was appointed as 'defenders of Yangchun Commandery'. When the Lady and her family suppressed the 'rebellion' by the Guangzhou Regional Inspector Ouyang Ge in 569 C.E., she was appointed as Commandery Lady, Grand Mistress of Shilong. Then, for her assistance in enabling the Sui rulers to take control of Lingnan in 590 C.E., she was given the prestige title 'Unequalled in Merit', the seventh highest of eleven merit titles. Finally, for success in suppressing a 'rebellion' against the Sui by the Lingnan chieftain Wang Zhongxuan (王仲宣) in 591 C.E., Lady Sinn was given the title of 'Jiaoguo furen' (Lady Defender of the Country) with her own Private Secretariat, or *mu-fu* (幕府).

The late sixth-century military victory against Wang Zhongxuan was obviously very important for the Sui court, as their representative Wei Guang (韋洸) had been surrounded in Nanhai, and the power of the Sui in Lingnan had been thereby threatened. It was thus through this victory by Lady Sinn and her forces against Wang that new power relationships were shaped in Lingnan. The Sui court, through Lady Sinn, recognised the rulers of Cangwu (蒼梧), Gangzhou (岡州), Lianghua (梁化), Tengzhou (藤州), and Luozhou (羅州), while Lady Sinn and her family continued to

40 *Geoff Wade*

govern Gaozhou (高州). The wife of Feng Pu was also assigned control over Songkang District (宋康邑). Lady Sinn was further 'provided with a seal and permitted to despatch troops and cavalry of the tribes and the six regions.' As such, she became essentially the major agent of the Sui court west of the Pearl River.

However, this was not to be without cost to her independence. The Private Secretariat established to 'assist' the Lady in her new administrative duties provided her with a range of Chinese advisers. In this way, it also provided the Sui court with a further avenue for influencing and monitoring the activities of Lady Sinn. Such administrative arrangements were in fact repeated throughout Chinese history as a transitional structure by which the traditional non-Chinese rulers of newly conquered or incorporated regions were first recognised by, and guided in the ways of, the Chinese state. They were then eventually removed and replaced by members of the formal bureaucracy. This was the antecedent of the later *tu-si* (土司) system, whereby through the threat or use of military force, Chinese polities dominated surrounding polities, appointed a traditional ruler to govern the polity, and demanded the submission of taxes and military servicemen. It can be assumed that the Private Secretariat played an important role in ensuring that Lady Sinn governed the region in ways which were in accord with the needs of the Sui court, and in turn played a role in bringing Lingnan further within the Chinese sphere.

The rhetoric of the Lady's biography in *Sui shu*, however, needs to be read within the context of traditional Chinese historiography. She is depicted as being a woman loyal to the Confucian standards which mark the standard histories. The Lady is quoted as saying to her son: 'We are loyal and virtuous, and we have been so for two generations. I cannot suddenly turn my back on the country just because I love you.' To her sons and grandson, she is also recorded as saying: 'You should be absolutely loyal to the Son of Heaven. I have served rulers of three dynasties, loyally with one heart. Now, here we have the goods which they conferred upon me. These are the rewards of loyalty and filial respect. I hope that you will all fully consider this!' It is, if some conjecture might be here excused, highly unlikely that a wily and astute military and political leader like Lady Sinn would have used such terminology in speaking to her descendants. However, the topoi and rhetoric of traditional Chinese historiographical moralising is satisfied by recording that she spoke in this way.

The deification of Lady Sinn

Even during her lifetime, Lady Sinn was apparently held in high esteem by her own society as well as being respected by the Chinese people who moved into Lingnan. In the early 580s, during the political chaos which ensued following the fall of the Chen dynasty, it appears that she assumed regional control of Lingnan under the title of 'Sacred Mother' (聖母). The respect she was accorded seems to have derived from her own personal qualities as well as her strategic and military skills. It also, no doubt, was a product of her capacity to mediate between her own society and Chinese polities. It thus appears that even during her own lifetime, there was great respect for this woman, often a prerequisite for veneration and deification.

Temples dedicated to Lady Sinn are today fairly numerous in the southern part of Guangdong and in Hainan Island. In Gaozhou County, for example, there are over 200 such temples.[27] The Maoming County Gazetteer (Maoming County is today's Gaozhou City) tells us that of the 153 temples in the county, those devoted to Lady Sinn totalled sixty-three, while those devoted to Guandi numbered twenty-three. The spread of the Lady Sinn cult to Hainan is dealt with in a volume by Chen Xiong, *Xian furen zai Hainan* (冼夫人在海南).[28] The only example so far identified of a temple outside of China dedicated to Lady Sinn is that at Jinjang near Kuala Lumpur, established by the Gaozhou Association members.[29] The Lady's birthday is celebrated in the temples devoted to her on the twenty-fourth day of the eleventh lunar month.

How and when did this deification take place? It is impossible to know whether, after her death, she became a subject of worship within Yue society. However, it seems clear that the Chinese people of the region did come to regard her with veneration. What likely began as some sort of ancestor worship by the Feng family subsequently spread to where there was region-wide veneration of Lady Sinn. The earliest textual evidence for the worship of Lady Sinn dates from the tenth century.

While a number of historical figures have been deified in Chinese culture and become the subjects of popular veneration—figures such as Ma Yuan, Guan Di, and Lin Mo/Ma-zu—there seem to be few examples of non-Chinese persons who were so venerated (excepting perhaps Gautama Buddha). As such, a study of Lady Sinn within the pantheon of popular deities in China should prove a valuable exercise in understanding the processes of popular deification. Was the Lady worshipped because of the role she played in assisting the Chinese states expand to the south? Ma Yuan seems to have gained great veneration for his role in this process, and the number of place names which celebrate the suppression or 'pacifying' of the recalcitrant peoples of Lingnan suggests that the process was seen as a glorious task. The deification of Zheng He and fellow eunuchs as 'San-bao-gong' (三保/寶公) in Southeast Asia during and after the fifteenth century seems to have resulted from their voyages which likely made the Southeast Asian ports safe for Chinese to reside in. Perhaps the deification of Lady Sinn resulted from a similar mechanism.

The Hainan connection

There is no firm textual evidence that Lady Sinn ever travelled to the island of Hainan, and yet Hainan was a place in which many of the later

42   *Geoff Wade*

descendants of the Feng family settled, and today is one of the major centres of Lady Sinn worship. At the end of the *Sui shu* biography of the Lady, we read the following:

> Gaozu[30] was very pleased with her, and rewarded the Lady with 1,500 households in Tangmu City (湯沐邑), Linzhen District (臨振縣).[31] The position of Commander-in-Chief of Yazhou (崖州総管) and the title of Duke of Pingyuan Commandery (平原郡公) were also conferred upon [Feng] Pu.

We can thus see that towards the end of Lady Sinn's life, the Sui both authorised control by herself and her family members over households in the island of Hainan, and assigned the family members Hainan-related titles. This suggests either that Lady Sinn's writ extended to the island at this time, or that the Sui rulers were anxious to extend their own control over the island through the influence and power of Lady Sinn and her clan.

Following the death of Lady Sinn, her grandson Feng Ang appears to have been successor to her position of authority. In his biography contained within the *Xin Tang shu*,[32] it is noted:

> After the fall of the Sui, he hurried back to Lingbiao, and assembled the various chieftains. He thereby brought together forces of 50,000 men. The prominent bandits Gao Facheng (高法澄) and Xian Baoqi (冼寶沏) of Panyu and Xinxing were subject to Lin Shihong's (林士宏) command and killed the Sui officials. Ang thus led forces to smash them....Subsequently, he gained control over Panyu, Cangwu and Zhuya, and he assumed the title of commander-in-chief...In the fifth year of the Wude reign (622 C.E.), he surrendered the territory to [Tang] Gaozu.[33] This was then divided into the eight *zhou* of Gaozhou, Luozhou, Chunzhou, Baizhou, Yazhou, Danzhou, Linzhou and Zhenzhou. Feng Ang was promoted to Pillar of the State, appointed as Commander-in-Chief of Gaozhou and was enfeoffed with the title of Duke of Yueguo (越國公).

Again we see a reference to Zhuya in Hainan as a place over which Feng Ang gained control, and a further suggestion that through Feng Ang's efforts, the Tang gained some sort of administrative fiat over the island of Hainan. The Hainan Feng family genealogy also notes Feng Ang as the primal ancestor who came to Hainan.[34] Fuller details of the subsequent spread of the Feng clan in the island of Hainan are provided in Feng Ren-hong's *QiongYa shihai gouchen* (瓊崖史海鈎沉), but such study falls beyond the scope of this paper.

The modern rediscovery of Lady Sinn

Many of the local gazetteers of the region we have been examining—Dianbai (電白), Maoming (茂名) and Gaozhou (高州) in particular—contain references to Lady Sinn and the Feng family members. However, it was only in the middle of the nineteenth century that attention was again drawn to Lady Sinn. In the 1860s, the Guangdong regional inspector Guo Songdao (郭嵩燾) submitted a memorial to the Tongzhi emperor requesting that the emperor confer an honour title on Xian furen (Lady Sinn). This was approved, and the title 'Ciyou' (慈佑) was conferred upon her. This seems to have been an effort at appeasing local sentiments. In the late Qing, a Maoming native, Tan Yingxiang (譚應祥), compiled the materials then available relating to Lady Sinn and included these in a volume entitled 'Xianfuren quanzhuan' (洗夫人全傳), but this has apparently been lost.[35]

In the mid-1950s, the party committee of Gaozhou County organised people to collect and study materials on Lady Sinn. The collection of materials which resulted was entitled 'Xian Furen ziliao huiji' (洗夫人資料匯集), but this was never printed. The incentive for compiling this work is not spelled out in the available materials, and nor is the reason for the failure to take the work to completion.

December 1983 saw the convening of a week-long conference 'Academic Research and Exchange Meeting on Xian Furen' by the Guangdong Provincial Nationalities Affairs Committee, attended by about fifty scholars, which met successively in Maoming City, Zhenjiang City, and Haikou City. Various of the papers presented at this conference were published in *Lingnan wenshi*.[36] The motive behind the conference can be gleaned by the first article in the *Lingnan wenshi* issue, where Zhou Zongxian writes on 'The Contribution of Lady Feng (nee Xian) in Safeguarding the Unity of the Motherland and Good Relations between the Nationalities'.[37]

A Gaozhou City Xian Furen Academic Research Committee was established in March 1995, directly under the city government. Interest in the subject of Lady Xian in recent years has derived mainly from the Guangdong Nationalities Affairs Committee, which obviously needed the story of an 'ethnic minority' heroine for their campaigns, and from the Gaozhou City Government which appears to want the Lady for the purpose of promoting a regional identity and possibly also for tourism.

The political needs of the PRC state are often quite apparent in the assessments of the modern scholars who write on Lady Sinn. These include the following: 'Through three dynasties, the Liang, the Chen and the Sui, she always safeguarded the country's unity'; 'She firmly struck out against the splittist tendencies of the local warlords, and safeguarded the country's political unity'; and 'she assisted the Court to govern Ling-nan.'[38] In addition, she is seen as having 'upheld ethnic unity and promoted a melding between the Han and the Li', and 'advocated advanced feudal culture, and promoted the civilizing of Li society.'[39]

Conclusions

After considering the various aspects of the life and times of Lady Sinn, as recorded in *Sui shu, Bei shi*, and other works, and analysing them in a context beyond that provided by the historians of China, there are a number of

44   *Geoff Wade*

points which might be made, and these collectively suggest that there is a real need to revise the existing histories of the Lingnan region.

We need to recognise that the Chinese historical atlases available to us are premised on an eternally existing China, ranging over the geographical scope of the modern PRC. It is, however, more realistic to see Chinese presence in Lingnan, up until at least the Tang, as small pockets in urban commandery seats, with the area having little connection with the courts based in the areas around the modern Nanjing or Xi'an. An essential element in this is to work towards more accurate historical atlases of the region, which reflect what was 'China' at particular periods. That is to say, they need to indicate which places were controlled by Chinese regimes and agents and which were not. Only thereby will we be able to begin to understand the processes by which places in non-China became China. In particular, we must recognise that there existed major non-Chinese/Southeast Asian polities in Lingnan prior to the Tang. Because they have not left us with written records, we must in this endeavour proceed through critical reading of the Chinese texts as well as fully exploiting the archaeological record. These Southeast Asian polities need to be studied far more fully than they have been, in order to break down the hegemony of Chinese historiography as the sole arbiter of the past in much of East Asia. These societies must be seen as Southeast Asian societies which were subsequently incorporated (and which are in some cases still being incorporated today) within Chinese polities.

As a necessary corollary, the processes of Chinese expansion southwards (and in other directions) need to be investigated in a concerted and coordinated manner. In the case of Lady Sinn, it was through marriage with an influential Chinese family that the Chinese generals came to control many of the non-Chinese/Southeast Asian peoples. This could usefully be compared to the methods of European colonialism, whereby the European colonialists co-opted the indigenous ruling elite in Southeast Asia and used them to control their colonial appendages (albeit not usually through marriage).[40] This policy of 'using yi to control yi' (以夷治夷), whereby the Chinese state used non-Chinese persons to economically or politically control other non-Chinese persons, or to engage in military actions against them, marks much of Chinese history and should be investigated together with the role of the *tu-si* (土司) system of indirect rule in the processes of Chinese expansion. But this was only one of many means of incorporation, which included military conquest, economic incorporation, and cultural incorporation. A study of these processes on all Chinese borders throughout the last several millennia would open up new areas for understanding the Southeast and East Asian pasts.

Lady Sinn was a major political and military player for a period of close to sixty years in much of what is today southern Guangdong. It is important to investigate to what degree the Chinese incorporation of Lingnan was a result of Lady Sinn's great influence over the non-Chinese/Southeast Asian tribes of Lingnan. This would also provide useful input in studying the social

Lady Sinn & the Chinese incorporation of a SEAn region   45

systems in place in the Lingnan societies prior to Sinicisation. The ethnic relations which existed in this period can only be explored through very few texts. However, it appears that the marriage of Lady Sinn to the Feng family (and likely many other such unions which were taking place in this period) gave rise to a new creole generation which operated both in the Yue cultural and linguistic sphere as well as the Chinese sphere. Similar interactions over the subsequent 1,400 years have given us the Guangdong cultures we know today. These creole Southeast Asian-Chinese cultures of Guangdong and Guangxi need to be examined far more deeply in terms of their non-Chinese elements. This has long met obstacles, as many such people today are anxious to demonstrate how 'Chinese' they are, rather than investigating those elements which distinguish them from other Chinese people.

The manner by which a Southeast Asian person such as Lady Sinn was deified in Chinese society also needs to be further investigated. A study of Lady Sinn within the pantheon of popular deities in China should prove a valuable exercise in understanding the processes of popular deification, and also illumine the relationship between the Lady's deification and the southward movement of Chinese culture into the polities and societies of Southeast Asia. Comparisons with the deification of other Southeast Asian women such as the Trung sisters in Vietnam and the process by which the Cham deity of Pô Nagar ('Lady of the Kingdom') was transformed into the Viet deity Thien Y A Na[41] would likely offer useful insights, as would an examination of the deification and worship of *Chao Mae Yu-hua* (Lady White Blood) in southern Thai society.[42]

Acknowledgement

The author would like to acknowledge with gratitude the assistance provided by Professor Claudine Salmon of Paris who provided a range of very useful materials and by Dr Elizabeth Sinn of Hong Kong who supplied a copy of a Sinn family publication which includes various references to Lady Sinn.

Notes

1 This is a difficult term to define. Essentially, within this paper, 'non-Chinese' refers to those people or cultures which the Chinese documents represent as being 'beyond China' (cultural and/or political China), through such epithets as Yue (越), *man* (蠻), *yi* (夷), or *di* (狄). Some of these terms were descriptive but often they were imbued with pejorative implications of being 'uncivilised'.
2 A recent valuable addition to the scholarship on the region and these peoples is Catherine Churchman's *The People between the Rivers: The Rise and Fall of a Bronze Drum Culture, 200–750 CE* (Lanham, MD: Rowman & Littlefield, 2016).
3 Although we must, of course, mention the following: Owen Lattimore, *Inner Asian Frontiers of China* (New York: American Geographical Society, 1940); Herold J. Wiens, *China's March toward the Tropics* (Hamden, CT: Shoe String Press, 1954); Wolfram Eberhard, *The Local Cultures of South and East China*

46 *Geoff Wade*

(Leiden: E. J. Brill, 1968); Claudine Lombard-Salmon, *La Province du Gui Zhou au XVIIIe siècle: un exemple d'acculturation chinoise* (Paris: École française d'Extrême-Orient, 1972); Charles Patrick FitzGerald, *The Southern Expansion of the Chinese People: 'Southern Fields and Southern Ocean'* (London: Barrie and Jenkins, 1972).

4 Some work in this direction is included in Geoff Wade (ed.), *Asian Expansions: The Historical Experiences of Polity Expansion in Asia* (Abingdon, Oxon: Routledge, 2015).

5 'Xian fu-ren' (洗 夫人). I am here opting for the modern Cantonese pronunciation of the surname.

6 'Account of Qiaoguo furen' in 'Biographies of Outstanding Women', *Sui shu*, juan 80. An English-language translation of this biography is provided in the appendix of Geoff Wade, 'Lady Sinn and the Southward Expansion of China in the Sixth Century', in Shing Müller, Thomas O. Höllmann, and Putao Gui (eds.), *Guangdong: Archaeology and Early Texts / Archäologie und Frühe Texte (Zhou Tang)* (Wiesbaden: Harrassowitz Verlag, 2004), pp. 125–150.

7 601–605 C.E.

8 Zhang Junshao (張均紹), *Xian furen kaolüe* (洗夫人考略) (Guangzhou: Guangdong sheng ditu chubanshe, 1996), pp. 45–49.

9 Mo Lun (莫侖), Su Hancai (蘇漢材), *Xian furen shilüe* (洗夫人史略) (Hong Kong: Tianma tushu youxian gongsi, 2000), pp. 13–17.

10 *Sui shu*, juan 80, 'Jiaoguo furen'.

11 *Bei shi*, juan 91, 'Jiaoguo furen Xian shi'.

12 The *Sui shu* and the *Bei shi* accounts of Lady Sinn use the character 'Xian' with the 'san dian shui' (三點水) radical, but all the Sinn families of Lingnan today use the 'liang dian shui' (兩點水) radical. This chapter follows the Lingnan practice.

13 Zhang Junshao, *Xian furen kaolüe*, pp. 2–7.

14 Ibid. p. 8.

15 *Taiping yulan*, juan 785.

16 During the Three Kingdoms period, Jiaozhou referred to the area which included most of modern Guangdong.

17 In the 210s B.C.E.

18 Zhao Tuo was a 'King of Nan Yue'. Sent south by the Qin ruler in the second century B.C.E., he established himself as 'King of Nan Yue' after the collapse of the Qin. He was later recognised by the Han rulers, but subsequently opposed them and declared himself emperor.

19 There appears to have been no extant text from which Qu Dajun, the author of *Guangdong xinyu*, could have obtained such information. Also, the work was compiled in a period when genealogies of regions were being created by Qing scholars to assist in creating a 'Chinese history' for regions, with longer genealogies than previously known. It appears that Qu Dajun's efforts were aimed in this direction and we can be somewhat sceptical about his claims of people of the Xian family assisting Zhao Tuo 200 years before the beginning of the Common Era.

20 Here, the definition of Chinese being employed is 'people who use a Chinese language/script as their primary language/script'.

21 Again these terms were often imbued with the idea that persons so described were beyond Chinese culture.

22 An area suitable for agriculture and often controlled by a political leader. In some ways similar to a Thai *muang*.

23 Much as is the case today among the people known as the 'Chinese Shan' and who reside in northern Burma and Yunnan.

24 Zhang Junshao, *Xian furen kaolüe*, p. 81.

25 *Liang shu*, juan 33.
26 For comparative studies of later slave-raiding and slave-trading of other Southeast Asian peoples, see Anthony Reid (ed.), *Slavery, Bondage and Dependency in Southeast Asia* (St. Lucia: Queensland University Press, 1983); and James Warren, *Iranun and Balangingi: Globalization, Maritime Raiding and the Birth of Ethnicity* (Singapore: NUS Press, 2002).
27 Zhang Junshao, *Xian furen kaolüe*, p. 14.
28 Chen Xiong (陳 雄), *Xian furen zai Hainan* (冼夫人在海南) (Guangzhou: Zhongshan Daxu chubanshe, 1991).
29 My thanks to Professor Claudine Salmon for confirming its existence and providing publications from the temple.
30 Referring to the Wen Emperor of the Sui Dynasty, Yang Jian (reigned 589–604 C.E.).
31 Both Wang Xingrui and Tan Qixiang locate Linzhen in Hainan, the former situating it in Yazhou in the north of the island, the latter in the very south of the island. The basis for these identifications is not clear. See Wang Xingrui (王興瑞), *Xian furen yu Feng shi jiazu* (冼夫人與馮氏家族) (Beijing: Zhonghua shuju, 1984), p. 73. See also Xu Junming (徐俊鳴), *Lingnan lishi dili lunji* (嶺南歷史地理倫集) (Guangzhou: Zhongshan daxue xuebao bianjibu, 1990).
32 *Xin Tang shu* [New History of the Tang], juan 110.
33 The Tang emperor.
34 Feng Renhong (馮 仁 鴻), *Qiong-Ya shihai gouchen* (瓊崖史海鈎沉) (Hong Kong: Tianma tushu youxian gongsi, 2000), p. 297.
35 Zhang Junshao, *Xian furen kaolüe*, p. 5.
36 See *Lingnan wenshi* (嶺南文史), 1984, p. 1. For example, Pan Xiong (潘雄), Cai Licai (蔡理才), 'Xian furen de zushu ji liren yiyi kao' (冼夫人的族屬及俚人 遺裔 考), *Lingnan wenshi* (嶺南文史), 1984, No. 1, pp. 3–8.
37 Zhou Zongxian (周宗賢), 'Feng Xian furen weihu zuguo tongyi he minzu hemu de gongxian' (馮冼夫人維護祖國統一和民族和睦的貢獻), *Lingnan wenshi* (嶺南文史), 1984, No 1, pp. 3–8.
38 Zhang Junshao, *Xian furen kaolüe*, pp. 65–68.
39 Ibid., pp. 70–73.
40 Although the Europeans, in their colonising of places within Europe (e.g. England's colonising of Scotland) did employ marriage alliances.
41 For which see Nguyên Thê Anh, 'The Vietnamization of the Cham Deity Pô Nagar', in Keith W. Taylor and John K. Whitmore (eds.), *Essays into Vietnamese Pasts* (Ithaca, NY: Cornell University Press, 1995), pp. 42–50.
42 Lorraine Gesick, *In the Land of Lady White Blood: Southern Thailand and the Meaning of History* (Ithaca, NY: Cornell University Press, 1995).

3   Querulous queens, bellicose *brai*

Cambodian perspectives toward female agency

Trude Jacobsen

> Formerly, [Funan] had for its sovereign a woman named Liu Ye... Liu Ye saw the ship and organized her soldiers to resist it. But Hundien raised his bow and shot an arrow which, penetrating the side of a boat, struck someone. Liu Ye was afraid and surrendered. Hundien then made her his wife...[1]

Cambodia is a land of dichotomies. One of the strangest of these is the acceptance, on one hand, that the mythical founder of Cambodia was an unmarried warrior queen; and on the other, that Cambodian women are and always have been submissive, timid, and powerless. The supernatural realm abounds with violent and bloodthirsty female spirits, while women of the everyday world are cast in a '(preferably silent) supporting role rather than as an agent'.[2] There is a belief in Cambodia today that agency[3] is acceptable for female beings in one world but not the other. Agency is constrained in the human world, irrespective of gender, by the complex network of relationships known as *khsae* (patron-client ties) or *omnaich* (literally, 'influence'); nobody is ever free of social obligations. Women are also restricted by the responsibility of observing 'correct' behaviour. At the same time, it seems extremely unlikely that there were never any 'women warriors' in Cambodian history. Did such women exist? If so, why are they unknown to Cambodians today?

The spiritual realm

In the third century, Chinese observers related that a Cambodian polity called 'Funan' had had as its original ruler a woman warrior, Liu Ye ('Willow Leaf'; sometimes she is called Ye Ye, 'Coconut Leaf', in other dynastic histories), who led her navy against an invading force from South Asia.[4] Until the eighth century, the brahmanical goddess Durga Mahishasuramardini was extremely popular in early Cambodia.[5] The name of this goddess translates as 'Durga, the slayer of the great demon [buffalo]'. Sculpturally, she was depicted as a fierce warrior standing atop the disembodied head of her prey. The autonomous representation of other goddesses – implying agency independent of male intercession – is also indicative of a more aggressive

Cambodia: querulous queens, bellicose brai & female agency   49

aspect of femaleness in the celestial realm. Goddesses were almost never shown as accoutrements of their male counterparts during the preclassical period (third–ninth centuries).[6]

In the classical period (tenth–fourteenth centuries), although the brahmanical goddesses began to be depicted in terms of their relationships to the gods upon whom their existence depended, the *apsara* emerged, and carried on the tradition of female 'warriors' in the supernatural world. The *apsara* hovered near battlefields, waiting to pounce upon the souls of dead soldiers, or incite jealousy, which would in turn lead to violence and death.[7] Similarly, the women who dwelt in the palaces of kings – and therefore in a space wherein the mundane and celestial worlds converged – were forceful and passionate. Some inflicted 'the marks of amorous games' upon their king, at times with their teeth.[8] Perhaps most significantly, each night, the king of Cambodia was expected to climb the many steps to the gold-covered tower of the Baphuon temple, where a *nagini*, a nine-headed serpent in the form of a beautiful woman, appeared. If the king failed to please her, through either performance or attendance, disaster would befall the kingdom; if the *nagini* chose not to keep the appointment it was a sign that the king was doomed.[9] Either way, agency devolved upon the *nagini*.

After the Cambodian court moved away from 'Angkor' in the fourteenth century, the historical record poses more of a problem. Cambodian sources are few, and dates must be ascertained or estimated from context and corresponding regional histories. Nevertheless, as Ashley Thompson has remarked, the agents of both supernatural and mundane Middle Cambodia (fifteenth–eighteenth centuries) seem to be distinctly *female* in collective Cambodian cultural memory.[10] Recorded for the first time at the end of the nineteenth and the beginning of the twentieth centuries, oral traditions implied that the many ghosts and spirits residing in Cambodia then had been fixtures for centuries. One category of supernatural being, the *me sa*, are by their name female – *me sa* is, quite literally, 'white lady'. The most well-known of these is the *me sa* of Ba Phnom.[11] It appears to have been customary to offer this particular *me sa* human sacrifices in order to earn her favour, the last taking place in 1877. Interestingly, the *me sa* of Ba Phnom resided in a female image of a much earlier period – Durga Mahishasuramardini.[12] Certain *neak ta*, 'ancestor spirits', who were female also inhabited stone or wooden objects[13] and required constant appeasement lest their violence be unleashed upon unsuspecting bystanders. Sometimes no offerings would suffice, however, as in the case of *neak ta* 'Lady Mau':

> From 1866 until 1944 this *neak ta* was very wild, very noisy; if people walked along the road toward Kampot in front of her place they would be prevented. She could not be pleased with offerings of this or that.[14]

Other female *neak ta* had no name; these were *araks brai*, 'wild spirits', and took on different forms, one of which was *srei khmau*, 'black lady'.[15] One

50 *Trude Jacobsen*

such *araks brai* inhabited the governor's sword in Battambang. Known as *Srei Khmau*, once released from its scabbard it had to taste blood twice before being resheathed.[16]

Some female *neak ta* had specific victims in mind. Those that dwelt next to stairs going down to a *srah*, or artificial lake built as part of a temple complex, were to be avoided by pregnant women, lest they miscarry through the malevolent power of the *neak ta*. This was especially the case in places wherein women had been killed in the area. In the late eighteenth century, *Neang* Teav,[17] wife of a Cambodian official at the court of Siam, became homesick and fled to Battambang province. Her husband sent his retainers to capture and kill her for deserting him. They caught up with her on the Sangkhe River, killed her, and buried her body on the riverbank. From that time on, passengers on the waterway felt compelled to offer a gift of some sort to *Neang* Teav or risk drowning or losing their boatloads of goods in the suddenly treacherous waters.[18] When a dike was later built at the site, again, pregnant women were warned to steer clear.[19]

Key events in the life-cycle of women were opportunities for fearsome female spirits to emerge. Pregnancy and childbirth were times when a particular kind of spirit, a *brai*, would attempt to take the child or inhabit the body of its mother in order to fulfil their own thwarted maternal instincts. One type of ghost in this genre was the *brai krala plerng*, 'spirit of the fire-chamber'. A woman who had died in childbirth or very soon afterward haunted the room in which women gave birth – the *krala plerng* – waiting for an opportunity to seize the infant or invade its mother. As a precaution against the *brai krala plerng*, for three days after delivery the mother and child slept on a raised platform under which a fire was kept constantly burning. Women who died in childbirth or in the third trimester of pregnancy were said to have been killed by the *brai krala plerng*. *Brai* could also be created by audacious men from such a corpse through ritual. If he carried out the ceremony correctly, the woman would eventually be resurrected as a *brai*; if he withstood her horrific attempts to frighten him, he could take her unborn child and make it into a *koan kroach*, an object of immense power, by smoking it over a ritual fire. The dead mother would follow her child and protect it from harm, thus protecting the man who carried it on his person as a talisman.[20]

Women of childbearing age who died sexually inexperienced were also violent inhabitants of the supernatural world in late nineteenth- and early twentieth-century Cambodia. Beautiful at first glance, with long, lustrous hair, the *brai kramom* ('unmarried female spirit') lured her victim – usually a man who had broken her own heart, leading to her death or the death of another young woman under similar circumstances – to a secluded spot and then revealed her true appearance. This was calculated to frighten the victim to death and included bulging, rolling eyes, a long, lolling tongue, and matted and wiry hair. Again, these *brai* could be created for a purpose and their potentially dangerous energies could be ritually transformed into protective forces; according to local legend, when Wat Vihear Thom, in Kratie

Cambodia: querulous queens, bellicose brai & female agency   51

province, was being built, one hundred virgins were crushed to death in the foundation rubble. The hundred *brai kramom* would then protect the *wat* and its inhabitants from harm.[21]

The folktales and legends of Middle Cambodia, written down for the first time in the late nineteenth or twentieth century, also bespeak immense agency for women. Legends such as *Rioeng Neang Rasmey Sok* ('The tale of the young lady of the beautiful hair') and *Neang Kangrei* ('Tale of the young lady Kangrei') tell of *yaksini,* female demons, leading their supernatural armies into battle and fighting to the death.[22] In *Rioeng Kang Han* ('Tale of Lucky Han'), Han is chased up a tree by a tiger: a coward, he remains there until his wives rescue him, driving the beast away so that he may descend from his undignified roost. In addition to being represented as physically braver, women are often more intelligent and quick-witted than men, whose greed and laziness land them in hot water time and time again.[23] The Cambodian *Jataka*, tales of the Buddha's lives, similarly reflect women as purposeful agents rather than passive.[24] Similarly, the presence of *Preah Neang Dharani*, the Earth Goddess whom Buddha calls forth from the earth to vanquish the armies of the demon Mara is testament to the acceptability of agency for women in Cambodia throughout the premodern period, even within the usually conservative tenets of Buddhism.[25]

The powerful women of the supernatural realm continued to have resonance for Cambodia throughout the twentieth century. *Neak ta*, male and female, continued to be venerated by 'modernised' Cambodians as they had for centuries. A statue of a female *neak ta* named Yeay Deb, 'Grandmother Deb' ('Deb' is a corruption of *Devi*, 'goddess') housed within a *wat*, posed a danger for pregnant women in the 1940s.[26] In 1968, six girls fell victim to a malevolent *brai* dwelling near a river in Sisophon province.[27] The spirit of Princess Krapum Chhuk, who had been eaten by a crocodile at the site of Wat Vihear Thom (mentioned above) in the sixteenth century, regularly sent messages to Prince Sihanouk throughout the 1960s via a spirit medium. The last message, received in 1969, stated that Prince Sihanouk would fall from power; some months later he was deposed in the *coup d'état* of March 1970 that brought Lon Nol to power and ushered in the Khmer Republic (1970–1975). Preah Neang Dharani remained popular and images of her continued to be constructed or refurbished. In the early 1970s her iconography was co-opted into an anti-communist propaganda poster in which she is shown vanquishing the Viet Cong. In 1972, a possessed woman climbed onto the roundabout near Psar Orussei in Phnom Penh on which a statue of Preah Neang Dharani had been erected in 1966, and rained prophecies down upon passers-by.[28] Around this time, a man attempting to create a *brai* murdered his pregnant wife in southeastern Cambodia.[29]

The three years, eight months, and twenty days of the Khmer Rouge regime (1975–1979) – during which all 'superstitious' practices were forbidden, at least in theory – did little to change the way that female power in the supernatural world was received in the Cambodian collective consciousness.

Figure 3.1 Earth goddess Preah Neang Dharani standing guard at the entrance to the Ministry of Water Resources and Meteorology, Phnom Penh, Cambodia.
Source: Photo by Trude Jacobsen (2007).

Indeed, there is evidence to suggest that a few Khmer Rouge cadres attempted to create *brai* from their victims.[30] Today, malevolent *kmouch*, 'ghosts', including *brai* and *ap,* 'sorceresses', congregate near stagnant water; many people living in Chamcar Mon district in Phnom Penh, through which a polluted canal runs, believe that one of the key reasons that the municipality is agitating to fill in the canals is the proliferation of *kmouch*. Female *neak ta* continue to inhabit statues, trees, caves, and stones. Legendary women of the past and goddesses, including 'Lady Naga', Parvati, Srei Khmau, Preah Neang Dharani, and Umavati, regularly occupy the bodies of male and female mediums, imparting predictions and knowledge.[31] The best visual representation of the way that female agency in the supernatural world continues to be appreciated is at the gates of the Ministry of Water Resources and Meteorology, where Preah Neang Dharani stands guard (Figure 3.1).

Querulous queens

Contrary to the way in which supernatural women and other female agents in the supernatural realm were, and continue to be, regarded in Cambodia, there is a belief in present-day Cambodia that women should not be

Cambodia: querulous queens, bellicose brai & female agency   53

aggressive or forceful. Agency is considered to be not quite appropriate for Cambodian women – in the everyday world, at least. There is a widespread view that the 'natural' timidity of women makes them incapable of independent thought and decisive action.[32] Men are the leaders, with women relegated to a supporting role. The idea that a woman should put herself 'forward', especially if in so doing she eclipses a man, attracts severe censure.[33] The source of this notion of model behaviour is the *Cbpab Srei*, 'Code of conduct for women', of which there are at least three versions. Its authorship is attributed variously to the *oknha* (lord) Nong (late eighteenth/early nineteenth century), King Ang Duong (1837), the scholar Minh Mai (mid-nineteenth century), and the Cambodian poet laureate Ind (late nineteenth century).[34] All were inspired by their education in Siamese-influenced monasteries or households in which their tutors were invariably Buddhist monks.

All versions of the *Cbpab Srei* concur in admonishing daughters and wives to be obedient to their fathers and husbands. Agency is only permissible within the context of contributing positively to the well-being and reputation of the family – which meant taking a subservient position to their husband. Women were instructed that the 'master of the chamber is our superior; never mistake it';[35] they owed their husbands 'unwavering respect' and should 'support and believe him, as you are a woman; avoid putting yourself as his equal'.[36] Respect for one's husband was essential:

> If you are proud, and harden your heart, and make yourself the equal of he who is your superior,
> If you get carried away and speak without thinking, you are a woman who invites trouble.
> Do not protest or respond sarcastically to excite his anger,
> Do not persist, do not look at him with stony eyes, do not provoke a quarrel with your lack of respect.[37]

The relationship between husbands and wives within the household serve as a microcosmic exemplar for gender roles in Cambodian society at large. As Judy Ledgerwood has explained, texts such as the *Cbpab Srei* never discuss Cambodian women in terms of their strength or power, but in terms of virtue.[38] This virtue may take the form of correct obedience within the family or observance of Buddhist piety but never through aggressive action or agency, which was reserved for men. *Cbpab Preah Rajasambhir* ('Code of conduct for kings'), produced earlier, advised that in order to evaluate a king, 'one must look at his conquests; in order to form an estimate of a queen one must look at her pious acts'.[39]

The earliest extant Cambodian histories, the court chronicles, were composed at the very end of the eighteenth or early nineteenth century, although they purport to date from pre-Angkorian times. Deviation from the 'correct' model of female behaviour as expounded in these elite-authored

54 *Trude Jacobsen*

texts attracted censure. This is not surprising as court chronicles and didactic codes were written by the elite; both genres could therefore be expected to espouse similar perspectives toward female agency. Mae Yuor Vatti is one example, although her story is largely sympathetic. Forced to marry her uncle Paramaraja Udaiy in 1627, she fell in love with her half-brother Dhammaraja. She tricked her husband into giving permission for her to take a pleasure-trip to the Tonlé Sap; once out of sight of his guards, she changed course and joined Dhammaraja at Oudong. Once Paramaraja discovered the truth, he sent Portuguese mercenaries to bring her back. A civil war broke out between uncle and nephew, culminating in Dhammaraja's death. Mae Yuor Vatti was executed for treason to her king and disobedience to her husband, even though the chronicles imply that the love between the siblings was appropriate and their desire to be together understandable.[40]

There are three tropes employed to explain historical incidences wherein women stepped beyond the accepted notion of correct female behaviour and displayed agency, aggression, or violent tendencies, apart from the 'condemnation and punishment' model described above. The first, exigent agency, occurs when women were 'driven' to agency or violence through extraordinary circumstances. Devikshatri, principal queen of Paramaraja I (r. 1556–c.1570), is recorded in the chronicles as having acted with a high degree of independence (and remained a powerful presence behind the throne after his death). When her grandson Paramaraja III died in 1600, Devikshatri brought another grandson, the sixteen-year-old Nom, to the throne, but finding him unsatisfactory, she sent word to the king of Siam in 1603 asking that her husband's second son, Suriyobarna, be returned to Cambodia, as his country needed him. Summoning the court, she 'stripped her grandson prince Nom of sovereignty…and offered the throne to Suriyobarna'.[41] These actions hardly imply passivity, yet Devikshatri was not censured for stepping outside the parameters of correct conduct for women.

Similarly, Baen (1807–1840), the eldest daughter of Ang Chan (b. 1792, r. 1797–1834), received favourable treatment in the chronicles although her actions could be construed as treason. King Chan had welcomed a Vietnamese military presence into Cambodia in 1811 in an effort to resist the over-involvement of Siam in Cambodian political life. Upon his death, the Vietnamese crowned his second daughter Mei queen, becoming increasingly enmeshed in the administrative and political life of Cambodia. Meanwhile, the Thai king set about assisting Chan's brothers Ang Duong (b. 1796; r. 1848–1859) and Ang Im (b. 1794–1844) to 'liberate' the country. In 1840, Princess Baen was discovered to have been planning to escape to her mother Queen Tep and uncle Ang Im in Battambang. She was charged by the Nguyen advisors at court with 'collaborating with the enemy' and imprisoned until her trial, after which, according to most versions of the story, she was executed by drowning.[42] Despite the fact that Baen had been actively plotting

Cambodia: querulous queens, bellicose brai *& female agency* 55

against her queen and half-sister, she was depicted in the chronicles as a heroine. The story of Baen confirms two models: women exercising agency should be punished, but they are also capable of exigent agency.

The second trope employed in the chronicles to explain female behaviour deviating from the purported ideal was to dismiss the women concerned as not 'truly' Cambodian by dint of ethnicity. Stepping outside the parameters of appropriate behaviour and acting with aggression and violence was only to be expected in women who were not constrained by civilized social mores. It was never condoned, however, even when their agency resulted in positive outcomes for the Cambodian court. The removal of King Ramadhipati I (r. 1642–1659) from power is a case in point. Having married a Cham girl, Neang Hvas, whom he discovered in a fishing village and raised to be his 'left-hand queen',[43] Ramadhipati I converted to Islam and forced all the nobles at court to convert likewise. This, and in particular circumcision, proved deeply unpopular.[44] Ramadhipati I is described in the chronicles as having been enchanted by the beauty of Neang Hvas and thus led astray; she maintained his devotion by making him drink potions concocted by Cham and Malay sorcerers.[45] It was Neang Hvas, therefore, not Ramadhipati I, who erred; yet this is explained by her 'foreignness'. Her allegiance is naturally to her true people, not to her husband and sovereign. Similarly, although Ang Chuv, a Nguyen princess who married King Jai Jettha II around 1620, was instrumental in deposing Ramadhipati I, she is described in the chronicles as an immoral woman of 'extraordinary powers' who forced her husband to relinquish the land around Prei Nokor (Saigon) to the Vietnamese.[46]

'Otherness' could still be invoked as an explanation for un-Cambodian behaviour in cases wherein the princess or queen was the child of a Cambodian king and a non-Khmer queen. Ang Li Kshatri, daughter of Ramadhipati I and Neang Hvas, was forced to marry her uncle, Padumaraja II, when he usurped the throne in 1672. The following year, she plotted with her Cham and Malay retainers (inherited from her mother) to assassinate him. Having secured permission for a large group of these retainers to remain in the palace overnight in order to tend to her during a feigned illness, she ordered them to kill the king in his bed.[47] The plot was successful, and the throne passed to a more popular king. This is not in keeping with Cambodian ideals of female passivity in the mundane world; yet because the woman concerned was *not* fully Cambodian, and demonstrated this through her identification with Cham and Malay peoples to the apparent exclusion of all others, her agency could be tolerated.

The final trope employed was to completely disregard the existence of women who displayed characteristics that were not viewed as appropriate according to received social mores by writing them out of court chronicles – although evidence remains elsewhere. It is clear that this occurred in at least two occasions in the eighteenth century, when queens broke away from the established court and set up their own rival seats of power; yet no mention

56   *Trude Jacobsen*

is made of them in the chronicles. Inscriptions, however, have preserved some tantalising evidence, corroborated by Thai sources. After the death of King Ang Im (r. 1710–1722 and 1729–1730) in 1736, Queen Sijhata, married to Ang Im's son Sattha, left the court at Longvaek in order to establish her own court at Samrong Saen. She was accompanied by members of the royal family and officials who, presumably, saw Sijhata, the daughter of King Jai Jettha IV, as a more legitimate ruler than Sattha, the heir apparent Dhammaraja then sequestered in Siam. Her title in the inscription is *anuj kshatri*, 'young queen'.[48]

The same inscription mentions a *kshatri*, 'great queen', daughter of 'the king *kaev hva*'. Jai Jettha IV had given the title *kaev hva* to Ang Im in 1699, and he was usually referred to in this manner.[49] In all likelihood this queen was the daughter of Ang Im and his principal queen, another sister of Dhammaraja. The *mahakshatri*, therefore, was Dhammaraja's niece. The implication is that in 1736 or shortly thereafter, Sijhata broke away from the Ang Im-Sattha faction, perhaps to establish a seat of power from which her brother Dhammaraja could set about winning over the populace once he returned. He was ultimately successful, yet the *mahakshatri*, obviously a member of the Ang Im-Sattha faction, held out against him. The title *kaev hva* had been inherited by a male member of the clan after Ang Im died in 1730 and in 1737 acknowledged Dhammaraja as king.[50] By 1747, however, things appear to have soured between the two factions of the family and the *mahakshatri* and Dhammaraja were at war. One interpretation is that one of Ang Im's queens was another sister of Dhammaraja; a daughter of Ang Im and grand-daughter of Jai Jettha IV would be perceived as a legitimate contender for the throne. The *mahakshatri* posed too great a threat to Dhammaraja's legitimacy, and he engaged her in civil war. He was successful; Dhammaraja's general 'captured the princess and a mass of goods, and escorted her to the king in order to prostrate herself and offer her slave and her belongings [to him]'.[51] Neither of these relatively recent women warriors are known to Cambodians today, nor do they appear in any of the surviving court chronicles.

There is no awareness in Cambodian society at large that *any* of the women discussed in this section ever existed. They do not feature in school textbooks. They are not held up as examples by those seeking to instill a greater sense of gender equality in Cambodia. Angkorian times, however, are believed by some to have been ones in which women were warriors. One advocate of women's rights, lamenting the lack of egalitarianism in the early 2000s, stated that women had been 'actively involved in wars' in that period, and asked why this had not translated into greater numbers of women standing for election.[52] Yet almost everyone born in Cambodia, if asked, would be able to give detailed explanations of the different forms of *brai* and how to avoid them, not to mention the significance of Preah Neang Dharani. Why has it been necessary to explain or omit female agency in the mundane world when its presence in the supernatural realm has been universally accepted?

Constructing context

Part of the answer lies in the way that 'traditional' Cambodia has been constructed. The reign of King Ang Duong (r. 1848–1859) is considered a 'golden age' in Cambodian history,[53] a brief interregnum of political and cultural autonomy between Vietnamese hegemony and French colonialism. For this reason, any material dating from this period is regarded uncritically as representing true 'Cambodian-ness'. Thus the tenets of the *'Cbpab Srei'*, a collective term meaning any and all versions, are viewed as indicative of the prevailing social mores of Cambodian society, even though the earliest possible version dates only from the late eighteenth century.

There are two problems with this assumption. First, the possible biases of the authors must be placed in context. The *oknha* Nong and the future king Ang Duong spent long periods at the Thai court during a time when Buddhism was undergoing a conservative restoration. Cambodian monks at the court of the Thai King Rama I (r. 1782–1809) were deeply involved in the revision of Buddhist texts along the more austere lines of the *Dhammayut* sect. There is no doubt that Ang Duong and other members of the Cambodian court sequestered in Siam in the late eighteenth and nineteenth centuries were heavily influenced by Dhammayut Buddhism and its conservative mores, particularly regarding agency for women. Prior to writing his *Cbpab Srei* in 1837, Ang Duong wrote *Rieong Neang Kaki*, modelled upon the work of a Thai court poet and derived from two *jataka* tales. The central theme of the text is that women – particularly their sexuality – must be controlled lest disaster result for the kingdom.[54] The antecedents of Minh Mai are less well known, but it seems safe to assume that a court official of the nineteenth century would have been exposed to the same influences as Ang Duong. In any case, all noblemen were expected to observe a period as a novice monk, another possible avenue for the inculcation of conservative views toward female agency. *Oknha suttanta prachea* Ind, 'lord poet of the land', hailed from the province of Battambang, subject to Thai hegemony from 1774 until 1907 and therefore exposed to the influences emanating from the Thai court. He also spent over a decade as a monk.[55] All of these men were elite, educated, and came from religiously conservative backgrounds. Their status ensured that their literature would be well received by their peers. We are told that people in Battambang waited avidly for Ind's next creation: 'Everyone in Battambang praised his works and speeches. While Cambodia had no printed books, the people of Battambang borrowed his work from one another, copying them out by hand to keep and distributing them one to the other.'[56]

The second issue with accepting that the *Cbpab Srei* represented the true state of pre-colonial Cambodian society is that the mores enshrined in the text are at variance with ethnographic and other information of Cambodia at the time. Most of the Cambodian population was illiterate until the mid-twentieth century; the only time that rural people would have had an opportunity to hear works of literature such as the *Cbpab Srei* was when

58   *Trude Jacobsen*

they were set to music and recited by travelling folk-singers like Phiroum Ngoy.[57] Legal codes, the observations of French explorers and administrators, and the Cambodian folktales bespeak a high degree of autonomy for women generally, at the same time that more conservative texts disallowing female agency were being written and, allegedly, read.[58]

The Cambodians who searched their past for a 'true' Cambodian identity in the 1930s and 1940s did not remark upon this disparity, or, if they did, ignored it. By this time, the French too had accepted the *Chpab Srei* as a literal reflection of traditional gender norms, bolstered by their own impressions of Cambodian women as passive and powerless, and enshrined this view in the colonial education system. Their assumptions were imparted to what Penny Edwards has termed the *neak che doeung*,[59] 'people knowing knowledge', who were the first to seize upon the educational opportunities offered by French patronage and establish themselves as the new elite in the colonial era. This group, in conjunction with both Buddhist *sangha*, the royal family, and the French administration, was responsible for determining which elements of the past (or newly created ones) constituted Cambodian 'tradition', not the far greater number of Cambodians in the countryside. Thus, agency for women in the twentieth century was constrained by having to remain within the parameters allowed by the *Chpab Srei*, as the reflection of a 'pure' Cambodian society.[60] Observance of the *Chpab Srei* came to symbolize harmony in Cambodia as a whole. A book published in 1967 suggested that women were 'forgetting the *Chpap Srei*' and putting society at risk.[61]

This has persisted even when Cambodian women have been called upon to be warriors. During the Cambodian civil war of the early 1970s, women were mobilized into civilian units and the revolutionary forces in the countryside, yet there is an almost apologetic sense to statements praising their participation. The heroine depicted in one pro-Lon Nol propaganda poster was described in 1970 as having 'for a moment abandoned her natural gentleness….nevertheless being also firmly resolved to oppose the aggressors'.[62] On the other side of the conflict, women would carry out armed manoeuvres with their male counterparts, but only they would don aprons and prepare food upon return to camp.[63] Once the revolutionary struggle was achieved, women were expected to cast off their 'warrior' personas[64] and return to the lives of passivity set out in the *Chpap Srei*. Any attempt on the part of women to step beyond these parameters is met with hostility. Such women are not merely causing dissonance in society – frowned upon because of the tragic consequences that resulted from the total inversion of Cambodian society under the Khmer Rouge – but endangering Cambodian culture.

***

Epigraphic, sculptural, textual, and ethnographic evidence indicates that women warriors in the supernatural realm have been an accepted part of

Cambodia: querulous queens, bellicose brai *& female agency* 59

life in Cambodia for two millennia. Their counterparts in the mundane world, however, are denied similar agency. When women warriors are acknowledged in the Cambodian histories, three tropes are employed to explain this departure from correct behaviour for Cambodian women: (1) exigency, in which the circumstances in which the women are 'forced' to act are extraordinary; (2) 'otherness', wherein the women concerned cannot be expected to observe 'correct' behaviour as they are not Cambodian; and (3) omission, in which women are left out of Cambodian versions of events, but their existence is known from other sources such as epigraphy or the histories of other courts. The lack of agency for women in the everyday world is articulated by the *Cbpab Srei*, the code of conduct that most Cambodians believe reflects 'traditional' Cambodian society. In fact, this text dates from the late eighteenth or nineteenth century at the earliest, and depicts the ideal society as perceived by its authors (who borrowed heavily from Siam) rather than a likeness of true gender roles. Yet there is more than one world of significance in Cambodia; the supernatural and the mundane are inextricably linked, and perhaps is not for western sensibilities to determine which is the more important, querulous queens or the bellicose *brai*.

Notes

1 Excerpt from the *History of the Southern Qi*, in Paul Pelliot, 'Le Fou–nan', *Bulletin de l'École Française d'Extrême-Orient* (BEFEO), Vol. 3 (1903), p. 256.
2 Kate Frieson, *Women in the Shadows: Power and Politics in Cambodia* (Victoria, British Columbia: University of Victoria Centre for Asia-Pacific Initiatives Occasional Paper 26, 2001), p. 3.
3 For the purposes of this paper, the notion of collective human agency (cf. Hegel and Marx) is eschewed in favour of action realizing outcomes for specific individuals.
4 Pelliot, 'Le Fou–nan', p. 256.
5 Kamaleswar Bhattacharya, *Les religions brahmaniques dans l'ancien Cambodge, d'après l'épigraphie et l'iconographie* (Paris: École Française d'Extrême-Orient [EFEO], 1961), p. 92.
6 For a more detailed explanation of this phenomenon, see Trudy Jacobsen, 'Autonomous Queenship in Preclassical Cambodia, 1st–9th centuries AD', *Journal of the Royal Asiatic Society*, Vol. 13, No. 3 (2003), pp. 357–375.
7 K. 834, verses B29, B59, B72, in *Inscriptions du Cambodge* [hereafter *IC*], ed. George Cœdès (Paris and Hanoi: Imprimerie de l'EFEO and Imprimerie Nationale, 1937–1966), Vol. 5, pp. 244–269; K. 191, verse B29, *IC* 6, pp. 300–311; Vittorio Roveda, *Khmer Mythology* (London: Thames and Hudson, 1998), p. 56.
8 K. 692, v. C39, *IC* 1, pp. 227–249; K. 661, vv. A22, A24., *IC* 1, pp. 197–219.
9 Zhou Daguan, *The Customs of Cambodia*, trans. J. Gilman d'Arcy Paul, 2nd ed. (Bangkok: Siam Society, 1992), p. 5.
10 Ashley Thompson, 'Introductory Remarks between the Lines: Writing Histories of Middle Cambodia', in Barbara Watson Andaya (ed.), *Other Pasts: Women, Gender and History in Early Modern Southeast Asia* (Honolulu, HI: University of Hawaii at Manoa, 2000), p. 47.

60   *Trude Jacobsen*

11 Two documents list the names of hundreds of *me sa*. One of these documents is dated 1859; the other is not dated, but it is reasonable to place it slightly later. See David Chandler, 'Maps for the Ancestors: Sacralized Topography and Echoes of Angkor in Two Cambodian Texts', in David Chandler, *Facing the Cambodian Past: Selected Essays, 1971–1994* (St. Leonards, NSW: Allen & Unwin, 1996), p. 42.

12 For more detailed information on this goddess see David Chandler, 'Royally Sponsored Human Sacrifices in Nineteenth Century Cambodia: The Cult of *nak ta* Me Sa (Mahisasuramardini) at Ba Phnom', in Chandler, *Facing the Cambodian Past*, pp. 119–135. A similar phenomenon occurred in Vietnam with the Cham goddess Po Nagar.

13 See, for example, *Neak ta Srei neung Yeay Bos*, in *Prajum rieong bring khmei: Krom jomnuon tomniem tomleap khmei* (Phnom Penh: Buddhist Institute, 2001), Vol. 8, pp. 107–113; *Neak ta Yeay Nguon*, in *Prajum rieong bring khmei*, Vol. 8, pp. 155–175.

14 *Neak ta Jamdev Mau*, in *Prajum rieong breng khmei*, Vol. 8, pp. 123–133.

15 *Neak ta Yeay Khmau*, in *Prajum rieong bring khmei*, Vol. 8, pp. 51–56; Etienne Aymonier, *Notes sur les coutumes et croyances superstitieuses des cambodgiens, commenté et présenté par Saveros Pou* (Paris: Cedorek, 1984), pp. 58–59, 77.

16 Tauch Chhong, *Battambang during the Time of the Lord Governor*, 2nd ed., trans. Han Sithan, Carol Mortland and Judy Ledgerwood (Phnom Penh: Cedorek, 1994), p. 50; Judith Jacob, *The Traditional Literature of Cambodia: A Preliminary Guide* (Oxford: Oxford University Press, 1996), pp. 139, 142; *Kambujasuriya*, vols. 7–9 (1937), pp. 327–337.

17 *Neang* is a polite title by which to refer to a young woman.

18 Tauch Chhong, *Battambang during the Time of the Lord Governor*, pp. 27–28.

19 Ang Chouléan, *Les êtres surnaturels dans la religion populaire khmère* (Paris: Cedorek, 1986), p. 219; Tauch Chhong, *Battambang during the Time of the Lord Governor*, p. 82. A small boat kept at Wat Kantoeng in Battambang itself also had the same unfortunate effect as it was inhabited by such a spirit.

20 *Kram montiro bal*, in Adhémard Leclère, *Les codes cambodgiens* (Paris: E. Leroux, 1898), t. 1, pp. 191–192; Ang Chouléan, *Les êtres surnaturels dans la religion populaire khmère*, p. 105; Ang Chouléan, 'Grossesse et accouchement au Cambodge: Aspects rituels', *ASEMI: Asie du Sud-Est et du Monde Insulindien*, Vol. 13, No. 1–4 (1982), p. 100; Aymonier, *Notes sur les coutumes et croyances*, p. 69. It was also possible to make *koan kroach* by forcibly removing the fetus from its mother while she still lived.

21 Ang Chouléan, *Les êtres surnaturels dans la religion populaire khmère*, pp. 132; 213, note 503.

22 Tauch Chhong, *Battambang during the Time of the Lord Governor*, p. 50; Jacob, *Traditional Literature of Cambodia*, pp. 139, 142; *Kambujasuriya*, vols. 7–9 (1937), pp. 327–337.
     FTR: I added the comma, in line with the earlier note 12

23 Jacob, *Traditional Literature of Cambodia*, p. 15; *Rieong maya srei*, in *Kambujasuriya* 7–9 (1938), pp. 327–337; *Rieong Kang Han*, in *Kambujasuriya* 8, 4–6 (1938), pp. 45–53.

24 Muriel Paksin Carrison (comp.), *Cambodian Folk Stories from the Gatiloke*, trans. Kong Chhean (Rutland, Vermont, VT; Tokyo, Japan: Charles E. Tuttle, 1987), p. 16; Adhémard Leclère, *Le Buddhisme au Cambodge* (Paris: Ernest Leroux, 1889), pp. 223–224, note 6.

25 Carrison, *Cambodian Folk Stories from the Gatiloke*, p. 16; Leclère, *Buddhisme au Cambodge*, pp. 223–224, note 6. See also Elizabeth Guthrie, 'Outside the sima', *Udaya: Journal of Khmer Studies*, Vol. 2 (2001), pp. 7–18.

26 Ang Chouléan, *Les êtres surnaturels*, pp. 134, 219.

Cambodia: querulous queens, bellicose brai *& female agency* 61

27 *Ibid.*, pp. 150, 162–163.
28 Milada Kalab, 'Buddhism and Emotional Support for Elderly People', *Journal of Cross-Cultural Gerontology*, Vol. 5 (1990), pp. 12–13; Ang Chouléan, *Les êtres surnaturels*, pp. 40–41, 222; Guthrie, 'Outside the sima', p. 13; fieldnotes 2001, 2005; Harris, *Cambodian Buddhism*, note 72, page 282; Osborne, *Before Kampuchea*, pp. 46–47; Milton Osborne, *Sihanouk: Prince of Light, Prince of Darkness* (St. Leonards, NSW: Allen & Unwin, 1994), p. 70.
29 Ang Chouléan, *Les êtres surnaturels*, pp. 40–41, 222.
30 Haing S. Ngor, *Cambodian Odyssey* (New York: Macmillan, 1987), pp. 223, 245–246; fieldnotes, 2004, 2005. Six informants insisted that this had occurred during the Khmer Rouge period. Only one claimed to have witnessed such an occurrence; the others had been told by others.
31 Didier Bertrand, 'A Medium Possession Practice and its Relationship with Cambodian Buddhism: The *grū pāramī*', in John Marston and Elizabeth Guthrie (eds.), *History, Buddhism, and New Religious Movements in Cambodia* (Honolulu, HI: University of Hawaii Press, 2004), pp. 153, 159.
32 See, for example, Peter S. Hill and Heng Thay Ly, 'Women are Silver, Women are Diamonds: Conflicting Images of Women in the Cambodian Print Media', *Reproductive Health Matters*, Vol. 12, No. 24 (2004), p. 108.
33 See, for example, Judy L. Ledgerwood, 'Politics and Gender: Negotiating Changing Cambodian Ideas of the Proper Woman', *Asia Pacific Viewpoint*, Vol. 37, No. 2 (1996), pp. 141–142.
34 A *Cbpab Srei* ostensibly authored by Ang Duong was published by the Buddhist Institute in 1962. It lists the types of wives and their characteristics in a similar fashion to the Minh Mai text and to *Kram tous bhariya*. See Khing Hoc Dy, *Contribution à l'histoire de la littérature khmère* (Paris: L'Harmattan, 1990), p. 90; Judy L. Ledgerwood, 'Changing Khmer Conceptions of Gender: Women, Stories, and the Social Order' (PhD thesis, Cornell University, 1990), pp. 82, 86; Jacob, *Traditional Literature of Cambodia*, p. 70. The travelling folk-singer Ngoy, popular in the early nineteenth century, had a *Cbpab Srei* in his repertoire that is very similar to that of Ind – perhaps unsurprising as they both hailed from Battambang.
35 *Cbpab Srei*, v. 5. The version of the *Cbpab Srei* referred to in this paper is the *Cbpab Srei* of Minh Mai, reproduced in *Cbpab srei-broh* (Phnom Penh: Phsep pseay juon koan khmei, 2001). A transliterated version with French translation is available in Saveros Pou (ed.), *Guirlande de cpāp* (Paris: Cedorek, 1988), 2 vols.
36 *Cbpab Srei*, verses 51–52.
37 Ibid., verses 69–72.
38 Ledgerwood, 'Changing Khmer Conceptions of Gender', p. 24.
39 *Cbpab Preah Rajasambhir*, verse 37, in Saveros Pou and Philip N. Jennar, 'Les cpāp' ou "codes de conduit" Khmers IV: Cpāp Rājaneti ou cpāp' brah Rājasambhīr', *BEFEO*, Vol. 65 (1978), p. 375.
40 *Chroniques royales du Cambodge*, vol. 2: *De Bonea Yat à la prise de Lanvaek (1417–1595)*, trans. and ed. Khin Sok (Paris: EFEO, 1988), pp. 99, 104, 111, 158,186, 214–215; *Chroniques royales du Cambodge* (Paris: EFEO, 1988), vol. 3: *De 1594 à 1677*, trans. and ed. Mak Phoeun, pp. 79, 122, 127, 168, 171, 175–177, 423–424.
41 *Chroniques* 3, pp. 76, 82–84, 88–89.
42 Bun Srun Theam, Cambodia in the Mid-Nineteenth Century: A Quest for Survival, 1840–1863 (MA thesis, Australian National University, 1981), pp. 71–72; David Chandler, 'Cambodia before the French: Politics in a Tributary Kingdom, 1794–1848' (PhD thesis, University of Michigan, 1973), p. 151. According to the *Veang Thiounn* chronicle, Princess Baen was tortured to death and her body

62   Trude Jacobsen

thrown into the river in a sack. See Khin Sok, *Le Cambodge entre le Siam et le Vietnam (de 1775 à 1860)* (Paris: EFEO, 1991), p. 94.

43 The women of the Cambodian court were arranged according to direction, usually cardinal points, but also left and right upon occasion.

44 The chronicle indicates that the king forced all male courtiers to undergo circumcision as part of their conversion, after which the Chams at court collected the foreskins and placed them in a temple, thus symbolically emasculating their rival officials. See Trudy Jacobsen, 'The Temple of the Thousand Foreskins', *Phnom Penh Post*, December 16–29, 2005, p. 7.

45 See Carool Kersten, 'Cambodia's Muslim King: Khmer and Dutch Sources on the Conversion of Reameathipadei I, 1642–1658', *Journal of Southeast Asian Studies*, Vol. 37, No. 1 (February 2006), pp. 16–17.

46 *Chroniques 3*, pp. 79, 122, 127, 168, 171, 176–177, 423–424.

47 Ibid., pp. 207–208.

48 She was the younger half-sister of Dhammaraja. See Saveros Pou, 'Inscriptions modernes d'Angkor 35, 36, 37 et 39', *BEFEO*, Vol. 61 (1974), p. 322; David Chandler, 'An Eighteenth Century Inscription from Angkor Wat', in Chandler, *Facing the Cambodian Past*, pp. 18, 22. Both are correct, as Sijhata was the half-sister of Dhammaraja. See also IMA 39, lines 17–20, in Pou, 'Inscriptions modernes d'Angkor 35, 36, 37 et 39', p. 319."

49 Chandler, 'An Eighteenth Century Inscription from Angkor Wat', pp. 18, note 10.

50 IMA 39, lines 11–13, Pou, 'Inscriptions modernes d'Angkor 35, 36, 37 et 39', p. 319.

51 IMA 39, lines 32–43 (French translation), in Pou, 'Inscriptions modernes d'Angkor 35, 36, 37 et 39', p. 324. David Chandler suggests that the *kaev hva* was Cun, a nephew of Dhammaraja, and the *mahakshatri*, Cun's daughter. The civil war erupted when, upon Cun's death in 1743, his title and widow were given to two sons of Dhammaraja. See Chandler, 'An Eighteenth Century Inscription from Angkor Wat', pp. 17–21.

52 *Gender in Election and Female Leadership at the Communal Level* (Phnom Penh: Women's Media Centre of Cambodia and the Royal Embassy of the Netherlands, 2000), p. 17. This belief derives from the fact that one of the most aesthetic temples in Siem Reap is called *Banteay Srei*, 'Fortress of Women'. It has been called this because it boasts remarkable *bas-relief* carvings of female figures.

53 David Chandler, *A History of Cambodia*, 3rd ed. (Boulder, CO: Westview Press, 2000), p. 135. 'Coffee-table' books and travel guides are particularly prone to this perspective. See, for example, Julio A. Jeldres, *The Royal House of Cambodia* (Phnom Penh: Monument Books, 2003), p. 20.

54 Somboon Suksamran, *Political Buddhism in Southeast Asia: The Role of the Sangha in the Modernization of Thailand* (New York: St Martin's Press, 1976), p. 26; Meas Yang, *Le Bouddhisme au Cambodge* (Brussels: Thanh Long, 1978), p. 38; Klaus Wenk, *The Restoration of Thailand under Rama I, 1782–1809*, trans. Greeley Stahl (Tucson, AZ: University of Arizona Press, 1968), pp. 39–41; Klaus Wenk, *Thai Literature: An Introduction*, trans. Erich W. Reinhold (Bangkok: White Lotus, 1995), p. 30; Ang Duong, *Rieong Kaki* [1813] (Phnom Penh: Buddhist Institute, 1997).

55 Tauch Chhong, *Battambang during the Time of the Lord Governor*, pp. 98–100; 'Supasit cbpab srei', *Kambujasuriya* 6, 4–6, pp. 46–80, p. 48; *Gatilok ke oknha Suttanta Prachea Ind*, in *Kambujasuriya* 7 (1927), pp. 75–93; *Gatilok ru chbpab tunmean khluon*, in *Kambujasuriya* 9 (1928), pp. 25–41 and 10 (1928), pp. 21–58. A neighbour of Ind named Chheum, a fortune-teller by profession, claimed to have written *Neang Chhantea*, but Ind's son said that his father had written it.

56 Tauch Chhong, *Battambang during the Time of the Lord Governor*, p. 99.

Cambodia: querulous queens, bellicose brai & female agency   63

57 *Kambujasuriya* 6, 7–9, pp. 176–179; *Gatilok ke oknha Suttanta Prachea Ind, Kambujasuriya* 7 (1927), pp. 75–93; *Kambujasuriya* 9 (1928), pp. 25–41 and 10 (1928), pp. 21–58; *Kambujasuriya* 4, 7–12 (1932), pp. 149–180; *Kambujasuriya* 4, 7–12 (1932), pp. 181; Ngoy, 'Cpbap kram thmei', *Kambujasuriya*, Vol. 4, No. 7–12 (1932), p. 149.

58 See Trudy Jacobsen, *Lost Goddesses: The Denial of Female Power in Cambodian History* (Copenhagen: NIAS Press, 2007), Chapter 6.

59 Penny Edwards, *Cambodge: The Cultivation of a Nation, 1860–1945* (Honolulu, HI: University of Hawaii Press, 2007), p. 136.

60 For an excellent treatment of the development of gender roles during the emergence of Cambodian nationalist thinking, see Kate Frieson, 'Sentimental Education: *Les sages femmes* and Colonial Cambodia', *Journal of Colonialism and Colonial History*, Vol. 1, No. 1 (2000) [available online at Project Muse].

61 San Neang, *Socheavatadar samrap broh neung srei* (Phnom Penh: n.p., 1967), p. 26.

62 San Sarin, 'For Victory', *New Cambodge*, Vol. 5 (September 1970), pp. 65–68, at p. 67.

63 *Democratic Kampuchea is Moving Forward* (Cambodia?, n.p., August 1977), p. 11; *New Cambodge* 4 (August 1970), p. 50.

64 The return of women warriors to their pre-revolutionary lives seems a pervasive phenomenon as illustrated by various papers in this volume. In the Cambodian context, opposition politician Mu Sochua is continually beset by reprimands from the ruling Cambodian People's Party that she is not acting in accordance with 'traditional' Cambodian womanhood.

4   The *Regio Femarum* and its warrior women

Images and encounters in European sources

Christina Skott

In 1784, a volume entitled *Allehanda Utländska Märkvärdigheter och Sällsamma Händelser* [All Kinds of Foreign Curiosities and Strange Events] was published in Västerås, Sweden. The purpose of the book was to provide an overview of the most unbelievable and marvellous facts from around the known world. From the island of Java it was reported:

> Various travelers can confirm, that the King of Bantam[1] on Java, has six, or some say twelve, hundred women equipped with rifles. These women guard the King night and day. They also wait on the King and carry out duties which only men do in royal courts elsewhere.[2]

This image of armed women guarding local rulers constituted one of the most persistent themes in European knowledge of Southeast Asia, and Java in particular, throughout the early modern era. The large number of court women caught the attention of the earliest European visitors to the region, and reports that some of these women carried arms were eagerly extracted by compilers of knowledge to be included in cosmographies, geography books, and other compendia of knowledge. So powerful was this image of the armed women that the very first visualisations of Southeast Asia, seventeenth-century engravings based on accounts generated by the earliest Dutch expeditions to Southeast Asia, depicted the powerful king of Aceh being waited on by pony-tailed, sturdy, and rather un-feminine ladies carrying spears, clearly evoking classical images of the ancient Amazons.

Historians of early modern Southeast Asia have affirmed that local rulers did surround themselves with armed female bodyguards, but, as we shall see, the scarce information on how these corps functioned in fact originates from the same European reports which created the image of the armed Amazons in European imagination. Instances of female participation in actual combat have however been suggestive and mostly related to mythical queens and royal consorts.[3] Arguing that women were more trustworthy than men, and that women were less prone to betrayal and rash action to defend honour, Anthony Reid has proposed that women could have taken part in battle on the grounds that female participation in war was not improbable in a society where social status had always played a bigger role than gender.[4]

It was in fact this aspect of society that would colour European knowledge of Southeast Asian women. Throughout the early modern era, women in their 'different' capacities gained a remarkable prominence in European reporting. This was very much linked to the visibility of women in the trade encounter, but could also be seen as an 'ethnography of difference', where Europeans witnessed women in unfamiliar roles, of which women as armed guards was only one.

Regional historians such as Reid have long since argued that the relationship between Southeast Asian men and women in the early modern era had a distinct pattern, which gave women a strong social and economic position that was unique in the world at the time.[5] Leaning heavily on European sources, Reid further placed the position of women within his argument for a regional 'age of commerce', seeing a deteriorating status of women as a reflection of political and economic decline during the seventeenth century. In the past decades gender and the role of women in early modern Southeast Asia has become a more firmly established field of study. The anthology *Other Pasts: Women, Gender and History in Early Modern Southeast Asia* crucially expressed criticism of a picture of gender relations as derived from European sources, but writers were also faced with the difficulties of reading women's lives out of indigenous literary traditions.[6] An extensive survey of female roles and the history of women in a regional context followed in Barbara Watson Andaya's *The Flaming Womb: Repositioning Women in Early Modern Southeast Asia*, which presented a cautious defence of the 'high status' of women but also highlighted the ways in which women's lives and roles changed with socioeconomic developments. This work also offered a detailed and nuanced account of how 'outside' influence, in particular the arrival of Europeans, often reduced options for women.

This chapter sets out to provide a contextualised overview of the ways in which outsiders (mostly Europeans) associated Southeast Asia with women in arms and as warriors, from classical times until the nineteenth century, by highlighting the relationship between the origins, transmission, and the processes of 'recycling' of knowledge. As historians have already pointed out, early European observation and interest in the region's warrior women leaned heavily on classical and medieval images of the East, where armed women easily fitted into older images of Amazons, long associated with the unknown East. The armed female guards in early modern European travel accounts were therefore easily recognisable as one of the ancient marvels. But this also eventually meant that nineteenth century calls for new, 'scientific' knowledge resulted in earlier accounts of armed women being dismissed as 'travellers' tales', ancient fables catering to European taste for the fantastic.

The chapter has a twofold aim. Firstly, I examine ways in which this region since earliest time became associated with queens and female warriors. By surveying pre-modern perceptions and knowledge of the region, I suggest the possibilities of conjecturing 'other', former roles for women in the Malay world prior to contact with outsiders. A second aim is to clarify

66 *Christina Skott*

and disentangle European reporting, to examine the origins of information about Southeast Asia's warrior women, and consequently to highlight the problematic status of travel literature and other related types of European sources for early modern Southeast Asian history. Although the institution of female guards was not confined to the Malay world (the best known are the bodyguards of the king of Siam) European references to females carrying weapons focus on the corps of guardswomen at the royal courts of Aceh and in Java. Our discussion will therefore revolve around these crucial sites of European contact with the region.

Throughout the early modern era, women acquired a unique visibility in European writing on Southeast Asia, something which was clearly linked to the unfamiliar roles in which Europeans encountered women here.[7] It is therefore useful to first see how the position of women, and female roles more widely, was perceived and reported by Europeans.

Female roles and the early modern encounter

When in 1617 the cosmographer and publisher of travel literature Samuel Purchas (c.1577–1626) for the first time introduced an English reading public to the Malay world, its women received generous attention. Describing the Malay sultanate of Patani, Purchas reported that Patani had a female ruler, and that Europeans who arrived there were assisted by local women in trading matters. These women were seen as 'carelesly frolick, and fearelesly merry' who 'let Venus predominate'.[8] This passage introduced themes which would engage European observers of Southeast Asia throughout the early modern era: women were described as 'loose', their eagerness to engage with Europeans interpreted as lasciviousness. Purchas had culled his information from the published accounts of the first Dutch expeditions to the region only a few decades earlier. The leader of the second Dutch expedition (1598–1600), Jacob Corneliszoon van Neck (1564–1638), had reported how local dignitaries had offered their daughters and even wives to stay with the Dutch for the duration of their stay in Patani.[9]

In early modern Southeast Asia, daughters and associates of local dignitaries were often crucial players in the trading process. Contracted out to visiting European traders, they had multiple roles as sexual partners, as providers of domestic services, but were importantly also facilitators of commerce and acted as translators. Van Neck was the first European to provide a description of the arrangements of these so-called 'temporary marriages'. A deterioration in this mutually beneficial arrangement, by which the 'wives' were gradually seen and treated as mere prostitutes, has been interpreted as an illustration of how a region-wide economic change which took place in the late seventeenth century also affected the status of women.[10] It is clear that it was the perceived eagerness to engage with Europeans that principally generated comments about female sexual behaviour, creating an image of the women of Southeast Asia as promiscuous and lacking in morals.[11]

The *Regio Femarum & its warrior women* 67

Apart from female participation in the trade encounter, women were also observed by Europeans in other unfamiliar capacities: as market traders, working the fields, as musicians and dancers, but also involved in customs which in Europe were associated with men such as smoking tobacco.[12] Europeans also encountered women as diplomats, messengers between rulers, and as brokers of trade deals.[13] One circumstance that had long-term consequences for European perceptions of Southeast Asia was that the earliest English and Dutch expeditions to Aceh and Patani coincided with female rule in these major trading ports. The female rulers of the Malay world have parallels in other Austronesian societies, and numerous polities were ruled by queens during the early modern era. Most of these examples are known only through indigenous sources, where the queens are portrayed as caring mother figures ruling with justice.[14]

Due to the scarcity of new publications in the later seventeenth century, the earliest Dutch and English accounts describing 'East-Indian' queens were repeated and recycled. As late as 1703 the editor of an English cosmography found it called for to explain the origins of this curiosity: 'The inhabitants of this island are so curious to have a lawful Heir upon the Throne, that the Husband not being certain the Children which he has by his wife are his own, but she is certain they are hers, therefore they rather chuse to be Governed by a woman to whom they give the Title of Queen; her Husband being only her Subject and having no power but what she gives him.'[15]

These remarks do not only refer to contemporary queens observed by early modern Europeans, but reflect a long-standing tradition of associating the furthest East-Indies, i.e. Southeast Asia, with powerful warrior queens.

Medieval warrior queens: the image of the Amazon

In scholarship concerned with the origins of Europe's knowledge of the outside world, the figure of the Amazon has attracted attention within a variety of fields, feminist theory, literary criticism, anthropology and cultural history. To the ancient Greeks, Amazons were female warriors associated with the northern shores of the Black Sea, and more generally the periphery of the Greek world. Herodotus famously described an ancient war between the Greeks and the Amazons, who were said to fight both on horseback and on foot; dressed in trousers and leather boots; and equipped with spears, bows and arrows. Amazonian society consisted solely of women, who mated with males only on rare occasions. Any male offspring were used as slaves, as Amazon mothers chose to rear only healthy female children.

During the time of European exploration, the figure of the Amazon was frequently evoked. Renaissance drama and poetry, for example, made use of the trope of Amazons inhabiting unknown lands.[16] The strongest geographical association was South America, where Sir Walter Raleigh (c. 1552–1618) famously met and obtained information from Amazons. In a gendered proto-colonialist 'imagining' of the New World, the Amazons have been

68   *Christina Skott*

seen as instrumental in the 'feminising' of the continent; a land seen as a woman which was easily turned into a land of women, and so fit to be exploited.[17] As part of a theorised colonial discourse, Amazons have been associated with areas of vast natural resources, especially precious metals, but the figure of the Amazon has also been appropriated into the role of the autonomous and threatening woman: a figure through which difference was expressed, especially as a trope by which racial difference was constructed.[18]

These literary interpretations have, however, entirely focused on images of the New World. Rarely mentioned by scholars is the long and unbroken chain of Amazon lore which portrays islands of warrior women in the furthest East. The main transmitter of these ideas seems to have been the Alexander romance, a well-known legend in medieval Europe.[19] One of its most popular stories, known in several versions, tells of Alexander's meeting with the queen of the Amazons. These women were armed and fought battles with men, and were said to live on an island in the ocean, where they were visited by men from the mainland only once a year.[20] Transformed into an Islamic setting, the Alexander romance became important in Malay tradition as *Hikayat Iskandar*. The Malay hero Iskandar does not encounter islands of women, but, like Alexander, communicates with a powerful queen of an island next to that of the wild dogs (*Anjing Hutan*) situated between Ceylon and China.[21]

However, these ideas were not exclusive to European classical mythology, as both Chinese and Arab traditions embraced the theme of islands in an eastern ocean inhabited separately by men and women.[22] Before the first European descriptions of Southeast Asia, several Arab writers elaborated on eastern islands ruled by women, one claiming to have visited such an island and seen the queen herself sitting naked on her throne, surrounded by 4,000 virgin slaves.[23] The Arab chronicle 'Aja'ib al-Hind' [Miracles of India], compiled around 1000 C.E., related the story of how a storm-shaken ship in the 'Sea of Malauy' drifted to an unknown island where the crew were abducted by a multitude of women who made the men 'the instruments of their pleasure'. The unbridled passion of these women in the end killed all but one sailor, who lived to tell the story of the curious island, initially given to the women by men who had agreed to give up all their power.[24] Similar tales are found in several other Arab travel accounts. The most influential of these is the *Rihla* of Ibn Batuta (1304–1369), known in Europe only in the nineteenth century, which describes how the author landed on Tawalísi, an island governed by a warrior princess, who had only female servants. Her army consisted of both men and women, 'who ride on horseback and are skilful archers, and fight exactly like men', and the princess herself was said to lead her armies in war. Various editors of Ibn Batuta's travelogue have identified the island as Tonkin, Cambodia, Sulawesi, or Sulu in the Philippines.[25]

In medieval European literature, references to islands of women in the Eastern Ocean are commonplace. Amazon stories in the Letter of Prester John might have been the inspiration for the fictitious author Sir John

The Regio Femarum *& its warrior women* 69

Mandeville, whose *Travels* became the main source of information on the East in the Middle Ages.[26] Also Marco Polo (1254–1324), who gave Europe one of the first eyewitness reports of East and Southeast Asia, described two islands of men and women, called 'Male' and 'Female' in the Indian Ocean.[27] Although it has been suggested that Marco Polo had been inspired by Chinese folklore, the wide transmission of this text meant that the Amazon islands came to be associated with the Malay Archipelago and Sumatra in particular.[28]

Medieval maps were strongly influenced by these images. Most intriguing in this respect is the depiction of Southeast Asia in the so-called Catalan World Atlas, thought to have been produced around 1375. In this map, two islands are of particular interest here: Taprobana, which in the Ptolemaic tradition was associated with Ceylon or Sumatra, and 'Iana', thought to be referring to Java (or, alternatively, 'Pentan' (Bintan) or Melayu mentioned by Marco Polo). In the explanatory text, the island of Iana is said to produce camphor, sandalwood, and several kinds of named spices. Marked place names in Iana include *Malao*, but also *Regio Femarum*, the kingdom of women. This is visualised by an impressive image of a crowned queen holding a long sword. Although the Catalan World Map is decorated with a variety of images of both kings and queens, this is the only female figure holding a weapon.[29]

The first recorded European eyewitness descriptions of Southeast Asia after Marco Polo all mention islands of women. The Venetian Nicolo Conti (1385–1469), who visited mainland Southeast Asia and Sumatra, only made vague references to islands in the Indian Ocean inhabited by men and women separately.[30] In contrast, several sixteenth-century travellers tell of islands of women in Southeast Asia and, interestingly, make references to native information. Hence Antonio Pigafetta (1491–1534), the Venetian chronicler of Magellan's circumnavigation of the world, reported hearing about an island called Ocoloro south of 'Java Major' (Sumatra) from one of his local navigators, a place inhabited solely by women, who become pregnant by the wind. Another collector of local stories was Tomé Pires (c. 1468–c. 1540), a Portuguese apothecary based in Malacca from 1512 to 1515. Pires was the first European to use sources such as the *hikayat*, later known as the *Sejarah Melayu*, to glean information on local history. Leaning on Sumatran lore about the ethnically different Engano islanders of Nias, Pires wrote that some people indeed say that the island women get pregnant by the wind, whereas others maintained that 'they are got with child by others who go there to trade and who go away again at once'. However, Pires urged caution, writing that 'the people believe in this, as others believe in the Amazons and the Sybil of Rome.'[31] Much later, William Marsden (1754–1836), an English East India Company official stationed at the British trading post of Bencoolen in Sumatra in the 1770s, returned to the female islands in his *History of Sumatra* (1783). To Marsden it was now important to record 'native' legends, and this story was told as a curiosity, as part of a then novel project of mapping native literary traditions.[32]

70   *Christina Skott*

From these examples it is clear that islands of warrior women were a recurring and persistent theme in early European knowledge of Southeast Asia. The strength of this image is illustrated in the popular *Mundus Alter et Idem* (1605), an imaginary travel account of a journey to Terra Australis, written by the English Bishop Joseph Hall. After visiting the Moluccas, the traveller found himself on an island called 'Womandecoia', inhabited by women only, where any interaction with men was severely punished.[33] This idea was mirrored in Renaissance maps; both the Gastaldi world map (1529) and Italian map-maker Benedetto Bordone's *Isolario* (1528) firmly placed islands of women in the region.[34]

Early modern European publications: women in arms

By the time Joseph Hall published his fictitious travel account, European knowledge of Southeast Asia had already entered a new phase. Selected Spanish and Portuguese texts describing the East had been published elsewhere in Europe in the sixteenth century, and travel compilations such as the *Navigationi et Viaggi* [Navigations and Travels] published by the Venetian geographer Giovanni Battista Ramusio (1485–1557) in the mid-sixteenth century had greatly enhanced awareness of the region.[35] Central to this emerging body of travel literature was the account of Ferdinand Magellan's circumnavigation in the early 1520s, in which the chronicler Antonio Pigafetta established a new way of reporting, characterised by more systematic observations of peoples and customs.

Ramusio made use of selected passages from Pigafettas's account, but there are further extant manuscript versions of Pigafetta's journal, some published only in modern times, which are of empirical interest. Among islands inhabited by cannibals and 'Gentiles', Pigafetta described an island named 'Mallua' where the Spaniards had to stay for several weeks to repair their ship. It is here that we find the first 'eye-witness' report of women in arms. In one version Pigafetta recorded his arrival in Mallua thus (in translation): 'and when the women saw us, they came to meet us with their bows. But after we had given them some presents, we were immediately their friends'.[36] This passage was later incorporated into numerous compendia of travel literature. In England, the easternmost islands were bluntly described by the cosmographer Samuel Purchas in 1625: 'The people are man eaters. The Women use Bowes and Arrowes.'[37]

Some eighty years after Pigafetta's visit the armed women were visualised in a series of watercolour drawings depicting the peoples of New Guinea. The draughtsman was the Portuguese explorer Don Diego Prado de Tovar who accompanied the Torres expedition to the Pacific around 1600. Here, only the women of the north-western parts of the island are seen holding bows, as well as large quadrilateral shields which reveal influences from the culture of the Indonesian archipelago.[38]

Only a few years later another European sighting of warrior women was reported. In 1601, a Dutch ship under Olivier van Noort (1558–1627) made first contact with Borneo. The island was found to be populous, and most people were said to be armed, with 'Bowes, Javelins pointed with Iron, Forkes, Ouivers and venomed Darts'. Prominent in van Noort's account were Borneo's women, 'wittie, warie in trading, bold and coragious: one of them rudelier handled by a Hollander, with a Javelin [would have] had dispatched him, if her force had not beene intercepted'.[39] Van Noort's landing in Borneo was part of the first Dutch circumnavigation, of which accounts were published in various languages. Furthermore, due to the lack of new information on Borneo, van Noort's account was copied and recycled for a long time. At the beginning of the eighteenth century, a British travel compendium could still claim that in Borneo 'the very women have so much of the soldier in their composition, that if affronted, they'll revenge themselves with sword or javelin'.[40]

Although these 'eyewitness' sightings of armed women are few in number, they were part of a new, more detailed and informative European reporting generated by the first actual European encounters with the island world of Southeast Asia. As such, these reports moved away from the reliance on ancient and classical sources, and could be argued to provide more 'reliable' information, indicating that women of the island world were indeed trained in the use of arms.

Court women

The most enduring theme relating to women in arms originated from European fascination with the various groups of women surrounding local rulers. The practice of keeping women enclosed in inner apartments of royal courts was probably brought from India and came to Southeast Asia with the spread of Buddhism and Hinduism. In Sumatra, rulers of the Srivijaya Empire are recorded to have kept harems in the twelfth century.[41] In the early modern era both rulers and high-ranking men surrounded themselves with court women and concubines in great numbers. Court women had distinctive ceremonial roles, but they were also kept to express social status, and bonds between ruler and ruled could be confirmed by the acquisition of women from hinterlands and from prominent families.[42] In local sources the royal women are given a variety of roles, some which would be unfamiliar to Europeans, but did not necessarily indicate influence outside the court circles. Javanese courtly poetry makes court women visible mainly in praise of their beauty. In Bali, a strong female presence in court literature such as *Kidung* poetry has been seen as 'mere decorations' in a patriarchal system.[43] In Siam, on the other hand, where the king's consorts had the higher status of royal wives, women were entrusted with management of the palace, and women are also thought to have supervised diplomatic correspondence.[44] In Malay courts, women would raise royal children and were responsible for music making and dance. Although the official role of Malay court women was limited, their indirect political influence behind the scenes is documented in court chronicles.[45]

72   *Christina Skott*

The role and status of the court women have been discussed by Europeans since the earliest Portuguese accounts. In the early nineteenth century, the British Lieutenant-Governor of Java, Stamford Raffles (1781–1826) considered these women little more than prostitutes, and early European historians of the region claimed that palace women prostituted themselves with the rulers' consent.[46] In contrast, sixteenth-century references to court women in the eastern part of the Indonesian archipelago, in particular the coveted Spice Islands, make no reference to prostitution. Tomé Pires simply stated that the ruler of Ternate housed 400 women inside his compound.[47] The account by Duarte Barbosa, written in 1518 (but not fully published until the nineteenth century), reported a curiosity from the court of the king of 'Maluquo' (Maluku):

> He is served by hunchbacked women, whom he keeps for display, whose backbones he has broken in their childhood. He may have five of these, old and young, who always go with him and serve him in everything. Some give him betel, another carries his sword on feast days.[48]

It could of course be argued that later images of armed court women simply originated from these early observations of women ceremonially carrying rulers' swords. In any case, both Pires' and Barbosa's accounts were selectively used by the above-mentioned compiler Ramusio, whose travel collection has subsequently been acknowledged as an important source for images of island princesses and Amazons in Elizabethan literature.[49]

Also in Java, early observers mention the great numbers of women at royal courts. Pires described in some detail the procession of the ruler of Majapahit, where the royal women rode on richly decorated elephants and where 'each of the concubines and wives is followed by thirty women on foot, each according to her rank.'[50] In 1586, the English circumnavigator Thomas Cavendish (1560–1592), whose account received wide publicity in England, met with the Javanese ruler 'Raja Bolamboan', a man who had a hundred wives. Cavendish also maintained that after the death of the ruler of Java all his wives assembled to kill themselves with a *kris*.[51] Likewise, Oliver Noort visited 'Sorbay', where he saw 'Pagodes' and idols associated 'ancienter Indian Rites'. A man referred to as the 'Chiefe Priest' was said to be residing outside the city, keeping 'many wives to keepe him warme, & with their milke to nourish him, eating no other meat'.[52] These earliest European sources, perhaps underused by historians, can at best provide valuable information about pre-Islamic practices in the island world, such as earlier roles and functions of women surrounding rulers.

The tradition of associating courts of Java and Aceh with armed female guards became firmly established with the string of publications which appeared in Holland and England in the wake of the first expeditions to Southeast Asia. These trading enterprises, which preceded the formation of the English East India Company in 1600 and the Dutch East India Company in

The Regio Femarum & its warrior women

1602, generated a body of accounts which transmitted first-hand and much sought after information on trading conditions in the East. As English and Dutch traders were unable to approach Portuguese-held Malacca, these accounts are mainly concerned with Aceh, Patani, Bantam and the Moluccas.

The most important point of contact in the first decades was Aceh, where the northern European newcomers were at first welcomed, given audiences with the ruler and entertained, giving them a unique and later unobtainable glimpses of life within the royal palace. In 1603, the Dutch Admiral Vybrandt van Varwiijk (Warwick), provided a vivid description of the royal court of Aceh, where the Dutch visitors were treated to a grand meal, guarded by female guards equipped with blow pipes, lances, swords and shields. This tantalising scene was chosen by the German engraver Theodor de Bry for a series of engravings depicting selected scenes taken from accounts of the first Dutch trading expeditions to the East, Historia *Indiae Orientalis*, published in twelve folio volumes between 1601 and 1616. The engraving portrays the Sultan and his Dutch guests being waited on by a group of women, who are presented here in a manner very different from that of other women in this series. Armed with spears and bows, sturdy and muscular, most with naked upper bodies, these figures carried clear associations to European perceptions of Amazon women.

Figure 4.1 Dutch traders entertained by the Sultan of Aceh.
Source: Engraving from the German version of *Historia Indiae Orientalis Pars Octava* (1607) by Johann Theodor and Johann Israel de Bry. Author's collection.

74 *Christina Skott*

BOX 4.1

Similar to comics and graphic novels, the engraving narrates a complex event by breaking it up into two panels. Based on the German language commentary, the upper panel features the 1603 encounter of Dutch Admiral Wybrandt van Warwijk's group with the Sultan of Aceh, whereas the lower part imagines the following invitation by the Prince of Aceh and his female servants. The German language commentary, roughly summarised, explains the key sequence of events.

After landing, van Warwijk's party, which brings along one or two pieces of artillery as a gift of honour, makes its way to the palace from where the Sultan, who had been lying in a corridor, addresses them. One interesting detail captured by the engraver is how he imagines the three Dutchmen closest to the Sultan performing the local style of greeting. It is hence not a pudic reaction to seeing the partially clad women in the lower part of the engraving, which instead focuses on the next stage of the Dutch-Acehnese encounter, namely with the Sultan's son.

After the Acehnese customary greetings, the Prince invited them to sit on the ground and had them served with food and drink. As clearly seen here, the Prince's staff is entirely female, including body guards armed with swords, bows, spears, and rifles (archebuses).

Published in both Latin and German, *India Orientalis* came to reach a wide readership through the Frankfurt book fairs, and had a profound impact on early modern Europe's 'imagining' of the East.[53] This particular engraving was also copied in the Dutch travel compilation *Begin ende Voortgang*, edited by Isaac Commelin and published in 1646, one the most influential publications describing Dutch eastward expansion.[54]

In seventeenth-century England, knowledge of Asia and Southeast Asia in particular was greatly enhanced by publications produced by Richard Hakluyt (c. 1552–1616) and the earlier mentioned Samuel Purchas (c. 1577–1626). These cosmographers translated and published Dutch accounts, but Purchas in particular was also able to obtain letters, original reports and other documents from the English East India Company.[55] In the volume *Purchas His Pilgrimes*, which appeared in a string of editions, we find a different account of Aceh, describing audiences given by the Sultan to the English traders, based on letters by John Davis. Again, a vivid scene from the voluptuous court of Aceh is painted, with the ruler attended by 'fortie women at the least, some with Fannes to cool him, some with Clothes to dry his sweat, some give him Aqua vitae,[56] others water: the rest sing pleasant songs. He doth nothing all the day but eate and drinke, from morning to

The Regio Femarum *& its warrior women* 75

night there is no end of banqueting'. There is no mention of armed guards here, but Davies wrote that the court women were in fact the king's 'chiefest counsellors', furthermore he claimed that 'a woman is his admiral, for hee will trust no men'.[57] This statement is not found in any of the other early sources, but has been seen by modern historians as evidence for the prominence of women in Acehnese politics and society.[58] Other English accounts of Aceh from this time, such as that of Thomas Best, provide no further information about the royal women. By the time of Best's visit, the sultan of Aceh was the feared Iskandar Muda (r. 1607–1636), whose absolutist reign and harsh administration of punishment caught European fascination.[59] However, new trade regulations introduced in Aceh at this time meant that English commercial interest in Aceh waned. In addition, misbehaviour by individual English traders caused the relationship between the ruler of Aceh and the British to sour.[60] The English were no longer invited to dine in the palace, and we have no further eyewitness accounts of the armed palace women.

The most important European description of Aceh in the mid-seventeenth century, upon which much of the chronology of events has been based, was composed by the Frenchman Augustin de Beaulieu (1589–1637) in the 1620s. Like Davis slightly earlier, Beaulieu had not himself been inside the royal palace, but wrote that the inner palace was restricted to women, who numbered 3,000 and never left the palace. None of these women were allowed to be seen by outsiders; still Beaulieu maintained that many of them were armed.[61] Due to the decline in European trade with Aceh and consequently a lack of new information during the later seventeenth century, Beaulieu's description of Aceh was widely copied and quoted, so giving the 'myth' of Aceh's Amazons a new and prolonged life in Europe.

The opulence and the number of women at the court of Aceh would become a persistent theme, but there was another curiosity which also caught the imagination of European readers, namely the fact that Aceh was ruled by a succession of four queens between 1641 and 1699. As European contact with the Acehnese court became more restricted, travellers increasingly had to resort to hearsay. Some reported having been told that Aceh was always ruled by women, whereas others disputed this.[62] The exposure given to Davis' account in Purchas' publications meant that the remark about the female admiral was widely quoted. The English compiler of travel literature John Harris wrote about the sultan of Aceh in 1705: 'His whole life is spent among women, and women manage all his concerns. They are his attendants and his companions, his councellors, and chief ministers of state: nay, a woman is his admiral, and gives orders at sea; such a confidence he has in the Prudence of that sex.'[63] Other eighteenth-century treatises and compilations of knowledge such as *Histoire des Indes* (1744) by the Abbé Guyon (1699–1771) still maintained that the King of Aceh was the most 'voluptuous prince in the world', who surrounded himself with an 'incredible number of women', ready to satisfy his desires in every way, but who also took turns

76   Christina Skott

to guard the sultan night and day. The Abbé, who had not himself travelled to the East, added: 'It has been observed, that his palace is the theatre of jealousy, hatred, disputes, and perpetual complaints.'[64]

While the above examples suggest that the Amazons of Aceh took on a life of their own in European publications, it is essential to note that other early seventeenth-century observers of Aceh, whose accounts were published only in modern times, in fact confirmed the existence of armed guardswomen. One of these was the Englishman Peter Mundy (fl. 1600–1667), who in the 1630s described a royal procession in Aceh in great detail: the King riding on an Elephant, 'a guard of Drummes going before him, Another guard of Weomen Following him on Foote with bowes and arrowes in their hands'.[65]

As mentioned earlier, references to female guards of the 'king of Java' were commonplace. This appears to have spread in Europe mainly through German publications, such as Jürgen Andersen's much copied *Orientalische Reise* (1669). Andersen had himself visited Mataram in central Java and seen 400 of the ruler's 1,200 female attendants keeping guard at night. Other visitors to Javanese courts, however, do not mention women as guards in the seventeenth century. The gem trader Jean-Baptiste Tavernier (1605–1689) described the court at Bantam in great detail, but reported that the king himself was guarded by 2,000 armed men, while the 'harem' was characterised as a 'small affair'.[66]

It was, however, the female corps at the court of Mataram which received increasing European attention, as this sultanate became the focus of Dutch polity in Java. The Amazons of Mataram first appeared in the (unpublished) records of the VOC (Dutch East India Company) as women were reported to have taken part in the defence of Sultan Agung at the beginning of the seventeenth century, and the 'wrouenwacht' ('female guard') of the ruler is mentioned several times.[67] The most detailed Dutch account of Mataram originates from the mid-seventeenth century and was compiled for the VOC by Rijklof van Goens (1619–1682), who was sent as ambassador to the court of Mataram. From the *kraton*, van Goens could report that the corps of guards consisted of about 150 women, of which 30 escorted the ruler whenever he appeared in audience. Ten of these carried his paraphernalia: water vessel, betel set, tobacco pipe, sunshade and perfume boxes, whereas twenty women carried pikes and blowpipes. These women, van Goens wrote, were trained in handling weapons, but also in singing, dancing and the playing of musical instruments. Although these girls were chosen for their beauty, they were seldom taken as concubines, but could sometimes marry nobles.[68]

This report was published in full only in the twentieth century and has remained one of the main historical sources about the female corps of Mataram.[69] At the time, however, parts of this report was utilised by François Valentijn (1666–1727), who through his five volume *Oud en Nieuw Oost-Indiën* (1724–1726) became the main transmitter of knowledge of the island world in the eighteenth century. Quoting van Goens' descriptions of the female guards almost word for word, Valentijn added that there were almost

The Regio Femarum *& its warrior women*   77

10,000 women in the *kraton* area of Mataram. These included 3,000 older women who had the task of controlling the entrances to the compound, and another 4,000 who were engaged in handicrafts.[70] Valentijn's passage was, needless to say, quoted and retold by many commentators throughout the eighteenth century.

From the above it is clear that although European writing on Aceh and Java abounded with references to armed females, actual first-hand observation was scarce, and overall there was very little detailed information to be had. Furthermore, while Europeans marvelled at the multitude of women and the splendour of the royal processions which included armed guardswomen, no European could report seeing these women using their weapons.

Still, an assortment of both Javanese and Dutch sources testify to the existence of elite female 'warriors', the *prajurit estri*, into the late eighteenth and early nineteenth century. A vivid insight into the lives of these women is found in the diary of an anonymous woman (referring to herself as a 'lady scribe and soldier') of the court of Surakarta during the reign of Mangkunegara I (r. 1757–1795). This manuscript has been examined in detail by Ann Kumar, revealing that women at this time were still trained in the use of arms.[71] The governor of Semarang, Jan Greve, who visited the court of Yogyakarta in the late 1780s, reported seeing these women being drilled in horsemanship and the use of firearms, and a few decades later Dutch officials observed mounted exercises at the court of Yogyakarta.[72] During the British occupation of Java (1811–1816), the *prajurit estri* were said to be in attendance in the Sultan's private apartments at night, equipped with *krises* and daggers.[73] In 1821, a Frenchman who visited the nearby Surakarta court described forty women sitting below the royal throne each holding a sabre and musket.[74] Furthermore, women dressed in the traditional Javanese fighting costume, *prajuritan*, were found among the dead Javanese combatants in the early stages of the Java War (1825–1830).[75] From these examples, there seems little doubt that the Amazon women continued their presence in the Javanese *kraton* into modern times.

Although the examples above have been concerned with the Malay world, there is evidence that rulers in other parts of Southeast Asia indeed surrounded themselves with armed female guards. A Chinese envoy to Cambodia in the 1290s gave a vivid description of the king's women: some were his private guards and carried lances and shields, but they were also said to form a separate military unit.[76] The ruler of Siam had a similar corps of guardswomen, described in great detail by a French visitor to the court of Siam in 1857. These women were said to be trained in the use of firearms and took part in duels, but seem otherwise to have had a merely ceremonial function.[77] It also appears that in Patani the wives of high ranking officials could be called on to guard the royal compound.[78]

Another striking and well documented parallel to the Southeast Asian Amazon guards can be found in Africa. Again, the earliest references are found in European accounts, wherein the sixteenth century Portuguese

78   *Christina Skott*

explorers observed that the armies of the king of Benamatapa on the West Coast of Africa included thousands of women. In the Kingdom of Dahomey in Benin, West Africa, women formed a full-time professional elite force in the standing army into modern times. As in Java, these women were initially selected to guard the ruler, since no man was allowed to enter a royal palace after sunset.[79] Renowned for their ferocity the women provided fierce resistance to colonisation well into the twentieth century.[80]

Conclusion

The Dahomey example suggests that the female warrior corps survived so long because of the continued strength of African religion. The women formed a sisterhood, bound by oaths of loyalty, where religious ritual and ceremony played a central part. For Southeast Asia, a region which has been defined by its openness and adaptability to outside influences, the Dahomey model opens up the intriguing question of whether the tales of Amazon women and warrior queens, so prevalent in pre-European sources, in fact reflected 'other', historical roles of women, in pre-Islamic or even pre-Indianised societies.

The consistency of the earliest eyewitness reports from the island world, some of which have been discussed above, could possibly invite a reinterpretation of classical and medieval writing on Southeast Asia, so often dismissed as fable, with a stubborn reliance on European ideas derived from images of a marvellous East.[81]

Incidentally, the Southeast Asian Amazon is not the only image that appears familiar from ancient texts. A few examples will suffice. Already the ancient Roman naturalist Pliny (23–79 C.E.) described small people living in caves among his 'monstrous races'. Pigafetta's earlier mentioned report from the Eastern Archipelago does not only mention women equipped with bows and arrows, he also reported hearing stories of islands inhabited by very small people living in caves. It is easy to recall the recent 'discovery' of the disputed *Homo Floresiensis*, found on the island of Flores and suggested by some scientists to have constituted a separate species of dwarf humans which could possibly have existed until historical times.[82] There is a long and unbroken tradition of associating the furthermost east, and Taprobana (Sumatra) in particular, with *anthropophagi*, man eaters, vividly described by several classical writers.[83] As is well known, cannibalism among the Batak of Sumatra has been eagerly studied by modern anthropologists, and remains a source of wonder and excitement which still supports the local tourism industry. Another marvel reported by Pigafetta was people with long ears.[84] The practice of elongating earlobes has, as we now know, survived in Borneo until today. Another incredible fact was reported from the island of Bangaya by the early Portuguese chronicler Barbosa: 'the inhabitants thereof have, according to my information, a custom which cannot be believed, that is that while they are yet young they saw off their teeth close to

The Regio Femarum *& its warrior women*   79

the root'.[85] Similarly, tooth filing continues to be practised in parts of island Southeast Asia. These rather haphazard examples go some way at least to show how outsiders have dealt with the human diversity of this region.

The German author of the medieval Walsperger Map echoed Europe's fascination with a marvellous East when he noted of the southeastern parts of Asia: 'around this pole there are most wonderful creatures, not only beasts, but men'.[86] And women, we might add. Suggested here is the possibility of conjecture that the earliest European observations could in fact have reflected earlier, more prominent roles for women in warfare and defence, and that the armed guardswomen seen by Europeans in modern times could be seen as relics of older practices.

Feminist theory has long attempted to show that societies with egalitarian gender relations have been more likely to transform their gender roles through encounters with societies with clearer gender stratification. This has been considered with reference to European colonialism, and recent studies have given examples of how the arrival of Islam and Christianity impacted on women. In the Philippines, for example, women's position in religious rituals and as spiritual mediators was fiercely attacked and undermined by Spanish missionaries.[87] As for the function of pre-Islamic court women in Java, early European observers, such as Tomé Pires, alluded to practices and rituals which later seem to have disappeared, and later reports provide clues to suggest 'different' tasks carried out by women, such as the early modern female fire brigade described in Mataram in the 1660s.[88] Indigenous sources also provide clues to changing gender roles both inside and outside the royal sphere. For example, in the Javanese version of the Hindu epic, the *Mahabharata,* the ruler's spouse took a more active role in warfare than in the Indian version.[89] Furthermore, as Barbara Andaya has shown, women traditionally played an important part in the ancient custom of headhunting.[90]

Recent research on gender in early modern Southeast Asia has demonstrated the interchangeability of gender roles through actions and dress, as well as the close links between royal authority and the power of women.[91] By highlighting the different ways in which women contributed to the life of the Central Javanese courts in the eighteenth and early nineteenth centuries, historians have concluded that court women in central Java initially enjoyed more freedom to contribute to domains which later became male dominated, as colonialism and western education changed elite perceptions of women's roles within the court.[92] It is then perhaps not too far-fetched to suggest that these developments could have included an earlier more active role taken by women in military matters and defence.

This chapter has shown that most of the European descriptions of armed women in the Malay world emerged in the sixteenth and seventeenth centuries, a 'honeymoon' period when European traders were still welcomed and entertained by local rulers. These reports therefore provide unique glimpses of life inside royal courts.[93] But, complex and intricate ceremonies were

80 *Christina Skott*

sometimes too elaborate and tiresome for the European traders, who had to sit through endless dance performances and rituals. James Lancaster, an early visitor to the court of Aceh, wrote about the intricacies of court ritual: 'with (for brevities sake) I omit to trouble the Reader with all: for, my purpose is to shew the effect of this first setling of the Trade in the East-Indies, rather then to particularize of them.'[94] Further information about the armed women might have been lost this way, but the number of females who took part, their roles and behaviour became a new marvel at a time when the idea of the luxurious harem associated with the Ottoman Empire was beginning to emerge in European writing on the 'Orient'.[95]

Barbara Andaya has pointed out that instances where 'European material can play off indigenous texts' are essential for the mapping of female roles and women's histories in Southeast Asia.[96] I have here attempted to highlight the origins, spread and use of one group of European sources extensively relied on by historians of early modern Southeast Asia. By the beginning of the nineteenth century these older forms of knowledge, mainly based on travel literature, were increasingly dismissed, as calls were made for systematic, new and more precise information, which clearly also was intended to inform and propel an increasingly assertive European expansion in the region. The first publications on Java in English, Stamford Raffles' *History of Java* (1817) and John Crawfurd's *History of the Indian Archipelago* (1820), make no mention of the armed women. But Crawfurd, now keen to invoke indigenous sources and histories, told his readers the curious story of how in the sixteenth century a Javanese Princess, 'accoutered as a warrior', led an army to victory, explaining that this was, after all, a place where women 'assume a tone, and insist on privileges, unknown to their sex in the east'.[97] In the end, the Amazon women who had excited Europeans for centuries had to give way for more 'scientific' inquiries into Southeast Asian societies, but it would remain a source of fascination that women here could and would take on roles not witnessed anywhere else.

Notes

1 Present day Banten, western Java.
2 *Allehanda Utländska Märkwärdigheter och Sällsamma Händelser* (Wästerås: Johan Laur. Horrn, 1784), p. 30.
3 Michael W. Charney, *Southeast Asian Warfare, 1300–1900* (Leiden; Boston: Brill, 2004), p. 4.
4 Anthony Reid, *Southeast Asia in the Age of Commerce, 1450–1680*. Vol. 1: *The Lands below the Winds* (New Haven, CT; Yale University Press, 1988), p. 167.
5 Ibid., pp. 146–158, 162–172.
6 Barbara Watson Andaya (ed.), *Other Pasts: Women, Gender and History in Early Modern Southeast Asia* (Honolulu, HI: Center for Southeast Asian Studies, University of Hawaii at Manoa, 2000).
7 For an overview of female roles in early modern Southeast Asia, see Anthony Reid, 'Female Roles in Pre-Colonial Southeast Asia', *Modern Asian Studies*, Vol. 22, No. 3 (1988), pp. 629–645.

The Regio Femarum & its warrior women   81

8 Samuel Purchas, *Purchas his Pilgrimage, or Relations of the World and the Religions Observed in all Ages* (London: William Stansby for Henry Fetherstone, 1617), p. 316.

9 'Het tweede boek, journael oft Dagh-Register Amsterdam 1601', in *De tweede schipvaart der Nederlanders naar Oost-Indië onder Jacob Cornelisz. van Neck en Wybrandt Warwijk, 1598–1600*, Vol. 3. ed. J. Keuning, Verken uitgegeven door de Linschoten-Vereeniging, XLVI ('s-Gravenhage: Nijhoff, 1942), p. 225.

10 See Barbara Watson Andaya, 'From Temporary Wife to Prostitute: Sexuality and Economic Change in Early Modern Southeast Asia', *Journal of Women's History*, Vol. 9, No. 4 (1998), pp. 11–34; Andaya, *The Flaming Womb*, pp. 123–127.

11 Reid, 'Female Roles', p. 631; Barbara Watson Andaya, *The Flaming Womb: Repositioning Women in Early Modern Southeast Asia* (Honolulu, HI: University of Hawai'i Press, 2006), pp. 21–22; See also Donald Lach, *Asia in the Making of Europe. Vol. III: A Century of Advance. Book Three: Southeast Asia* (Chicago, IL: University of Chicago Press, 1993), p. 1372.

12 See, for example, Thomas Herbert, *A Relation of some Yeares Trauaile, begunne anno 1626...* (London: W. Stansby and I. Bloome, 1634), p. 199.

13 For an early example, see Edmund Scot, 'An Exact Discourse of the Subtilties, Fashions, Pollicies, Religion and Ceremonies of the East Indians, as well Chyneses as Javans, there Abiding and Dealing', in Sir William Foster (ed.), *The Voyage of Sir Henry Middleton to the Moluccas* (London: Hakluyt Society, sec. series, 88, 1943), pp. 81–176. A nineteenth-century account of the continued role of female messengers is found in John Anderson, *Mission to the East Coast of Sumatra in 1823*. Facsimile reprint of the 1826 edition, with an introduction by Nicholas Tarling (New York: Oxford University Press, 1971), p. 45.

14 See Andaya, *The Flaming Womb*, pp. 166–169. See also the discussion of Malay sources on the queens of Kelantan in Cheah Boon Kheng, 'Power behind the Throne: The Role of Queens and Court Ladies in Malay History', in *Journal of the Malaysian Branch of the Royal Asiatic Society* (JMBRAS), Vol. 66, No. 1 (1993), p. 10.

15 The editor could reinforce this view by referring to the tropical environment, writing 'it may here be observed, that all these female Kingdoms are in the hot Countries, and seem to be an effect of the Raging Lust of the Men, who overvaluing the soft Sex not only call them, but really make them their Mistresses'. Peter Heylyn (ed.), *Cosmography in Four Books: Containing the Chorography and History of the Whole World: And All the Principal Kingdoms, Provinces, Seas, and the Isles thereof* (London: Edw. Brewster et. al., 1703), pp. 830–831.

16 Julie Wheelwright, *Amazons and Military Maids: Women who Dressed as Men in Pursuit of Life, Liberty, and Happiness* (London: Pandora, 1989); Simon Shepherd, *Amazons and Warrior Women: Varieties of Feminism in Seventeenth Century Drama* (New York: St. Martin's Press, 1981).

17 Louis Montrose, 'The Work of Gender in the Discourse of Discovery', in Stephen Greenblatt (ed.), *New World Encounters* (Berkeley, CA: University of California Press, 1993), pp. 177–217. For the allegorical representation of America as a woman, see Hugh Honour, *The New Golden Land: European Images of America from the Discoveries to the Present Time* (New York: Pantheon Books, 1975), Chapter 4.

18 Laura Brown, *Ends of Empire: Women and Ideology in Early Eighteenth-Century English Literature* (Ithaca, NY: Cornell University Press, 1993), p. 157.

19 The collection of legends about Alexander the Great is known from around 300 C.E. and derived from a number of classical as well as Christian sources. For a bibliography, see W. J. Aerts, 'Alexander the Great and Ancient Travel Stories', in Zweder von Martels (ed.), *Travel Fact and Travel Fiction: Studies on Fiction, Literary Tradition, Scholarly Discovery and Observation in Travel Writing* (Leiden: Brill's Studies in Intellectual History, 55, 1994), p. 30, n. 4.

82 *Christina Skott*

20 There are similarities in this story to the Brahmans of India visiting their wives. In other versions the Amazons cross over to live with the men. See Aerts, 'Alexander the Great', pp. 33–34. See also W. W. Tarn, *Alexander the Great, II: Sources and Studies* (Cambridge: Cambridge University Press, 1948), pp. 326ff.

21 R. O. Winstedt, 'The Date, Authorship, Contents and Some New Mss. of the Malay Romance of Alexander the Great', *JMBRAS*, Vol. 16, No. 2 (1938), p. 17. In classical and medieval literature, the island of dog-headed men referred to the Andaman Islands.

22 For an overview of male-female islands in different traditions, see Sir Henry Yule (transl. & ed.), *The Book of Ser Marco Polo the Venetian Concerning the Kingdoms and Marvels of the East*, third edition, revised throughout in the light of recent discoveries by Henri Cordier (of Paris), Vol. II (London: J. Murray, 1903), pp. 405–406.

23 Thomas Suárez, *Early Mapping of Southeast Asia* (Singapore: Periplus, 1999), pp. 119–121.

24 'The men were dying of exhaustion one after another; and each time that one died, they fell again on him, taking no notice of the foul odour of his corpse. A single one survived and he was a Spaniard. He was taken care of and nursed by one single woman, who also led him to a gold mine that she had discovered.' At least three Arab writers mention these islands. See G. R. Tibbetts, *A Study of the Arabic Texts Containing Material on South-East Asia* (Leiden: Brill, 1979), pp. 182–183.

25 Ibn Batuta, *Travels in Asia and Africa, 1325–1354* (London: Routledge & Kegan Paul, 1983), pp. 279–280, 368, n. 9.

26 Malcolm Letts, *Sir John Mandeville: The Man and His Book* (London: Batchworth Press, 1949), pp. 54–55.

27 Yule (transl. & ed.), *The Book of Ser Marco Polo*, pp. 404–405.

28 John Larner, *Marco Polo and the Discovery of the World* (New Haven, CT: Yale University Press, 1999), p. 219, n. 28. The Gastaldi world map (1520) placed the male and female islands in the eastern archipelago. See also Suárez, *Early Mapping of Southeast Asia*, pp. 120–121.

29 *Mapamundi: The Catalan Atlas of the Year 1375*, edited and with commentary by Georges Grosjean (Dietikon-Zurich: Urs Graf, 1978), sheet 6b, pp. 88–89. The Catalan Atlas consists of six large sheets of parchment. It appeared in the library of the King of France in 1380 and is now kept in the Bibliothèque Nationale de France in Paris.

30 Nicolo Conti, 'The Travels of Nicolò Conti in the East in the Early Part of the Fifteenth Century', in R. H. Major (ed.), *India in the Fifteenth Century* (London: Hakluyt Society, 1857), pp. 21–22.

31 Tomé Pires, *The Suma Oriental of Tomé Pires*, transl. and ed. by Armando Cortesão, Vol. 1 (London: Hakluyt Society, 1944), pp. 162–163.

32 William Marsden, *The History of Sumatra*, a reprint of the third edition, introduced by John Bastin (Singapore: Oxford University Press, 1986), p. 297.

33 Joseph Hall, *Another World and yet the Same: Bishop Joseph Hall's Mundus alter et idem*, transl. and ed. by John Millar Wands (London: Yale University Press, 1981). This book was first published in Latin and translated to English in 1609.

34 See Suárez, *Early Mapping of Southeast Asia*, pp. 119–121.

35 *Primo Volume delle Nauigationi et Viaggi* was published in Venice in 1550, containing excerpts from the travel journals of Marco Polo, Nicolo Conti and Pigafetta. Ramusio also used material compiled by Tomé Pires, although he was not aware of the identity of the author.

36 Antonio Pigafetta, *Magellan's Voyage: A Narrative Account of the First Navigation*, transl. and ed. by R. A. Skelton (London: The Folio Society, 1975), p. 164.

The *Regio* Femarum & *its warrior women* 83

This is a translation of the so called Beinecke manuscript. However, another version of Pigafetta's journal is more ambivalent regarding this encounter: 'Their bows and arrows are of bamboo, and they have a kind of a sack made from the leaves of a tree in which their women carry their food and drink. When people caught sight of us, they came to meet us with bows, but after we had given them some presents, we immediately became their friends'. 'Mallua' is thought to be an unidentified island of the Alor group, east of Ambon. Antonio Pigafetta, *The First Voyage around the World 1519–1522: An Account of Magellan's Expedition*, ed. by Theodore J. Cachey, Jr. (Toronto; Buffalo; London: University of Toronto Press, 2007), p. 114, 116, 178. The 'original' Italian version clearly states, 'Le sue femine, quando ne vistenno, ne venirono incontra con archi'. Antonio Pigafetta, *Relazione del primo viaggio attorno al mondo*. Testo critico e commento de Andrea Canova (Padova: Editrice Antenore, 1999), p. 332.

37 Samuel Purchas, *Hakluytus Posthumus, or, Purchas His Pilgrimes*. Reprint of 1625 edition, Vol. 2 (Glasgow: J. MacLehose and Sons, 1905), pp. 115–116.

38 William Eisler, *The Furtherst Shore: Images of Terra Australis from the Middle Ages to Captain Cook* (Cambridge: Cambridge University Press, 1995), pp. 48–49, 76. See also Charney, *Southeast Asian Warfare*, p. 39.

39 Purchas, *Hakluytus Posthumus*, Vol. 2, p. 203.

40 John Harris (ed.), *Navigantium atque Itinerantium Bibliotheca, or, a compleat collection of voyages and travels: consisting of above four hundred of the most authentick writers....*, Vol. 1 (London: Thomas Bennet, John Nicholson and Daniel Midwinter, 1705), p. 32.

41 Barbara Watson Andaya, 'Delineating Female Space: Seclusion and the State in Pre-Modern Island Southeast Asia', in Andaya (ed.), *Other Pasts*, p. 239.

42 See Andaya, *The Flaming Womb*, pp. 172–178; Leonard Y. Andaya, *The World of Maluku: Eastern Indonesia in the Early Modern Period* (Honolulu, HI: University of Hawaii Press, 1993), pp. 66–67.

43 See Helen Creese, 'Inside the Inner Court: The World of Women in Balinese *Kidung* Poetry', in Andaya (ed.), *Other Pasts*, pp. 125–146, esp. p. 142.

44 Junko Koizumi, 'From a Water Buffalo to a Human Being: Women and the Family in Siamese History', in Andaya (ed.), *Other Pasts*, p. 258.

45 In Johor, for example, a number of powerful women are known to have influenced politics in the eighteenth century, and there are numerous cases where women behind the throne influenced royal succession. See Cheah Boon Kheng, 'Power behind the Throne'. The female intervention in politics was here seen in the use of 'slander and scandal' as the most efficient means of achieving political ends.

46 W. E. Maxwell, 'The Law Relating to Slavery among the Malays', *Journal of the Straits Branch of the Royal Asiatic Society*, Vol. 22 (1890), pp. 252–253.

47 Pires, *The Suma Oriental*, Vol. 1, p. 215.

48 Duarte Barbosa, *The Book of Duarte Barbosa: An Account of the Countries Bordering on the Indian Ocean and their Inhabitants, Written by Duarte Barbosa, and Completed about the Years 1518 A.D.*, transl. and ed. by Mansel Longworth Dames, Vol. 2 (London: Hakluyt Society, sec. ser., 49, 1921), pp. 203–204.

49 In Beaumont and Fletcher's play *Island Princess*, for example, the islands of the East Indies were presented as an Earthly Paradise.

50 Pires, *The Suma Oriental*, Vol. 1, p. 178.

51 Purchas, *Hakluytus Posthumus*, Vol. 2, p. 180.

52 Ibid., p. 204.

53 See Isabella Matauschek, 'Exotic Knowledge as Commodity: De Bry's Historia Indiae Orientalis', in Richard Kirwan and Sophie Mullins (eds.), *Specialist*

84   *Christina Skott*

Markets in the Early Modern Book World (Leiden: Brill, 2015), pp. 110–122; Michiel van Groesen, *The Representations of the Overseas World in the de Bry Collection of Voyages (1590–1634)* (Leiden: Brill, 2008).

54 Isaac Commelin (ed.), *Begin ende Voortgang van de Vereenigde Nederlantsche Goectroyeerde Oost-Indische Compagnie* (Amsterdam: Facsimile Uitgaven Nederland, 1969).

55 See Parker, 'Contents and Sources', pp. 392–393.

56 Distilled alcohol.

57 Parker, 'Contents and Sources', p. 321.

58 See, for example, Reid, *Southeast Asia*, Vol. 1, p. 167.

59 See Thomas Best, *The Voyage of Thomas Best*, ed. by Sir William Foster (London: Hakluyt Society, sec. ser., 75, 1934), p. 176.

60 Lee Kam Hing, *The Sultanate of Aceh: Relations with the British, 1760–1824* (Kuala Lumpur: Oxford University Press, 1995), p. 15.

61 Augustin de Beaulieu, *Mémoires d'un voyage aux Indes Orientales, 1619–1622. Un marchand normand à Sumatra*, introduction, notes et bibliographie de Denys Lombard (Paris: EFEO/Maisonneuve & Larose, 1996), p. 204.

62 See Cornelius LeBruyn, *Travels into Muscovy, Persia, and Part of the East-Indies*, Vol. 2 (London: A. Bettesworth and C. Hitch, 1737), p. 116.

63 Harris (ed.), *Navigantium atque Itinerantium Bibliotheca*, Vol. 2, p. 52. Beaulieu's account was also translated in this volume.

64 Abbé Claude Marie Guyon, *A New History of the East Indies, Ancient and Modern*, Vol. 1 (London: R. and J. Dodsley, 1757), p. 39.

65 Peter Mundy, *The Travels of Peter Mundy in Europe and Asia, 1608–1667*, Vol. 3, Part I (Cambridge: Hakluyt Society, 45, 1919), p. 131.

66 Jürgen Andersen and Voquard Iversen, *Orientalische Reise-Beschreibunge, in der Bearbeitung von Adam Olearius*, reprint of the 1669 edition, published by Dieter Lohmeier (Tübingen: Niemeyer, 1980), p. 12; Jean-Baptiste Tavernier, *Travels in India by Jean-Baptiste Tavernier Baron of Aubonne*, translated from the original French edition of 1676 with a biographical sketch of the author, notes, appendices, &c by V. Ball, 2nd edition, Vol. 2 (Oxford: Oxford University Press, 1925), p. 275.

67 H. J. de Graaf, *De Regering van Sultan Agung, Vorst van Mataram, 1613–1645 en die van zijn voorganger Panembahan Séda-ing-Krapjak 1601–1613* ('s-Gravenhage: KITLV, 23, 1958), pp. 90, 107, 123.

68 Rijklof van Goens, *De vijf gezantschapsreizen van Rijklof van Goens naar het hof van Mataram, 1648–1654*, published by H. J. de Graaf ('s-Gravenhage: M. Nijhoff, 1956), pp. 259–260. For a summary of van Goens' account, see Lach, *Asia in the Making of Europe*, III. 3, pp. 1345–1348.

69 See Kumar chapter, and, for example, Andaya, *The Flaming Womb*, pp. 175–176.

70 François Valentijn, *Oud en Nieuw Oost-Indiën*, Vol. 4 (Dordrecht & Amsterdam: Joannes van Braam, 1726), pp. 59–60.

71 See Ann Kumar's contribution to this volume. Also see Ann Kumar, 'Javanese Court Society and Politics in the Late Eighteenth Century: The Record of a Lady Soldier. Part I: The Religious, Social and Economic Life of the Court', *Indonesia*, Vol. 29 (1980), pp. 1–46.

72 Merle C. Ricklefs, *Jogjakarta under Sultan Mangkubumi, 1749–1792: A History of the Division of Java* (Oxford: Oxford University Press, 1974), p. 304; Peter Carey and Vincent Houben, 'Spirited Srikandhis and Sly Sumbadras: The Social, Political and Economic Role of Women at the Central Javanese Court in the 18th and early 19th Centuries', in Elsbeth Locher-Scholten and Anke Niehof (eds.), *Indonesian Women in Focus: Past and Present Notions* (Dordrecht: KITLV 127, 1987), p. 19.

The *Regio Femarum & its warrior women* 85

73 William Thorn, *Memoir of the Conquest of Java; with the Subsequent Operations of the British Forces, in the Oriental Archipelago* (London: T. Egerton, 1815), p. 293; Peter Carey (ed.), *The British in Java, 1811–1816: A Javanese Account*, with a foreword by John Villiers (Oxford: Oriental Documents, X, 1992), p. 413, n. 73.

74 Quoted in Peter B. R. Carey (transl. & ed.), *Babad Dipanagara: An Account of the Outbreak of the Java War, 1825–1830* (Kuala Lumpur: Council of the M. B. R. A. S., 1981), p. lxxi, note 215.

75 Carey, *Babad Dipanagara*, p. xiii.

76 Chou Ta-kuan quoted in George Coedès, *The Indianized States of Southeast Asia*, ed. Walter F. Vella, transl. Sue Brown Cowing (Honolulu, HI: East West Center, 1968), p. 216.

77 John Laffin, *Women in Battle* (London; New York: Abelard-Schuman, 1967), pp. 46–47.

78 See Andries Teeuw and David. K. Wyatt (ed. & transl.), *Hikayat Patani: The Story of Patani*, Vol. 2 (The Hague: Martinus Nijhoff, 1970), p. 188.

79 Stanley B. Alpern, *Amazons of Black Sparta: The Women Warriors of Dahomey* (London: Hurst & Co, 1998).

80 See Robert B. Edgerton, *Warrior Women: The Amazons of Dahomey and the Nature of War* (Boulder, CO: Westview Press, 2000), pp. 18–19. Although the warrior women were killed almost to the last woman by better equipped French troops in the 1890s, modern anthropologists were able to interview some of the surviving women themselves in the 1920s.

81 See R. Wittkower, 'Marvels of the East: A Study in the History of Monsters', *Journal of the Warburg and Courtauld Institutes*, Vol. 5 (1942), pp. 159–197.

82 See Christina Skott, 'Linnaeus and the Troglodyte: Early European Encounters with the Malay World and the Natural History of Man', *Indonesia and the Malay World*, Vol. 42, No. 123 (2014), pp. 164–165.

83 *Mapamundi, the Catalan Atlas of the Year 1375*, pp. 88, 92; See John Block Friedman, *The Monstrous Races in Medieval Art and Thought* (Cambridge, MA: Harvard University Press, 1981), Chapter 8.

84 Pigafetta, *The First Voyage*, pp. 116–117.

85 Barbosa, *The Book of Duarte Barbosa*, Vol. 2, p. 205.

86 George H. T. Kimble, *Geography in the Middle Ages* (London: Methuen & Co, 1938), p. 198.

87 Andaya, *The Flaming Womb*, Chapter 3; Carolyn Brewer, 'From Animist 'Priestess' to Catholic Priest: The Re/gendering of Religious Roles in the Philippines, 1521–1685', in Andaya (ed.), *Other Pasts*, pp. 69–86.

88 'They have a particular course for quenching fire, which happens but too often among them; for the Women have this office imposed on them, while the men stand in Arms to defend them in the mean time from pillage.' 'Mandelslo's Travels into the Indies', in *The Voyages and Travells of the Ambassadors Sent by Frederick Duke of Holstein, to the Great Duke of Muscovy, and the King of Persia…* (London, 1662), p. 116.

89 Andaya, 'Delineating Female Space: Seclusion and the State in Pre-Modern Island Southeast Asia', p. 239.

90 Barbara Watson Andaya, 'History, Headhunting, and Gender in Monsoon Asia: Comparative and Longitudinal Views', *South East Asia Research*, Vol. 12, No. 1 (2004), pp. 13–52.

91 This is particularly the case with regard to individuals who did not fit into ordinary categories of male and female, such as the *bissu* in South Sulawesi, also to a large extent studied through later European sources.

92 Carey and Houben, 'Spirited Srikandhis', p. 33.

86 *Christina Skott*

93 Purchas, *Hakluytus Posthumus*, Vol. 2, p. 409.
94 James Lancaster, in Purchas, *Hakluytus Posthumus*, Vol. 2, p. 430.
95 See Rana Kabbani, *Imperial Fictions: Europe's Myths of Orient: Devise and Rule* (London: Pandora, 1986), p. 18; Leslie P. Pierce, *The Imperial Harem: Women and Sovereignty in the Ottoman Empire* (Oxford: Oxford University Press, 1993).
96 Andaya, *The Flaming Womb*, p. 228.
97 John Crawfurd, *History of the Indian Archipelago*, Vol. II (London: Cass, 1967), pp. 331–332.

5 Geisha warriors? The incomparable *prajurit estri* at the court of Mangkunĕgara I

Ann Kumar

What, exactly, does *prajurit estri* signify? It is the name of a rather special institution of the old Javanese courts. *Prajurit* means 'soldier' or 'warrior', and is the name used to designate the different warrior corps that made up Javanese armies, each of which bore its own name: examples are the Nyutrayu and Jayengasta corps mentioned below. *Estri* is a *krama* (high Javanese) word for a woman, which because of its polite and respectful character may be translated as 'lady'. The *prajurit estri* corps of earlier Javanese rulers, the Sultans of Mataram, was remarked upon by the earliest Dutch visitors to the court, during the reign of Sultan Agung (1613–1645). Rijklof van Goens, who visited Mataram in the mid-seventeenth century, gives some interesting information on the corps as it existed then.[1] He estimates that it contained about 150 young women altogether, of whom 30 escorted the ruler when he appeared in audience. Ten of them carried the ruler's impedimenta – his water vessel, *sirih* set, tobacco pipe, mat, sun-shade, box of perfumes, and items of clothing for presentation to favoured subjects – while the other twenty, armed with bare pikes and blow-pipes, guarded him on all sides. Van Goens says that members of the corps were trained not only in the exercise of weapons but also in dancing, singing, and playing musical instruments – hence my use of the term 'geisha' in the title of this chapter. He also says that, although they were chosen from the most beautiful girls in the kingdom, the ruler seldom took any of them as a concubine, though they were frequently presented to the great nobles of the land as wives. They were counted more fortunate than the concubines, who could never entertain an offer of marriage so long as the ruler lived, and sometimes not even after his death. Valentijn, writing a description of the court of Mataram in the first decade of the eighteenth century, repeats van Goens' description almost word for word, adding, however, that the young women proved 'not a little high-spirited and proud' when given as wives, knowing as they did that their husbands would not dare to wrong them for fear of the ruler's wrath.[2] They were evidently not like the fictional Patient Griselda, that exemplar of wifely submission to extreme abuse whose story was so popular in Europe from medieval to early modern times.

The *prajurit estri* were an enduring institution, and in the late eighteenth century there were at least two corps – one belonging to the future second sultan of Yogyakarta, and the other described in this chapter.[3]

88 *Ann Kumar*

European travellers give a number of accounts of a somewhat similar institution in seventeenth-century Aceh. The Dutchmen who sailed under Admiral Wybrandt van Warwijk in 1603 saw a large royal guard formed of women armed with blow-pipes, lances, swords, and shields, and a picture of these women is to be found in the journal of the voyage.[4] The French Admiral, Augustin de Beaulieu, who visited Aceh in 1620–1621, reported that the Sultan of Aceh had 3,000 women as palace guards; he claimed that they were not generally allowed outside of the palace apartments, nor were men allowed to see them, but he may just have been out of favour with the Sultan.[5] On his visit to Aceh in 1637 the Englishman Peter Mundy saw a guard of women armed with bows and arrows.[6] It is possible that women were employed for guard duties in other Indonesian courts, but the Javanese *prajurit estri*, the most cultivated and privileged group among the hierarchy of ranks which made up the female population of the court, are unlikely to have had close equivalents elsewhere.

These European accounts are sketchy and tell us little of the life of the women in this corps. It is only due to the survival of a single primary source, a diary, that we have a first-hand account of this life.[7] There are hardly any surviving pre-modern Javanese diaries, so it is a stroke of the greatest good fortune that we have an unusually interesting and comprehensive example actually written by a member of the *prajurit estri* corps and describing their life. It covers a full decade (1781–1791) and was written at the court of Mangkunĕgara I, one of the major figures of eighteenth-century Javanese history, and one of the last of the 'old style' princes whose rise to power was based on their prowess on the battlefield.

The author identifies herself in a short introductory note in prose, which forms the first lines of the manuscript itself: 'Note: the writer is a lady scribe and soldier, bringing to completion the story of the Babad Tutur, in the month of Siyam [Ramadan], on the 22nd day, still in the year Jimawal[8] numbered 1717, in the city of Surakarta'. This passage is followed by the first stanza of (*macapat*) verse, which reads: 'The work then is in Mijil meter; its basis is something else, it follows a different story. Because of the length of the story it was written [in an abridged form in verse??] It was still a [the?] lady scribe who transmitted it'.[9] It is clearly a matter of regret that the information given on the authorship of the diary should be so tantalizingly brief and cryptic: the authoress is not identified by her name – conforming to the widespread Javanese custom of anonymous authorship – and it is not even clear whether the women referred to in the introductory note and in the first stanza of verse are one and the same person.

The descriptive material of the diary follows immediately, and there is no further information on the writer either here, at the beginning, or at the end of the manuscript. The small amount of information which is given seems to suggest that the diary in its present form is a revision of an earlier version, probably an abridgement, since the 'length' of the story which formed its basis is given as the reason for (re-)writing. The last entries in the diary are in fact from the first half of the month of Mulud 1718 A.J. (November 1791 AD), that is, nearly half a year after the date, Siyam 1717 A.J., given in the opening passage, above: presumably, the authoress of the revised version which we have went on to extend the original text to cover the half-year period which had elapsed since it was written. The revision retained the diary form, for it consistently indicates the day,[10] and, at least once a week, also the date[11] on which an event took place. There is not an entry, or provision for an entry, on every day, however, and the coverage of the first two years of the decade reported is much less detailed than is the case for the later years. Checked against Dutch archival records, the diarist's dates prove accurate, except for occasional slips. More importantly, it provides many insights unattainable elsewhere in its reporting of a whole decade of central Javanese politics and provides much new light on the political and social history of Java.

The representation of women in armed combat and on the battlefield occurs quite frequently in modern Javanese literature, such as the Panji stories, and is particularly prominent in the Menak epic, which centres on the career, mainly on the battlefield, of the Islamic hero Hamza b. Abd al-Muttalib. The Javanese version is based on a Malay version fairly close to the Persian original,[12] but it is very greatly expanded and interpolated, no-where more so than in the description of the martial exploits of the women characters, which were already striking in the original. Especially remarkable in the Javanese version are the sections devoted to the 'Chinese' princess (she is Chinese only in the Malay and Javanese versions) and to the lovely Rěngganis.[13] The Chinese princess of the Menak story is probably the basis of the simile in the following diary passage, in which the diarist describes the *prajurit estri* corps on a ceremonial occasion, the reception of a Governor of the Northeast Coast:

On Thursday, Sawal
the twenty-seventh,[14] in the late afternoon
the Governor[15] and the Company officials
came to the Mangkunĕgaran.
The Pangeran Dipati[16]
went to the factory[17] to meet
the Governor,
taking the lady soldiers.

They wore krises in the Balinese style,
ornamented with gold filigree leaves, in a gold filigree belt.
Their clothes were glittering.
Those who went first
were the Nyutrayu corps,[18] on foot carrying bows and arrows,
and then the Jayengasta corps,
not properly [?] dressed,

90   *Ann Kumar*

and then the Pangeran Dipati,
ceremonially escorted by the lady soldiers,
without peer,

like a god descended from heaven,
attended by princesses from China:
that is the [only] comparison.
The élite soldiers went behind
– only these brought up the rear,
for the ordinary soldiers
were none of them taken along.
Even so the spectators crowded around;
the all- gold clothing was really beautiful.
They arrived in the factory and were met

by the Resident,[19] and all the officers,
coming to meet the Pangeran Dipati.
They all greeted one another;
the Governor paid his compliments and sat down.
They were offered arak[20] to drink.
The lady soldiers
sat down in the proper fashion
and were offered drinks.
Then the Resident went to the palace in a carriage,
to summon the heir to the throne[21].

Then, correct in their ranks, the lady soldiers
descended to the compound of the factory.
The Pangeran Dipati descended,
with the Governor, delighted at the sight
of the lady soldiers in their lines.
The heir to the throne
and the Resident arrived,
at the factory, with the escort.
Then the Pangeran Dipati[22] gave the order
to the lady soldiers.

The salvos of the lady soldiers sounded in unison;
it was the Pangeran Dipati who gave the order.
They were well-matched and in time
as they fired a three-fold salvo.
The watchers were astonished and amazed,
and the Governor was staggered, and
completely captivated by the sight.
After this,

Geisha warriors? Java's prajurit estri   91

the lady soldiers mounted their horses first,
followed by the Pangeran Dipati
who withdrew first, with all his armed men,
leaving the heir to the throne at the factory.

Once home, the corps changed from the gold masculine clothing they had worn for these manoeuvres to plain white women's clothes – and proceeded to archery practice. Later, the Governor came to Mangkunĕgara's residence where an elaborate entertainment awaited him, and where the lady soldiers again displayed their skill with firearms. The diarist comments on this occasion that none of the Company officers had seen anything like them in Surakarta, Yogyakarta, or Semarang.

Since the diarist was herself a *prajurit estri* and takes an undisguised pride in the different achievements of the Mangkunĕgaran, her claims to a disciplined skill at arms might be regarded with indulgence. But the Governor, Jan Greeve, for whose benefit this exhibition was made, also wrote a diary of his visit to Surakarta, and the entry for Thursday 31 July included descriptions of this reception at the Dutch factory and of the later entertainment at Mangkunĕgara's residence. Of the first, he says that the three-fold salvo was fired 'with such order and accuracy as must cause us to wonder', and of the second that the women 'dragoons' 'once more fired a three-fold salvo from their hand weapons with the utmost accuracy, followed by various firings of some small [artillery] pieces which had been placed to the sides, after which he went to see the Dalem[23] and the house, both fashioned after a very wonderful style of architecture. . . .'. This was, moreover, a period when skill with firearms was by no means universal among Javanese troops: when Greeve visited Yogyakarta the following month he recorded that the crown prince's troops were so unhandy in this respect that they exploded one of their weapons, wounding a European artilleryman.[24] The description of the *prajurit estri* as dragoons seems to imply that Greeve considered them to be battlefield troops as well as palace guards, which their skill in artillery also suggests. As noted above the term 'prajurit', soldier or warrior, was used to designate battlefield troops, though no involvement in this area is described in the diary.

The military origins of the Mangkunĕgaran

The diarist lived and wrote in a small principality that had its origin in warfare and proudly retained its martial character. The eighteenth century was wracked by wars of succession, in which the VOC was also involved. The 'Chinese war', which actually began as an anti-Dutch rebellion in the Chinese community of Batavia, rather than as a conflict among princes, broke out in 1740. Mangkunĕgara was one of the parties of the aristocracy who joined the Chinese against the Dutch. He did not surrender with the 'Chinese' Sunan (Sunan Kuning or Raden Mas Garĕndi) and remained at large with a

92 *Ann Kumar*

number of other princes, insolently close to the capital, Surakarta. The ruler's half-brother Pangeran Arya Mangkubumi was one of those who joined forces with him. This was a formidable alliance. Mangkunĕgara was, without doubt, a man of great leadership qualities, possessing in superabundance the capacities which had made a prince preeminent among his peers in the old way of life. He was a military commander of notable subtlety, and himself a great warrior, excelling in archery and horsemanship. He was widely respected and beloved, and his vivid personality drew men to him. The alliance between the two rebel princes was confirmed by the marriage of Mangkunĕgara to Mangkubumi's eldest daughter.

On 10 February 1753, the crown prince himself, Pangeran Buminata, fled the capital to join forces with Mangkunĕgara.[25] After deliberation, the VOC decided that Mangkunĕgara would be offered the position of crown prince (since Buminata had conveniently forfeited his claims to this). At the conference of 28 July, however, Mangkunĕgara demanded to be installed not as crown prince but as ruler. The alliance with Mangkubumi had now broken down, and Mangkunĕgara had just defeated Mangkubumi and his forces in an engagement east of Surakarta. At this point Mangkunĕgara clearly felt that he was well placed to dictate the terms of peace to the Company.[26]

This proved to be a mistake. Mangkubumi was quick to open negotiations with the Dutch and asked for only *half* of the kingdom. His request was granted, and at the beginning of 1755 the kingdom was formally and finally divided into two.[27]

Despite the fact that the rulers of both the half-kingdoms thus created (the Sunan of Surakarta and the Sultan of Yogyakarta), and the VOC, all directed their military forces towards Mangkunĕgara's defeat, this was a surprisingly long time in coming. Eventually, Mangkunĕgara agreed to submit to Pakubuwana III, becoming a subject of Surakarta in return for a grant from the Sunan of 4,000 *cacah*.[28] He and his followers then built the Mangkunĕgaran *kraton* in the city of Surakarta itself.

The diary begins more than twenty-six years after Mangkunĕgara had laid down his weapons, yet we find in it strong echoes of those mid-century years of warfare. His court would still have included some who in their youth had chosen to fight by his side, and, even apart from this, something of the character of the period when court and army were on the move seems to have persisted. We see this in the descriptions of the great ritual celebrations of its unity: the tournaments where the Mangkunĕgaran soldiery competed in horsemanship and other military arts, and the theatrical and dance performances which now, decades later, still re-enacted in dramatic form the victories of past battles. Mangkunĕgara maintained the court's standards for war (still at this period personally drilling his men), for the arts (he himself instructed his court dancers), and for religion (the third area in which Mangkunĕgaran unity expressed itself). Mangkunĕgara and his followers would carry out together the regular requirements of Islam,

Geisha warriors? Java's prajurit estri   93

such as the weekly vigil on the eve of Friday. Major observances would be held for important annual festivals, such as the *slamĕtan* held on the 26th of Mulud, some days later than the more public ceremony of the Garĕbĕg Mulud. It is noteworthy that even at such a major 'Islamic' occasion place was found for dances commemorating not the Prophet's life but the victories of Mangkunĕgara. A male dancer, accompanied by a male singer, re-enacted the battle at Pranaraga where Mangkunĕgara had displayed his prowess as an archer and defeated Mangkubumi and a Dutch Major in command of a force of Dutchmen, Buginese, and Balinese.[29]

The sinews of war

Cicero's famous statement that 'endless money forms the sinews of war' applied no less in Java than in Europe.

The diarist did not just record the many twists and turns of high-level politics during this period – she also kept the *kraton* accounts, which are set out in the diary in considerable detail.[30] Wages were paid half-yearly, in the months of Mulud and Sawal. The second of these two payments was known as the *gajihing (wulan) Siyam* (Ramadan/fast month salary) but was actually paid in the following month, Sawal. It is clear that the wages of the soldiery comprised of a very large proportion of the total: in comparison, the amounts received by the other court servants (the *abdi*), and by Mangkunĕgara's own sons and further descendants, are quite small.

The accounts clearly reveal a rather dangerous balance between income and expenditure. With an income of about 6,000 *real*[31] from his lands, Mangkunĕgara was paying out about 10,000 *real* per annum on wages, not to speak of the sums required for participating in the obligatory present-giving in which the Javanese courts and the VOC were always involved, and for other expenses unavoidable for a man of his station. Even when he began to receive a further 4,000 *real* per annum from the VOC, this sum would barely have closed the gap between his previous income and his wages bill.

The fact that the largest amounts for wages were paid to the soldiery raises another interesting point. At this period, Mangkunĕgara was apparently losing more followers to the Sultan than he was attracting to his own kraton. Ricklefs has suggested that the preponderant direction of the movement of courtiers is an indication of which court was 'stronger in terms of legitimation'.[32] The above analysis suggests that it should rather be explained in terms of relative economic strength and the ability to meet a large wages bill, which was clearly taxing Mangkunĕgara's finances to their utmost. Particularly important was the capacity to pay the soldiery – who, as we have seen, received the lion's share of wages – in view of the implications this had for the relative military strength of the rival courts. One should note, however, that Mangkunĕgara's court was not suffering from a large-scale exodus, that significant numbers of followers (who were subsequently

94   *Ann Kumar*

enlisted in the Mangkunĕgaran military forces) did come over to him from the Sultan's people, and that there is evidence of a strong *esprit de corps* existed among Mangkunĕgara's dependents.

Given the unhealthy relationship between his income and expenditure, what could Mangkunĕgara do? It was not in his power to increase the size of his landholdings, and, though he might have tried to obtain for himself a larger share of the tax-bearing capacity of his existing lands, it is questionable how far he could succeed in this. One way of increasing his income was to adapt to new opportunities and changed circumstances by beginning to produce those cash crops which could be sold to the VOC, and this he did. In a letter of 1792, we find him requesting the Company to provide instruction in the cultivation of pepper and indigo, which his men did not then know how to grow.[33] In the nineteenth century, the cultivation and processing of sugar and coffee was a major element in the Mangkunĕgaran's finances.[34]

So from the late eighteenth century onwards, the economic viability of the Mangkunĕgaran became increasingly dependent on its connection first with the VOC and then with the colonial government, which obviously diminished Mangkunĕgara's political independence and ability to wage war alone, a major factor in the most serious armed conflict described in the diary, to which we now turn.

Chronicling military conflict

Unlike many diaries, that written by the *prajurit estri* deals with matters beyond the local and commonplace: it gives an account of high-level political intrigue and the subsequent military actions. So the juxtaposition of the diary record and the account given in the VOC letters of the period gives the historian a perhaps unique opportunity to compare two types of original record, one Dutch and one Javanese, before their reworking into official 'histories'. One might very well expect that records from two such divergent organisations as a Javanese princely kraton and a Dutch trading company would differ greatly in their perceptions of the important issues of the period. The comparison made here reveals that this is not the case. There is a general agreement between the diary and the Dutch records, though each contains some information not provided by the other.

Relationships between the three principalities (Surakarta, Yogyakarta, and the Mangkunĕgaran) placed cheek by jowl in close proximity, involved more or less constant muscle flexing, sabre rattling, and champing at the bit. This sometimes developed into minor spats and on one occasion, in 1790, escalated to the point of threatening the whole political structure established in 1755–1757.

Readers interested in the many twists and turns of this complex scenario are referred to my earlier article which aimed to discover the intentions of the protagonists and the nature of the relationship between the Javanese courts and the VOC.[35] Here I do not intend to revisit, reprise, recapitulate, revise, or reassess that exercise. Instead, I will look particularly at those events which are most illuminating for an understanding of the diarist's position and activities. I have used italics for passages taken from the diarist's account, to make it easier for the reader to follow her analysis of the political and military situation.

The political events of the period in which the diary was written may be compared to an extremely protracted chess game with not two but four players, and many more pieces than the standard chess set. In its partition of the kingdom of Mataram in 1755–1757 the VOC had made, and subsequently perpetuated, the mistake of leaving Mangkunĕgara and his large household of family and followers, without a secure provision for their support, in immediate proximity to one of the two major Javanese princely houses. The Company envisaged Mangkunĕgara as a 'wall' between these two houses, and its officials referred to him as 'our prince', expecting loyal service from him. Yet he had profited from his alliance with the VOC only to the extent of receiving a small endowment, which was, moreover, not even secured to his heirs.

As we shall see, the VOC had given Mangkunĕgara reason to believe that he might succeed to the throne of Yogyakarta. Given the VOC's record of delivery on its promises, however, he had to consider all alternative possibilities. The weak and old Pakubuwana III in the last years of his reign showed interest in finding out whether or not Mangkunĕgara was prepared to intensify his quarrel – a bitter one – with Yogyakarta. On the death of Pakubuwana III, the diarist reports that both the heir to the Surakarta throne and the Sultan of Yogyakarta moved to increase their power. She also says the heir to the throne had requested, as the reign of Pakubuwana III approached its end, that the VOC Resident not overturn any of his decisions relating to the aristocracy and to rebels. She says this request was agreed to by the Resident who reportedly said that the heir could rule him as he did the Dipati [his lords of the realm[36]] and he [the Resident] would carry out all his wishes (*dika reh cara dipatya, pan sakarsa-karsa andika kadadi*).[37] After the death of Pakubuwana III, Mangkunĕgara was denied entry to the kraton by Greeve, in accordance with the old custom (*adat*) of closing it against potential usurpers after the ruler's death. This was done, the diarist says, even though Greeve thought times had changed (*sejen mangke lan nguni*) making princely coups less likely, because Greeve regarded Mangkunĕgara as a 'great man and senior in rank'.[38] The Sultan of Yogyakarta sent a threatening letter to Greeve saying that there would be trouble if Mangkunĕgara was elevated in rank, a threat which prompted an angry reaction from the heir and the Resident.[39] And when Pakubuwana IV (belying the 'sweet and lovable' character with which some VOC officials endowed him) embarked upon a policy of 'standing firm against Mataram and the Company', Mangkunĕgara had to decide how much he stood to gain or lose if he agreed to join the Sunan. He therefore enquired from Greeve

96 *Ann Kumar*

whether the Company did in fact intend to give him or his descendants the throne of Mataram when the Sultan died, as he claimed he had been promised. It is clear that his sons and grandsons, moved by the fire of youth and their uncertain prospects, were also exerting considerable pressure on him to grasp the initiative firmly at this point. When (by 4 September 1790) he had ascertained that the Company denied his claims to the throne of Mataram (and even reproached him for making them), he formed an alliance with Pakubuwana IV, at the same time demanding of Greeve such an impossibly high price for his continued cooperation with the VOC that he must have felt himself to be in a position to take a very hard line with the Company. Whether he calculated that he would be able to reduce his price in subsequent negotiations should it begin to look as if rapprochement with the VOC was the wiser course, we are not really in a position to know.

Provocation

One of the forms that sabre-rattling took was the gravely insulting appropriation of someone else's royal title. The first example of this took place in the reign of Pakubuwana III, who bestowed the name and title 'Pangeran [Prince] Mangkubumi' on Mangkunĕgara's grandson, a name subsequently withdrawn after a protest from the Sultan of Yogyakarta, who had borne this name before he ascended to the throne.[40] (A title of comparable significance would be 'Prince of Wales', conferred by the reigning monarch of England or Britain on the heir to the throne.) The second example took place on 22 Arwah 1716 A.J. [7 May 1790] when the new Sunan, Pakubuwana IV, proclaimed at a public audience that he had bestowed names and titles on two of his brothers: Pangeran Arya Mataram was henceforth to be known as Pangeran Mangkubumi, and Raden Mas Saidi was to be known as Pangeran Buminata. He soon received a letter from Greeve, conveying the Sultan of Yogyakarta's displeasure at the use of Mangkubumi, his former title, and suggesting alternative names. Pakubuwana IV hesitated, but eventually stood firm.

Then on 20 Bĕsar [31 August 1790] the diarist records the first news of raiding parties from Mataram causing serious damage. Neither Mangkunĕgara nor the Sunan reacted immediately: the diarist explains that they were waiting to see what the Company *did*.

Greeve now received letters from Mangkunĕgara claiming that van Straalendorff (First Resident of Surakarta 1767–1784) had promised him that he would be given the throne of Mataram on the Sultan's death. It seems clear that Mangkunĕgara knew that something was in the wind, and was endeavouring to find out what profit he could expect if he remained on the Company's side instead of joining the Sunan in his planned aggression against Mataram. He claimed that van Straalendorff had made this promise to him in the name of the 'Edelheer at Sĕmarang' (the Governor of the Northeast Coast) on 2 Jumadilakir 1700 A.J. and again on 26 Sapar Je 1710 A.J., i.e.

Geisha warriors? Java's prajurit estri   97

20 January 1784 C.E.[41] The first date falls outside the period covered by the diary, but under the second date the diarist[42] has in fact entered a note recording just such a promise. This indicates that Mangkunĕgara genuinely believed he had been given such an undertaking. Further, it is not at all improbable that van Straalendorff had at least hinted at such a possibility: the Company was very prone to the use of threats or bribes with Javanese princes and, as de Jonge has remarked,[43] frequently did not keep its word. This was, indeed, a technique which Greeve himself was to use later with Pakubuwana IV.[44]

Greeve was alarmed to hear of Mangkunĕgara's claims on Yogyakarta. He postponed giving Mangkunĕgara an answer while he made enquiries about the military situation. These revealed that Mangkunĕgara had at least 500 men in his household, on wages, and could easily summon another 3,000 to 4,000 thousand. His informant remarked that Mangkunĕgara was popular among his men – 'criminal wretches' as many of them were – because of his former leadership in war and because of the good treatment and protection which he had always given them. Greeve himself was of the opinion that Mangkunĕgara could in fact call up as many as 10,000 men within three days. The Company's military reserves, in contrast, currently numbered exactly 243.[45]

Finally (and reluctantly) Greeve decided he had to intervene in person. He left Sĕmarang on 15 September with an escort of dragoons; a further 374 men awaited the arrival of porters.[46] This step was partly motivated by a letter he had received from the Sunan suggesting that, since there were likely to be many pretenders to the Sultan's throne after his death, trouble could be avoided by dividing Yogyakarta among his children. Greeve felt this proposal would destroy the necessary equipoise between the two kingdoms, which was the foundation of the Company's mastery of Java, and that it was probably a cover for the Sunan's plan to swallow the fragments of Mataram one by one.

Armed combat

The diarist notes that the Sunan and Mangkunĕgara were concerned to see how the Company would react, and on the first day of the new year, 1717 [11 September 1790 AD], the Sunan himself called on Mangkunĕgara to discuss the situation, an unprecedented departure from normal protocol. According to the diarist, the Sunan said that he would follow Mangkunĕgara's lead in deciding whether he would stand firm against the Company, and Mangkunĕgara decided to do so.[47] Afterwards, he discussed the matter with his sons, and a few days later Governor Greeve arrived from Sĕmarang.[48] By now, Mangkunĕgara's dĕmang were bringing in heads of fallen Yogyakarta warriors.[49] On 11 Sura [21 September 1790] a deputation from Yogya was brought by the Dutch Resident to Sala to speak with the Sunan, who, according to the diarist, addressed them with open insults, bringing

98   *Ann Kumar*

Greeve to the point of tears. Mangkunĕgara himself bought up large stocks of rice, readied his army, and sent Pangeran Prang Wadana to consult with the Sunan.[50]

Greeve tried to give Mangkunĕgara a letter from the Sultan, but the prince refused to receive it.[51] He went to see the Sunan, who remained unbending, and advised him not to try to apply pressure to his 'uncle'[52] who was a man not to be frightened once he had made up his mind – in fact, he might actually stab Greeve. The diarist then notes that Greeve decided not to visit Mangkunĕgara after all. Now 300 South Indians in the Company's service (described by the diarist as unbelievers who physically resembled Middle-eastern Muslim traders, whom Greeve had brought to Sala hoping they would terrify the Javanese into submission) arrived in Sala from Sĕmarang. The Residents of Surakarta and Yogyakarta and Greeve continued to try to intimidate Mangkunĕgara, in vain. They succeeded however in persuading the Patihs of Sala and Yogyakarta to swear an oath in the Dutch factory. This was on 18 Sura 1717 [28 September 1790].

The Company had decided to offer Mangkunĕgara 4,000 *real* per annum, but he refused: only 4,000 *cacah* would do. He also asked for the return of his wife and *sĕlir*.[53] Greeve refused this last request, but promised to try to get the *cacah*.

On 21 September a Yogyakarta party arrived and asked if the Company would agree to the Sultan's bestowing the name 'Mangkubumi' on his own grandson, the son of the Crown Prince, by way of compensation for its use in Surakarta. This solution having proved acceptable to all sides, the matter of the name was no longer an issue.

The armed encounters between Mangkunĕgara and the Sultan were, however, not so easily brought to an end. Both sides claimed that the other had been the first to attack. Greeve proposed a peace plan, evidently based on van Ijsseldijk's earlier suggestion, by which all parties would sign a Contract of Reconciliation *(Contract van Bevreediging)*. The Yogyakarta reaction to this suggestion was much more favourable than Greeve had hoped, but Mangkunĕgara continued to insist that the only acceptable token of the Sultan's peaceable intentions would be the return of Ratu Bĕndara and his two *sĕlir*. This was clearly an impossible demand and could only signify that Mangkunĕgara meant to obstruct the road to peace. On the 26th of September, however, Mangkunĕgara sent his European equerry, Corporal Pieter Bloemhart, to tell Greeve that his children, Pangeran Purbanĕgara and Pangeran Padmanĕgara, were pressing him to adhere to the Sunan's counsel, so that he was not able to oblige Greeve in what he had requested. This can be interpreted as a tactic on Mangkunĕgara's part to avoid totally closing off the possibility of striking a deal with the VOC. Greeve also received reports that the Mangkunĕgaran forces were continuing their attacks.

Moreover, the Sunan's behaviour still presented considerable difficulties, even after the 'Mangkubumi' issue was resolved, as he put a long series of procedural difficulties in the way of the Contract of Reconciliation.

Geisha warriors? Java's prajurit estri   99

Although Greeve's diary does not record that the Sunan verbally abused the Yogyakarta party – as described in the diary – he does record that the Sunan unduly delayed sending his Patih on a reciprocal visit to Yogyakarta. The Sunan also, one can only surmise from the record, enjoyed embroiling the cowardly Greeve in fraught or perilous situations: when Greeve later went to Yogyakarta, he asked him to request the Sultan to agree to giving the Surakarta *pengulu* authority over all Islamic marriages conducted in Yogyakarta and Semarang – an astonishing claim to Surakartan supreme authority over Islam that the Sultan of Yogyakarta would never have accepted. At the same time, he also actually asked Greeve to select for him the most beautiful of the Yogyakarta Crown Prince's daughters so that he could marry her. The hapless Greeve reported to the Sunan that though he had seen the princesses *en déshabillé* he could not say which was most pleasing to the eye.[54]

After the Patihs of Yogyakarta and of Surakarta had finally put their seals on the Contract on 28 September, Greeve told Mangkunĕgara that he too must put his seal on it, on the following day. Mangkunĕgara continued, however, to insist on the return of his wife and *sĕlir*, and his equerry Bloemhart told Greeve that Mangkunĕgara had had a conference with his sons and his grandson Prang Wadana. Later in the day, Mangkunĕgara told Greeve that, if he were compelled to renounce his wife and *sĕlir*, the Company should do something to compensate him, as it had so often said that he was under its protection, and he had put up with so much bitterness in its name. He asked for 4,000 *cacah*; Greeve offered 4,000 *real* per annum, but Mangkunĕgara said that he could not 'sell his wife for money'. He also told Greeve that it was the Sunan who was forcing him to be intransigent; Greeve himself knew that five of Mangkunĕgara's sons held appanages from the Sunan, and could lose these if he were alienated. At the same time, Greeve was receiving information, via the VOC's chief ally, Pangeran Purbaya, that 'serious things' were happening in the kraton, and that he should be on his guard. The Sunan's generally uncooperative behaviour gave added credence to these rumours, as he refused to put his seal on Mangkunĕgara's request to the Sultan of Yogyakarta to provide the 4,000 *cacah*.

The Mataram raids continued; Mangkunĕgara's dĕmang and a large force under Pangeran Prang Wadana pushed the invaders back, conquered some Yogyakarta villages, and took the heads of four men of rank (Raden). Greeve ordered the fighting to be stopped, and the Mangkunĕgaran forces obeyed. The diarist explains that this was done for two reasons: first, Greeve had undertaken to get the 4,000 *cacah*, and second, the Yogyakarta forces had Dutchmen with them. She also says that Pangeran Prang Wadana was extremely exasperated by this stop to the fighting, and had to be calmed by his father. The Mangkunĕgaran troops too were disappointed and did not like to retreat before the 'Kumpĕni's' pressure.[55]

Greeve however returned from Yogyakarta unsuccessful: he had not persuaded the Sultan to allocate 4,000 of his *cacah* to Mangkunĕgara.[56]

100 *Ann Kumar*

The prince refused to accept money, and Greeve, having annoyed the Sunan too (by pretending to be ill and causing a kraton party to be cancelled), left in humiliating disarray for Sĕmarang.[57]

Dutch sources confirm that Greeve had indeed been unsuccessful in Yogyakarta. The Sultan would not even speak of Ratu Bĕndara, and the *sĕlir* could not be returned because they had borne the Crown Prince's children. He asked Greeve to intervene on his behalf and rescue one of his regents from Mangkunĕgara's men. It appears that, at this stage, Mangkunĕgara's men had captured considerably more of the Sultan's villages than the Sultan's men had of his, so that the military advantage was with Mangkunĕgara.

Greeve reported to Mangkunĕgara his failure to obtain the 4,000 *cacah*, and the prince once again refused to accept the 4,000 *real*, saying that this would not compensate for the shame he had suffered. Greeve then left, explaining that his refusal to attend the reception given by the Sunan was due to his fear of treachery.[58]

As soon as Greeve left, Mangkunĕgara created new corps of soldiery which went out to fight the Yogya forces on 8 Sapar 1717 [18 October 1790 C.E.]. This time, however, they had to retreat before the Yogyakarta forces. The diarist explains that this was because the Sultan's men had Dutchmen with them, and because the Sunan did not keep his promise to support the Mangkunĕgaran forces. The prince himself did not take part 'because he had boils'.[59]

News of further attacks by Mangkunĕgara's men, in the Gunung Kidul region, had come as early as 13 October, the day Greeve left Surakarta, so he continued to strengthen his military backing with Madurese and other troops.[60] The VOC advanced Greeve large sums of money – over 100,000 *rijksdaalders* – for hiring these troops. A *rijksdaalder* was very close in value to the *real* – both maintained a value which varied only between £0.22 and £0.23 over the period 1651–1781.[61] So this figure tellingly illustrates the enormously greater VOC resources, in comparison with Mangkunĕgara's annual income from his lands of c. 6,000 *real*.

On 23 Sapar [2 November 1790] Mangkunĕgara's men finally dispersed on Kumpĕni orders and he accepted the offer of 4,000 *real* per annum. He rationalized his position by saying that he was now old and sick, and obeyed all the Company's commands, so as to be able to sit and sleep in peace; and that the Sunan had betrayed him, going back on his promise.[62] On 27 Sapar [6 November 1790] he signed a solemn agreement (sĕrat prajangji) in the Dutch factory.

In his letter to Batavia of 28 October,[63] Greeve had remarked that the Sunan appeared to be withdrawing his support from Mangkunĕgara. The Sunan continued to refuse to hand over to the VOC five of his advisors.[64] The impasse was so serious that the Sunan put his army on the alert,[65] and the Company began to bring in troops from Sumĕnĕp, Madura,[66] and South India, and later from Yogyakarta and Kaduwang.[67] On 8 Mulud [16 November] the Resident visited Mangkunĕgara and told him that

Geisha warriors? Java's prajurit estri   101

the Company had broken with the Sunan and intended to depose him.[68] Garěběg Mulud [the 12th of the month, 20 November 1790] was a time of deserted markets, and panic and confusion among the Sunan's subjects.[69] The Sunan himself did not even appear for the customary celebrations. But now he decided to play for time, summoning representatives both of his santri advisers and of the opposing party, led by the Patih. More troops, from Sampang, Suměněp, and Yogyakarta, moved in, and these forces were disposed at strategic points around the city. By 17 Mulud [25 November], Mangkuněgara had already received the first payment of his annual 4,000 *real*. The next day, the Sunan capitulated, handing over five of his advisers – Wiradigda, Kanduruhan, Saleh, Pangeran Paněngah, and Bahman – to Pangeran Purbaya, who brought them to the Dutch factory. From there they were taken to Sěmarang.[70]

The information from Greeve's diary on the events of these weeks can be summarized as follows: on 5 November, Greeve decided that it was essential that the 'popes' be handed over to the Company. When he was informed by Pangeran Purbaya on 9 November that the Sunan had decided to 'live or die' with them, he made a contingency plan in case the Sunan should flee his kraton. Mangkuněgara – chosen, as Greeve later explained, because he was a formidable man who could 'maintain himself', whereas the Sunan's son and heir was still a child[71] – would replace him. On the 10th, the 300 Suměněp troops left Sěmarang for Surakarta, accompanied by fourteen sepoys and some European troops. On the 16th, Greeve received news that the Sunan had called up his regents and their armed men, some of whom (those from Banyumas) had already reached Surakarta. On the 18th, news arrived from Yogyakarta that the Sultan had strengthened his forces in the field to far more than 2,000 men, and that his *mancanagara* regents with another 2,000 would approach Surakarta from the east by the morrow. On the 19th, the 500 west Madurese troops left for Surakarta.[72]

Greeve's estimates of the relative strength of the different central Javanese forces readied for combat were as follows – those of the Sultan of Yogyakarta, between 4,500 and 7,000 men; those of Mangkuněgara, now 2,000 [considerably less than the 3,000–4,000 foreshadowed above]; and those of the Sunan himself, 7,000.[73]

In the event it did not come to war; for on 20 November the Surakarta Resident sent news that the Sunan had decided to relinquish the 'popes'. Greeve asked the Sunan that the replacements to the posts vacated by the popes should be 'honest men' (*brave lieden*) and, for these appointments only, should swear an oath of loyalty to the Company. On 26 November, news came that the Sunan had handed over the five 'chief popes' (as named in the diary) to Pangeran Purbaya, who took them to the VOC fort. The Sunan was granted the Company's forgiveness and the troops began to disperse.

On 1 December, Greeve wrote to Batavia explaining his strategy: he had not – however, it might have appeared from what he had said – intended actually to depose the Sunan without the Governor-General's authorization, but had judged it useful to give the impression that he did in fact intend to

102   *Ann Kumar*

take this ultimate step. His plan to put Mangkunĕgara on the throne had been purely a precaution for the eventuality that the Sunan himself took the step of leaving his capital.

From this point on, a 'reconciliation' between the Sunan and the Dutch began, and the troops and officers and Company officials began to return to their normal posts.[74] The Sunan dismissed another of his officers on the Company's request,[75] and resumed the social niceties. He visited the Dutch in their factory and even, the diarist records, drank alcohol (as did his dignitaries) to please them, although he usually took only tea or coffee.[76] He had not drunk alcohol in earlier gatherings with Dutch officials.[77]

It is clear from the VOC letters of the period immediately following this development that the alliance of interests between the two Surakarta princely houses had now definitely broken down, as a result of the different ways in which Pakubuwana and Mangkunĕgara had withdrawn from confrontation with the Company. The Company, however, once it had brought about the peaceful installation of the Yogyakarta Crown Prince (this took place on 2 April 1792), also moved to ensure the succession of Mangkunĕgara's heir, Prang Wadana, to his grandfather's position, supported by the same grant of land and labour, the 4,000 *cacah* granted to Mangkunĕgara by Pakubuwana III.

Near the end of the diary,[78] the diarist gives an analysis of Mangkunĕgara's political position. She compares him with a wong anggur[79] (lir nganggur saumpama), but claims also that he is 'acknowledged as the child' (ingakĕn anak) of the Company, in contrast to the rulers of Sala [Surakarta] and of Mataram [Yogyakarta], who, with all the people of Java, are ruled (kareh) by the Governor [of the Northeast Coast], for it is the Company which possesses supreme authority. She goes on to say that, because Mangkunĕgara does not owe service to the Sunan, he does not have to attend court at the Garĕbĕg celebrations, as the Bupati does – which was not in fact true, as Mangkunĕgara was contractually bound to attend these celebrations, but avoided doing so.

This is an extremely interesting formulation. First, we see Mangkunĕgara, who had for so long relied on his own strength, now in his old age brought to accept the fact that it was the Company that guaranteed his present position. Second, we find – in marked contrast with the conclusion of Ricklefs that the relationship was one of alliance[80] – an acknowledgment of Company *rule* over the whole of Java, including the Sunan and the Sultan.

Conclusion

In the title of this piece, I suggested that the *prajurit estri* possessed both military skills and the beauty and refined arts of the geisha. This is a very rare combination – especially since the military skills were in this case of an exceptionally high order. Yet, as the diary shows, the *prajurit estri* had in fact significantly *more* skills than those of geishas and warriors combined.

Geisha warriors? Java's prajurit estri   103

As is evident from the account of the 1790 crisis given above, the diarist is also a political commentator who has provided a detailed coverage of high-level political developments. Her reportage is not written from the perspective of the lowly foot-soldier or of the bystander. She is clearly well informed about the motives and moves of all the most powerful actors in the political and military contest for power. Nor does the diarist deal in empty theorizing about the nature of power. Rather, she provides a detailed coverage of the economics and realpolitik of war. As she was also the keeper of Mangkunĕgara's accounts, she knew how much his soldiers cost him and the need for the income-bearing *cacah* he was trying to obtain from the VOC, as constantly reiterated in the diary. And at the conclusion of the crisis described above, the diarist reflects on the nature of the relationship between the VOC and Javanese principalities and its implications for their relative power – the earliest example of an awareness of the passing of sovereignty from Javanese rulers to the VOC that I know of.

In sum this unique and detailed account of the colourful life of such an extraordinarily talented corps of women is a wonderful antidote to what van Leur (1908–1942) called the 'grey and undifferentiated' picture of Indonesian society provided by Dutch sources,[81] and to clichéd assumptions concerning the limitations surrounding Indonesian women.

In addition, the diary also provides an extremely rare insight into the process of history writing, constituting as it does a basis for the production of a Babad. It also raises the question, since most historians wrote anonymously, how many of them were women?

Notes

1 See H. J. de Graaf (ed.) *De Viif Bezantschapsreizen van Rijklof van Goens naar het hof van Mataram 1648–1654* (The Hague: Nijhoff, 1956), pp. 259–260.

2 François Valentijn, *Oud en Nieuw Oost-Indiën*, Vol. 4, *Beschryving van Groot Djava ofte Java Major* (Dordrecht, Amsterdam: n.p., 1726), pp. 59–60.

3 Merle C. Ricklefs, *Jogjakarta under Sultan Mangkubumi, 1749–1792: A History of the Division of Java* (Oxford: Oxford University Press, 1974) p. 304, n. 42: apparently the Yogyakarta crown prince's corps was the occasion of 'notoriety'. See Koloniaal Archief [henceforth KA] 3708, Vereenigde Oost-Indische Compagnie Overgekomen Berichten [henceforth VOCOB], 1789, Semarang to Batavia, 19 August, Greeve's diary for 13 August.

4 *Begin ende Voortgangh, van de Vereenighde Nederlandtsche Geoctroyeerde Oost-Indische Compagnie*, Vol. 1, *Historische Verhael Vande Reyse gedaen inde Oost-Indiën, met 15 Schepen voor Reeckeninghe vande vereenichde Gheoctroyeerde Oost-Indische Compagnie: Onder het beleydt van den Vroomen ende Manhaften Wybrandt van Waerwijck* (Amsterdam: n. p., [1644], pp. 31–32 (of last fascicule).

5 See Beaulieu's account in *Navigantium atque Itinerantium Bibliotheca*, ed. John Harris (London: Bennet, 1705), Vol. 1, p. 744.

6 R. C. Temple (ed.), *The Travels of Peter Mundy 1608–1667*, 5 vols. (Cambridge: Hakluyt Society, 1907–1936), Vol. 3, p. 131.

7 The source is described in Ann Kumar, 'Javanese Court Society and Politics in the Late Eighteenth Century: The Record of a Lady Soldier: Part I: The

104　*Ann Kumar*

Religious, Social and Economic Life of the Court', *Indonesia*, Vol. 29 (May 1980), pp. 1–46: pp. 2–3, fn. 5.

8　The third year of the Javanese eight-year *windu* cycle.

9　The Javanese wording of this introductory passage is given in Kumar, 'Part I', p. 3.

10　The day of the seven-day week (Sunday to Saturday) is always given, sometimes in combination with the day of the Javanese five-day week (Lĕgi or Manis, Paing, Pon, Wage and Kliwon), as in Salasa-Manis (Tuesday-Manis).

11　Because of the importance of the Friday prayer observances, the date of the month is given on every Friday for which there is an entry, for example, 'Friday-Wage the 26th of the month of Bĕsar', Wage being the day of the five-day week, and Bĕsar the twelfth month of the Javanese lunar calendar. The year is given on the first day of every new year, for example, 'then it was the day Saturday-Wage, the first day of the month of Sura [Javanese New Year: Sura is the first month of the lunar calendar]. The year changed to Jimawal [the third year of the eight-year *windu* cycle] "one horse, voice of the ruler" [chronogram for 1717 AJ]'. The year is also noted on the occasion of some particularly important event, such as the installation of a new ruler.

12　The facts of Hamzah's career have been enormously elaborated and expanded in the epics it inspired. Both Arabic and Persian versions exist, and the Malay and Javanese versions derive from a Persian original: see Ph. S. van Ronkel, *De Roman van Amir Hamza* (Leiden: Brill, 1895), pp. 91–98, 165–166, 176, 184, 245–251. The Islamization of Java has sometimes been attributed to the congruence between Sufi mysticism and Hindu-Javanese religion. It seems to me however that there is an equally good 'fit' between the Islamic and the Javanese martial traditions – as attested by the popularity of the Menak.

13　For a synopsis of the Rĕngganis story, an original Javanese composition which grew out of the Menak saga, see R. M. Ng. Poerbatjaraka, P. Voorhoeve and C. Hooykaas, *Indonesische Handschriften* (Bandung: Nix, 1950), pp. 1–17.

14　The year was 1714 AJ and the date converts to 31 July 1788.

15　The Governors of Java's northeast coast, the most important of the Company's officials so far as the central Javanese courts were concerned, are usually referred to by the diarist as 'the Dĕler', which is derived from Dutch *edelheer*, the title they bore as members of the Governor-General's Council.

16　That is, Mangkunĕgara, who is nearly always referred to in the diary simply by his title, 'Pangeran Dipati'.

17　This word is used in its original sense of 'an establishment, such as a trading station, where factors or agents reside and transact business for their employers'.

18　The Nyutrayu and Jayengasta (see next line) were names of corps in Mangkunĕgara's armed forces.

19　The VOC (First) Resident at Surakarta, the head of the Company's representation.

20　Arak is a strong drink prepared from a base of sugar-cane and a glutinous type of rice.

21　That is, the future Pakubuwana IV, who is referred to here as 'the younger Pangeran Dipati' in contradistinction to 'the elder Pangeran Dipati', i.e., Mangkunĕgara.

22　Lit. 'the elder Pangeran Dipati'.

23　In the Dutch original, dalm, from Jav. *dalĕm*, noble or princely residence.

24　See entries of Thursday 31 July and Wednesday 13 August, in Greeve's diary, which is found under Semarang to Batavia, 19 August, in KA 3708, VOCOB, 1789.

25　Ibid., p. 73.

26　Ibid., pp. 80–81.

Geisha warriors? Java's prajurit estri   105

27 On the details of the partition, see Ricklefs, *Jogjakarta*, pp. 61–95.
28 On the nature of the *cacah* as a revenue or land unit, see Kumar, 'Part I', pp. 27–28.
29 For a translation of this passage, see ibid., pp. 22–25.
30 See Ibid., pp. 26–35.
31 The hard Spanish dollar, *peso duro*, generally known in the Indonesian world – where it was the standard currency for a long period – as the *real*, an abbreviation of *real de a ocho* ('eight-real piece'). See further Kumar, 'Part I', p. 27, n. 156.
32 Ricklefs, *Jogjakarta*, p. 234.
33 See van Overstraten to Batavia, 3 November 1792, KA 3859, VOCOB, 1793.
34 See G. P. Rouffaer, 'Vorstenlanden', *Adatrechtbundel*, Vol. 34, Series D81 (1931), pp. 233–378: p. 273.
35 Kumar, 'Javanese Court Society and Politics in the Late Eighteenth Century: The Record of a Lady Soldier: Part II: Political Developments: The Courts and the Company 1784–1791', *Indonesia*, Vol. 30 (October 1980), pp. 67–111.
36 Dipati was a title for men of extremely high rank, such as princes, chief ministers, and some regional overlords.
37 Kumar, 'Part II', p. 78.
38 Ibid.
39 Ibid., p. 79.
40 Ibid., pp. 76–78.
41 See enclosures ten and eleven, Mangkunĕgara to Greeve, received at Sĕmarang on 15 and 17 May respectively, in Greeve to Batavia, 19 May, in KA 3802, VOCOB, 1791.
42 31R – see further Kumar, 'Part II', p. 68. '31R' refers to the right-hand side of page 31. As only the left side of each of the 303 double pages is numbered, the number of pages would rise to 606 if following modern convention. Javanese paper bark was used.
43 J. K. J. de Jonge, *De Opkomst von het Nederlandsch Gezag in Oost Indië* (The Hague: Nijhoff, 1878), Vol. 10, p. LXXIII.
44 See below.
45 See F. J. Rothenbuhler to Greeve, 16 May, in Greeve to Batavia, 19 May, in KA 3802, VOCOB, 1791.
46 See Greeve's diary, 15 September, in KA 3833, VOCOB, 1792.
47 249R: see Kumar, 'Part II', p. 92 for the Javanese original.
48 251L.
49 252L.
50 253L.
51 253R–254L, 15 Sura 1717 [25 September 1790].
52 Mangkunĕgara's grandfather, Pakubuwana I, was the Sunan's great-grandfather, though they were descended from different wives of Pakubuwana I.
53 The wife referred to was Ratu Bĕndara, the daughter of the Sultan of Yogyakarta, who had now been back with her father for twenty-seven years. Two of Mangkunĕgara's *sĕlir* ('concubines' or 'secondary wives', who were married when they fell pregnant) had defected to Mataram and had apparently joined the Crown Prince's household: see below.
54 See Greeve's diary, under 1 October, in KA 3833, VOCOB, 1792, and for more detail on the Sunan's behaviour Kumar, 'Part II', pp. 93–95.
55 256R.
56 257.
57 258.
58 See also Ricklefs, *Jogjakarta*, p. 329 on this episode.

106 *Ann Kumar*

59 260L. *dasar karingĕn* (i.e *korengĕn*) *gĕrahe*.
60 See Greeve to Batavia, 8 November, in KA 3833, VOCOB, 1792.
61 See further Kumar, 'Part I', p. 27.
62 260R: see Kumar, 'Part II', p. 96 for the original Javanese text. The diarist says, however, that the Sunan's brother Mangkubumi had taken part in the fighting (260L).
63 In KA 3833, VOCOB, 1792.
64 In the Dutch sources, these men are always referred to as 'popes', a singularly inappropriate term frequently used to designate men highly respected for their Islamic learning.
65 261R.
66 'Madura' is used in the diary, as it was generally until a much later period, to mean only west Madura, from Bangkalan to Sampang.
67 262.
68 262.
69 262R.
70 263R.
71 Greeve to Batavia, 1 December, in KA 3833, VOCOB, 1792.
72 Diary, 18 November, and Greeve to Batavia, 20 November, in KA 3833, VOCOB, 1792.
73 See Greeve's diary, 5 and 18 November, in KA 3833, VOCOB, 1792.
74 264L–268L.
75 268L.
76 265R: The diarist makes it quite clear that the drinking of alcohol was a special departure from the Sunan's usual custom. In the Mangkunĕgaran, of course, alcohol was regularly served at festivities, and there are numerous reports in the diary about Mangkunĕgara being drunk, or very drunk, although he was an observant Muslim and even used to write out copies of the Quran for presents.
77 See, for example, 251R (the Sunan's reception of Greeve).
78 292L.
79 The *wong anggur* were a specific class of people in Javanese society. However, this class was differently defined from region to region: as landless people with no obligation to perform the customary labour services, for instance, and elsewhere as people who performed specified services for the village head but were otherwise free of obligations, thus constituting a sort of élite. See further Kumar, 'Part II', p. 76, note 45, and p. 100.
80 See Ricklefs, *Jogjakarta*, pp. 371–425.
81 Jacob Cornelius van Leur, *Indonesian Trade and Society: Essays in Asian Social and Economic History* (The Hague: W. van Hoeve, 1955), p. 153.

Part III

Southeast Asian women warriors and revolutionaries in the modern period

6 Heroines and forgotten fighters

Insights into women combatants' history in Aceh, 1873–2005[1]

Elsa Clavé

In late 2014, an Indonesian language Facebook posting drew an unusual wide audience by claiming that Indonesian textbooks projected erroneous visual representations of Tjut Nyak Dhien (c. 1848–1908), the Acehnese – and later also Indonesian – national heroine in the armed anti-colonial struggle against the Dutch. Posted by a group with the name of Seuramoe Mekkah (Verandah of Mecca), a synonym for Aceh, it was claimed that the proud heroine was improperly attired. This was because her beautiful black hair remained visible, neatly tied up in a bun held together by silver jewellery. The post contrasted this with a sepia-coloured photograph of a woman seated on a chair, wearing the *jilbab* (Islamic headscarf in Indonesia), which it asserted to be the real Tjut Nyak Dhien (see Figure 6.1).[2] Implicit in this post were not just claims about how Muslim women should be dressed, but also that the only extant photo of Tjut Nyak Dhien (see Figure 1.1), just after her capture in 1905, was an explicit Dutch humiliation because the photograph represents her bare-headed.

Although the online post was quickly debunked as an ahistorical reading of present-day proclivities and styles of fashions into the past, it nevertheless provides an interesting and fitting metaphor for the present chapter, which goes back to field work and interviews in December 2006 and May 2007, and engages with questions relating to the representations of Acehnese women warriors by the Dutch, the Acehnese themselves, and the Indonesians. Why has there been a tendency in the historiography to focus on elite women who resisted the Dutch and to omit the efforts of ordinary Acehnese women? Why is it that the *Gerakan Aceh Merdeka* (GAM, Free Aceh Movement) used women in its armed struggle for more autonomy from Jakarta and also to attract international support, but is now keen on downplaying if not forgetting the contribution of these women?

The first part of this chapter focuses on the heroines of the resistance to the Dutch, but also attempts to bring in the less well-known and even anonymous women occasionally mentioned in Dutch reports, and ends with a brief coverage of Acehnese female soldiers during the Indonesian War of Independence against the Dutch (1945–1949). The second part of this chapter deals with the GAM, in particular during the 1998–2005 period, when

Nyak Dien Tanpa Jilbab

Figure 6.1 Creating controversy online: Tjut Nyak Dhien without jilbab, late 2014.
A less fierce looking portrait of the Acehnese and Indonesian heroine also covers the obverse side of the 10,000 Indonesian rupiah note introduced in 1998–1999 that ceased to be legal tender a decade later following the introduction of notes in 2004–2005. Interestingly, the watermark of the new 1,000 and 5,000 rupiah notes series features a portrait of Tjut Nyak Meutia, the other Indonesian heroine of Acehnese descent. Like Tjut Nyak Dhien, her contemporary, she is represented wearing her hair in a bun.
Source: Screenshot dated 31 March 2015 from www.tribunnews.com/nasional/2014/12/23/terkuak-kontroversi-potret-resmi-cut-nyak-dientanpa-jilbab.

the traditional term *inong balëë* gained new currency to denote both female civilian activists and also female soldiers of its military wing, the *Teuntra Neugara Aceh* (TNA, or Aceh National Army).[3] It traces the contours of their hardly recognised contribution to the armed struggle, which ended in mid-August 2005 with the Helsinki Agreement. The main sources for the first part are Dutch accounts, local biographies, and nationalist historiographies, whereas the second part considerably draws on the author's in-depth interviews with former *inong balëë*, which were conducted in December 2006 and May 2007 in Aceh.[4]

Part I: Women in the light and women in the shadows: the Dutch and independence wars

When the Dutch launched their first attack on the independent Sultanate of Aceh in 1873, they did not expect that it would take about four decades to subdue the population. This struggle did not only involve capturing the sultan (1903) and eventually abolishing the sultanate (1907), subduing a combative territorial aristocracy, the *ulèëbalang*,[5] and religious scholars, but it also required dealing with Aceh's women as the guerrilla resistance could hardly have been maintained without female support and even leadership. Women belonging to the elite classes were consequently monitored in order to gain intelligence and assert control over their kinship and other networks. If they took up arms against the Dutch, they risked with their lives, a fate valued over the humiliation of imprisonment and exile.[6] Perhaps such female resistance should not have been too surprising, since the region was known for having produced a legendary female Admiral Malahayati, whose existence is deeply anchored in the Acehnese consciousness,[7] but also four well-documented sultanahs (queens) who ruled for nearly two thirds of the seventeenth century (1641–1699).[8] Moreover, early European visitors to Aceh noted that the sultan had a corps of female body guards, the training and maintenance of which would have required considerable resources.[9] An additional, Acehnese system of organising female armed units is the legendary seventeenth-century corps of *inong balèë* under Admiral Malahayati, which allegedly comprised of 2,000 women trained in armed and naval combat, and based in a fort (*benteng*) on the northern Acehnese coast.[10]

Tjut Nyak Dhien and Tjut Meutia: Iconic Acehnese and Indonesian national heroines

The most prominent Acehnese woman warrior, then and now, is Tjut Nyak Dhien (c. 1848–1908).[11] Not only did she attract the curiosity of the Dutch during the Dutch-Acehnese wars (1873–1913), but Indonesia's first president, Ahmed Sukarno, elevated her in 1964 to the status of 'National Hero[ine]'.[12] She is therefore familiar to all Acehnese and Indonesians, since her name is used alongside that of Javanese Prince Diponegoro (1785–1855) and others to symbolise 'Indonesian' resistance to colonial conquest and foreign rule. But if Tjut Nyak Dhien's life is so extensively known, it is thanks to Magdalena (Madelon) Hermina Székely-Lulofs (1899–1958), who wrote the first detailed, and romantic, biography.[13] This would serve as a basis for many other biographies of the heroine.[14]

The author, a Dutch woman who was born in Java and lived in the Sumatran plantation belt with her Hungary-born husband, knew Aceh very well as she had spent the first years of her life in a military outpost there. It is during this time that she heard and read about Tjut Nyak Dhien through Dutch and Acehnese records. While it can be assumed that she had access to Dutch reports or accounts, we also do know that H. T. Damsté, a scholar on Aceh, had read to her a translation of the Acehnese chronicle *Hikayat Prang Gompeuni*. Written by the Acehnese poet Dôkarim, the chronicle would have given her a clear view of the Acehnese version of history.[15] Although based on historical facts, Székely-Lulofs' work therefore is a novel, with a large part of invention in the dialogues. The factual information that can be gleaned is as follows:

112   *Elsa Clavé*

Of noble birth, Tjut Nyak Dhien grew up in the village of Lampadang (North of Aceh) where, as a teenager, she was match-made with Teuku Ibrahim, the son of the ulèëbalang[16] of Lamnga (North of Aceh). In 1873, when Dutch-led forces first attacked Aceh, Tjut Nyak Dhien supported her first husband's participation in the war against the foreign invaders. But five years later, in 1878, Teuku Ibrahim was killed in a battle. Some months after his death, Tjut Nyak Dhien, by now aged about 30, married Teuku Umar. She was to be his third wife, after Tjut Nyak Sapiah and Tjut Nyak Meuligoe, and had a child named Tjut Gambang with him.[17]

Fifteen years later, on 30 September 1893, Teuku Umar and fifteen of his followers surrendered to the Dutch and vowed allegiance to the colonial government as represented by General Deijckerhoff, Aceh's Military Governor.[18] Unlike other female resistance fighters, who divorced their collaborationist husbands (as we will see later), Tjut Nyak Dhien followed her husband and thereby accepted Dutch authority. But after having helped the Dutch to fight Acehnese troops for more than two years, Teuku Umar finally defected on 29 March 1896, taking along weapons and ammunitions. The background to his defection remains unclear but, from an Acehnese point of view, his surrender to the Dutch most likely was a ruse, a *tipu muslihat* (smart trick), which was a perfectly acceptable strategy often used by the Acehnese. When he was eventually entrusted with military equipment, Tjut Nyak Dhien's husband was able to abscond with 380 modern rifles, 800 old-fashioned weapons, 25,000 bullets, 500 kilos of gun-powder, 120,000 gun-powder wicks, and 5,000 kilos of lead.[19]

Together with her husband, Tjut Nyak Dhien fled to the Acehnese West Coast (Daya, Woyla and Meulaboh). But three years later, in 1899, Teuku Umar was killed in an ambush by a *Marechaussee*[20] unit at Suak Ujung Kalak (West of Aceh). Tjut Nyak Dhien, by then already in her early fifties, did not surrender and continued the fight in the jungle of the western coast area. Six years later, almost blind and considerably weakened, she was betrayed, but in a way also saved, by her war companion Pang Laot Ali, who revealed her position to Lieutenant Veltman.[21] On 4 November 1905, she was arrested with several of her companions. According to the tradition, she tried to kill herself with her *rencong*[22] but failed. A Dutch photograph shows her shortly after being captured, sitting on a bench near Pang Laot Ali, looking dejected and angry (see Figure 1.1). She was then brought to Meulaboh, and from there transferred to prison in Kutaraja (today's Banda Aceh). Despite blindness and a weak physical condition, the Dutch decided to exile her – a not uncommon strategy typically reserved for people of high status – because they thought that her charisma still represented a danger to Dutch authority. In December 1906, she was exiled to Sumedang (Java), where she died nearly two years later, on 9 November 1908, refusing to acknowledge Dutch authority up to her last breath.[23]

Tjut Nyak Dhien was not the only Acehnese resistance fighter to be widowed twice in the fight against the Dutch, although she is by far the most famous.

Tjut Meutia (1870–1910), the heroine of the region of Pase (Eastern Aceh), suffered the same fate. In 1964, President Sukarno proclaimed her as an Indonesian National Hero[ine]. The Dutch war journalist Zentgraaff, who recorded events of her life, describes her as being 'not only of remarkable beauty, but also a proud and stately figure [...] an apparition of rare elegance and charm'.[24]

Born in 1870 in Keureutoe (North of Aceh), Tjut Meutia was the daughter of Teuku Ben Daud, an *ulèëbalang* who resisted Dutch authority by refusing to sign the *Korte Verklaring* (Short Declaration), an act that would have signalled his submission to the Dutch.[25] Tjut Meutia married Teuku Syamsarif upon the prompting of the female *ulèëbalang* of Keureutoe, Tjut Nyak Asya.[26] Because her first husband cooperated with the Dutch, the latter appointed him as the *ulèëbalang* in place of his mother. Shortly thereafter, probably dissatisfied with her husband's collaborationist stance, Tjut Meutia divorced him and married his brother instead, Teuku Tjut Muhammad alias Teuku Chik Tunong, to continue the anti-Dutch resistance. But in 1905, her second husband was arrested by Lieutenant Van Vuuren, imprisoned, and sentenced to death. Following his execution, Tjut Meutia married for a third time, her war companion Pang Nanggroe, to continue the fight against the Dutch, bringing along her five year old son Teuku Raja Sabi.[27]

The attacks launched by Pang Nanggroe varied from major battles to small offensives. In a mere three months in 1907, the Dutch recorded him as having attacked Dutch trains twice, shot at them, attacked the camp at Lhoksukon and Dutch patrol troops five times, and sabotaged the railway twenty-two times and the telephone system fifty-four times.[28] All these actions, which were attributed to Pang Nanggroe, also increased his wife's standing and charisma, but in September 1910, he was shot dead during a battle in Paya Cicem. While Tjut Meutia and her son managed to escape, one month later, on 22 October 1910, they were caught in a battle in which she and several of her followers were killed.[29]

Other prominent but less well-known women warriors from the Acehnese elite

Although Tjut Nyak Dhien and Tjut Meutia are the most iconic because they were made Indonesian national heroines, there are several other prominent female Acehnese anti-Dutch resistance fighters who are all well known. Thus, Dutch sources attest to the existence of women warriors who belonged to the political – usually the territorial *ulèëbalang* nobility rather than court circles – or the religious elite. Among the former are Potjut Baren (1880–1933), Potjut Meurah Intan (?–1937), and Potjut Meuligo (dates unknown), whereas Teungku Fakinah (1856–1938) and Teungku Tjutpo Fatimah (?–1912) belong to the latter category.[30] Although belonging to the elite, these women appear far less present in the oral tradition and in popular

114   *Elsa Clavé*

history, not to mention re-narrations in Indonesian or Acehnese nationalist historiographies.

The most detailed account about one of these women relates to Potjut Baren. Her story was captured by Teuku Zainal Harun – a scribe in the Dutch military camp in Kuala Bheë – in a long narrative.[31] Her fate is particularly interesting because she eventually accepted Dutch authority and would serve as *ulèëbalang*, which also made it extremely unlikely that she would gain the status of national heroine. Born in 1880, Potjut Baren was the wife of the *ulèëbalang* of Tungkop and Gome, who was also the resistance leader of the Woyla region (Western Aceh). After the death of her husband at the hands of the Dutch in 1898, Potjut Baren, then just aged eighteen, continued in her husband's footsteps. In charge of two strongholds in the Kuala Bheë and Tanoh Mirah regions (West of Acch), she forced the Dutch to reorganise their troops to put an end to her resistance. Her leg was severely injured when the Dutch struck a decisive attack in 1906, which also destroyed her centre in Kuala Bheë, on mount Macang. Defeated and captured, she was then brought to Meulaboh as a prisoner of war. Her injured leg eventually had to be amputated in Kutaraja.[32] Like Tjut Nyak Dhien, she was exiled to Java, but unlike her much senior counterpart, she eventually recognised Dutch authority. In return, the latter commuted her sentence and facilitated Potjut Baren's return to her native land. She was finally reinstated as an *ulèëbalang*, after the suggestion of Captain Veltman, as a way to break any future contestation, but kept under supervision.[33] Lieutenant H. Scheurleer, the camp commander of Tanah Miraj, reported that she tried to create order, security, and prosperity. This eventually earned her the Dutch honorific distinction of being 'De vrouwelijke Oeleebalang met het houten been [The female Ulèëbalang with the wooden leg]'.[34]

Potjut Baren's submission to the Dutch is unusual, not just in comparison with the iconic Tjut Nyak Dhien and Tjut Meutia, but also the other prominent but less well-known female guerrillas, including Potjut Meurah Intan (?–1937). Also known as Potjut Meurah Biheue, from the name of her birthplace, she was the offspring of a noble family from the Sultanate of Aceh. She married Tuanku Abdul Majid, the son of Tuanku Abbas bin Sultan Alaiddin Jauhar Alam Syah, an official of the Sultanate assigned to collect customs and duties at the port of Kuala Batèë. After her husband's surrender to the Dutch, she separated from him and urged her three sons Muhammad, Budiman and Nurdin to continue the fight. Consequently, they were part of the fugitive persons listed by the *Marechaussee* force.[35] A colonial report, from early 1904, states that she was the only figure from the Aceh Sultanate who had not yet surrendered and maintained an anti-Dutch attitude.[36]

As narrated by the Dutch war journalist Zentgraaff, Potjut Meurah Intan was finally captured in her headquarters at Padang Tiji:[37]

> ...Veltman who was well known as 'Tuan Padoman [Mister Guide]' was also a kind man, and he once knew a certain Acehnese woman

whom he highly respects even until this day. One of the patrol units in the Pidie region had captured this woman of Acehnese nobility named Potjut Meurah [...]. That woman was suspected of hiding a single-edged sabre within the folds of her clothes. Suddenly she withdrew this Acehnese dagger and shouted: 'In that case let me die!' Then she attacked the brigade. It seemed that members of the troop were not very interested in fighting a woman who was acting like a madwoman, stabbed around [sic] her, and a moment later she lay heavily wounded on the ground. She had two wounds on her head and two more on her shoulder, and one of her Achilles tendons had been severed. There she lay on the ground, full of blood and mud as if she were a piece of meat which had been cut up. A sergeant who looked at her with compassion said to his commander: 'May I end her life'? which was harshly responded to by Veltman: 'Are you crazy?' Then they continued their journey. They wanted that woman to die in the hands of her own people. Several days later while Veltman was walking in the shops of Biheue (between Sigli and Padang Tiji), he heard that Potjut Meurah was not only alive but even had a plan to murder all inhabitants in that settlement! [...] Maybe it seems too credulous that a very noble spirit still remained within a body which had been so ravaged. [...] Cow dung was smeared on her wounds. Her condition was very weak as a result of a lot of blood loss and her body shivered while she moaned in pain. In spite of that she refused medical assistance; she preferred to be dead rather than have a 'kaphé'[38] touch her body. Veltman who was fluent in the Acehnese language had a long discussion with this woman in a very respectful manner, as accorded to someone of her social standing. Finally she accepted this soldier's assistance which she had rejected from a doctor.[39]

Finally, in 1905, Potjut Meurah Intan, who was lame, was exiled to Blora, in eastern Java, with her two sons and a family member of the Sultan.[40] Like Tjut Nyak Dhien, she refused to collaborate with the Dutch and therefore remained in exile for more than thirty years. Her tombstone mentions that she passed away on 20 September 1937.

If women combatants are often presented as following the cause defended by their fathers or husbands, the example of Potjut Meurah Intan, who divorced her collaborationist husband and continued the anti-Dutch struggle with their three sons, also shows considerable female agency. A slightly different example is Potjut Meuligoe,[41] whose anti-Dutch engagement would open the way to a new generation of prominent fighters. She is the grand-aunt of Teuku Hamid Azwar, one of the founders of the Parindra (*Partai Indonesia Raya*; Greater Indonesia Party) in Aceh, and hero of the Indonesian War of Independence of 1945–1949. Although she is seldom mentioned in local historiography and is only cited in the prominent genealogy of Teuku Hamid Azwar, Potjut Meuligoe made important contributions in her own right in the war against the Dutch.

116   *Elsa Clavé*

As the war commander (*pang prang*) of the Samalanga region (North of Aceh), Potjut Meuligoe distinguished herself by defeating the Dutch in 1880 when they tried to take Batëë Ilie. She was used to wielding authority ever since she had stood in as the *ulèëbalang* for Samalanga when her brother Teuku Chik Bugis (alias Chik Samalanga) had sailed to Lahore (British India, today's Pakistan) in 1857 to trade and purchase weapons. When a Dutch naval blockade prevented her brother from returning from a later voyage, it naturally fell upon Potjut Meuligoe to lead the first battle against the Dutch. According to Captain Schoemaker, her hatred of the *kaphé* was such that she urged every able-bodied person to participate in the war, even if this meant abandoning vital work in the fields. She also threatened that a heavy price awaited those who would not follow her orders. Potjut Meuligoe also supported other regions in their efforts to resist, sending funds, weapons and volunteers to Aceh Besar (North of Aceh), a region where the Dutch were already installed.[42] As we do not have details about the end of her life, it is likely that she was never captured, but we do know that her region and the fort of Batëë Ilie were finally captured by the Dutch in 1904, thirty-one years after the beginning of the war in Aceh.[43]

Although the above cases suggest that the women combatants and leaders were exclusively from *ulèëbalang* families, and in the case of Potjut Meurah Intan from the Sultanate, some also had a strong religious background. These women can be identified by the respectful title of *teungku*, which was given to them in accordance to local tradition. Teungku Fakinah (1856–1938) lived in Lam Diran (North of Aceh) where she and her husband, Teungku Ahmad, served as religious teachers in her parents' *dayah* (coranic school) in Lam Pucok.[44] Following the beginning of the hostility with the Dutch, the couple engaged in the war and went to Pantai Cermin to join forces resisting the *kaphé* invasion.

After her husband's death, Teungku Fakinah continued the fight on her own, displaying considerable vision and skills.[45] She extended her activities to recruiting among women for the holy war and also to fundraising. This brought her in touch with the wives of some important Acehnese chiefs with whom she organised the resistance: Teungku Fakinah's network hence included Potjut Lamgugup, the wife of Tuanku Hasyim; Tjut Njak Meuligoe, married to Teuku Tjut Tungkop; Tjut Njak Lamreung, Teuku Tjut Lamreung's wife; and Tjut Nyak Dhien.[46] Her organisational skills and charisma must have been considerable because her greatest achievement consisted in the formation of a regiment (*sukey*) made up of four battalions (*baling*). One of these battalions, which was headquartered at Kuta Cot Weu fort, was entirely composed of women. Local history records women such as Tjutpo Fathimah Blang Preh, Njak Raniah Lam Urit, Tjutpo Habi, Tjutpo Njaktjut, and Tjut Puteh as forming part of Teungku Fakinah's troops.[47]

The resistance mounted by Teungku Fakinah did not go unnoticed by the Dutch. In June 1896, Colonel J. W. Stempoort led the attack on the forts of Lam Krak and forced Teungku Fakinah and her troops to sound the retreat.

After the capture of the sultan in 1903 and upon his orders, some of Aceh's *ulama* (Islamic religious scholars) wound down their engagement in the guerrilla. Teungku Fakinah was among those who followed the sultan's call to return to their religious activities and to rebuild *dayah*. Ever so enterprising, she married a third time and accomplished the holy pilgrimage (*hajj*) in 1915, just one year short of her sixtieth birthday. She stayed in Mecca for three years and would return there once more for a second time. Teungku Fakinah died in her *dayah*, where she is also buried, at the ripe old age of eighty-two in 1938.[48] Her name remains associated with a road, 'Ateung Teungku Faki', which she initiated and helped to build with other villagers.[49]

Another *teungku*, about whom very little is known, is Teungku Tjutpo Fatimah, the wife of Teungku di Barat. She appears to have been from Gampong Sialëet Perak (North of Aceh) and, according to Dutch reports, fought at the sides of Tjut Meutia and Pang Nanggroe. After the death of the latter two in 1910 (see above), Tjutpo Fatimah and her husband took care of Raja Sabil, Tjut Meutia's son (see above), who was around eleven years old at that time. They lived for a year and half in the jungle of Pase before being killed in the mountains on 22 February 1912 by a *Marechaussee* unit commanded by Lieutenant H. Behrens.[50] Zentgraaff describes Teungku Tjutpo Fatimah as an example of bravery because she took the firearm of her husband, who was so severely wounded that he could not use it anymore, and resumed firing until both of them were dead.[51]

Besides these more or less well-known historical figures, we also find traces of groups of unnamed women combatants. These anonymous women villagers are mentioned in Dutch reports but not acknowledged as the individual heroines previously mentioned. These women, far from the exclusive circle of Acehnese nobility, show a more popular face of the *inong balèë*, not noticed as such by the Dutch, and completely absent from Indonesian and Acehnese historiography.

Anonymous village women combatants of the Dutch and the Independence Wars

According to war journalist H. C. Zentgraaff, 'hundreds and perhaps thousands'[52] of Acehnese women were actively involved in war. He explained that they did not stay at home but went to the battlefield, then added: 'if they also fought, they did so with energy and contempt of death which often exceeded that of men'.[53] Archival evidence of 'common' women combatants can be found in Dutch telegrams sent from Aceh to the Netherlands East Indies' Governor-General in Java.[54] They mention women villagers armed with *rencong* attacking the *Marechaussee*, hiding weapons and munitions, and said to be 'disguised' in black-coloured men's clothes. The Dutch reports reveal the lack of information that the Europeans had at that time on Acehnese society, especially with regard to village life. Hence, the black

118   *Elsa Clavé*

men's clothes in reality were traditional dark pants known as *luweu tham asèe* (dog-chasing trousers), which were commonly used by women in Aceh.

In reports these women remained, often quite literally, a question mark. Surprisingly, they were not qualified as enemies (*vijanden*), a term reserved for men, but were classified as women (*vrouwen*) who were typically viewed as 'accidentally' killed by Dutch police. The daily telegrams sent from Aceh to Buitenzorg, the administrative seat of the Governor-General of the Netherlands East Indies, from 1905 to 1930, often bore mentions of 'vrouwen in mannenkleeren' (women in men's clothes) or 'als man verkleede gewapende vrouw' (armed woman disguised as a man).[55] Despite the red-inked questions written by the officers in the margins ('why so many women casualties?'), it never appears that they could conceive of these women as female combatants wearing their own clothes.[56] This suggests that the Dutch could not imagine female resistance as a general phenomenon, and thereby ignore the depth of indigenous resistance, although it might also betray official concerns about exactions against the civilian population.

This Dutch unwillingness to consider ordinary women as combatants oddly contrasts with the Dutch recognition of noble women as warring parties. Women at the top of society thus are generally recognised by name in the Dutch reports, although usually in connection with their husband or male relatives. This practice to trace genealogy through women was indeed noticed by Snouck Hurgronje, the Dutch scholar turned Advisor for Native Affairs, as particularly helpful to understand and track circles of resistance among the Acehnese nobility, the *ulèëbalang*.[57] But in the case of ordinary village women (and their male counterparts), names were typically not recorded and therefore remained anonymous, as in the following, deadly encounter.

A Dutch source hence describes the following violent encounter: 'During a house search in the village of Beu'ah, a *Marechaussee* [member] was unexpectedly attacked by an Acehnese woman with a hidden knife (*grasmes* – used for cutting grass), wounding his face. Out of self-defence, he was forced to kill her. In the house were found, besides individual blank weapons, also gunpowder and munitions-cargo, together with two barrels of guns and accessory parts'.[58] Numerous episodes where single Acehnese women attacked the *kaphé* are narrated by Zentgraaff. In the region of Pidie (East of Aceh), for example, an Acehnese man was shot when attacking a *Marechaussee* patrol. His wife took the *kelewang* (knife) from his body and attacked a soldier who tried to take it from her hand. She was shot dead and died as a 'martyr'.

Ordinary, and usually anonymous, female soldiers were also a common feature during the Indonesian War of Independence (1945–1949) against the Dutch who tried to re-assert their authority after three years of Japanese rule. This included involvement in more traditional guerrilla resistance, but also participation in formal troops that were formed to defend the newly proclaimed Republic of Indonesia. In October 1945, the *Pemuda Republik*

Indonesia (later called PESINDO, *Pemuda Sosialis Indonesia*) called all young people above the age of eighteen years to join them and form a local branch in Aceh. This led to the formation of a women's regiment named after resistance heroine Potjut Baren, which was one of seven regiments of the Rencong Division.[59] The Potjut Baren Regiment was based in Kutaraja and under the command of a female leader known as Zahara.[60] Women combatants were also found in another division, the Tengku Cik Paya Bakong Division, where a special group/staff for women's mobilisation (*staf istemewa/mobilisasi wanita*) was formed, although this appears not to have led to the creation of a full-fledged female regiment. Among the very few names recorded are Ibu Maryan, Tengku Aisyah Amin, Ti Aman I Latif, and Khadijah Aba.[61]

These women, barely mentioned in Indonesian history, took part in the national struggle alongside male combatants and sometimes in all-female units. But in contrast to the earlier forty-year war of resistance against the Dutch, there is not one single female leader who was later elevated to the iconic status of a Tjut Nyak Dhien or a Tjut Meutia, or at least left more than her name in the records. This amnesia about Acehnese women's involvement might well have been due to the overall rather messy situation throughout the Indonesian archipelago during the Indonesian War of Independence and the years following it. It might have been further accentuated by the complexity of post-independence developments, notably the Darul Islam rebellion (1953–1962), the violent elimination of the Indonesian Communist Party following General Suharto's counter-coup in October 1965, but also the promotion by the Sukarno and Suharto regimes of a conservative view of women.[62] Regardless of the gaps in the historiography, they deprive us of a better understanding of Acehnese women's involvement in warring in between the forty-year war of anti-Dutch resistance (1873–1913) and the thirty-year resistance against the central government in Jakarta (1976–2005). Whereas the celebration of the icons of the past is central to war propaganda, the period is characterised by the minimisation of women's roles during the conflict, hence limiting the position they could have in society in the post-conflict era.

Summary: the Dutch and independence wars

We have seen that women's participation, including in leadership and in combat roles, in the anti-Dutch struggles must have been considerable. Despite the recorded acts of female resistance and of slain female bodies found, we know very little about these 'ordinary' women who remain anonymous most of the time. Even the innovative and relatively large all-female units that were organised by Teungku Fakinah at the beginning of the twentieth century and the Potjut Baren Regiment of the Pemuda Republik Indonesia during the Indonesian Revolution / War of Independence of 1945–1949 are largely forgotten.[63] It is likely that the women on historical record are just

120 Elsa Clavé

the tip of the iceberg and that many more participated by providing intelligence, logistical, and moral support to the anti-Dutch resistance.

In contrast to the ordinary and anonymous female resistance fighters, and the two all-female units, Dutch, Indonesian, and Acehnese historiographies clearly have a preference for the iconic heroines and female leaders who originated from the traditional *ulèëbalang* elite or from religious families. The Dutch clearly privileged the noble warrior women, whom they called 'Groote Dames', such as Tjut Nyak Dhien and Potjut Baren, the latter of whom eventually submitted to the Dutch and was instated by them as the 'female ulèëbalang with the wooden leg'. President Sukarno preferred elite women too, but his choice of Tjut Nyak Dhien and Tjut Meutia suggested that he preferred heroines whose resistance against the Dutch remained unwavering until death. It is interesting that Teungku Fakinah, who appears to be the most astute and organisationally capable of these elite women, does not receive more attention, even though she raised a female battalion alongside three male ones.

The portraits of the 'Groote Dames' suggest considerable independence of spirit and initiative in the face of adversity. This is evident in their decisions to continue the anti-Dutch fight after a husband had died and, perhaps more importantly, the decision to divorce a husband after he had begun collaborating with the enemy. Likewise, Potjut Baren showed considerable independence of mind when she eventually submitted to the Dutch and returned to Aceh to serve her people as *ulèëbalang* rather than languishing in Javanese exile, even though some people might have questioned her motives. Elite women could thus be a driving force and locus of anti-Dutch resistance, something the Dutch were clever enough to realise. From the existing portraits we consequently learn quite a lot about family relations and combat engagements, but regrettably, information about their life as female fighters is not available. In contrast, the following section will look at women in the struggle against the Indonesian central government (1976–2005), notably the third phase of the conflict between the Free Aceh Movement and the Republic of Indonesia (1998–2005), and will be able to draw on direct face-to-face access to some of these women.

Part II: Rediscovering the *inong balèë*

Involvement and role of women combatants in the Free Aceh Movement (GAM)

In 1949, the Dutch finally conceded defeat and recognised an Indonesian Republic that also comprised of Aceh. The phenomenon of Acehnese women combatants appeared then to come to an end. In the early years of the Republic, Indonesian governmental programmes had an ideological tendency to restrict women to household activities and thereby to undermine their previous social position. This started with President Sukarno's

Aceh: heroines & forgotten fighters, 1873–2005   121

'Family Welfare Guidance' (*Pendidikan Kesejahteraan Keluarga*, PKK) programme, which was implemented in villages throughout Indonesia. Although Sukarno asked all the nation's forces, both male and female, to continue their effort to free Indonesia from post-colonialism's influence, governmental and societal trends – in Indonesia and Aceh – suggested that the era of mythical and real heroines was over. This was even truer under President Suharto's New Order regime, which cultivated restrictive notions of women's social role through organisations such as *Dharma Wanita*.[64]

At the same time, nationalist policy brought about the immortalisation of quintessentially Acehnese heroines such as Tjut Nyak Dhien as Indonesian heroines in the post-colonial era. Historical publications and school books, from the 1950s to the 1980s,[65] contributed to this trend, but also, as mentioned previously, through President Sukarno's elevation of Tjut Nyak Dhien to the status of a 'National Hero[ine]' in 1964. The 'Indonesianisation' of this quintessentially Acehnese and Muslim heroine went hand in hand with her 'hinduisation' as many publications likened Indonesian women warrior heroines to Srikandi, the combative character from the famous Hindu epic, the Mahabharata.

On the ground, however, Acehnese women warriors seemed to be on their way out. While the *Darul Islam* (The House of Islam) rebellion of 1953–1962, which involved Aceh and other provinces against the central government, could have provided fertile ground for the renewed involvement of women, there is no written evidence that Acehnese women actively supported it.[66] It was not until the late 1990s, after the downfall of the authoritarian Suharto regime and the political opening during the *Reformasi* (reform) period, when Acehnese women warriors made a dramatic resurgence on the national and global stage under the banner of the Free Aceh Movement).[67] In 1999, the AFP (French Press Agency) distributed photographs that showed numerous women in Pandrah Kandeh village (North Aceh) wearing military uniform and a white veil, marching and praying during a flag-raising ceremony on the occasion of the movement's twenty-third anniversary.[68] Then still presented as 'srikandi', they were indigenised one year later at a celebration of the anniversary (*milad*) of the GAM in 2000 when Sofyan Dawood, the military commander of the Pase region and GAM spokesperson for military matters, referred to them as the *Pasukan Inong Balèë* (Inong Balèë Forces).[69] On this occasion, troops of *inong balèë* paraded in military uniform, a posture in which they were also displayed on the official website of the Acehnese government-in-exile in Sweden.[70]

This clearly shows that the *inong balèë* were part of the military propaganda of the GAM, and it appears that they had also been employed as a part of GAM's strategy of internationalisation. It showed to the world that the GAM was determined to mobilise the entire population, men and women, against the might of the Indonesian state. One year later, in 2001, two young *inong balèë* of seventeen and nineteen years old even participated in the Geneva Call against anti-personnel mines organised by the

122   *Elsa Clavé*

International Committee of the Red Cross. They were sent by Muzakir Manaf, the commander of the TNA (State of Aceh Military), on the request of Nur Djuli, who later explained that during the conflict, women's inclusion in the army was a strategy for campaigning for the Acehnese cause abroad.[71] This strategy worked in that the images of the *inong balèë* were not only showcased by the international media but also led to the rather exaggerated perception, internationally and domestically, of massive and organised women combatants all around Aceh. This was a surprising turn for the organisation, which apparently had neither actively sought women's participation earlier nor publicised their role for propaganda purposes.

Organisation of the civilian and military *inong balèë* in the third GAM

While the above suggests that the inong balèë were key to the GAM's propaganda and the projection of its will to mobilise completely during the *Reformasi* period, how did this translate into the organisation of the *inong balèë*? When I interviewed, former GAM officials and women who belonged to the movement's civilian branch or to its military wing, the TNA, I began to realise that clear answers would be difficult to come by a mere two to three years after the Helsinki Agreements of 2005 had ended civil war in Aceh. Indonesian repression and the fog of guerrilla war had led to a strong culture of secrecy within the GAM, whereas losses on battlefield and in the floods of the tsunami deprived me of key interview partners. Moreover, as an outsider who interviewed in the historical conjuncture of 2006–2007, which was characterised by uncertainty about whether the Peace Agreement would hold and where Aceh was headed to politically and socially, I realised that piecing together the different snippets of information from a diverse range of sources would be difficult.

Even ascertaining whether there was an overall GAM strategy to attract women into its movement and armed forces, let alone what the organisational structure was, proved to be challenging. When I interviewed Nur Djuli, the GAM's senior representative in Malaysia during the conflict, and later head of the Office for Reintegration in Aceh (*Badan Reintegrasi Aceh*, BRA) from 2007 to 2010, he said it was the GAM that decided to actively recruit and train women soldiers even though some women also spontaneously helped the guerrillas.[72] In contrast, Sofyan Dawood, the former military commander of the Pase region and spokesperson for the GAM relating to military matters, denied any overarching plan for the GAM leadership and claimed that women got involved in the struggle spontaneously, even though it was he who had actively put forward the Pasukan *Inong Balèë* on the local and global stage in 2000. He asserts that women joined the GAM in the mountains because their identity as GAM supporters had been uncovered or because they wanted to be with their husbands. For Sofyan Dawood, these were ad hoc decisions and there was

Aceh: heroines & forgotten fighters, 1873–2005 123

no overarching GAM plan to form *inong balèë* units and to use them as field soldiers.[73]

These two versions highlight different perceptions of the *inong balèë*. The first account, by Nur Djuli, insists on the active role of the GAM in recruiting women and their effective armed training. The other, by Sofyan Dawood, denies any planning from the male leadership and systematic recruitment, and minimises the role of women as field combatants. In these two cases the image of Acehnese women's role is completely different: the first one considers women as soldiers, the second one as mere helpers doing traditional feminine tasks, cooking and nursing.

Regardless of these different accounts by leading GAM members, the Indonesian National Armed Forces (Tentara Nasional Indonesia, TNI) preferred to err on the side of caution. An interview published in the TNI's weekly GATRA thus counted 472 women soldiers among the GAM in 2001.[74] GATRA even suggested that a certain Tjut Meutia was the women's commander and therefore that the TNA had a women's section under unified command. In 2003, the Indonesian authorities even arrested Tjut Nur Asyikin, an Acehnese activist, on the grounds of being the *inong balèë*'s national commander.[75] Civil society activists suggested that the arrest was meant to stop an influential activist woman from doing her humanitarian work and advocacy, as she was not even part of the GAM.[76] In my interviews, I have never been able to confirm any *inong balèë* organisational superstructure in which the *inong balèë* would have had their own war commandant for all Aceh.

Motivation and roles

All my interviews in 2006 and 2007 suggest that women became *inong balèë* largely due to three main factors. Indonesian pressure and punishment, especially between 1989 and 2005, against themselves or family members – in particular male family members such as a brother, father, husband – were a key factor for enrolment in the conflict.[77] Anyone, including relatives, could be beaten up, arrested, tortured, or simply could disappear if suspected of separatism. The GAM exploited the Indonesian state's violence and repression as an important motivational factor in its recruitment campaigns. Finally, the GAM also promised a modicum of security for those Acehnese women whose security was threatened – regardless of whether they actively supported the GAM or not – by the Indonesian armed forces or the police forces.

Like in many other guerrilla conflicts, the women in Aceh were the ones who still had relative freedom of movement. Consequently, they were in a strong position to communicate information, and deliver ammunition, weapons, and food to GAM soldiers who stayed mainly in the mountains of Aceh.[78] While some of this already happened during earlier phases, the opening up of political space after the fall of Suharto in 1998, the reduction

124 *Elsa Clavé*

of Jakarta's troops during the transitional presidency of Bacharuddin Jusuf Habibie (May 1998–October 1999), and the return of GAM activists from exile created a favourable environment. The GAM exploited this by recruiting Acehnese men, women, and youth at unprecedented levels. This was not limited to the training of female activists, but also included women joining the TNA and the movement's civilian structure. Women thus served in a wide range of functions: they were part of mixed gender units, and they served as individual women fighters, but also as cooks, nurses, in logistics, as treasurers and secretaries, and as part of the GAM's intelligence service.[79] Moreover, they also served as mobilisers and recruiters, for instance by educating villagers in clandestine night-time lectures about the goals of the GAM and how to participate in the movement.

Military and ideological training

Despite the existing limitations on how much we can know about the organisation of the *inong balèë* – whether at the civilian or military level – we do know far more about their training than we do for the women leaders and anonymous women who had fought against the Dutch during the 1873–1913 period, during the interwar period, and in particular the Indonesian Revolution of 1945–1949.

Military training was largely reserved for those women who joined the GAM's armed forces, the TNA. Among the 'civilian' branches of the GAM, military training was not compulsory and mostly restricted to those of the civilian *inong balèë* who were regarded as most in need of defending themselves, namely those in the intelligence network and those who lived in the mountains. All my interviews confirm the general format of the military training, which lasted between two and three months, and was conducted in camps located in the Pidie region on Aceh's eastern coast. The training was conducted by male or female instructors, or mixed teams, with many of the male instructors having received military training in Libya.

The first month of basic military training was dominated by heavy physical exercises that tested the women's grit and resolve. Starting early in the morning, they drilled, ran, and marched for a total of nine hours. This was followed up by religious readings, recitation or prayer, and rest towards the end of the afternoon, while the evenings were reserved for lectures on ideology, ethics, and military attitude. Taking good care of weapons and radios was emphasised because they were the property of the State of Aceh and, by extension, represented a sacrifice on the part of Acehnese people who had contributed to buy the equipment. Several of the interviewed *inong balèë* emphasise that the TNA slogan 'Our weapon is our soul' made them consider weapons as important as their own life.[80]

While the first month of basic military training was already extremely tough and trying, the second and third months were even more demanding. Regular equipment was now introduced for training purposes, including

Aceh: heroines & forgotten fighters, 1873–2005 125

carrying heavy backpacks full of sand, while exercises were conducted during the hottest time in the afternoon. The women were also taught to assemble, dismantle, and use a range of weapons, including assault rifles such as the Russian AK-47 and the American M-16, handguns, and the throwing of grenades. They learned how to jump over fire and into water, and how to land safely after jumping from heights. Lessons now also included strategy and guerrilla tactics. Their military training concluded with official induction into the TNA as *inong balèë* by means of a formal ceremony during which they swore 'I promise to Allah to sacrifice my possessions and my life for the nation because there is but one and only God'.[81]

Deployment as teachers and mobilisers

Although the tough military training would suggest otherwise, quite a few of the women in the TNA would come to serve as teachers and mobilisers. This arguably was because they had, unlike their male counterparts, relatively easy access to villagers, including women. Within the TNA, a woman who fulfilled this function was known as *guru penerangan*, literally translated as 'information teacher'. Her job profile included the giving of lectures (*ceramah*) on the goals and values of the GAM to ordinary villagers, both men and women. These lectures appear – based on my interviews – to have become a common feature in Aceh after 1998, during the early *Reformasi* period when the previously heavy-handed military control of the region gave way to a slightly more open political climate. Despite her official name, the *guru penerangan* would not just explain the movement to its rural audience, but also aim to mobilise the population. Attesting to the success of this method, Kak S., one of the *inong balèë* whom I interviewed in the Meureuhom Daja region, enrolled in the GAM after such a *ceramah* in 1999. She then recruited other women to organise communal reunions in every other group of villages (*permukiman*).

According to several testimonies, each *ceramah* was attended by around 1,000 people, and largely followed the same structure. Lasting about five hours, each *ceramah* began at nine in the evening and would last until around two in the morning. Chants, Quranic readings, and prayers were important elements in the 'performance' of the *ceramah*, opening and closing it, and kept the audience energised throughout. Content wise, each lecture was divided into three parts: the first dealing with war and guerrilla strategy, the second with ideology, and the third narrating the history of Aceh's glorious past and resistance. All the components of GAM's struggle were presented to the villagers in order to get their full support and to boost enrolment. Thus, not only positions for women in the TNA were advertised, but also that *inong balèë* could enter the civilian arm of the GAM by becoming cooks, nurses, treasurers, or secretaries. These last two positions entailed inducting these *inong balèë* into the official GAM structure, the speaking of a vow, and some training concerning codes and secret language.[82]

126 Elsa Clavé

Civilian and military *inong balèë* on the ground: a comparative sketch of three regions

While the structure of the military training and also the *ceramah* suggest a certain uniformity and central guidance, the situation on the ground was far more complex and varied considerably in Aceh's seventeen regions (*wilayah*).[83] Based on my interviews during the 2006–2007 period, each of these administrative units was headed by a commander (*pang wilayah*) who was in charge of his region's affairs, including the recruitment of the *inong balèë* and other matters relating to them.[84] To consider the particularities of each region, and how this influenced the *inong balèë*'s roles and actions, we will examine three *wilayah* with the aim of comparing and contextualising some of the regional differences and complexities.

The ethnic make-up of the first *wilayah*, Linge (Central Aceh), was unique because this region featured the largest Javanese population in Aceh. They had been settled there by state-sponsored 'transmigration' programs that sought to relieve over-populated areas, such as in Java, by facilitating migration to areas considered under-populated, including Aceh.[85] Although the mechanisms are not entirely clear, the presence of a relatively big Javanese community of transmigrants in Linge seems to have prevented the GAM from gaining more substantial traction. While the women from Linge appear not to have participated in direct fights on the ground, the region had civilian *inong balèë* who managed logistics, such as providing food or ammunition, and also acted as intelligence agents (*pateung*).

Based on my interviews with civilian *inong balèë* from Linge, any estimate of their numbers is near impossible because data were not recorded during the conflict for security reasons. Moreover, a lot of them could not be interviewed anymore because they had been arrested or killed by the military, anti-GAM militias, and villagers. If the *pang wilayah* and TNA knew about the existence of *inong balèë*, they would sometimes assume command over them, but there was no female chief to lead them. Instead the situation was so diffuse and subject to daily change that the existing, fragile networks were frequently disrupted. In fact, most of Linge's civilian *inong balèë* found out about each other only after the Helsinki Peace Agreement. It is therefore only in conditions of peace in 2005–2006 that existing links and organisations became more visible to activists and could be strengthened.[86]

In contrast to the Linge region with its many non-Acehnese transmigrants, the situation in Meureuhom Daja on Aceh's western coast was quite different. Conflict arrived late but the population became increasingly drawn into it due to the intensification of TNI military operations and GAM's propaganda. Women combatants assumed civilian roles in villages but also, unlike in Linge, military ones in the jungles, where they were part of TNA's male groups, such as in Lhok Sukhon *sagoë*.[87] Serving as spies, messengers, and suppliers, numbers are estimated to have been as high as a hundred at the time when President Megawati Sukarnoputri declared a state of emergency in 2003, but only twenty were still active at the signing of the Helsinki Peace Agreement in 2005.[88] A majority of the active ones had thus been killed or had left the area during the 2003–2005 period. A female unit, the *Pasukan Tjut Nyak Dhien* (Tjut Nyak Dhien Force), named after the heroine of anti-Dutch resistance, is said to have operated in the area. Regrettably, I could not confirm its existence, which may well have been due to the fact that the 2005 Peace Agreement did not lead to a lifting of the secret of military organisation and structure.

Despite these limitations, it is clear that even though most of the *inong balèë* in the Meureuhom Daja region remained in their villages under civilian cover, some of them progressed to jungle-based roles. This usually occurred, similar to men, when their safety could no longer be guaranteed in a civilian, village setting. Kak I., for instance, was part of the GAM for two years, but eventually had to leave her village for the mountains when the state of emergency was declared in 2003. She was one of about five women among the TNA's roughly 240 soldiers in the region, which were organised into four groups of 60 soldiers.

For the very small minority of five women among the 240 soldiers of the Meureuhom Daja wilayah, numerical inferiority coupled with religious values translated into gendered access onto the battlefield. Hence, Kak I. was prevented from joining attacks because her status as an unmarried woman would have required the presence of a *mahram* – that is a brother, father, husband, or any other male relative who could guarantee her moral and physical protection outside of the confines of the family home – during night-time operations. In contrast, a married *inong balèë* bearing the war name of Krueng Sabe is said to have joined attacks several times because she did so alongside her husband.

The situation in the wilayah of Pase, a traditional GAM stronghold, on Aceh's eastern coast was relatively similar to Meureuhom Daja. Pase was a traditional rebel-controlled region and a hot spot of the conflict, to the extent that it was known as a 'red zone' (*daerah merah*).[89] In Pase, the *inong balèë* had a presence not only in villages but also in the mountains, where they were organised as the *Pasukan Inong Balèë* (Inong Balèë Forces). Some of these Inong Balèë Forces lived partially, some permanently, in an all-female camp (*asrama*) and conducted guerrilla attacks. A leading *inong balèë* in Pase was Kak T., who was married to a GAM fighter, and who had returned with her family from Malaysian exile in 1998.[90] She began to organise women to demonstrate when people were arrested by the police. Then, starting in 1999–2000, she organised the delivery of medical assistance to the war area, the hiding of fallen GAM martyrs after deadly engagements with the enemy, handled the TNA's logistics, and gradually built up the regional *inong balèë* network in Pase. She was the commander in charge of the *Pasukan inong balèë* camp and reported in that capacity to the regional commander, the *pang wilayah*. She never completely stayed in the mountains

128   *Elsa Clavé*

because it would have prevented her from moving from village to village, which was key to growing her network and to building the movement.

Even though I interviewed a leading female member of the Acehnese resistance in Pase, in the person of Kak T., the region's all-female troop remains difficult to evaluate. Important information was lost during the state of military emergency, when documents were destroyed both intentionally and accidentally, but it seems that the unit could not have represented more than fifty to a hundred women, with a small number staying permanently in the mountain camp.[91] This *pasukan* conducted guerrilla operations such as acts of sabotage and ambushes.[92]

Similar women troops, reflecting more of a concerted effort at the supra level rather than simple reaction at the local level, seem to have existed in other regions under the name of *Malahayati Darah Juang*[93] in Aceh Besar and the *Pasukan Inong Balèë* in Pidie. If in the state of actual research it is impossible to establish any certainty, the existing evidence suggests that some regions displayed an elaborate organisation of the *inong balèë* with all-women troops and even inter-regional meetings between groups of *inong balèë*.[94] As my interview partners and informants were bound by official vows of silence with regard to the organisation of the GAM's military, they could not reveal the leadership for these meetings. Therefore, it is difficult to conclude to what extent the existence of these various groups of *inong balèë* was the result of a concerted effort by the GAM's leadership, a response to bottom-up developments, or a combination of both. Overall, the available information suggests that the situation on the ground varied depending on regional conditions, but also that the GAM's leadership might have played a coordinating or even centralising role at some point.

Conclusion: Rethinking women combatants' position in Acehnese history and society

A few months after the signing of the Memorandum of Understanding (MoU) between the Indonesian government and the GAM in Helsinki on 15 August 2005, the separatist movement transformed itself into the Transitional Committee of Aceh (*Komite Peralihan Aceh, KPA*) and officially dissolved its military structure. Interestingly, with the beginning of this new period of peace and reconstruction, the *inong balèë* were almost forgotten by the GAM leadership. If not for the intervention of the international community, the *inong balèë* would not have been part of the planned reintegration program for ex-combatants.

Considering that the GAM, during its thirty-year existence, had a very short history of mobilising women for armed activities, roughly from after the fall of the Suharto regime in 1998 to the Helsinki Peace Agreements in 2005, this fact is perhaps not surprising. It is also in line with the typical gendering of post-conflict trajectories elsewhere, in which the aim is to return to real or perceived traditional, pre-conflict gender norms.[95]

Aceh: heroines & forgotten fighters, 1873–2005 129

However, in the specific context of Aceh, where the participation of women in war is a common trope in popular history, notably with reference to the legendary Admiral Malahayati and also the noble heroines of the anti-Dutch resistance, it raises the question of how women's roles in the struggle for Acehnese independence from Indonesia can simply be downplayed.[96] It is thus interesting to compare the exaltation of female heroic leaders of the earlier periods with the post-conflict forgetting of the GAM's *inong balèë*.

As shown previously, since the anti-Dutch resistance, the only transmitted image of female combatants was the one highlighting the role of exceptional women leaders, usually from the religious or aristocratic elite. Although the 1905 Dutch photo of the captured Tjut Nyak Dhien showed an old woman with dishevelled hair and angry in despair, the vivid accounts of war reporter Zentgraaff, in combination with Marie van Zeggelen's influential historical novel on the legendary Malahayati and Hermina Székely-Lulofs' 1948 book on Tjut Nyak Dhien, helped in setting up the notion of a noble anti-colonial heroine.

This trend continued after Indonesian independence when historical publications and school books conjured an archetypal image of a woman warrior, always brave and daring, often beautiful, usually a widow of noble background fated to die a martyr's death. With President Sukarno's formal integration of Tjut Nyak Dhien into the national pantheon of heroes in the mid-1960s, the quintessentially Muslim and Acehnese women warriors became Indonesianised and even 'hinduised', as the mythical Hindu warrior Srikandi from the *Mahabharata* became a key reference point. As a result, romanticised stories of a select few figures have become the sole historical reference points for Acehnese women warriors in general.

In stark contrast to the warrior heroines of the anti-Dutch resistance, a 'heroine' from the GAM period has yet to emerge. This might well have had to do with the necessity, during the conflict, to keep a low profile and to maintain secrecy in order to ensure the safety of the GAM and TNA members. This pattern might have been extended into the post-conflict period due to the initial uncertainty about whether the peace process would work out, and with the larger post-conflict focus on rebuilding Acehnese society. Moreover, similar to other post-conflict societies, it is likely that many *inong balèë* desired to leave behind or downplay their war-time past in order to re-integrate into society, whilst the GAM's male leaders wanted to return to real or perceived pre-conflict societal norms. The six- or seven-year period in which the GAM had actively courted, mobilised, and even armed women was hence seen as a social anomaly due to war-time and propaganda considerations.

In fact, the legal framework for a religiously more conservative society had already been laid in 2001, when President Abdurrahman Wahid (1940–2009) introduced Islamic sharia law in the restive province with the aim of placating the GAM, but also in line with a radicalisation of Indonesian Islam since the 1990s.[97] This suggests that future studies of Aceh's women

130 *Elsa Clavé*

warriors would profit from being more attentive to societal changes on the ground in order to tease out not only the considerable continuities but also the significant differences between then and now. What was specific, and what was not, to Acehnese women's participation – and the representation thereof – in Aceh's anti-Dutch wars and resistance, in the Indonesian Revolution, and in the GAM's struggle against Jakarta? Could differences be explained, among other factors, by changes in the gendering of Acehnese society?

Of particular promise, at least for the present, is oral history as a method to learn more about the everyday lives of female soldiers, regardless of social status or rank. This would not only add the voice of ordinary women fighters to previously elite-centric histories, but it would also lend a richer texture to the previously exalted or romanticised experiences and sacrificial roles of warrior heroines from the religious or socio-political elite. In line with this, I expect that this chapter will contribute to the opening up of new space(s) for research and reflection on the gendered positions and experiences of women in warfare more generally, and in Southeast Asian and in particular Acehnese history and society more specifically.

Notes

1 This chapter is a revised version of Elsa Clavé-Çelik, 'Silenced Fighters: An Insight into Women Combatants History in Aceh (17th–20th c.)', *Archipel*, Vol. 87 (2014), pp. 273–306. I thank the journal's editor Daniel Perret for granting permission to publish it here in slightly revised form.
2 The two representations are shown, for instance, in the following article, by Reza Gunadha, 'Terkuak, Kontroversi Potret Resmi Cut Nyak Dien Tanpa Jilbab', 23 December 2014, *Tribunnews*, which rebuts the claims: www.tribunnews.com/nasional/2014/12/23/terkuak-kontroversi-potret-resmi-cut-nyak-dientanpa-jilbab (last accessed 31 March 2015).
3 The term *inong balèë* literally refers to a woman who has been left by her husband. In Aceh, the term can designate a divorced woman, a widow, and by extension, a female combatant because she would usually have lost her husband in armed conflict.
4 To preserve the identity of informants, only the initial of the name will be given except for some public figures.
5 Ito Takeshi and Anthony Reid define them as 'originally war-leaders, becoming a territorial aristocracy through their benefices' in their 'Introduction: A New Source for Seventeenth Century Aceh', in Ito Takeshi (ed.), *Aceh Sultanate: State, Society, Religion, and Trade (2 vols.): The Dutch Sources, 1636–1661* (Leiden: Brill, 2015), p. 10.
6 The 'Dutch forces' in fact were a multi-national and multi-racial force that comprised Dutchmen, Europeans, and Eurasians, but the majority were from the Netherlands East Indies, most notably Javanese and Ambonese. See Gerke Teitler, 'The Mixed Company: Fighting Power and Ethnic Relations in the Dutch Colonial Army, 1890–1920', in Karl Hack and Tobias Rettig (eds.), *Colonial Armies in Southeast Asia* (London: Routledge, 2006).
7 The evidence is discussed in Clavé-Çelik, 'Silenced Fighters', pp. 277–281.
8 See Sher Banu A. L. Khan, 'The Sultanahs of Aceh, 1641–1699', in Arndt Graf, Susanne Schröter, and Edwin Wieringa (eds.), *Aceh: History, Politics and Culture*

Aceh: heroines & forgotten fighters, 1873–2005   131

(Singapore: ISEAS, 2010), pp. 3–25. Three Muslim women ruled as regents during the thirteenth and fourteenth centuries in the North Sumatran sultanate of Pasai. See Claude Guillot and Ludvik Kalus, *Les monuments funéraires et l'histoire du Sultanat de Pasai à Sumatra (13e–16 siècles)* [Funeral Monuments and the History of the Sultanate of Pasai in Sumatra, *thirteenth–sixteenth* centuries] (Paris: Association Archipel, 2008), pp. 101–102.

9 For armed court women, see the chapter by Christina Skott in this volume; for parallel practices in Javanese courts, see the chapter by Ann Kumar. Also see Clavé-Çelik, 'Silenced Fighters', pp. 282–285.

10 I discuss the evidence for the *inong balèë* armada in Clavé-Çelik, 'Silenced Fighters', pp. 281–282.

11 Tjut (sometimes also 'Potjut' or 'Tjutpo') is a term used for Acehnese noble women. Following Indonesia's post-independence language reform, these terms are now written 'Cut', 'Pocut', or 'Cutpo'. Similarly, 'Tjut Njak Dhien' is now written as 'Cut Nyak Dien' or 'Cut Nyak Dhien'. In this chapter, I will use the original Acehnese spelling when referring to local terms or expressions, the exception being the notes in which I will use the titles of published works, written according to the Indonesian spelling.

12 Indonesian nouns are gender-neutral.

13 Hermina Székely-Lulof, *Tjut Njak Din: Kisah Ratu Perang Aceh* [Tjut Njak Din: History of an Acehnese War Queen] (Depok: Komunitas Bambu, 2007), translated from her *De geschiedenis van een Atjehse vorstin* (Amsterdam: Moussault's Uitgeverij, 1948).

14 Tanzil Hazil, *Teuku Umar dan Tjut Nja Din* [Teuku Umar and Cut Nyak Dhien] (Djakarta: Djambatan, 1955); Panitia Peringatan Almarhumah Srikandi Nasional Tjut Nja' Dhien, *Kenang-kenangan Tjut Nja' Dhien* [Memories of Cut Nyak Dhien] (place and editor unknown, 1956); M. Kasim, *Kisah-Kisah Perwiraan Wanita Aceh Dalam Perang Gerilya Melawan Belanda* [Heroic Stories of Acehnese Women in the Guerrilla War Against the Netherlands] (Medan: Pandraman, 1959); Soekarno, *Skrikandi Tjut Njak Dhien: Pahlawan Nasional* [Srikandi Cut Nyak Dhien: National Hero] (Djakarta: Senjan Djakarta, 1964); H. M. Zainuddin, *Srikandi Atjeh* [Srikandi of Aceh] (Medan: Pustaka Iskandar Muda, 1966); Badan Pembina Pahlawan Pusat, *Sri Kandi Bangsaku: Heroines of Indonesia History* [Srikandi of my Nation: Heroines of Indonesia History] (Jakarta: Central Board for National Heroes Affairs, 1974); Emi Suhaimi, *Wanita Aceh dalam Pemerintahan dan Peperangan* [Acehnese Women in Government and in War] (Banda Aceh: Yayasan Pendidikan A. Hasjmy, 1993); Muchtaruddin Ibrahim, *Cut Nyak Din* (Jakarta: Departemen Pendidikan dan Kebudayaan/ Balai Pustaka, 2001).

15 Dôkarim, from his full name Abdul Karim, lived during the second half of the nineteenth century in the region of Peukan Bada Geulumpang Dua (Aceh Besar district, North of Aceh). He is known for his contribution to Acehnese oral literature with his *Hikayat Prang Gompeuni* [History of the War against the Company; Company here referring to the Dutch even though the Dutch East India Company had already been disbanded in 1800], a long narrative poem covering several episodes of the war against the Dutch. The reading of this *hikayat* to Hermina Székely-Lulofs is mentioned in Rob Nieuwenhuys, *Mirror of the Indies* (Hong-Kong: Periplus Editions, 1999), pp. 170–175.

16 The term *ulèëbalang* designates the head of a *nanggroë*, a region equivalent to the present district (*kabupaten*) within the Indonesian administrative division. *Ulèëbalang* were from local noble lineages and ruled under the Sultan's power. They were destroyed by the Dutch or co-opted by them.

17 We do not have information about children from a first marriage. All the information given has been taken from several passages in Székely-Lulof, *Cut Njak Din*.

132   *Elsa Clavé*

18 Teuku Umar's vow was made at the graveside of the late Tengku Anjong in the village of Pelanggahan near Kutaraja (today's Banda Aceh), the site having been deliberately chosen by the Dutch government as it was considered a sacred grave.

19 J. A. Kruijt, *De Atjeh Oorlog* [The Aceh War] (s'Gravenhage: Lomann and Funke, 1896), pp. 69, 89–91.

20 A lightly armed, and thus very mobile, elite counter-guerrilla force operating in small units of 15–18 men, the majority of which were 'natives'. See Teitler, 'The Mixed Company', p. 162.

21 H. C. Zentgraaff, *Atjeh* (Batavia: Koninklijke Drukkerij 'De Unie', 1938), p. 64.

22 *Rencong* are Acehnese knives, forged in the stylistic form of *bismillah* (In the name of Allah).

23 Ismail Suny (ed.), *Bunga Rampai Tentang Aceh* [Anthology on Aceh] (Jakarta: Bhratara, 1980), pp. 280–289.

24 Zentgraaff, *Atjeh*, p. 87.

25 This document was designed by the Dutch scholar and advisor for Native affairs, Snouck Hurgronje, in order to simplify the process of getting the political agreement of local rulers. Implemented by the Dutch for the first time in Aceh in 1898, it was then extended to the rest of the Dutch East Indies. Merle Calvin Ricklefs, *A History of Modern Indonesia since c. 1200*, 3rd edition (Basingstoke: Palgrave, 2001), p. 188.

26 As mentioned earlier with regard to the sixteenth century sultanahs, kinship ties could trump sex if there was no direct male descendant, if the husband was absent, or if other factors spoke in favour of a woman.

27 M. H. Du Croo, *Generaal Swart: Pacificator van Atjeh* [General Swart: Pacificator of Aceh] (Maastricht: Uitgrave N.V. Leiter-Nypels, 1943), pp. 94–95.

28 Ibid., p. 97.

29 Ibid., p. 98. Her son survived until 22 February 1912 (see later under Tengku Tjutpo Fatimah).

30 While the terms 'Tjut' and 'Potjut' refer to noble status, 'Teungku' designates a religious person.

31 Zainuddin, *Srikandi Atjeh*, pp. 114–127.

32 Zentgraaff, *Atjeh*, p. 79.

33 Zainuddin, *Srikandi Atjeh*, pp. 119–121.

34 A. Doup, *Gedenkboek van het Korps Marechausse van Atjeh en Onderhoorigheden, 1890–1940* [Commemorative Book of the Marechaussee Corps of Aceh and Dependencies, 1890–1940] (Medan: N.V. Deli Courant, 1940), p. 204.

35 Ibid., p. 179.

36 Zainuddin, *Srikandi Atjeh*, p. 128.

37 T. J. Veltman, 'Nota over de Geschiedenis van het Landschap Pidie' [Note on the History of the Area of Pidie], *Tijdschrift Bataviaasch Genootschap*, Vol. 58 (1919), pp. 151–152, 154.

38 *Kaphé* is the Acehnese for *kâfir*, the Arabic word to designate the unbeliever in general. In Aceh it was used as a synonym for the Dutch.

39 Zentgraaff, *Atjeh*, pp. 73–74.

40 Zainuddin, *Srikandi Atjeh*, p. 131.

41 'Meuligoe' is sometimes also written as 'Meuligo' or 'Maligo'. Her dates of birth and death are not known.

42 Abdul Karim Jakobi, *Aceh dalam Perang Mempertahankan Proklamasi Kemerdekaan 1945–1949 dan Peranan Teuku Hamid Azwar Sebagai Pejuang* [Aceh during the War of Independence 1945–1949 and the Role of Teuku Hamid Azwar as Combatant] (Jakarta: Gramedia, 1998), pp. 31–34, Mohammad Said, *Atjeh Sepanjang Abad* [Aceh through the Centuries], Vol. 1 (Medan: Published by the Author, 1981), p. 141.

Aceh: heroines & forgotten fighters, 1873–2005   133

43 Said, *Atjeh Sepanjang Abad*, Vol. 2, p. 148.
44 Zainuddin, *Srikandi Atjeh*, p. 70.
45 Teungku Fakinah remarried at an imprecise date, but her second husband, Teungku Njak Badai, from the prominent *dayah* Tanoh Abey, died soon after.
46 Ibid., pp. 72, 74–75.
47 Ibid., p. 73.
48 Suaka Peninggalan Sejarah dan Purbakala, *Laporan Arkeologi Aceh Utara: Laporan Teknis Pemugaran Masjid Teungku Fakinah* [Archaeological Report on North Aceh: Technical Report on the Restoration of Teungku Fakinah Mosque], (Banda Aceh: Departemen Pendidikan dan Kebudayaan, 1993).
49 Ali Hasjmy, *Bunga Rampai Revolusi dari Tanah Aceh* [Anthology on the Revolution of Aceh] (Jakarta: Bulan Bintang, 1978), pp. 127–142; Zainuddin, *Srikandi Atjeh*, pp. 82–84.
50 Zainuddin, *Srikandi Atjeh*, p. 132.
51 Zentgraaff, *Atjeh*, p. 64.
52 Ibid., p. 65.
53 Ibid., p. 44.
54 Jacqueline Siapno, *Gender, Islam, Nationalism and the State of Aceh: The Paradox of Power, Co-optation and Resistance* (Richmond: RoutledgeCurzon, 2002), p. 27.
55 These telegrams have been given as example by Siapno, but her book regrettably does not provide the source. Siapno, *Gender, Islam, Nationalism*, p. 27.
56 Ibid., p. 27.
57 Zentgraaff, *Atjeh*, p. 64.
58 Siapno, *Gender, Islam, Nationalism*, p. 28.
59 The name of this regiment is interesting because Potjut Baren had later submitted to the Dutch. The actual size of a regular regiment at the time is not known.
60 Regrettably, I have not been able to find any additional information about this female commander. One can speculate that the regiment's link to PESINDO made it inopportune to advertise one's role in it. Hence, in October 1965, Aceh was the first area to be 'purified' by the Indonesian Army in its drive to eliminate the Indonesian Communist Party and suspected members and sympathisers, including children, in the aftermath of the 30 September 1965 coup that eventually led to the fall of President Sukarno and the rise of future President Suharto. See Anthony Reid, *A History of Southeast Asia: Critical Crossroads* (Chichester, UK: Wiley Blackwell, 2015), p. 356.
61 Ibrahim Alfian I. et al., *Revolusi Kemerdekaan Indonesia di Aceh, 1945–1949* [The Indonesian Revolution for Freedom in Aceh, 1945–1949] (Banda Aceh: Departemen Pendidikan dan Kebudayaan, 1982), pp. 51–52, 150, 153.
62 The Darul Islam was a rebellious movement that aimed at the creation of an Islamic state. First emerging in Java in 1942, offshoots appeared in parts of South Sulawesi and Aceh in the 1950s. For comprehensive studies, see Cornelis van Dijk, *Rebellion under the Banner of Islam: The Darul Islam in Indonesia* (The Hague: M. Nijhoff, 1981) and Chiara Formichi, *Islam and the Making of the Nation: Kartosuwiryo and Political Islam in 20th Century Indonesia* (Leiden: KITLV, 2012).
63 Teungku Fakinah's female unit was raised four decades before the Rani of Jhansi Regiment (1943–1945) of the Indian National Army, the recruitment of which is covered in this volume in the chapter by Frederik Rettig.
64 Siapno, *Gender, Islam, Nationalism*, pp. 174–176; Barbara Leight, 'Women in Integration and Disintegration of Nation and Region: Indonesia and Aceh', *México y la Cuenca del Pacífico*, Vol. 10, No. 29 (May – August 2007), p. 4, *http://148.202.18.157/sitios/publicacionesite/periodl/pacifico/Revista29/Analisis BarbaraLeight.pdf,* [last accessed 1 November 2010].

134   *Elsa Clavé*

65 Apart from the eight publications already cited in *note 14*, which focus entirely on Tjut Nyak Dhien, see the following: Ali Hasjmy, 'Srikandi Teungku Fakinah', *Sinar Darussalam*, Vol. 66 (1976); Alibasjah T. Talsya, *Cut Nyak Meutia: Srikandi yang Gugur di Medan Perang Aceh* [Cut Nyak Meutia: Srikandi who Died on the Battlefield in Aceh] (Jakarta: Mutiara, 1982); Tentara Pelajar Resimen II Aceh Divisi Sumatera, *Pocut Meurah Intan Srikandi Nasional dari Tanah Rencong* [Pocut Meurah Intan, National Srikandi from the Land of the Rencong] (Jakarta: Yayasan TP Aceh, 1987); Ali Akbar, *Perjuangan Cut Nyak Meutia di Rimba Pasai* [The Fight of Cut Nyak Dhien in the Jungle of Pasai] (Lhokseumawe: Departemen Pendidikan dan Kebudayaan Aceh Utara, 1987); Z. Ahmad and al., *Cut Nyak Meutia* (Jakarta: Departemen Pendidikan dan Kebudayaan, 1993); Solichin Salam, *Malahayati: Srikandi dari Aceh* [Malahayati: Srikandi from Aceh] (Jakarta: Gema Salam, 1995).

66 In Aceh, support for the *Darul Islam* was caused by the central government in Jakarta's abolishment of Aceh's special status as a province in 1951. This weakened Acehnese political power, its prerogative on education and social reforms, and caused the suspension of the right to trade directly with Singapore and Penang. See van Dijk, *Rebellion under the Banner of Islam*, and Edward Aspinall, *Islam and Nation: Separatist Rebellion in Aceh* (Stanford, CA: Stanford University Press, 2009).

67 The GAM was first founded in 1976 but had a very limited membership base and was almost wiped out by 1979. It was revived in 1989 with Middle Eastern financial support and training but President Suharto's government countered this 'second' GAM with a large-scale military operation, which included massive human rights violations against the civilian population. In 1996, Jakarta declared its counter-insurgency operations victorious, with the GAM incapacitated and surviving members in exile or lying low. There is very little information on the participation of women in the first and the second GAM, although it is likely that women were involved in the movement on an ad hoc basis as couriers, supporters, suppliers, and in other functions. For the conceptualisation of the three historical phases of the GAM, see Michael L. Ross, 'Resources and Rebellion in Aceh, Indonesia', in Paul Collier and Nicholas Sambanis (eds.), *Understanding Civil War: Evidence and Analysis* (Washington, DC: The World Bank, 2005), pp. 35–58.

68 www.imageforumdiffusion.afp.com/ImfDiffusion/Search/IndexMediaNew. aspx?numPage=2&srchMd=8&FastAGGREG=aceh%20woman%20soldier& FastDATE=FastSearch_AnyDate&ID_Fulcrum=371363172_0&Display Mode=Mosaic (last accessed 1 November 2010).

69 Interview with Nur Djuli, Banda Aceh, May 2007. Nur Djuli was the GAM's senior representative in Malaysia during the conflict.

70 www.asnlf.com (last accessed July 2007).

71 Interview with Nur Djuli, Banda Aceh, May 2007. It has to be added that Nur Djuli's opinion has changed since then because, for a few years already, he has become a strong supporter of empowering women.

72 Interview with Nur Djuli, Banda Aceh, May 2007.

73 Interview with Sofyan Dawood, Banda Aceh, May 2007.

74 Cited in Shadia Marhaban, 'The Reintegration of Ex-Combatants in Post-War Aceh: Remaining Challenges to a Gender-Blind Planning and Implementation Process', in Véronique Dudouet, Hans J. Giessman, and Katrin Planta (eds.), *Post-War Security Transitions: Participatory Peacebuilding after Asymmetric Conflicts* (London: Routledge, 2012), pp. 192–205.

75 Adward and Evorosita, 'Inong Balee, Kue Kecil di Medan Terakhir' [Inong Balee, Small Cakes on the Last Field], *Aceh Magazine* (June 2007), pp. 12–23.

Aceh: heroines & forgotten fighters, 1873–2005 135

76 I could not interview her because she died when the tsunami hit her prison on 26 December 2004.
77 As put forward in the following post-conflict civil society report: KontraS, *Aceh Damai Dengan Keadilan? Mengungkap Kekerasan Masa Lalu* [Is Aceh in Peace with Justice? Expressing the Violence of the Past], Seri Aceh II (Jakarta: KontraS, 2006).
78 Interview with Nur Djuli.
79 Although possible and claimed by a few interviewees, we have not come across any strong evidence to support the existence of female units.
80 'Senjata itu nyawa bagi kita.'
81 'Kita berjanji dengan Allah akan korban harta benda jiwa raga kita untuk bangsa karena Allah lillahi tah Allah.'
82 Interview with Bang M, GAM Governor of Sabang, Banda Aceh, May 2007.
83 Ibid.
84 Interview with Kak T., *Inong Balèë*'s head for Aceh (a position created after the Helsinki Peace Agreement as the EU provided funding to reintegrate women combatants), Lhokseumawe, May 2007; Interview with Bang M., GAM Governor of Sabang, Banda Aceh, May 2007.
85 The post-independence Indonesian government's transmigration (*transmigrasi*) programmes originated during the Dutch colonial period. Apart from the Javanese, Aceh also received state-supported internal migrants from other ethnic groups, most notably from the Minangkabau, Batak, Madurese, and Bugis. These transmigrant groups often were hostile to the GAM.
86 Interview with Kak A., *inong balèë* of Linge, Takengon, December 2006; Interview with Kak S., *inong balèë* of Linge, Banda Aceh, May 2007.
87 GAM's administrative and military division of Aceh followed the pre-colonial administrative order when territory was divided in *wilayah, sagoë, mukim*, and *gampong*. These roughly correspond to region, district, subdistrict, and village. A *wilayah* would be comprised of three to four *sagoë*.
88 Interview with Kak I., *inong balèë* of Meureuhom Daja, Banda Aceh, May 2007.
89 It is a term that often came up during interviews and was also commonly used by the Indonesian media for a region with a potential for conflict.
90 Interview with Kak T., *Inong Balèë*'s head for Aceh, Lhokseumawe, May 2007.
91 Ibid.
92 Interview with Kak L., *inong balèë* of Pase, Lhokseumawe, May 2007.
93 'Darah Juang' means 'the blood of struggle', whereas Malahayati (also known as Keumalahayati) was a female Admiral who reportedly served sultan Ala al-Din Riayat Syah (r. 1596–1604). Her historical existence is deeply anchored in the popular Acehnese conscious, but also the subject of prolific Dutch author Marie van Zeggelen's *Oude glorie: Indische roman* [Past Glory: (Dutch East) Indian Novel] (Amsterdam: Nederlandsche Keurboekerij, 1935). For more on Malahayati, see my 'Silenced Fighters', pp. 277–281 in particular.
94 Interview with Kak I., *inong balèë* of Meureuhom Daja, May 2007.
95 For similar patterns, see the chapters by Blackburn and Siapno in this volume.
96 Clavé-Çelik, 'Silenced Fighters', pp. 277–281.
97 See Andrée Feillard and Rémy Madinier, *La fin de l'innocence ? L'islam indonésien face à la tentation radicale de 1967 à nos jours* [The End of Innocence? Indonesian Islam Facing the Temptation of Radicalisation from 1967 to the Present] (Paris/Bangkok: Les Indes Savantes/Institut de Recherche sur l'Asie contemporaine, 2006), Chapter 5.

7 Women in the early Vietnamese communist movement
Sex, lies, and liberation[1]

Sophie Quinn-Judge

The Vietnamese communist movement was not the first to discover the plight of women in French Indochina.[2] Before the emergence of a Vietnamese proto-communist movement in the mid-1920s, which was consolidated with the foundation of the Vietnamese Communist Party (VCP) in early 1930, the issue was widely discussed there in the first decades of the twentieth century, as both David Marr and Hue-Tam Ho Tai have shown in their studies of the origins of Vietnamese radicalism.[3] Both traditionalists and radical nationalists realised that women had a right to education and a place in the modernising society being constructed under the French, even though they disagreed as to what that place should be.[4] The question of women was so central to the debates of the literati that both Pham Quynh (1892–1945), who worked from within the system, and the classically trained scholar Phan Boi Chau (1867–1940), who rejected French rule outright and advocated violent methods, wrote at length on the topic.[5]

Chinese reformist thinking associated with the New Culture Movement surely contributed to these early Vietnamese debates. By calling into question the Confucian hierarchy of state and family, male Chinese radicals, as well as females, found themselves confronted with a variety of issues connected to women's place in society. The link that they discerned between personal liberation from patriarchy and national renewal was at the root of new attitudes, which early Asian communists absorbed.[6] In 1921 Chen Duxiu, the first leader of the Chinese Communist Party (CCP), was an active collaborator of the Marxist journal *Women and Labour*.[7] Ho Chi Minh[8] (1890–1969) would also adopt a strong interest in women's issues – while he was in Moscow in 1923–1924, and later in Canton, he contributed to a Soviet paper called *Rabotnitsa* [Working Woman].[9]

In this chapter I will look at the fate of two Vietnamese women, Nguyen Tri Duc (c. 1911–n.d) and Nguyen Thi Minh Khai (1910–1941), who were attracted to the communist revolution, starting with its proto-communist precursors, largely for nationalist reasons. I will do so by drawing on materials that reflect the international networks and alliances of Vietnamese anti-colonialism and communism, as documented in the records of the Communist International (Comintern) contained in Russian archives, but

Women in the early Vietnamese communist movement 137

also by drawing on the materials collected and generated by the French surveillance and intelligence apparatus that extended beyond French Indochina into key southern Chinese cities and whose files are now held in the French colonial archives. As we will see, due to the strong systems of control and intelligence that the French had erected, these networks extended beyond French Indochina, into Siam, where Nguyen Tri Duc was born, into Southern China, where she and Nguyen Thi Minh Khai could tap into contacts with Vietnamese émigrés and with the Chinese Guomindang or the CCP, and as far as Moscow, where Nguyen Thi Minh Khai would address the Seventh Comintern Congress and attend the University of the Toilers of the East in the mid-1930s.

Despite their exceptional revolutionary careers, both Nguyen Tri Duc and Nguyen Thi Minh Khai became caught up in the rapid changes in morality and views of women that were prevalent in China and Vietnam in the 1920s. After the initial outburst of what we think of as Western feminism, emphasising individual liberation and rights, a shift to a more traditional view of women took place in these communist movements in the late 1920s. In the case of China, this change has been attributed in part to the influence of socially conservative peasants who joined the Chinese party in large numbers during the first united front in Guangdong.[10] A similar conservative influence arguably came from the working-class members who joined the CCP in Shanghai.[11]

In contrast, David Marr describes the Vietnamese communists' increasing emphasis on the rights of working people in general, as opposed to those of middle-class women.[12] This change was in part due to the class-against-class tactics advocated by the Comintern in the years following its Sixth Congress in 1928. By March 1931, when the newly established Indochinese Communist Party (ICP) held a second plenum, party members would be instructed to dissolve the Associations for Women's Liberation in favour of unions composed entirely of working-class women.[13] But for those young women who had thrown in their lot with the proto-communist revolutionary movement, there may have been no turning back to conventional feminine behaviour. These women came almost exclusively from the petty bourgeois intelligentsia, and needed to prove that their commitment to the revolution was no weaker than that of their working-class sisters. As more radical factions of the movement began to proletarianise in 1928, all the Vietnamese activists were called on to sacrifice their old lives for the sake of the communist revolution and the working class. Members who were 'lacking in virtue' or unable to put up with the hardships of party life were to be cleansed from the ranks, a meeting of revolutionary youth leaders decreed in September 1928.[14] How precisely 'virtue' was to be defined is unclear at this point. For the female activists, however, the new sacrifices demanded seem to have been particularly onerous. They had to renounce their right to raise their children, and sometimes seem to have been expected to put their bodies at the service of the revolution by living as the 'wives' of male activists.

138   *Sophie Quinn-Judge*

In the end it appears that only women with extreme strength of character, or extremely good connections, could survive as full-time activists with their self-confidence and faith in communism intact.

Rejecting tradition

In Southeast Asia, women had never been subjected to the extreme form of patriarchy which crippled the lives of Chinese women. There was no foot binding in Vietnam, and ordinary women played an active economic role in society, working in the fields alongside men and trading in the markets. Vietnamese women were even expected to play a part when national sovereignty came under threat. The cult of the Trung sisters, who led a revolt against Chinese invaders in 43 C.E., is the best known example of the honoured role allotted to Vietnamese women in times of national resistance. This tradition was still alive in the early days of anti-French resistance. Ho Chi Minh's older sister, known as Bach Lien [White Lotus], was sentenced to hard labour in 1918 for stealing rifles from the indigenous militia in Vinh (north-central Annam) for her rebel friends. She was still in prison when her younger brother circulated his demands for Vietnamese rights at the Paris Peace Conference in 1919.[15]

But, in the main, women could perform these roles without departing from their place in Confucian society. Their courage and devotion to the nation could be seen as a form of service to their menfolk. This service was expected to be given modestly and chastely. The ideal of patriotic female conduct is represented in the stories of fearless village women feeding visiting rebels and guerrillas under the noses of the French. Such tales abound in the literature of Vietnamese resistance.

In the 1920s, however, a wave of revolt against the restrictive old morality erupted. In these early days of communist proselytising, young women ran away from home, lived in largely male collectives, and seem frequently to have discarded their virginity without regrets.[16] Sexual licence may not have been part of the communists' political programme. Ho Chi Minh, in fact, reported to the Krestintern [Peasant International] in 1925 that peasants in Guangdong Province had to be reassured that the communist party's programme did not advocate 'socialisation of women'.[17] But according to the confessions made to the French police by arrested activists, the female comrades were often pressured by their male peers to sleep with them: at least in some cases it would seem that the male and female revolutionaries had different understandings of the new freedom they were seeking. In the revolutionary hotbed of Canton, where groups of young Vietnamese travelled for communist training between 1925 and 1928, there may even have been an organised pairing-off of couples, which did not always answer the wishes of the women involved. The story of Nguyen Tri Duc, also known as Ly Phuong Duc, points to that conclusion.[18]

Nguyen Tri Duc

Nguyen Tri Duc was born in the émigré community in northeastern Siam, to a Vietnamese father who had been made a village official by the Siamese authorities. He was Nguyen Tri Minh, or Cuu Tuan, she relates in her police confession. He may have been related to the Ngo family, which settled in Nakhon Phanom after the failure of Phan Dinh Phung's resistance in the 1880s.[19] Her parents paid considerable attention to her education – her intelligence must have been evident from an early age. After a year's study in a local Siamese school, which she entered at age eleven, she was sent to a Chinese-English school in Chieng Mai, as her father wanted her to learn Chinese characters. In her new school she obtained the top grades, both in Chinese and in Thai. Her 'irreproachable behaviour' earned her the esteem of her teachers and classmates, she told the Sûreté, the notorious security police built up by the French to keep Vietnamese anti-colonialism at bay, when she was interrogated in 1931.

In 1925, however, her parents sent her with her brother, Ngo Chinh Quoc, to Canton to join the Vietnamese students there. She may still have been as young as fourteen at this time: she was probably one of a group of youth who emigrated from Siam to Hong Kong at Ho Chi Minh's invitation, possibly with the intent of continuing on to Moscow for schooling. In July 1926 he wrote to the Comintern to request funding for a group of Vietnamese 'pioneers' to travel to Russia. They were between twelve and fifteen, he said, and several of them had parents who had been imprisoned by the French.[20] The Comintern never provided the money for this plan, however, so the youth group remained in China for their training. They all took the family name Ly: Nguyen Tri Duc thus became Ly Phuong Duc. Another young revolutionary, Ly Tri Tong, was one of her brothers.

In Canton she stayed with Lam Duc Thu (1890–1947),[21] an émigré from northern Vietnam, who rented part of a house which served as a school and hostel for the students. (At that time none of the Vietnamese suspected that Lam was a French informer, but his frequent reports to the Sûreté, now accessible at the Archives d'Outre-Mer, make his status clear. By 1929 he had become known for his decadent lifestyle and was removed from the Thanh Nien leadership.)[22] Duc passed an entrance exam for the Trung Son School, where she became a boarder. She would return to live with her fellow Vietnamese during breaks and holidays. During her studies at this school she once again distinguished herself by earning the top marks in all her subjects. At the same time she began to participate in political activities: she became a member of the League of Oppressed Peoples, founded in mid-1925 by Ho Chi Minh and a group of Korean and Indian exiles living in Canton.

In Canton the women's movement was invigorated in 1924 and 1925 by the victories of the Guomindang-Communist united front. The Russian women in the Soviet aid mission contributed to this ferment. After Ho Chi Minh arrived from Moscow in November 1924, he wrote a description of the

140 *Sophie Quinn-Judge*

work of Fanya Borodin, Mikhail's wife, as a mobiliser of women: 'She devotes herself to making us understand and to making us work in the path of emancipation. Everywhere she goes, she organises, she educates, she shakes, she wakes us', he wrote, in the guise of a female activist.[23] In mid-1925, as the May 30th strike movement and Hongkong boycott were gathering force, Deng Yingchao, who became Zhou Enlai's wife that August, moved to Canton to join Mrs Borodin.[24] He Xiangning, wife of the left-GMD leader, Liao Zhongkai, was also a mainstay of the women's movement, and in 1926 sometimes came to speak to the Vietnamese trainees who had come to Canton for short-term courses. By late 1926, Ho's Viet Nam Thanh Nien Cach Mang Dong Chi Hoi [Association of Revolutionary Vietnamese Youth], usually known as Thanh Nien, had organised three of these training sessions. But it is not known if any women were among the early trainees (before 1927), or whether they participated in separate courses for women. Nguyen Tri Duc may have received separate training aimed at the 'pioneers'. It would be enlightening to learn more about the lessons which Fanya Borodin was imparting to the Chinese women. She was a respectable family woman, as was He Xiangning, so there would seem to be little likelihood that her message was as radical as that of Alexandra Kollontai, the early Bolshevik feminist who advocated free love.[25]

In August 1927, Nguyen Tri Duc agreed to marry one of her fellow revolutionaries, Le Hong Son (1899–1933), at the urging of Lam Duc Thu. She did so against her own wishes, she told the French, because she was in love with another of the émigrés, Le Quang Dat. As the doyen of the Vietnamese group, however, Lam Duc Thu seems at this time to have commanded respect. (Ho Chi Minh had fled to Moscow in May following Chiang Kaishek's anti-communist coup, so we do not know whether he would have approved of the arrangement.) In a report to the Sûreté, Lam Duc Thu also claimed to have provided Ho Chi Minh with a young consort, a Cantonese woman known as Tuyet Minh, in October 1926.[26] Although some of his fellow émigrés disapproved of the marriage, Ho persisted because, as Lam Duc Thu explained it, he needed someone to look after him and to help him learn Cantonese. (In this case Ho seems to have placed his own needs ahead of those of his companion, the daughter of a concubine, who in any case could not have expected to make an advantageous match. This relationship ended after Ho departed from Canton in the spring of 1927.)[27] Lam Duc Thu thus seems to have played the role of village match maker for the revolutionary group.

How these liaisons were regarded by the Vietnamese is unclear, however. There seems to have been a grey area between a real marriage and the pose of being a married couple, which the communists often adopted for the purposes of their clandestine work. The practice of living as couples was encouraged as good clandestine technique because a group of single men living together was considered more likely to arouse suspicion among the neighbours. But these fictive marriages may often have progressed to true relationships, whether sanctioned by a marriage ceremony or not.[28] At other times such relationships may have been a case of pure play-acting.

Women in the early Vietnamese communist movement 141

For example, Nguyen Thi Nghia, a young liaison agent from Tonkin, is said to have posed as the second wife of party member Le Doan Suu to avoid arousing suspicion when she was assigned to work in Vinh in 1931.[29]

Nguyen Tri Duc's marriage was not a success. Her husband, a hardened revolutionary credited by the French with two political assassinations, was imprisoned in 1928, and she found herself alone and pregnant. She had to give up her studies in April 1928, just two months before her graduation. She became 'sick with despair', she told the French, because she was going to bear the child of a man she did not love, and she was not going to be rewarded for her months of study. 'This explains my aversion to the communist party', she wrote.[30] Her baby died of an unnamed illness in November 1928. She divorced Le Hong Son in 1929 and married the communist Le Quang Dat when he was released from prison in Canton later that year. By that time she had moved to Kowloon and joined the growing number of communists who were 'proletarianising' themselves. She and another young Vietnamese woman, Ly Ung Thuan (referred to in several French reports as the partner of Thanh Nien leader Ho Tung Mau (1896–1951), who had left behind a wife in Nghe An),[31] had taken work in a Chinese electrical factory which produced dynamos. The two women both joined the factory's communist cell, according to the confession of another party member.[32]

Nguyen Tri Duc emphasised her good conduct and academic achievements in her 1931 statement to the French, as she knew that she had been accused of loose behaviour by some of her former comrades. 'I was extremely grieved to discover that, in spite of my merits, a few good-for-nothings slandered me, because I had refused their advances.... the truth is that I have had relations only with my current husband and with Hong Son', her statement reads. In fact, rumours of a sexual liaison with Le Duy Diem, another of the leading members of Ho Chi Minh's group, were the pretext for his exile to Siam by the Thanh Nien Central Committee in the autumn of 1929. In Siam, according to one report, Le Duy Diem would be brutally murdered by members of the Vietnamese community for his alleged misconduct with the local women.[33] His exile and death occurred when he was on the point of undertaking an important mission for Thanh Nien: he had been assigned to bring Ho Chi Minh back to southern China to mend the rift between the party's two feuding factions.

There is room to wonder, then, whether Lam Duc Thu or another French agent had manufactured the accusations against Nguyen Tri Duc and Le Duy Diem in order to disrupt the unification of the Vietnamese communists. (On the other hand, Nguyen Tri Duc seems to have withheld a good deal of information from her French interrogators and may not have told them the full truth about her wayward past.) In the summer of 1930, following the reunification of the feuding communist factions, she moved to Shanghai to join her new husband. In Shanghai they carried out agitational work among the Vietnamese sailors stationed on French ships, under the direction of the CCP. In spite of her 'aversion to the communist party', she continued this work until her arrest in June 1931.

142 *Sophie Quinn-Judge*

By the time of their interrogation in Saigon, however, the couple both seem to have reached the end of their patience with communist politics. Their statements to the French sound too heartfelt to be a story concocted to escape imprisonment. Their disillusionment may well reflect the disunity which existed among the Chinese communists in Shanghai at that time. Le Quang Dat complained that in Russia the peasants were being 'targeted', and that the workers were removing them from power: equality and happiness were being reserved for the working class. He also denounced the Vietnamese party's policies on women: liberty for women and equality between the sexes were 'hollow words'. 'A woman who is affiliated with the party is often forced to abandon her husband and must give herself continually to different men, because if she refuses she risks being knifed,' he said. 'Is this liberty of the sexes?'[34] This suggests, at the very least, that the party was accepting members who had a primitive understanding of communist morality. I have found no further information on this couple. One wonders if it was really possible for them to escape to an ordinary life outside politics.

The woman trap

The Rue Barbier murder in December 1928, described in detail by Hue-Tam Ho Tai, is another example of the seemingly feudal treatment of young women within the communist fraternity.[35] According to the information gleaned by the French, in 1928 the leader of the Cochinchina Regional Committee of Thanh Nien, Le Van Phat, pressured a young recruit from Ben Tre to become his mistress. When she agreed, the jealousy which this provoked between Phat and Ton Duc Thang[36] (1888–1980), his apparent rival for leadership in the South, eventually led to Phat's murder by a Thanh Nien assassination squad. But as in the case of Le Duy Diem's exile and murder in late 1929, we do not really know whether the accused was guilty of misconduct towards a female comrade, as charged, whether he had been framed by a rival faction in Thanh Nien, or whether this was a case of French provocation, perhaps with Lam Duc Thu pulling the strings. Between 1928 and 1935, however, accusations of uncomradely treatment of women were a regular feature of party life. In early 1931, a member of the Saigon-Cholon committee, Nguyen Van Son, was removed from his position for neglecting his activities and womanising.[37] In 1935, as the Moscow trainee Ha Huy Tap was taking charge of the party's Overseas Bureau in Macao, he accused the party veteran Nguyen Van Tram, a former liaison agent for Ho Chi Minh, of raping the fiancée of an absent comrade. Tram then stole 1,500 Hong Kong dollars from the party's funds and disappeared, perhaps fearing a fate similar to that of Le Duy Diem. The woman, already ill at the time of the rape, was said by Ha Huy Tap to have died ten days later.[38]

Ha Huy Tap accused another of the early communists, Nguyen Huu Can, known variously as Phi Van, Min, or Philippe, of an exploitative attitude towards his female comrades. Trained as a radio operator in Moscow, Min was reported to have complained when he returned to work in China that the woman assigned to play the role of his wife was too old and ugly. He requested a pretty young companion, and the Vietnamese Overseas Bureau, then in Macao, duly found one from the Chinese party. Around this time, however, Min was accused by Ha Huy Tap of betraying the party to the French and demoted in his responsibilities.[39] We know from another report which Tap wrote to Moscow in early 1935 that he was working to purge the party of the petty bourgeois influence of Ho Chi Minh and his acolytes.[40] So once again there is a hint of ambiguity regarding this catalogue of Min's sins. Possibly Tap's accusation included some embellishments to demonstrate the indiscipline and lack of communist morality of which Min was accused. The communists were not above manufacturing pretexts to get rid of those considered to be enemies. One Hanoi account of the uprising at the Phu Rieng rubber plantation in Cochinchina in early 1930 describes how accusations could be manufactured against suspected informers. As Tran Tu Binh explains, the plantation owners sent informers into the ranks of the rebels. 'But these secret agents were grabbed by the Red Guards and beaten half to death. The Red Guards accused them of thievery, seducing the girls, fomenting trouble, and all manner of crimes as excuses to give them a suitable thrashing.'[41]

There seems to have been an overlap between those communists accused of immoral behaviour towards women and those who were considered to be infected with the 'petty bourgeois' tendencies of the early Thanh Nien group. Perhaps these men really were guilty of abusing the trust of young female comrades: perhaps they had not imbibed the modern Western sensibilities of the younger, French-educated party members. They may have simply been unable to discard former notions of female virtue, according to which a woman brazen enough to leave home on her own was fair game.[42] Within Thanh Nien, it seems that some of the older males still viewed themselves as outlaw chieftains of a secret society: the young women perhaps became their prizes. (Unfortunately, sexual licence carried serious risks: in China at least, venereal disease seems to have been a common health problem among communist party members.)[43] On the other hand, the romance of underground existence may have led both male and female revolutionaries to embrace a bohemian lifestyle, which simply got out of control at times. The high level of tension must have intensified emotions. Especially within Vietnam, the underground groups had to live with the constant danger of arrest and torture by the French. Still, one must consider the further possibility that the accusations of womanising reflected the efforts of one faction in the party to weaken its opponents.

Nguyen Thi Minh Khai

In contrast to Nguyen Tri Duc and some of the other female recruits, the revolutionary career of Nguyen Thi Minh Khai, another early militant,

144   *Sophie Quinn-Judge*

lasted longer and was more successful. Although she seems to have been subjected to similar pressures to have affairs with her comrades, Minh Khai came through her political apprenticeship with her confidence and commitment intact. Perhaps the reason is that she did not come under the influence of the cynical Lam Duc Thu. Although she received only a primary school diploma (six years of schooling), she was, like Nguyen Tri Duc, a bright pupil who became involved in revolutionary activities at a young age. Born in 1910, she came from a family with roots in the revolutionary heartland of Nghe Tinh in north-central Annam.[44] Her maternal grandmother was the daughter of a poor scholar from Nam Dan District in Nghe An Province, the home of nationalist leader Phan Boi Chau, Ho Chi Minh, and both husbands of Nguyen Tri Duc. Her maternal grandfather was himself a scholar from Duc Tho District in neighbouring Ha Tinh Province. Typically in this age of waning Confucian influence, her father worked for the French. He was a northerner who had come to Nghe An to take up the post of railway station master in Vinh, the provincial capital.

While still a fifteen-year-old student in Vinh, Minh Khai was inducted into a revolutionary group for girls, perhaps by one of her schoolmasters, Tran Phu (1904–1931), who would become the first leader of the Indochinese Communist Party (ICP) in October 1930. She described her early political initiation as an 'awakening' [*giac ngo*] when she wrote an autobiography for the Comintern at the end of 1934.[45] In 1926 she became a member of a nationalist group, the Revolutionary Party, which was at that time closely allied with the Thanh Nien Association. She was given responsibility for mobilising women in Nghe An. In order to avoid causing concern to her family, she took up work as a trader: that gave her the freedom to travel around the province and recruit members for Thanh Nien. Her mother worked as a cloth merchant, so Minh Khai's commercial activities would not have been considered odd. (Later one of her party pseudonyms would be *Ba vai*, Mrs Cloth.) In the summer of 1928 the Revolutionary Party abandoned its efforts to merge with Thanh Nien and renamed itself Tan Viet [New Vietnam Party]. Minh Khai became a member of Tan Viet, although she considered herself by this time to be a communist. She was elected secretary of the Tan Viet women's group and was also made a member of the provincial standing committee (*ban thuong vu*). Thus by the age of eighteen she was a leading revolutionary in one of Vietnam's chief breeding grounds for activists. By the end of 1928, she told the Comintern, she had recruited a women's group of fifty people, including a group of twenty at the match factory on the outskirts of Vinh and fifteen people at the Ben Thuy sawmill. These two sites would figure in the early demonstrations which sparked the Nghe Tinh uprising in 1930.[46] By 1929 the Comintern was becoming aware of the increasing feminisation of the factory workforce in Asia, and advocating special attention to the mobilisation of women workers.[47] If Minh Khai's own account of her activities is accurate, she was well ahead of this trend.

Women in the early Vietnamese communist movement 145

A French crack-down on several nationalist parties – the Thanh Nien, the Tan Viet, and the Vietnamese Nationalist Party (Viet Nam Quoc Dan Dang)[48] – in mid-1929 brought about the destruction of the Tan Viet central and province-level committees. The leadership in Nghe An scattered, Minh Khai wrote, with many members being arrested, going into hiding, or looking for ways to leave their revolutionary activities behind.[49] Only the mass organisations remained after that: the workers' and women's groups were still strong, while the student group 'vacillated', she reported. Along with other members of the workers' and women's groups, she began to travel around central Vietnam to find the loyal elements of the party, and form them into a communist group. She became a liaison agent charged with carrying secret materials between Tonkin and the central provinces, and was one of the founding members of the Cong San Lien Doan [Communist League], a communist group which merged with the unified Vietnam Communist Party in March 1930. By late 1929 the situation in Nghe An had become extremely dangerous for revolutionaries, however, and Minh Khai was forced to go into hiding. A Sûreté report of 1930 stated that in 1929 Nguyen Thi Minh Khai was suspected of having emigrated to Siam with another young woman, Bui Trung Luong. By mid-1930 the latter was reported to be hiding in a Buddhist pagoda near Nam Dinh, disguised as a nun. But by that time Minh Khai had already made her way to Hong Kong (Figure 7.1).[50]

Figure 7.1 Nguyen Thi Minh Khai, at the age of 24 the youngest of the three members of the delegation of the Indochinese Community Party to the Seventh Congress of the Comintern, which was held in Moscow in July and August of 1935. Her delegate's card featured her as Tov[arisch] (Comrade) Fan-Lan, from the Communist Party of Indochina, with full voting rights. Note the intensive glare of her eyes that suggests a steely determination, vital for succeeding in a hierarchical and largely male-dominated communist revolutionary world, as represented here by the portraits of Stalin, Lenin, Engels and Marx to her right.

Source: Photo from Sophie Quinn-Judge's collection, courtesy of the Comintern Archives, Moscow.

146 *Sophie Quinn-Judge*

Soon after Ho Chi Minh unified the communist groups in February 1930, Minh Khai says that she received a party directive to go to Hong Kong to work as a liaison agent. She lived in the new party's headquarters in Kowloon for nine months. Her Vietnamese biography describes how each morning Ho Chi Minh provided individual lessons in revolutionary theory for Minh Khai and another young woman living with her, Ly Phuong, who was, as noted above, Nguyen Tri Duc.[51] As he was absent in Singapore and Thailand for all of May and a good part of June, however, these lessons would have been fairly intermittent. The French reported that Minh Khai was still living in Kowloon in the same house as Ho Chi Minh, near the Hong Kong airport, at the time of the Vietnamese Communist Party's first plenum in October 1930.[52]

Although Ho Chi Minh was twice the age of Minh Khai, this self-driven and confident young revolutionary from his home province, who may well have become acquainted with his sister in the course of her work with women, must have appeared to be a more trustworthy mate than the Cantonese consort furnished by Lam Duc Thu. Pictures taken in Moscow a few years later also show her to have been very pretty, with a round face and perfect teeth. By the winter, Ho Chi Minh was discussing his marriage plans with the Comintern's Far Eastern Bureau in Shanghai: in January 1931 they asked that he let them know the date of his wedding two months before it took place.[53] In a February letter to the Far Eastern Bureau he mentioned that his wife was busy with preparations for the New Year and the reception of visitors from Saigon and Tonkin.[54] So it appears that he either ignored the Comintern's instructions or that they arrived too late. Again, we do not know whether this was a 'revolutionary marriage' or how the two of them viewed their future. From Comintern reports of 1934, we learn that Minh Khai was considered to be his wife when she was chosen to represent Vietnamese women at the Seventh Comintern Congress.[55] When she filled in a questionnaire in Moscow in December 1934, she wrote that she was married and entered her husband's name as 'Lin', Ho Chi Minh's pseudonym at that time.[56] He, however, never mentioned having a wife on any of his Comintern forms.

Their life together did not last long, at least not in 1931. The French destruction of the communists' leadership structures in Vietnam also extended to southern China, leading to Nguyen Thi Minh Khai's arrest in Hong Kong in late April 1931, followed by deportation to Canton.[57] The British police arrested Ho in Hong Kong on 6 June. With the skilled legal assistance of the Red Aid International, Ho was finally allowed to depart from Hong Kong in January 1933 to a destination of his choosing. He got back to Moscow in mid-1934, after lying low in Shantou and Shanghai for a time. Minh Khai was held in prison for a year before being released and deported to Hong Kong in 1932.[58]

Her existence for the next few years was precarious, as she described it to the Comintern. In Hong Kong she joined forces with a newly returned student from Moscow, Tran Ngoc Danh, the younger brother of her former school teacher, Tran Phu, who had died in autumn of 1931 in police custody in Saigon. Minh Khai and Tran Ngoc Danh formed a twosome and began to reconstitute the party's communications networks. The French referred to her in intelligence reports at this time as his concubine.[59] The two linked up with Le Hong Son and travelled together to Shanghai in May 1932 to make contact with the Chinese party. But thanks to the double-crossing of a fellow party member who had close contacts with the Chinese communists in 1932, they did not succeed in getting any financial support for their work. Truong Phuoc Dat, their erstwhile comrade, accused them of petty bourgeois behaviour and claimed that he had never seen them before.[60] Minh Khai and her companions had to pawn some of their clothing in order to pay their hotel bill.

From Shanghai they travelled to Nanjing, where they were taken in by Ho Hoc Lam (1884–1943), a Nghe An native who served as a colonel in Chiang Kaishek's General Staff. The uncle of Thanh Nien member Ho Tung Mau, Lam protected numerous Vietnamese revolutionaries who fell on hard times. A floating population of Vietnamese lived with him in Nanjing during the 1930s. Minh Khai stayed in his house for five months, waiting for news from Shanghai. No messages arrived, however, and when in September Tran Ngoc Danh and Le Hong Son went to make another attempt to reopen contact with the CCP, they were arrested.[61] In November 1932 she thus returned to Hong Kong with the intention of going to Vietnam, Siam, or even France.[62]

A group of letters which the French intercepted from a party mailbox in Hong Kong, written by Minh Khai in February and March 1933, gives us a rather startling revelation of her thoughts. The French copies are translations from the Vietnamese, and thus make her voice somewhat stilted. But all the same, they reveal a strong-willed revolutionary romantic. One of her Nanjing companions, Bui Hai Thieu, had clearly been pressuring her to return to Nanjing to work with, or resume a liaison with, another exiled revolutionary. Her response, however, demonstrated no interest in further entanglements. If she really had been involved with her contemporary Tran Ngoc Danh, in addition to Ho Chi Minh, she may well have been burnt out. She wrote back to Bui Hai Thieu that she was 'deeply touched' by the sincerity of her admirer, 'Do', and that she was not 'made of wood'. 'But marriage is absurd, a bore, a burden…. Now everything is broken and I am no longer haunted by the idea of marriage or motherhood', she explained. 'Let's not speak of the past! My only husband is the Communist Revolution…. Do is an excellent comrade, a precious friend, a sincere and courageous patriot whom I deeply respect…. but nothing in the world could make me love him. He is too sincere and too intelligent not to accept and understand my feelings. And our former liaison has planted in our hearts a friendship which is far superior to love by its purity, its power and its endurance.'[63] In referring to her husband as the 'Communist Revolution' she seems to be echoing

148   *Sophie Quinn-Judge*

Phan Boi Chau's prescription to female activists. He had written in 1927 that young women, when asked whether they had a husband yet, should reply, 'Yes, his surname is Viet and his family name is Nam.'[64]

The French police assumed that Minh Khai's admirer, 'Do' [Red], was Tran Dai Do in Hankou (part of Wuhan). He was engaged in propaganda work among the Vietnamese and French sailors stationed there; he served as a cook for the junior officers aboard an escort vessel, the 'Craonne'.[65] At one point the French also suspected that Tran Dai Do might be Ho Chi Minh, who had just been deported from Hong Kong at the end of January 1933 on a ship heading north. But this seems unlikely, as Do had been in Hankou since 1932, when Ho Chi Minh was still in prison. Perhaps her admirer was a different 'Do'. Given the strength of Minh Khai's language, one feels that he must have been someone important. She may have rejected the invitation, fearing that it was a Sûreté trap. Unfortunately, given the confusion generated by the mere scraps of information available in the Sûreté's records, one can only guess the truth of Minh Khai's romantic life. Possibly she had learned that Ho Chi Minh, rumoured in mid-1932 to be dying from tuberculosis, was in fact alive and well, and had just been deported from Hong Kong. She would need to keep that fact a secret: but at the same time might have decided to give the brush off to the men she had been associated with since his arrest. In any case, her first thought in the spring of 1933 seems to have been to stay out of the clutches of the French police and to get back in touch with the Vietnamese party's central committee.

In a February letter to her friend Ly Ung Thuan, who was soon to give birth, she proposed that Thuan bring the newborn child to Hong Kong to be looked after by a childless married woman. Ly Ung Thuan, earlier identified as the wife of Ho Tung Mau (in prison since June 1931), had formed a new liaison with the activist in Nanjing, Bui Hai Thieu. (The fact that Thuan was having a baby by another man while her 'husband' was in prison does not seem to have shocked the revolutionaries.) 'The child will be very well off in the hands of the person I am proposing', Minh Khai wrote.[66] It would seem that Minh Khai expected her female comrades to place the revolution before love and children, just as she did. She also asked Thuan to send her 'the pages which I wrote in French, the texts such as "Pity the Peasants" and the others, such as those that deal with feminism; and "The Progress of Feminine Youth"'. She went on to complain about the economic situation in Hong Kong: 'the situation is really sad this year. There are lots of unemployed here. Be careful! The water is already in the bottom of the boat, hold on tightly to the oar. If you see any news in the papers, tell me in a letter.'

According to her Comintern autobiography, Minh Khai spent the next year trying to avoid arrest. She would settle in one spot, but soon have to move on when suspicious people started asking questions. For a time she shared the life of the union of revolutionary Vietnamese 'boys' (male domestic servants) and craftsmen in Hong Kong. She earned a living making shirts and contributed to the finances of the union. When that work finished, she

Women in the early Vietnamese communist movement 149

became a coolie. In November 1933 the French had to admit that they had completely lost track of her.[67] Around that time she met a party member who had come from Siam, but it was not until August 1934 that she made contact with the newly formed Overseas Bureau of the Vietnamese party.[68] Le Hong Phong (1902–1942) and Ha Huy Tap (1906–1941), two natives of the Nghe Tinh region who had received training in Moscow, took charge of this organ, and delegated Nguyen Thi Minh Khai to travel to Moscow for the Seventh Comintern Congress. Le Hong Phong, the de facto party leader, headed the delegation. He and Minh Khai were joined by one other delegate, Hoang Van Non, a member of the Tay ethnic minority from Cao Bang.

Nguyen Thi Minh Khai's arrival in Moscow marked her promotion to the upper ranks of the Indochinese Communist Party. On the surface her selection to attend the Congress may have looked like tokenism: she was not a member of any of the party's leading committees in 1934 (as yet no women were), and her selection for the Congress delegation could have been viewed as a reward for her devotion to the party. But by being given the opportunity to speak in front of the world communist leadership, to meet Lenin's widow, Krupskaya, and then to stay on for studies at the Stalin School (University for the Workers of the East), she became one of a small élite and perhaps the only Vietnamese woman who had first-hand knowledge of the revolution's mecca. She attained this status through her own dedication, but her ties to Ho Chi Minh must have helped her to get noticed. Ha Huy Tap, in a 1934 report which listed the Congress delegates, referred to her as 'Quoc's wife' and 'Ba Vai' [Mrs Cloth].[69] A Vietnamese biography of Minh Khai published in 1976, however, describes a romance with Le Hong Phong which supposedly began as the two sailed to Vladivostok. This source claims that they were married in Moscow.[70] However, I have seen no documentary evidence or contemporary reference to such a marriage, and the account above betrays its unreliability by stating that Ha Huy Tap (who was still in China) was present at the ceremony at which Minh Khai married 'Vuong'. (Vuong was one of the names by which Ho was known in China: I have never seen it attached to Le Hong Phong.) It appears more likely that Le Hong Phong and Minh Khai became linked when they shared a house in Saigon in 1937 and 1938. But again, there may be no proof of a sexual liaison beyond the French assertion that she was his concubine or wife.[71]

Minh Khai addressed the Seventh Comintern Congress towards its close on 16 August 1935, on the dangers of French militarism in the Pacific. She defined the task of the ICP as being 'to mobilise all its forces to create a broad popular front to struggle for peace'.[72] Although she mentioned the fact that there were very few Asian women at the Congress, her speech did not primarily concern women's issues, as Vietnamese summaries of its content often imply. By moving beyond the field of women's organising she had broken through a barrier which would later become almost insurmountable for women in the ICP. In fact, the records of her studies at the Stalin School during 1935 and 1936 show that she viewed herself as a leader within

150   *Sophie Quinn-Judge*

the small group of Southeast Asians who remained in Moscow. Notes on her progress described her as 'politically restrained', 'disciplined', and as showing 'great growth' in her political studies. 'But sometimes she reveals a desire to play the leading role and to dictate to the others', a report said. Another teacher (of natural science) described her as 'somewhat stubborn, but remarkably determined in pursuit of her goals. She can quickly make up for what she has missed.'[73] Ho Chi Minh himself (Comrade Lin) described her as 'knowing a lot about many things, but knowing little in depth.'

In February 1937 Minh Khai departed from Moscow, her biographical file tells us.[74] The final phase of her career, from her return to Asia until her execution in August 1941, is a particularly murky period in the history of Vietnamese communism. Her role as an educator and mobiliser of women during the Popular Front years is what she is remembered for in party histories. Her arrest at the end of July 1940 and execution just over a year later, along with a group of the party's male leaders, has assured her of immortality as a communist martyr. But there has been almost no official acknowledgement of her importance as an advocate of united front policies within a communist party which was highly resistant to the new Comintern line in 1936 and 1937. Two of her letters, one from the Comintern archives and another from the French colonial files, give us an inkling of the part which she played behind the scenes. Yet some male historians, both in Russia and in Asia, are reluctant to admit that she possessed the educational background to have played such a role.[75]

According to official histories of the Vietnamese party, the united front policy of the Seventh Comintern Congress was adopted at a Central Committee meeting held in Shanghai in June 1936, just as the Popular Front government was being installed in France. In the Comintern archives, however, there is a long letter written to Moscow in September 1937 which contradicts this version of events. This letter recapitulates, for the Comintern's benefit, the disagreements between Le Hong Phong, who headed the Hong Kong-based Overseas Bureau of the Vietnamese party, and Ha Huy Tap, who had re-established the Central Committee in Saigon in August 1936 under his own leadership.[76] As the writer signs herself 'F. L.', and describes her return to Hong Kong and subsequent meeting with Ha Huy Tap in Saigon, we can be fairly certain that the author is Minh Khai. The French picked up her trace in Saigon around the time of the Enlarged Party Conference and plenum held in late August and early September 1937.[77]

Minh Khai had travelled with Hoang Van Non back to Hong Kong via France and Italy in the spring of 1937. They had memorised a list of Comintern instructions on the formation of a united front. When they tracked down Le Hong Phong in July, he explained to them that the Central Committee had been critical of the Comintern's new emphasis on legal and semi-legal methods of organising: the new policies were viewed as 'liquidationist, opportunist and rightist'. Although the Overseas Bureau had written a brochure explaining the new policies, this had been kept out of circulation by

Women in the early Vietnamese communist movement   151

Ha Huy Tap. Le Hong Phong then sent Minh Khai to Saigon in August 1937 to deliver the Comintern's latest directives in person, whilst Hoang Van Non was sent to Hanoi to do the same. In response to these instructions, Ha Huy Tap once again stated that the tactics being promoted by Moscow were 'reactionary'. 'I wanted to write to explain all this to the comrades overseas', F. L. wrote, 'but comrade Sinitchkin told me that if I did, I would be expelled from the party.' But after the party plenum voted to accept the Comintern's instructions, Ha Huy Tap finally yielded. The presence of Maurice Honel (1903–1977), Member of Parliament for the French Communist Party, in Saigon at this time seems to have been critical in overcoming Ha Huy Tap's resistance to the new line. F. L.'s letter says that Honel criticised Tap's 'sectarianism', and that he encouraged her to write to the Comintern to make clear what was happening within the ICP.[78] When the party held its Third Plenum in March 1938, Ha Huy Tap was removed from his post as General Secretary and replaced by an amnestied political prisoner from Tonkin, Nguyen Van Cu. Tap was arrested and expelled to his home province of Ha Tinh in May 1938. At this time the Sûreté identified Minh Khai as a member of the party's Cochinchina Regional Committee and the Saigon Committee. She was also put in charge of the education of party members, the French believed.[79]

For the period from 1937 to 1939, Minh Khai's Hanoi biography emphasises her work in educating and mobilising women. (This dates her return to Vietnam from Moscow as 1936.) She may have been the author of a pamphlet on women, as well as a series of articles in the communist newspaper *Dan Chung* [The People], signed by Nguyen Thi Kim Anh, all of which appeared in 1938.[80] The *Dan Chung* articles rebutted the fascist philosophy that women should devote themselves to their families and renounce ideas of social activism. In an article cited by Nguyet Tu, '*Van de giai phong phu nu*' ['The problem of women's liberation'] the writer, identified as Minh Khai, expounds the Marxist idea that women cannot solve their problems as individuals, but only within the framework of class liberation, a framework which does not distinguish between men and women.[81]

By the autumn of 1939, however, after the declaration of the Molotov-Ribbentrop Pact and the French decision to ban the communist party, Minh Khai had to take on a broader leadership role. With the party forced back into illegality, its leaders were being expelled from the south or arrested, one-by-one. Le Hong Phong was picked up in June 1939; Nguyen Van Cu and Le Duan would be taken in January 1940. By mid-1939 Ho Chi Minh was attempting to make contact with the Vietnamese party from across the Chinese border in Guangxi Province, where he had arrived from Yan'an in February 1939. He wrote to Moscow in July 1939 to explain that his efforts to contact the ICP had met with failure, although in July he had managed to send on the Comintern's latest instructions via 'a friend'.[82]

Although official party histories do not record Minh Khai's role at this juncture, it would appear from a letter discovered by the French in 1940

152 *Sophie Quinn-Judge*

that she was involved in trying to bring Ho Chi Minh into contact with the Central Committee leaders in Saigon. By mid-1939 the ICP was once again wracked by disagreements over how it should implement the Comintern's united front policy. There was still resistance to the idea of joining an anti-fascist front which would force the party to moderate its opposition to France, as well as to reformist parties within Vietnam. That discord would have increased the urgency of contacting Ho, who was waiting in Guilin, sending articles to a left-wing Hanoi newspaper in the hope that his comrades would notice his pseudonym, 'P. C. Lin' or 'Line'. Minh Khai's letter chides her 'comrades' in the Central Committee for failing to appoint someone to bring back 'L': 'You haven't decided on the rendez-vous. Which means that L. has waited a long time, without anyone going to get him. I was counting on bringing him back, but I didn't know the meeting place, and anyway, I hadn't received instructions about this ...' She goes on to remind the Central Committee of the 'events of exceptional seriousness' which were taking place in China, and says that the committee must 'assign tasks more clearly'. She mentions that she had been working with the 'directing organs' for the past two years, so one can guess that she was writing around the time of the ICP's Sixth Plenum, held in Hoc Mon outside Saigon in early November 1939.

At the end of her letter she brings up the fact that her sex has been a disadvantage in her work with the party leadership. 'I know that the idea of a woman, even if she is just or has a good political character, does not inspire great confidence. However, I feel that since I have begun working with the comrades here, I have not made any suggestions or begun any activities which are against the principles or the policy of the Party ...'[83] The letter's tone of authority leads one to suppose that Minh Khai saw herself as a representative of the Comintern or the Overseas Bureau of the ICP at this point. With Le Hong Phong under arrest, this responsibility could have fallen to her. From what we know about Ho Chi Minh's difficulty in making contact with the ICP, it seems highly possible that the 'L' referred to in her letter is indeed 'Lin', the pseudonym which Ho was still using to sign newspaper articles aimed at a Vietnamese readership. It is possible that she travelled to China sometime in mid-1939, bringing him news of political developments in Vietnam, which he then passed on to the Comintern in his July report.

Minh Khai is known to have given birth to a daughter, believed to be the child of Le Hong Phong, at some point between early 1939 and early 1940.[84] Childbirth does not seem to have kept her out of action for long: she entrusted her baby to her younger sister, Quang Thai (1915–1944), the first wife of Vo Nguyen Giap (1911–2013). By the time of her arrest in Saigon at the end of July 1940, she was described by the French as a Central Committee Secretary.[85] Found in possession of documents regarding planned sabotage of French military installations, Minh Khai was handed over to the military court and sentenced to death in March 1941, as one of the instigators of the

Women in the early Vietnamese communist movement   153

Southern Uprising which occurred in November 1940. The day of her execution, 28 August 1941, marked the loss of the ICP's top-ranking female, and a group of its most important leaders from all parts of the country. Central Committee members Ha Huy Tap, Nguyen Van Cu, Phan Dang Luu, and Vo Van Tan were all sent before the firing squad on that same day. After that, the home of the Central Committee would move to Tonkin, and the early work of building the war-time united front, the Viet Minh, would occur under Ho Chi Minh's guidance on the Chinese side of the border.

Conclusion

While Vietnamese women were widely recruited into the ranks of the revolutionaries in the 1920s and 1930s, the communist independence movement did not bring them the escape from patriarchy which was so widely discussed in the 1920s. If there was any sort of equality within the Indochinese Communist Party, it was in the degree of self-sacrifice demanded of rank-and-file members. The Vietnamese family and party remained strongly Confucian: for communists, the party replaced the family as the object of their loyalty and the source of authority in their lives. In Vietnam, as Nguyen Khac Vien argued, the Marxist militants adopted the political morality of Confucianism as their own. 'Bourgeois individualism, which places its own individuality above society, petty bourgeois anarchism, which recognises no social discipline, are foreign to both Confucianism and Marxism', Vien wrote.[86]

We do not know how many Vietnamese women were willing to marry themselves to the revolution, as Nguyen Thi Minh Khai apparently did. But even she, with her training in Moscow and long record of activism, was not easily accepted into the ICP's leading ranks in the late 1930s. Her rise to membership of the Central Committee occurred only after a period of severe repression by the French. From 1930 onwards, her close relationship with Ho Chi Minh may have been both a help and a hindrance to her political fortunes. When she returned to Vietnam from Moscow in 1937, she became involved in implementing policies largely decided in Moscow. These, like Ho Chi Minh's leadership, were not popular with some factions of the party. Consequently, the resistance to her ideas to which she alludes in her letter of late 1939 may have arisen as much from her political alliance with Ho as from her gender.

There is little doubt that for the women and men who became involved in communist politics in the 1920s, family connections were often of central importance. Nguyen Tri Duc was herself a second- or third-generation revolutionary when she went to Canton. Her parents' willingness to send her off to Canton in 1925, although with her brother, seems to demonstrate a markedly modern attitude towards the role of women. But it also revealed a willingness to give their children to the national cause, a great sacrifice for a Vietnamese family. When Duc had to give up her education for an unwanted pregnancy and then go to work in a factory, she must have begun to

154   *Sophie Quinn-Judge*

question what sort of freedom the revolution would bring her. Minh Khai's commitment brought her a heroine's death, but Nguyen Tri Duc seems to have been rewarded for her loyalty with humiliation. For the generation of women who began the revolution in Vietnam, the traditional virtues of stoicism and self-sacrifice were the ones that dominated their lives.

Notes

1 I am grateful to John Edmondson, IP Publishing's director, for his kind permission to have my earlier article published here in slightly different form: Sophie Quinn-Judge, 'Women in the Early Vietnamese Communist Movement: Sex, Lies, and Liberation', *South East Asia Research*, Vol. 9, No. 3 (November 2001), pp. 245–269.
2 French Indochina, which also included Cambodia and Laos, comprised of three Vietnamese territories, namely Cochinchina in the south, Annam in the centre, and Tonkin in the north. Cochinchina was a French colony, whereas Annam and Tonkin remained protectorates, although the latter was effectively run as a semi-colony.
3 David Marr, *Vietnamese Tradition on Trial, 1920–1945* (Berkeley: University of California Press, 1981); Hue-Tam Ho Tai, *Radicalism and the Origins of the Vietnamese Revolution* (Cambridge, MA: Harvard University Press, 1992). In October 1930, following instructions from Moscow, the Vietnamese Communist Party would become the Indochinese Communist Party.
4 Ho Tai, *Radicalism and the Origins of the Vietnamese Revolution*, pp. 92–102.
5 Marr, *Vietnamese Tradition on Trial*, pp. 202–204 on Pham Quynh; pp. 200–201 and p. 210 on Phan Boi Chau.
6 Steve A. Smith, *A Road is Made: Communism in Shanghai, 1920–1927* (Richmond, Surrey: Curzon, 2000), pp. 46–47.
7 Ibid., p. 47.
8 For the purpose of this paper, which aims at an audience well beyond the narrow field of Vietnamese Studies, I will use the name Ho Chi Minh, unless it is necessary to elucidate points important to understand Nguyen Tri Duc's and in particular Nguyen Thi Minh Khai's relations with him. In reality, Ho Chi Minh would take on this name only in 1940, with the French documents of the interwar period largely referring to him as Nguyen Ai Quoc.
9 Russian Centre for the Preservation and Study of Documents of Modern History, Moscow (hereafter RC) 495, 154, 594, p. 16, 12 November 1924 letter from Ho Chi Minh to an unnamed women's journal. The latter is identified as *Rabotnitsa* in *Bien Nien Tieu Su* [A Year-by-Year Biography of Ho Chi Minh], Vol. 1 (Hanoi: Nha Xuat Ban Thong Tin Ly Luan, 1992), p. 238.
10 Christina K. Gilmartin, 'Gender, Political Culture, and Women's Mobilisation in the Chinese Nationalist Revolution, 1924–1927', in Christina K. Gilmartin, Gail Hershatter, Lisa Rofel, and Tyrene White (eds.), *Engendering China: Women, Culture and the State* (Cambridge, MA: Harvard University Press, 1994); see pp. 217–223 for a discussion of Peng Pai and women's issues.
11 Smith, *Communism in Shanghai, 1920–1927*, p. 125.
12 Marr, *Vietnamese Tradition on Trial*, pp. 235–248.
13 'Resolutions of the Second CC Plenum, 3–1931', *Van Kien Dang* [Party Documents], Vol. 1 (Hanoi: Ban Nghien Cuu Lich Su Dang, 1977), p. 247.
14 Nguyen Van Hoan, 'Phong Trao Vo San Hoa Nam 1930' [The Proletarianisation Movement of 1930], *Nghien Cuu Lich Su*, Vol. 134 (September–October 1970), p. 11.

Women in the early Vietnamese communist movement 155

15 Daniel Hémery, 'Jeunesse d'un colonisé, genèse d'un exil: Ho Chi Minh jusqu'en 1911', *Approches Asie*, Vol. 11 (1992), pp. 148–150, citing Interrogation of Nguyen Thi Thanh, sister of Nguyen Ai Quoc, May 1920.

16 Ho Tai, *Radicalism and the Origins of the Vietnamese Revolution*, pp. 88–89. The remarkable story of the author's aunt, Nguyen Trung Nguyet (1909–1976), also known as Bao Luong (Precious Honesty), who took part in a revolutionary assassination (see 'rue Barbier murder' further below), shows how far traditional female conduct was transformed within revolutionary circles. For a more detailed coverage, see Hue-Tam Ho Tai, *Passion, Betrayal, and Revolution in Colonial Saigon: The Memoirs of Bao Luong* (Berkeley: University of California Press, 2010).

17 RC, 535, 1, 42, report of 5 November 1925.

18 Archives d'Outre-Mer (hereafter AOM), Aix-en-Provence; Service de Protection du Corps Expéditionnaire (hereafter SPCE) 367, Statement of Nguyen Duc Tri, 10 July 1931.

19 Phan Dinh Phung (1847–1896), a native of Ha Tinh and high-ranking court official, had led the royalist Aid the King (Can Vuong) movement between 1885 and 1896. On the Ngo family, see Christopher Goscha, *Thailand and the Networks of the Vietnamese Revolution, 1885–1954* (Richmond, Surrey: Curzon, 1999), pp. 22, 68–70. The generations of this extended family are difficult to pin down: Nguyen Tri Duc may have been related to Ngo Thi Khon Duy, wife of the Vietnamese émigré Ho Hoc Lam. Ngo Thi Khon Duy was the daughter of Ngo Quang, one of Phan Dinh Phung's generals. Her brother Ngo Chinh Hoc became one of the leaders of the early Thai communist party, as did Ngo Chinh Quoc, brother of Nguyen Tri Duc.

20 RC, 495, 154, 594, letter of 22 July 1926 from 'Nilovsky', Rosta News Agency, Canton, China.

21 I bring in the years of birth and death where available and relevant because age, besides gender and other categories, was a clear marker of social hierarchies in Confucius-influenced Vietnam.

22 AOM, SPCE 368, Mission Noel, envoi no. 507, 11 June 1929. The son of a nationalist scholar, Lam Duc Thu had for a time been one of Phan Boi Chau's principal lieutenants. Although he seems to have joined Ho's circle of communist recruits in Canton, he remained an instructor in the Canton army and, unlike a number of his countrymen, did not become attached to the Whampoa Military Academy.

23 RC, 495, 154, 594, pp. 12–13, Letter from China no. 1, written in French under the name of Loo Shing Yan, for the Russian newspaper, *Rabotnitsa*.

24 Gilmartin, 'Gender, Political Culture, and Women's Mobilisation in the Chinese Nationalist Revolution, 1924–1927', gives a picture of the different currents of women's organising in Canton.

25 See Richard Pipes, *Russia under the Bolshevik Regime* (New York: Alfred A. Knopf, 1993), pp. 331–333 for a succinct discussion of Kollontai.

26 AOM, SPCE 368, Agent Pinot report, 18 October 1926.

27 AOM, SPCE 367, Intelligence provided by Lesquendieu relating to Tuyet Minh, Chinese woman, mistress of Nguyen Ai Quoc, Hanoi, 28 October 1931.

28 Smith, *Communism in Shanghai, 1920–1927*, p. 125, cites an example of a working-class couple in Shanghai who eventually married after starting their relationship as a fictive couple.

29 *Nhung Nguoi Cong San* [The Communists] (Ho Chi Minh City: Nha Xuat Ban Thanh Nien, 1976), p. 240.

30 AOM, SPCE 367, Statement of Nguyen Duc Tri, p. 8.

31 Hoang Thanh Dam and Phan Huu Thinh, *Doi Noi, Doi vi Nuoc: ke chuyen gia toc Ho Tung Mau* [The Generations who Lived for the Country: Telling the Story

156 *Sophie Quinn-Judge*

of Ho Tung Mau's Family] (Nghe An: Nha Xuat Ban Nghe An, 1996): see family tree of Ho Tung Mau's clan in the publication's appendix.

32 AOM, SPCE 367, Declaration of Duong Hac Dinh.

33 AOM, SPCE 367, Interrogation of Le Van Phan (Le Hong Son), 24 October 1932 and the following days, index.

34 AOM, SPCE 367, Declaration of Le Quang Dat, July 1931.

35 Ho Tai, *Radicalism and the Origins of the Vietnamese Revolution*, pp. 214–217. Colonial Saigon's Barbier Street now is Nguyen Phi Khanh Street, located in Ho Chi Minh City's district 1.

36 Ton Duc Thang would, after Ho Chi Minh's death in 1969, become the second president of the Democratic Republic of Vietnam and continued to serve, after formal unification, as the president of the Socialist Republic of Vietnam.

37 Young Soon Nho, 'A History of the Indochina Communist Party, 1930–1936', Ph.D. thesis, University of London, 2000, p. 88. Nguyen Van Son may have been the early Thanh Nien activist Nguyen Van Loi, to judge by Loi's own statement to the police in SPCE 371, dated 18 January 1932.

38 RC, 495, 154, 586, letter to Far Eastern Bureau of 20 April 1935, signed Cin, for Cinitchkin, one of the pseudonyms of Ha Huy Tap.

39 Ibid.

40 RC, 495, 154, 688, letter in French from the Overseas Bureau to the Comintern, 31 March 1935.

41 Tran Tu Binh (transl. John Spragens, Jr.), *The Red Earth: A Vietnamese Memoir of Life on a Colonial Rubber Plantation* (Athens, OH: Ohio University, 1985), p. 70.

42 In the more conservative Hangzhou in China, even women who took seemingly honourable work in silk factories were considered to be no better than prostitutes. Lisa Rofel, 'Liberation Nostalgia and Yearning for Modernity', in Gilmartin et al. (eds.), *Engendering China*, p. 234.

43 *BKP(B), Komintern I Kitai* [The Soviet Communist Party, the Comintern and China], Documents, Vol. 3, part 1 (Moscow: Russian Centre for the Preservation and Study of Documents of Modern History, 1999), p. 555. In a letter from the Chinese party's central committee to the Eastern Secretariat of the Comintern (6 May 1929), the writers complain that there were few comrades healthy enough to send to Moscow for training. Serious tuberculosis, contagious venereal disease, and contagious ailments of the eyes disqualified them, according to the Russian rules.

44 Nguyet Tu, *Chi Minh Khai* [Sister Minh Khai] (Hanoi: Nha Xuat Ban Phu Nu, 1976), pp. 9–11.

45 RC 495, 201, 35, p. 6, 'Ly lich Fan-Lan' [Autobiography of Fan Lan].

46 Also known as the Nghe Tinh Soviets (1930–1931), the uprising became a key foundational event in the history of the newly founded Vietnamese (from October 1930: Indochinese) Communist Party.

47 RC 495, 154, 412, p. 61; English-language document dated October 1929, 'The immediate organisational tasks of the militant trade unions in the Far East' listed one of the greatest weaknesses of the left-wing trade unions in the Far East as 'the organisation of the unorganised, particularly women, juvenile, plantation and agricultural workers . . .'.

48 This party was inspired, as its name suggests, by the Chinese Guomindang.

49 RC 495, 201, 35, p. 7; 'Ly-lich Fan-Lan'.

50 AOM, SPCE 385, confidential note n. 1568, Hue, 27 August 1930.

51 Nguyet Tu, *Chi Minh Khai*, pp. 43–49.

52 AOM, SPCE 368, Reference sheet no. 8752, 30 July 1931.

53 RC, 495, 154, 569; letter to 'Dear Friend', 12 January 1931.

54 AOM, SPCE 367, letter from Victor, 12 February 1931.

55 RC, 495, 154, 688, p. 14, letter from Overseas Bureau to Moscow, 31 March 1935.

Women in the early Vietnamese communist movement   157

56 RC, 495, 201, 35, 'Ankieta' [Questionnaire] dated 14 December 1934.
57 We had earlier seen that Nguyen Tri Duc was arrested a short time later, in June 1931, in Shanghai.
58 RC, 495, 201, 35, 'Ly-lich Fan-Lan'.
59 They may have received this impression from AOM, SPCE 367, Declaration of Truong Phuoc Dat, p. 51, where Dat claims that Tranh Ngoc Danh suspected him of 'fancying his mistress, Co Duy' (one of Minh Khai's aliases at that time).
60 AOM, SPCE 367, Statement of Truong Phuoc Dat, p. 53.
61 AOM, SPCE 367, Declaration of Le Van Phan [Le Hong Son], p. 45.
62 RC, 495, 201, 35, 'Ly-lich Fan-Lan', p. 8.
63 AOM, SPCE 385, Envoi no. 92 of 21 April 1933, Translation of three letters in quoc-ngu [romanised Vietnamese script] ... sent from Hong Kong on 31 March by Nguyen Thi Minh Khai, alias Truong Minh, alias Co Duy.
64 Cited in Marr, *Vietnamese Tradition on Trial*, p. 210.
65 AOM, SPCE 367, Statements of Truong Phuoc Dat to the Sûreté Générale, 22 May 1933 and following day.
66 AOM, SPCE 385, Envoi no. 92 of 21 April 1933 of Service de Renseignements [Intelligence service], Shanghai; translation of two letters in quoc-ngu sent from Hong Kong, 7 February 1933 by Nguyen Thi Minh Khai to Nanjing.
67 AOM, SPCE 385, letter from Debord in Hanoi to Cross, 19 November 1933.
68 RC, 495, 201, 35, 'Ly-lich Fan-Lan', pp. 8–8b.
69 RC, 495, 154, 688, p. 14.
70 Nguyet Tu, *Chi Minh Khai*, p. 60.
71 AOM, SPCE 385, Sûreté cable from Hue to Saigon, 16 October 1939 referred to her as the wife of Le Hong Phong; a letter from Hanoi to Langson, 9 June 1940, referred to her as his concubine.
72 RC, 494, 1, 379, p. 47.
73 RC, 532, 1, 386, notes on students, 26 June 1935.
74 RC, 495, 201, 35, *Ankieta* for Fan-Lan, 14 December 1934; written across the top are the words, 'Left for her country 2 February 1937'.
75 In one conversation with a specialist on Vietnamese communist history, I was told that Minh Khai 'couldn't write'.
76 RC, 495, 10a, 140, pp. 23–27, French translation of letter of 10 September 1937, which in the Vietnamese original is signed 'F. L.'. Ha Huy Tap describes the transfer of the Central Committee to Saigon in 495, 10a, 140, p. 33; letter written in approximately September 1937, signed 'Sinitchkin'.
77 AOM, SPCE 385, n. 5819-S, Saigon, 6 September 1937, describes her two meetings with Maurice Honel; or biography written 29 August 1941, after her execution.
78 RC, 495, 10a, 140, pp. 23–27 (references taken from the French translation of the letter).
79 AOM, SPCE 384, Confidential note n. 144-ss; Hue, 14 April 1938.
80 Marr, *Vietnamese Tradition on Trial*, p. 238, makes this suggestion.
81 Nguyet Tu, *Chi Minh Khai*, p. 99.
82 RC, 495, 10a, 140, p. 102.
83 AOM, SPCE 385, from French translation of a letter seized during a search made on 21 April 1940 of the home of Nguyen Van Cho, Hoc Mon, Gia Dinh. A photostat of the Vietnamese original is in the file, along with the translation.
84 Nguyet Tu, *Chi Minh Khai*, p. 112, gives the date of her daughter's birth as the start of 1940; other sources give the date as the spring of 1939, for example, *Nhung Nguoi Cong San* [The Communists], p. 223.
85 AOM, SPCE 385, note of May 1940 on 'Activités communistes, arrestation d'agitateurs'.
86 Nguyen Khac Vien, 'Confucianisme et Marxisme au Vietnam', in his *Expériences vietnamiennes* (Paris: Editions Sociales, 1970), p. 226.

8 Recruiting the all-female Rani of Jhansi Regiment

Subhas Chandra Bose and Dr Lakshmi Swaminadhan[1]

Frederik Rettig

In the middle of 1940, a twenty-five-year-old medical doctor from an elite family in Madras, Dr Lakshmi Swaminadhan, arrived in Singapore to set up a clinic with her doctor friend, 'K'. Although an unconventional, if not scandalous move, it gave her the opportunity to not only leave behind the social stigma of separation from her traditionalist husband, an airplane pilot, but also to rebuild her life and her professional career. Little did she know that her stay in the multi-ethnic and cosmopolitan, but politically rather placid, port city of Singapore would also allow her to connect with a more assertive and masculine Indian nationalism that she had first encountered as a fourteen-year-old girl, when she had first seen 'the rebel and *enfant terrible* of the Congress', Subhas Chandra Bose (23 January 1897–18 August 1945).[2]

Less than one year after the fall of Singapore to the Japanese, the firebrand Bengali politician and Indian nationalist leader, who repudiated Gandhian non-violence and also envisaged a far more active social and political role for women, was headed east. Subhas Chandra Bose's long submarine journey from the naval port of Kiel in northern Germany to the Japanese Imperial Navy's offshore outpost of Sabang just north of Aceh gave him ample time to meticulously prepare the blueprint for the mission that would occupy the last two and a half years of his life.[3] The former president of the Indian Congress (1938–1939) had been identified as the only credible leader to resuscitate the fledgling Indian National Army (INA), composed of former Indian prisoners of war from the defeated British forces in Singapore, and the Indian Independence League (IIL).[4] From at least late May 1942, Bose had sought out ways to leave Berlin for Asia because he realised that his best chances to end the British Raj – following Germany's defeat at Stalingrad on 2 February and the successful Japanese onslaught on Southeast Asia, including the surrender of Singapore on 15 February 1942 – now lay in Southeast and East Asia rather than in Germany.[5] In contrast to Germany, where he had managed to raise a 4,000-strong Indian Legion largely recruited from Indian soldiers captured in North Africa, he would be much closer to India if based in Singapore or even Rangoon.[6] Closer proximity aside, he could expect to resuscitate the INA and the IIL by mobilising the

Indian communities in Southeast Asia for the liberation of India.[7] Bose's ambitious blueprint for 'total mobilisation' therefore also included the creation of an all-female regiment, the Rani of Jhansi Regiment, which was in line with his earlier activism and politics.

This chapter will take the reader through the early months of the Rani of Jhansi Regiment, from its blueprint on to the early stages of its conception, including a twenty-woman strong guard of honour in Singapore on 12 July 1943, Bose's appointment one day later of Dr Lakshmi Swaminadhan to develop this nucleus into a proper regiment, and the initial growth of this rump unit to nearly hundred women by the end of August.[8] It also discusses Bose's rallies in Malaya that brought in additional commitments to join the regiment, including first-person accounts by two future 'Ranis'. The paper argues that Dr Lakshmi's tour of the Malayan mainland in September 1943 was crucial in convincing the many female volunteers, and also their parents if they were teenagers, that the regiment was for real.

As the INA and its Rani of Jhansi Regiment left barely any significant shred of paper trail,[9] I will therefore draw on autobiographies, interviews, and secondary literature to provide the first article-length account of the recruitment and constitution of the Rani of Jhansi Regiment. In particular, I refer to the autobiography of Dr Lakshmi Sahgal (née Swaminadhan) because her uncontested leadership position right from the start provided her with a unique overview of the regiment's constitution.[10] To a lesser extent, I draw also on the autobiographical chapter of one of her recruits, Rasammah Bhupalan (née Navarednam), and the recollections of Janaki Athi Nahappan (née Davar).[11]

Subhas Chandra Bose's conception of the regiment and identification of a suitable role model

From the start of his active political career in the 1920s, Bose appealed to women to make it their duty to look after the nation and not just their families, and he also encouraged them to 'boycott foreign cloths, carry on propaganda among women and organise' 'women's societies'.[12] In 1928, he organised a 300-strong women's section of the Bengali Volunteers who would parade in the streets of Calcutta on the occasion of the Indian Congress' gathering in the city.[13] This was an early prototype of the Rani of Jhansi Regiment, as evident in the section leader being referred to as 'Colonel Latika', even though the female volunteers marched unarmed and dressed in saris.[14] The women volunteers also served as a nucleus for a 'loose network' of young Bengali women revolutionaries, to the extent that Bose was, according to Geraldine Forbes, 'considered by many [of them] as Bengal's champion of women's rights.'[15]

In contrast to the female section of the Bengali Volunteers, Bose chose to give the regiment a suitable name that would allow for easy identification while also not being too controversial or radical. Lakshmibai, the Rani

160   *Frederik Rettig*

(Queen) of the princely state of Jhansi (c. 1828–1858), fitted his needs.[16] She had led her subjects against the British during the 1857–1858 Indian Rebellion (or Indian Mutiny) and following her death in battle had become the folk heroine of what not only Bose would later refer to as the First Indian War of Independence. Her fate, as the widowed and child-less caretaker of her late husband's interests and his adopted son, symbolised to many Indians the injustice of Company rule as the Governor-General used circumstances such as hers in order to swallow additional territories by means of the doctrine of lapse. The Rani had first defended her traditional rights by means of law and diplomacy, but the onset and then the spread of the Indian Mutiny to her territory created a situation in which it was difficult not to take sides. After insurgents massacred Company officials and their families, whose evacuation from Jhansi they had asked her to protect, she was accused of siding with the rebels. Having shown an inclination for the martial arts from young, Rani Lakshmibai organised a last stand against the British at Gwalior, personally led her military force into battle, and on 17 June 1858 died on the battlefield.

Rani Lakshmibai's exploits were immortalised in poems, literature, and the visual arts. She also cut a martial figure in representations showing her on horseback, sword and shield in hand, riding into battle. Other representations showed the horse-riding Rani with her adopted son bundled on her back and thus even further stressed her femininity and nurturing side. Moreover, her anti-colonialism could easily be given a subcontinental, nationalistic meaning that would appeal to twentieth-century audiences. Hers was a good story to tell and had the potential to appeal not only to women but also to men, not least because Lakshmibai also upheld the rights of her late husband and their adopted son. Importantly, the Rani was from the subcontinent's heartlands and Bose was always watchful about not being seen as partial to any one region, in particular not his native Bengal. She also created a link between the First Indian War of Independence and the Second War of Indian Independence that Bose was waging. Finally, the youth of the Rani was palpable, which most certainly must have appealed to the many young girls and women whom he sought to attract.

On the third day after his arrival in Singapore, Bose addressed the remaining 12,000 soldiers of the first INA at the Singapore Padang, the green playing field located between the town's imposing Municipal Building and the Straits of Malacca, in the late morning of Monday 5 July 1943.[17] Civilians attended too, including Dr Lakshminadhan, a twenty-eight-year-old medical doctor and member of the women's section of the IIL, who would become his most trusted female lieutenant. Appearing for the first time in military clothing, Dr Lakshmi recalls that Bose was announced as the Supreme Commander of the INA, and then addressed his audience, arguing that 'the final victory could only come through armed struggle' in the 'final and most crucial stage' of the Indian independence struggle.[18] When he asked for the consent of all INA soldiers and Southeast Asian civilians to follow his ambitious programme, he connected directly as 'the entire audience stood up, the jawans [soldiers] lifted their rifles above their heads and the civilians roared their consent'.[19] Continuing to work the crowd, Bose stressed that he 'wanted a total mobilisation of manpower and all the resources of the Indians in S.E.A.' The participation of Indian civilians was vital because 'he wanted the INA to be an absolutely independent army' and therefore recruitment for 'all physically fit Indians [...] would start immediately'.[20]

Bose then 'dropped a bombshell' when '[h]e said the Army of Liberation would be incomplete unless women also came forward and volunteered for the fighting ranks. It was his desire to raise a women's regiment called the Rani of Jhansi Regiment after Rani Laxmi Bai of Jhansi who fought so valiantly against the British in 1857 [sic]'.[21] For Lakshmi, 'this was the highlight of his speech' even though '[m]ost of the others felt it could never be done'.[22]

On Friday 9 July, at a mass rally that brought together 60,000 civilians,[23] Bose again stressed the importance of having male and female civilians joining the INA. If the INA remained made up of *jawans* and officers, then it would be easy for the British to depict this 'token force of ex-Indian army personnel' as Japanese 'stooges'.[24] 'Therefore', in the words of Lakshmi, 'if it was to be a true Indian National Army, every physically fit Indian should enlist. Above all, the Rani of Jhansi Regiment must be raised to dispel all talk of the INA being a puppet army. He stressed the need for this over and over again'.[25]

Creating the nucleus of the regiment: Bose and Lakshmi as proselytisers

Bose would find his twentieth-century reincarnation of Rani Lakshmibai in a twenty-eight-year-old medical doctor, Dr Lakshmi Swaminadhan (1914–2012). Born in Madras (today's Chennai, Tamil Nadu) on 24 October 1914 into an unconventional family, including an independent-minded and politically active mother, very much open to Western ideas but also critical of British imperialism,[26] Lakshmi arrived in Singapore in the middle of 1940 and was one of the few India-born women of the regiment. Her political engagement in the Singapore branch of the IIL, her privileged background that included playing sports and driving cars, her position as a gynaecologist and obstetrician whose client base included Indian migrants in Singapore, her knowledge of Tamil and Malayalam, and her tending to prisoners of war following the British debacle made her a natural choice for a leadership position, even if this meant breaking off her relationship with her doctor friend, 'K', whom she had followed to Singapore. Bose made her the commander of the Regiment and a few months later, on 21 October 1943, appointed her as the Minister in Charge of Women's Organisation of the Provisional Government of Azad Hind (Free India).

162 *Frederik Rettig*

Lakshmi had been part of the reception committee that waited for Bose's arrival in Singapore at Paya Lebar Airport on Saturday 3 July.[27] As a fourteen-year-old girl, she had first seen Bose when she 'had gone to watch the Congress volunteers doing their parade under him', but this time he was in command for real.[28] Having attended the 4 July ceremony in the Cathay building, where Bose formally took over from veteran revolutionary and IIL leader Rash Behari Bose (no relation), Lakshmi also closely followed Bose's other public appearances. In particular his Friday 9 July address, in which he had repeatedly stressed the need to form the Rani of Jhansi Regiment, had left her unsettled:

> I spent a sleepless night after this rally as I kept thinking of a women's regiment, wondering if it could ever be done. So far I had found little enthusiasm among Indian women for the Independence movement. Women of the middle and lower classes were mostly conservative, almost feudal in their outlook. But I was not the only one who had spent a sleepless night over this problem.[29]

Indeed, '[e]arly next morning [she] was summoned by [Attavar] Yellappa', a Southern Indian barrister and chairman of the Singapore branch of the Indian Independence League.[30] Together they hatched a plan as to how to make the regiment come alive: Dr Lakshmi was to mobilise women for the IIL's women's rally to be held two days later, on Monday 12 July, with '[t]he highlight [being] a women's guard of honour that would present arms to Netaji'.[31] Finding enough volunteers was not easy but '[b]y searching the length and breadth of Singapore we managed to collect 20 women willing to be trained to present arms.'[32]

In the afternoon of the same day, the twenty women, still dressed in saris, assembled for three hours to 'be drilled into how to present arms with the heavy.303 [Enfield] rifles the INA had.'[33] Instructed 'by two experienced NCOs', the volunteers first learned about the different parts of the rifles and then underwent rigorous drilling into 'how to present arms'. A further three hours of rigorous drilling took place 'the next morning till our arms ached as never before.'[34] 'Nevertheless we were able to click our rifles smartly and present arms when Netaji arrived.'[35] The women's guard 'came as a complete and pleasant surprise' to Bose because '[t]his part of the programme had been kept secret from him'. As in the previous rallies, he stressed 'how he was only continuing with the Indian tradition of women fighting shoulder to shoulder with men in the independence struggle.'[36]

'[T]he nucleus of the Rani of Jhansi Regiment had [thus] been formed with these 20 women'.[37] The next day, Tuesday 13, IIL branch chairman 'Yellapa came over and said that Netaji wanted to meet me and discuss details regarding the Rani of Jhansi Regiment'.[38] Lakshmi 'was thrilled at the honour but also slightly apprehensive because I knew that I would now have to make a complete break with my old life', because it would most likely mean breaking up with 'K', with whom she operated the clinic in Geylang

Recruiting the all-female Rani of Jhansi Regiment 163

and a more recently opened one in the centre, 'and embrace [a life] of adventure and danger.'[39] 'However', she 'had been waiting for just such an involvement so I brushed aside all my fears.'[40]

In the evening, Lakshmi went to Bose's official residence in Meyer Road, a massive two-storey beach-front building on Singapore's east coast, for an informal interview 'that went on for three hours'.[41] Bose said that 'he had great faith in women and felt that, given the opportunity, there was nothing they were not capable of doing.' Indeed, 'men and women were two equal halves of a whole.'[42] Therefore '[h]e believed that in the fight for independence women should not remain spectators', and instead they 'should play a positive role'. The benefits for women to play such a role were twofold as Bose linked the liberation of India with the 'end [of] our own oppression and subjugation by men.' This was because '[w]e would be in a position to demand and obtain equal rights and no longer be the exploited sex.'[43] Bose appears to have done most of the talking, also warning Dr Lakshmi 'of the dangers ahead' and eventually 'asked me if I would be prepared to take up the command of the Rani Jhansi [sic] Regiment', upon which '[I] gave him my unconditional support.'[44] The interview concluded with Bose 'telling me that I should start my duties the next day. I would be given an office at headquarters and from there I should start planning the raising of the Rani Jhansi Regiment.'[45] Thus began the multiplication of the Ranis.

Multiplying the Ranis

'The next morning, [Wednesday] 14 July, 1943, at 8 a.m., I found a staff car at my door to take me to the office.'[46] It is interesting that Dr Lakshmi mentions, unlike probably most autobiographers, that '[o]nce I got there, I did not know what to do next!', but this admission also accentuates the 'usual thoughtfulness' of 'Netaji' in the next sentence who 'sent [her] his personal secretary, Abid Hassan, to discuss matters.' Following the advice of Bose's trusted lieutenant, Dr Lakshmi started the project of producing Ranis by 'visiting the homes' of 'the women who had taken part in the guard of honour'. With some disappointment she notes that '[o]nly 15 of the 20 volunteered to join; the others were prevented from doing so either because they had small children or dependents whom they had to support by working full time. They were most disappointed.'[47]

With no training ground of their own yet, 'the fifteen recruits [...] started part-time training in a maidan[48] within the Indian Independence League grounds' 'for a few hours each afternoon', with Dr Lakshmi joining whenever she could.[49] The 'instructors were specially selected by Netaji who impressed upon them the need for enforcing military discipline without the help of barrack-room language or corporal punishment.'[50] They lived up to Bose's high expectations and made the volunteers feel welcome by accepting them as 'a part of the Indian National Army'; they were also the ones who started referring to the women as the 'Ranis'.[51]

164 *Frederik Rettig*

Throughout the rest of 'July and August', Lakshmi's 'time was taken up with military training and organising the women's section at headquarters', while the initial number of fifteen Ranis 'had grown to nearly a hundred and there were many more applications from girls on the [Malayan] mainland.'[52] The increasing number of Ranis and the prospect of getting even more from Malaya necessitated finding 'adequate grounds to house the regiment', but in the absence of Bose, the Japanese 'were most un-cooperative almost to the extent of obstructing my work'.[53] Indeed, Bose had gone on a fundraising tour for he needed the financial, political, and manpower support of the Indian communities in Southeast and East Asia in order to make the INA less dependent on the Japanese and also to show the Provisional Government of India that he was working towards a popular base.[54]

In fact, the incoming applications to join the Rani of Jhansi Regiment were at least partially due to Bose's touring of the region. Broadcasts, newspapers, and the local branches of the IIL announced his arrival and created a sense of expectation, while the rallies and his speeches left such a strong impact that people would volunteer themselves or their possessions for the liberation of India. In Kuala Lumpur, eighteen-year-old Janaki Davar, whose father had become a successful dairy farm owner since migration from Southern India in 1911, had read about Bose's call for the formation of a women's regiment in Bose's 'English-language newspaper'.[55] The day of Bose's widely announced appearance in Kuala Lumpur, knowing that her mother would forbid it, she 'made [the cook] cover for me, got out my bicycle, and went' to attend the rally at the *padang* of the Selangor Club (today's Merdeka Square).[56] Leaving her bicycle in a ditch, Janaki 'walked to the platform where Bose was speaking.'[57] She was so moved by Bose's speech 'in Hindustani and also in English' and his appeal to fight for the liberty of India that 'the feeling grew in me that I must join.'[58]

Bose called for the offering of 'money, jewelry, anything they had', and Janaki did not hesitate and 'went up, took off the earrings I was wearing, and put them into his hand.'[59] A 'cameraman' was there who 'took a picture of me doing this.'[60] Not knowing how to tell her parents about the 'loss' of her two earrings she stole her way back home by skipping family dinner and went to bed on an empty stomach. The next morning, at breakfast, Janaki found her father hidden behind the newspaper with last night's photograph facing her, but it was her older sister Papathi who could not help but excitedly draw her mother's attention to it. Janaki's mother was very angry and wanted to hit her, whereas her father was more 'broadminded'.[61]

About hundred miles north of Kuala Lumpur, Bose also left an indelible mark on many of those who witnessed his rally in Ipoh at the *padang* of the Ipoh Club.[62] Among those who attended was the entire family of Nancy Navarednam, a Christian widowed school teacher in British service who lived in government property in Ipoh's Green Town area and whose background suggested that she would be opposed to Bose's call to liberate India from the British. She was consequently shocked when her two youngest

Recruiting the all-female Rani of Jhansi Regiment 165

daughters, Ponnammah Ruth (b. 1925) and Rasammah Naomi (b. 1927), both of them roused by Bose's 'passionate appeal for volunteers', wanted to join the Rani of Jhansi Regiment.[63] 'We regarded our sacrifices to be far more important for India than our sheltered lives.'[64] Despite imploring their mother for weeks for permission, Mrs Navarednam was 'aghast' and 'not even slightly inclined into permitting her two youngest children to join the Regiment'. Rasammah notes that the situation was not different for other female volunteers because '[i]n each and every case there was strong opposition from the parents and relatives' for whom '[i]t was too shocking that young people – girls and women in particular, should leave the safe confines of their homes [...] in this our war for the freedom of India.'[65]

Dr Lakshmi harvests volunteers

While Bose had clearly planted the seeds for the Rani of Jhansi Regiment during his tour of the Malayan Peninsula, Lakshmi would play a crucial role in reaping the harvest of those women and girls who had declared their commitment to join the regiment. While making them donate their jewellery was relatively easy, enticing them to volunteer was already more difficult, and actually making them leave behind their previous lives as daughters, wives, and mothers was a real challenge, in particular if parental consent was required. This necessitated a more institutionalised effort and door-to-door follow-up as Lakshmi had already practised in Singapore when she mobilised the female guard-of-honour on 12 July and the first hundred or so women after she had been formally put in charge by Bose.

Hence during the month of September, Lakshmi went up to Kuala Lumpur, Penang, and Ipoh in order to 'convince all those who had volunteered that we meant business and that a camp would be started as soon as Netaji [had] returned' to Singapore.[66] She even made house visits to convince concerned parents to put their young daughters under her command.[67] This attention to detail and her perseverance, coupled with her experience of house visits as a doctor and her particular personality, allowed her to 'g[e]t some of my most outstanding recruits who later became officers in the Regiment.'[68]

In Kuala Lumpur, Janaki Davar used the opportunity of Lakshmi's presence to persuade her father, who had a friend at the local IIL office, to invite her to tea.[69] Lakshmi accepted Rengasamy Davar's invitation and left him 'terribly impressed'. Fearing that her father might change his mind later, Janaki immediately asked him to provide his parental consent on the 'application form' that she had already filled out.[70] As Davar was an important member of the Indian community in Kuala Lumpur, Janaki suggests that the paternal approval made it easier for other girls 'to go too'. In Kuala Lumpur, [albeit in early October] Lakshmi also won over a Mrs Satyavati Thevar, 'who was in her early forties and had been headmistress of a girls school', 'to join me as a second-in-command' (Figure 8.1).[71]

Figure 8.1 Mrs Satyavati Thevar (centre left) in front of Rani nurses and soldiers on a photograph that is less heroically choreographed than the others. Representing a slightly more casual moment, as though the photographer was familiar with at least some of those present, including the Japanese officer (or interpreter?), it does not feature Subhas Chandra Bose and Captain Lakshmi. The photo is notable also for showing the nurses side by side with the soldier Ranis. First row on the right, closest to the photographer, should be Janaki Davar, who would eventually be assigned a nursing role in Burma, where she would encounter the horrors of war in an INA-run military hospital.

Source: Puan Sri Datin J. Athi Nahappan Collection, courtesy of National Archives of Singapore.

In Ipoh, she won over 'the Navaratnam sisters, Ponnamma and Rosamma, and also Mrs. Blanche Thevar and Mrs. Das.'[72] Rasammah notes that it was '[a]fter the meeting with this vibrant, dynamic, dedicated leader' that the 'families who were opposed to their daughters being recruited' finally 'were persuaded to release their young fledglings.'[73] Even then, Rasammah's and Ponnammah's four older 'brothers and sisters continued to dissuade us' and their mother was 'torn', all contributing to a 'painful, agonising anxiety' that starkly contrasted with the two sisters' 'exuberant enthusiasm'. What really made a difference during the long weeks prior to departure for Singapore was that the 'parents of girls who were also to join the Regiment did meet on a few occasions and in a real sense this reinforced them in a profoundly positive manner'. Of equal importance was the 'on-going information on the plans for the INA from the bulletins and media', which 'helped dispel doubts and parents were convinced that the call for the freedom of India did demand sacrifice and this they were willing to accept' (Figure 8.2).[74]

Figure 8.2 Captain Lakshmi seated in full uniform surrounded by Indian girls and young women. The location and date are not known, but it could well have been during her recruitment trip to Kuala Lumpur, perhaps even in front of Janaki Davar's father's house, with Janaki seated to her right, still with long braids.

Source: Puan Sri Datin J Athi Nahappan Collection, courtesy of National Archives of Singapore.

Conclusion

When Subhas Chandra Bose formally opened the Rani of Jhansi Camp in Singapore's Waterloo Street on 22 October 1943, he had realised a dream that arguably dated back at least to the Calcutta Congress of 1928 and the women's section of the Bengali Volunteers.[75] In Dr Lakshmi Swaminadhan, recently promoted to Captain Lakshmi, he had found an outstanding leader who had not only assembled the first twenty women to stand guard of honour on 12 July but who, since her appointment on 13 July, had tirelessly worked to increase the initial nucleus to 156 women, and also built up the Rani of Jhansi Camp to accommodate up to 500 recruits.[76]

Together they had formed a formidable team. While Lakshmi was busy in Singapore expanding the initial nucleus of fifteen women to nearly hundred who were training part-time, Bose's touring of the mainland had roused in many more girls and women a desire to step forward in order to participate in the liberation of India, even though most of them had never set foot on Indian soil. Yet again it was Lakshmi's September tour of the mainland that proved crucial in this because it convinced anxious parents to sign the parental consent form and convinced others that the Rani of Jhansi Regiment

168   *Frederik Rettig*

was set on fulfilling its aims. This marked a radical departure from the past when Indian migrant fathers and husbands had called for the womenfolk to follow them to their overseas places of work, whereas now it was girls and women asking for permission to leave their families for the sake of a larger cause.

The Ranis that Bose and Captain Lakshmi, who was walking to his right, were inspecting that evening also matched his ideals of a more egalitarian and non-communal India: one where merit rather than ethnicity, religion, class, caste, language, or gender were key and in which communal differences could be overcome by training, eating, and living together. The momentum had to be sustained by providing full-time training as Bose must have been aware that the tides of war were tilting against his ambitious plan to invade India. On 30 March 1944, Dr Lakshmi's 'proudest day', the regiment's first passing-out parade celebrated the first batch of officers in Singapore.[77] The first Ranis from the Singapore camp, including Janaki and Papathi Davar from Kuala Lumpur and Rasammah and Ponnammah Navarednam from Ipoh, were soon on their way to Burma via the infamous Death Railway.

Acknowledgement

Thanks to various research assistants who have helped me over the years: the late Joanne Karen Chen, the late Rajan Rishyakaran, Adrian Cheng Sai Pong, Sugumaran Devaraja, Yeo Shan Hui, Surekha Ahgir Yadav, Sukanto Lacson Chanda, Siddarth Poddar, Sonika Kaur Dhaliwal, and Teo Kay Key. Thanks are due also to the Singapore Management University's Research Grant for financial support and in particular its late director, Professor Winston Koh, for encouraging me to leave early 1930s French Indochina behind to engage in 'more contemporary' research. I am most grateful to Rasammah Bhupalan and the late Janaki Athi Nahappan (1925–2014) for sharing their insights on their experiences in the RJR, Mr Poonampalan for sharing his experience in the INA, and to S. R. Nathan for confirming the location of the Singapore camp of the RJR. I am also very grateful to Mr Kesavapany, to Nilanjana Sengupta, Kevin Blackburn, Karl Hack, Vera Ingrid Hildebrand, and the Indian High Commission for their interest, invitations to events, or for sharing information. Finally, I am grateful to IP Publishing's director, John Edmondson, for his kind permission to have my *South East Asia Research* article published here in slightly different form.

Notes

1   This chapter was first published in a slightly different form. See Tobias Rettig, 'Recruiting the All-Female Rani of Jhansi Regiment: Subhas Chandra Bose and Dr Lakshmi Swaminadhan', *South East Asia Research*, Vol. 21, No. 4 (November 2013), pp. 657–668.
2   Lakshmi Sahgal, *A Revolutionary Life: Memoirs of a Political Activist, with an introduction by Geraldine Forbes* (New Delhi: Kali for Women, 1997), pp. 48f.

Recruiting the all-female Rani of Jhansi Regiment 169

3 The voyage, which began on 9 February and ended on 6 May 1943, with a change from a German to a Japanese submarine some 'four hundred nautical miles off the coast of Madagascar' on 28 April, is covered in Sugata Bose, *His Majesty's Opponent: Subhas Chandra Bose and India's Struggle against Empire* (Cambridge, MA: The Belknap Press of Harvard University Press, 2011), pp. 232–236.

4 The first INA had initially comprised about 16,000 Indian Prisoners of War and could have had up to 40,000 if not for Japanese unwillingness to provide more weapons. Tensions between its then leader, Captain Mohan Singh and the Japanese, but also internal tensions in the INA and uncertainties about the suitability of the leader of the IIL, the Bengali revolutionary Rash Behari Bose (1886–1945; no relation to Subhas), had led to a crisis at the end of 1942 and reduced the first INA to about 12,000 men. For a very good discussion of the most likely number, see Peter Ward Fay, *The Forgotten Army: India's Armed Struggle for Independence, 1942–1945* (Ann Arbor, MI: University of Michigan Press, 1993), pp. 525f. Following Subhas Chandra Bose's arrival in Southeast Asia in early July 1943, an additional 8,000–10,000 'ex-Indian Army men' and '18,000 Indian civilians' joined the second INA.

5 Bose, *His Majesty's Opponent*, pp. 213, 219; Joyce Chapman Lebra, *The Indian National Army and Japan* (Singapore: ISEAS, 2008) [reprint of *Jungle Alliance: Japan and the Indian National Army* (Singapore: Donald Moore, 1971)], pp. 110–112.

6 Bose had thus managed to recruit fewer than 25% of the 'nearly [17,000] Indian [POWs] in German and Italian captivity' for his Indian Legion; see Bose, *His Majesty's Opponent*, p. 210; Africa: Lebra, *The Indian National Army and Japan*, p. 109. She writes that 'approximately' 3,000 POWs joined.

7 In contrast to the civilian Indian population in Europe, which was negligible, one secondary source estimates the Indians in Southeast Asia to be 1.5 to two million, of which about one million were in Burma alone; see Leonard A. Gordon, *Brothers against the Raj: A Biography of Indian Nationalists Sarat and Subhas Chandra Bose* (New York: Columbia University Press, 1990), p. 465. Bose, *His Majesty's Opponent*, pp. 247f., estimates the numbers of the most important Indian communities in the region in mid-1943 as 'nearly a million' for Malaya, 'some [800,000]' for Burma, and 'about [60,000]' for Thailand.

8 Less is known about the Rangoon side of the Rani of Jhansi Regiment. A very brief overview is provided by Joyce Chapman Lebra, *Women Against the Raj: The Rani of Jhansi Regiment* (Singapore: ISEAS, 2008), pp. 81f. Even less is known about a camp in Bangkok, which is usually mentioned in one single sentence. See e.g. Geraldine Forbes, 'Introduction', in Sahgal, *A Revolutionary Life*, p. xxi; and Amritlal Seth, *Jai-Hind: The Diary of a Rebel Daughter of India with the Rani of Jhansi Regiment* (Bombay: Relief Fund for Families of the Azad Hind Fauj Soldiers, Janmabhoomi Prakashan Mandir, 1946), p. 68. For a more recent and in-depth treatment of Bose and the Rani of Jhansi Regiment, see Vera Hildebrand, *Women at War: Subhas Chandra Bose and the Rani of Jhansi Regiment* (Noida, Uttar Pradesh: HarperCollins India, 2016).

9 See the excellent discussion of the 'beggarly' state of sources in Fay, *The Forgotten Army*, pp. 553–563.

10 Sahgal, *A Revolutionary Life*. Ritu Menon's preface suggests that the autobiography was 'originally written in the late 1960s' (p. vi) at the request of 'Comrade E.M.S. Namboodiripad' (p. vii), with translations into Malayalam and Hindi. As Peter Ward Fay had started interviewing Dr Lakshmi Sahgal and her husband, Prem Kumar Sahgal (1917–1992), who had served as Bose's military secretary, in the mid-1960s, it is quite conceivable that his interviews and follow-up questions are also related to this first manuscript; see Fay, *The Forgotten Army*, pp. viii–ix, 559–560. In fact, Fay (p. 526) refers to an undated, privately printed

170   *Frederik Rettig*

'little book', given to him by Dr Sahgal's younger sister, Mrinalini, but he fails to mention when he received it.

11 Mrs Bhupalan's autobiographical chapter forms part of her biography by Aruna Gopinath, *Footprints on the Sands of Time: Rasammah Bhupalan: A Life of Purpose* (Kuala Lumpur: Arkib Negara Malaysia, 2007). The entire chapter of 56 pages, 'The Rani of Jhansi Regiment: A Will for Freedom' (pp. 49–104) is written in the autobiographical 'I' form, whereas the rest of the book (with the exception of a five-page section on 'My Family My Anchor', pp. 463–467) is in the biographical third person based on Gopinath's interviews with Rasammah over a two-year period from 2003 to 2005; see p. 503. Interview with Rasammah Bhupalan, August 2011, Kuala Lumpur. See Gopinath, *Footprints on the Sands of Time*, pp. 141f., 147f. She has a B.A. in History (Honours) from the University of Malaya and embarked on a postgraduate degree at the University of London's School of Oriental and African Studies (SOAS) that was cut short because of severe asthma problems.

12 Nilanjana Sengupta, *A Gentleman's Word: The Legacy of Subhas Chandra Bose in Southeast Asia* (Singapore: ISEAS, 2012), p. 23.

13 Ibid., pp. 23f.

14 Ibid., p. 24. Latika Ghosh, Sri Aurobindo's niece.

15 Ibid., p. 24; Sengupta directly cites from Geraldine H. Forbes, 'The Women Revolutionaries of Bengal', *The Oracle*, Vol. 2, No. 2 (1980), p. 7.

16 Lebra, *Women Against the Raj*, pp. 1–9 [Chapter 1, 'The Historical Rani'] provides a good overview. Her book-length study provides more depth and context; see Joyce Chapman Lebra, *The Rani of Jhansi: A Study in Female Heroism in India* (Honolulu, HI: University of Hawaii Press, 1986).

17 Bose, *His Majesty's Opponent*, pp. 4, 245. Land reclamations have since pushed the sea shore considerably further away, whereas the Municipal Building became City Hall in 1951. After a major overhaul and integration with the former Supreme Court, the new complex was renamed as the National Gallery Singapore in 2015.

18 Sahgal, *A Revolutionary Life*, p. 53. This section follows Lakshmi's narrative of events and her recollection of Bose's address.

19 Ibid., pp. 53f.

20 Ibid., p. 54.

21 Ibid.

22 Ibid. NB: the Rani had fought against the British in 1858.

23 Bose, *His Majesty's Opponent*, p. 245.

24 Sahgal, *A Revolutionary Life*, p. 55.

25 Ibid.

26 For this paragraph, see Sahgal, *A Revolutionary Life*, pp. 1–9 (Chapter 1, entitled 'Childhood and Student Days') and pp. 11–28 (Chapter 2, 'In Singapore'). Also see Fay, *The Forgotten Army*, pp. 33–49 ('Lakshmi's Youth'), notably for 'K', p. 43, and also pp. 201, 218.

27 Sahgal, *A Revolutionary Life*, pp. 47f.

28 Ibid., pp. 48f. It is interesting that she does not mention the female section of the Bengali Volunteers.

29 Ibid., p. 55.

30 For 'Early next morning', see ibid.; for Yellappa's background, see Fay, *The Forgotten Army*, p. 201; 'Attavar': see Sengupta, *A Gentleman's Word*, p. 204.

31 Sahgal, *A Revolutionary Life*, pp. 55f. 'Netaji', a compound made of the noun *neta* (leader) and the honorific suffix *ji*, is the rough equivalent of the German *Führer* or the Italian *Duce*, but the suffix gives it a more endearing twist. Bose, *His Majesty's Opponent*, p. 209, notes that it was his paternal grand-uncle's

Recruiting the all-female Rani of Jhansi Regiment 171

followers in war-time Germany who had come up with this honorific title, which 'is a very Indian form of expressing affection mingled with honour.' The glossary in Fay, *The Forgotten Army*, p. 550, translates *netaji* as 'beloved and respected leader'. Unlike Hitler or Mussolini, Bose stood for liberation from imperial rule and also made it very clear what he thought of Hitler's racial policies.

32 Sahgal, *A Revolutionary Life*, p. 56. The 'we' refers to Mrs Chidambaram, the chairwoman of the IIL's women's section, see Fay, *The Forgotten Army*, p. 216.

33 Sahgal, *A Revolutionary Life*, p. 56. Enfield: see Lebra, *Women Against the Raj*, p. 72. The location of the drilling is not indicated.

34 Sahgal, *A Revolutionary Life*, p. 56.

35 Ibid. The guard of honour appears to have been staged in the Bras Basah Road area, with the women looking towards Stamford Road, Bras Basah Road behind their backs, with Waterloo Street (which at the time extended to Stamford Road) to their left, and the old Indian prison building at the corner of Bencoolen Street / Bras Basah Road slightly behind to their right. See first photo in Lebra, *Women Against the Raj*, in between pages xvi and 1.

36 Sahgal, *A Revolutionary Life*, p. 56.

37 Ibid., p. 57. It is interesting that Lakshmi's memoirs do not mention any of the Singapore recruits by name. This is in contrast with some of her top recruits from Malaya and Burma.

38 Ibid. According to Fay, *The Forgotten Army*, p. 217, it was John [Aloysius] Thivy who was sent by Bose to ask whether she was willing to lead the regiment, whereas Thivy and Yellappa had suggested her to him. Thivy was a London-trained lawyer, well-acquainted with Lakshmi's family in Madras, and practicing in Ipoh at the time of the Japanese onslaught on Malaya.

39 Sahgal, *A Revolutionary Life*, p. 57. Information on clinics and 'K' from Fay, *The Forgotten Army*, pp. 201, 218.

40 Sahgal, *A Revolutionary Life*, p. 57.

41 Ibid., pp. 57f. Due to land reclamations, today's Meyer Road is located a little more than half a mile from the East Coast. The bungalow has since given way to a condominium, the Atria at Meyer Road. For the latter, see Sengupta, *A Gentleman's Word*, photos between pp. 134 and 135. For a description of the 'handsome building', see Fay, *The Forgotten Army*, p. 217.

42 Sahgal, *A Revolutionary Life*, p. 57.

43 Ibid.

44 Ibid., pp. 57f.

45 Sahgal, *A Revolutionary Life*, p. 58.

46 Ibid.

47 Ibid.

48 A 'maidan' (from Urdu) is a multipurpose open field that can be used for meetings, sports, as a parade ground, market place or esplanade.

49 Sahgal, *A Revolutionary Life*, pp. 58f.; 'for a few hours...': Fay, *The Forgotten Army*, p. 218. Fay also suggests that training did not begin until Monday 19 July, by which time the number of volunteers had already increased to fifty. The IIL headquarters were at Chancery Lane; see Sengupta, *A Gentleman's Word*, photo between pages 134 and 135.

50 Sahgal, *A Revolutionary Life*, p. 58.

51 Ibid., pp. 58f. It is not clear from the sources whether this initial group of 'part-time' Ranis received the same 'basic training' as the 'full-time' Ranis who lived in the Rani of Jhansi Camp which was opened in late October. Likewise, it is unclear if the part-time Ranis, who were living at home, later moved into the camp.

52 Ibid., p. 59.

172   *Frederik Rettig*

53 Ibid.
54 Fay, *The Forgotten Army*, pp. 214f.
55 Ibid., p. 219. Janaki's account is Fay's reconstruction of an interview with Janaki Athi Nahappan in Calcutta of January 1989; see p. 585n6.
56 Ibid. 'Padang' is the Malay equivalent of 'maidan': an open, multi-purpose, field.
57 Ibid. Sengupta, *A Gentleman's Word*, p. 218, mentions that the speech was translated into Tamil.
58 Fay, *The Forgotten Army*, p. 219.
59 Ibid. Sengupta, *A Gentleman's Word*, p. 218, who interviewed Janaki in September 2011, mentions that Janaki also gave Bose her necklace.
60 Fay, *The Forgotten Army*, p. 219ff.
61 Ibid., p. 220.
62 Gopinath, *Footprints on the Sands of Time*, p. 62.
63 Ibid., pp. 46–47. Rasammah was the youngest of six children; see p. 17.
64 Ibid., p. 63.
65 Ibid., pp. 62f.
66 Sahgal, *A Revolutionary Life*, p. 59. It is not clear how many days she spent on the peninsula.
67 Lebra, *Women Against the Raj*, p. 76.
68 Sahgal, *A Revolutionary Life*, p. 59.
69 Fay, *The Forgotten Army*, p. 220.
70 Ibid.
71 Sahgal, *A Revolutionary Life*, p. 60; Satyavati: Sengupta, *A Gentleman's Word*, p. 212.
72 Sahgal, *A Revolutionary Life*, p. 60.
73 Gopinath, *Footprints on the Sands of Time*, p. 63.
74 Ibid.
75 The Rani of Jhansi camp occupied the playing field (*padang*) of the Saint Joseph's Institution (today's Singapore Arts Museum). This parcel of land, then situated between Bras Basah Road, Waterloo Street, the (now covered) Stamford Canal and Stamford Road, and Queen Street, has since made way for the library of the Singapore Management University (SMU) and parts of SMU's Campus Green. In the process, the final stretch of Waterloo Street has disappeared.
76 Fay, *The Forgotten Army*, p. 221.
77 Sahgal, *A Revolutionary Life*, p. 77.

9 Women guerrillas of the Communist Party of Malaya

Nationalist struggle with an internationalist experience

Agnes Khoo

Women redefining nationalism and nationalist struggles

How can women be nationalists when they do not have equal rights as men in their country? Yet, how can they not be nationalists when they love their country, people and home? Given that citizenship is a gendered experience and defined mostly by state and political powers that privilege male dominance, revolutionary women who fight for their emancipation, as well as that of their communities inevitably challenge their given-nationality or national identity that jars with their internationalist experiences and world-views. Hence, the words of Virginia Woolf ring true, in view of the lived experiences of the revolutionary women and former guerrillas of the Communist Party of Malaya (CPM), who are the focus of this chapter, '... as a woman, I have no country. As a woman I want no country. As a woman my country is the whole world.'[1]

Different variations of nationalism in anti-colonial struggles including the Malayan one have been defined as oppositional to mainly western colonialism. In the case of Malaysia and Singapore, independence from colonialism extended from resistance against British imperialism to fighting the Japanese invasion and occupation, and further, upon Japan's defeat that brought the end of World War II to Asia—a war against neo-colonialism. For women to relate to the wider liberation struggles against colonialism, neo-colonialism and imperialism in Malaysia and Singapore, they must be able to claim a national identity—however gendered this may be.[2] Nationalism and national identity are 'gendered' in so far as they are constructed through predominantly male experiences, male status hierarchies and male bonding. Moreover, it is often defined in masculine terms and understood from male perspectives. As a result, women have too often been rendered '... invisible in definitions of nationalism and in discussions of state and nationalism'[3] except in the common abstract exaltations of 'women as the mother of nation' or as 'widows of wars'—both identities being defined in relation to men.

Kumari Jayawardena argued that even though women may have contributed substantially to Third World nationalist movements, it is often the

174　*Agnes Khoo*

male nationalists who have the power to organise and set the parameters for these movements.[4] In contrast, Lois West believed that women can 'redefine feminism with nationalism and civil rights by redefining the private and public realms as not mutually exclusive and binary but as complementary and unitary.'[5] Conversely, women must be included in the definition of any nationalist discourse for it to be relevant to both women's public and private experiences. Women must be given the space to shape their nationalism based on both types of experiences so that they are not only reacting to the process of nation-building, but their agency is also included in it. In other words, women should be the embodiment of their own ethnic and national cultures so that their subjectivity is valued and respected and they are not relegated to serving only as cultural symbols of the nation.

Today, feminists have recognised that women are 'constituted as citizens *differently* than men.'[6] According to this view, women need to transcend the narrow confines of nation-states and reconstruct their consciousness both as women and as citizens through a larger sense of internationalism and global solidarity that places women's concerns and interests at the centre of any nationalist discourse, analysis and actions. This is the main purpose of my book, *Life as the River Flows: Women in the Malayan Anti-Colonial Struggle*, which presents sixteen life narratives of former women guerrillas of the CPM. In order to engage more specifically with their internationalist and gendered revolutionary experiences, this chapter will concentrate on three ethnically Chinese women who joined the Malayan Communist Party in their teens: Lin Mei (b. 1937), Lin Dong (b. 1944) and Cui Hong (b. 1949).[7]

The suppressed voices of internationalist revolutionaries of Malaya

If biographies and autobiographies—let alone oral histories—of male Southeast Asian anti-colonialists are few, then the life stories of their female counterparts are even scarcer.[8] In the case of Malayan history, which would later bifurcate into the post-independence national histories of Singapore and Malaysia, respectively, the resurgence of public interest in this particular historical period is very much related to the yearning for more radical and alternative interpretations, particularly among post-independence Malaysians and Singaporeans, of their national histories, as opposed to those sanctioned or propagated by the state.[9] Unfortunately, independent, alternative perspectives and narratives that potentially conflict with or counter the official, national 'meta-script', have remained by and large ignored, discouraged, refuted, and contested, if not suppressed outright by their governments.[10] The banning by the Singapore government of Tan Pin Pin's documentary, *To Singapore with Love* (2014) in the same year, which features Singaporeans in exile since more than half a century ago, is a case in point.

The Communist Party of Malaya's women guerrillas 175

This has resulted in tensions between the state-sanctioned and the grassroots versions, as well as the women's accounts of Malayan history.[11] National histories of Malaysia and Singapore remain until today, an 'unfinished business'. The extent to which competing or even contradicting versions of histories—specifically, the subaltern histories of the grassroots and from those without state power—are allowed to be discussed and debated on the national stage shall be the litmus test of the extent of democratisation the ruling elites are prepared to accommodate.

This chapter draws on three out of the sixteen women's narratives in my book, aimed at breaking the above-mentioned 'conspiracy of silence'.[12] It also reclaims these 'subaltern' women's voices in the 'national' and 'transnational' histories of Malaysia and Singapore, and further shows how they extend to Indonesia, the People's Republic of China, Northern Vietnam and Southern Thailand. It is an attempt, inspired by Helena Grice, to tell the 'personal and national stories through women's voices, which are fractured, and at times, evasive; in contrast to the men's 'authorised' and 'authoritative' narratives.[13] As men and women generally tell their stories differently, my chapter reflects how these women's oral histories tend to be characterised by the ever-going back-and-forth between the personal, the national and the international, on the one hand, and their subjective and objective experiences embedded in their narratives, on the other. This 'inextricability of personal and collective experience and identity' in the construction and interpretation of women's histories is especially pronounced.[14]

Hence, presenting the life stories of specifically female grassroots guerrillas of the CPM is in effect, an attempt to re-examine and re-evaluate the national histories of Malaysia and Singapore from both gender and subaltern perspectives. The very act of putting memories into words and words onto paper is to claim one's place in the collective memory of a nation, no matter how contested it maybe.[15] The possibility of transforming oral narratives into widely accessible printed words helps to preserve the extraordinariness of many ordinary women's lives. And it is precisely this affirmation of the 'little people's (women's) extra-ordinariness' that is empowering to a people and nation.[16]

Since no one life story can be told in isolation from the others, just as all national histories inevitably exist within the wider context of world events, this makes the narration of national history not only both 'complex and collective' but also by definition, global.[17] Thus, by telling the marginalised accounts of the communist women's role in the history of Malaysia and Singapore, as well as their trajectories in Indonesia, China, Hong Kong, Macau, Vietnam, Southern Thailand and even Europe, we are restoring the internationalist character of the movements and the women's involvement. Moreover, their role in the social-political movements has traversed a long historical period, embracing the highs and lows, as well as the good and the ugly of the colonial, anti-colonial, post-colonial times, right up to the end of the Cold War, thereby spanning from early 1930s to late 1980s.

Brief background on the Communist Party of Malaya (CPM)

The CPM was formed with the support of the Communist International (Comintern) or Third International, and it was formally established on 30 April 1930.[18] Nguyen Ai Quoc (the future Ho Chi Minh), then a 'Vietnamese' representative of the Comintern, attended its founding meeting. The CPM, by virtue of its considerable grassroots support, then led and directed a broad, anti-colonial liberation movement that comprised of a wide variety of political groupings and front organisations. It was not only a nationalistic movement but also an international one because it had to look beyond 'nascent local nationalism' in colonial Malaysia and Singapore for its survival and expansion.[19] The multi-racial, cultural, and religious characteristics of the people of Malaya, which comprise the Malays, Indians, Chinese, Eurasians and other ethnic minorities, as well as indigenous populations, compelled the CPM to reach out to non-Chinese communities whose networks extended overseas, including the Netherlands East Indies (present-day Indonesia), Ceylon (Sri Lanka) and the rest of the Indian subcontinent.[20] The CPM and its front organisations, although dominated by ethnic Chinese who were either migrants from different parts of mainland China or were of Chinese descent but born in Malaya, had always consisted of people from different racial, ethnic and country origins—migrants of whom some were radicalised by their past experiences from home, as well as their exposures to British colonialism and multi-culturalism in the Malay Peninsula and Singapore. Thus, as part of a broader anti-colonial movement worldwide, the party had always advocated the formation of an independent nation—*Malaya*—that would be multi-racial, multi-cultural and multi-lingual.[21]

Before and during World War II, the party had relied on widespread anti-Japanese sentiment—particularly among the Chinese diaspora—to expand and consolidate its constituency, which was by and large ideologically and culturally influenced by the anti-colonial and anti-imperialist movements against Japanese imperialism that were surging through mainland China at that time. Further, with respect to women's position in society, Malayan Chinese women did experience and benefit from the impact of the early women's liberation movement in China.[22] The same can be said of their Malay counterparts, many of whom were inspired by anti-colonialists in Indonesia who fought against Dutch colonialism and then Japanese occupation.

After World War II, many Asian societies including Malaysia and Singapore were in the midst of momentous and unprecedented change, socioculturally, economically and politically. Particularly in port cities like Penang, Malacca and Singapore, new popular cultures were created. A spectrum of radical ideas revolving around class, national identity, national sovereignty and women's emancipation began to be articulated.[23] All these had culminated into a national movement for independence from the British, on the one hand, and various international movements against colonialism and imperialism, on the other hand. In the case of Malaysia and Singapore, the CPM had played a key role, right up to the promulgation of Emergency by the British colonial administration, aimed at exterminating the CPM and its supporters from mid-1948 onwards.[24]

The women of the CPM and its guerrillas

Towards the end of World War II, according to the CPM's own estimates, the Malayan People's Anti-Japanese Army (MPAJA) was about 10,000 soldiers strong, supported by a broader movement of tens of thousands of underground members. However, by the time the CPM guerrillas laid down their arms and left the jungle in 1989, only about 1,000 guerrillas remained.[25] Even though men had always outnumbered the women in the CPM and in its guerrilla army, women, nonetheless, played significant roles as leaders, cadres, rank-and-file members and foot soldiers. Most of the older, first generation of Chinese women in the party and army had their roots in China; they spoke diverse Chinese languages and came from different ethnic backgrounds. Many Malay women members of the same generation also claimed ancestral links to Java and elsewhere in what is today's Indonesia. However, later generations of CPM members were mostly born in Malaya, with some of them born in Siam / Thailand.[26]

Nevertheless, almost all of the Chinese women I interviewed speak Malay. This is partly due to CPM's policies of multi-racialism and internationalism, as well as its recognition of the Malay language as the national language of independent Malaya.[27] And also as a result of the multi-cultural milieu that these women lived and operated in. These women also came from very diverse socio-economic backgrounds: ranging from daughters of the well-to-do merchant class, families of artisans and petty traders to waged labour, landless peasants and the poor. Their varied motivations for joining the CPM or its guerrilla army included: a yearning to carve out a different but independent life for themselves; to have an education; to escape from domestic violence; to be free from marriage; to heed the call for national liberation and independence; to fight against feudalism; and last but not least, to liberate themselves from male domination and gender discrimination.[28]

By joining CPM or its guerrilla army as clandestine members and supporters, these women, regardless of their ethnicity, racial origin or family background, were seeking empowerment for themselves, for their communities and most of all, independence for their country. This political awareness and activism had expanded to include a progressive sense of 'internationalism' that stood for the liberation of nation-states from colonialism and imperialism, as well as the emancipation of the oppressed classes of the world from exploitation. This sense of 'internationalism' was particularly relevant to the time: the time of Third World independence struggles, followed by the Cold War and the Non-Aligned Movement as defined by Africa, Asia and Latin America.[29]

178 *Agnes Khoo*

Even though one may argue that these women's sense of 'internationalism' was nonetheless defined by the CPM, and thus, confined by the party's vision, their concrete political involvement and exposure had nevertheless enabled them to transcend the physical boundaries of the nation-state by embracing a much wider worldview that encompassed Asia and beyond. Through the education they got in the party and their experiences in the anti-colonial and independence struggles, they began to see themselves as part of a worldwide struggle for Third World liberation, not only against imperialism, feudalism and capitalism, but also against male domination.

This is the context in which the revolutionary lives of these communist women unfolded. This chapter hopes to give a more nuanced picture of their participation and role in a centralised, hierarchical political movement and armed struggle that remains outlawed, demonised and repressed by the Singapore and Malaysia governments until today. The three life stories that follow also show that despite the CPM's attempts at gender emancipation and equality, the movement as a whole had largely remained male-dominated and gendered.

Lives of three revolutionary women

The three women portrayed in this chapter became party cadres and subsequently soldiers of the CPM during the 1950s and 1960s, shortly before and after Malaysia and Singapore had gained independence from British rule. They are Singapore-born Lin Mei, Malaysia-born Lin Dong and Southern Thailand-born Cui Hong.[30]

This generation of communist women is important because their experiences straddled the end of the colonial era and the beginning of nation-state formation in the Third World. They experienced poverty and deprivation during the period of post-war reconstruction and also during the post-colonial era when Malaysia and Singapore had achieved formal independence. The CPM had regarded the newly formed governments as puppet regimes, serving the interests of their former colonial masters.[31]

These three women are highlighted for three reasons. First, they were born in different places of the Malay Peninsula. Lin Mei was born in Singapore, an island-city south of Malaya (or today's Malaysia); Lin Dong was born in the jungle of the State of Selangor on the peninsula; and Cui Hong was born in Southern Thailand near the border of what is today Malaysia. Even though they are considered ethnically 'Chinese', they represent different identities, as well as nationalities. Moreover, they speak different dialects and trace their ancestral origins to different parts of China but they share three common languages: Mandarin, Malay and Thai. Since the CPM has always considered the Malay language as the national language of Malaya, almost all members of the party and its army spoke and used this language.

After the 1989 Peace Agreement between the CPM, the Malaysia and Thai governments was signed, the guerrillas had descended from their military

The Communist Party of Malaya's women guerrillas 179

bases in the mountains and subsequently, settled into villages in locations designated by the Thai government. They had to clear the jungle areas and build their villages from scratch. Members and their families were given land to build their homes, as well as plantations of rubber trees, fruit trees and vegetables. They also studied the Thai language with teachers provided by the Thai government.

Among the three women, Lin Mei and Lin Dong have both spent considerable time outside the Malay Peninsula. Lin Mei was forced to leave Singapore and went into exile in neighbouring Indonesia in 1963 before the party sent her to the People's Republic of China in 1977.[32] Lin Dong's overseas journey began even earlier. As a teenager of thirteen years old, she was sent to China in 1957 to reunite with her parents who were party cadres, who were then based in Beijing. She was able to continue her study in China, and in 1964, she was sent to North Vietnam to study medicine for five years, specialising on tropical diseases and war-time injuries. Thus, Lin Dong had witnessed the Vietnam War first-hand and she recalled vividly the carpet-bombing of US forces in the then Northern Vietnam. Lin Dong then returned to China for two years before finally joining the guerrillas on the Thai-Malaysian border in 1971.[33]

Cui Hong, in contrast, is Thai by birth and by nationality. As a young woman of eighteen, she joined the CPM's guerrilla army in 1967 together with her siblings, and devoted her life to the struggle for Malayan independence until the Peace Agreement. She lost her first husband in combat in 1972, five years after their marriage. Two years later, she married a comrade who had joined the guerrillas from Malaysia.[34] It is evident that all three women embodied a profound sense of internationalism in their politics, political actions and personal lives, even if they did not always articulate it as such.

These three women represent a cross-section of the CPM, in terms of their educational background, as well as the roles and functions they undertook in the party and army. Lin Mei was a middle school student leader before she went underground in Singapore, followed by fourteen years of exile in Indonesia. She was later sent to mainland China to work as a teacher and carer for the children of her comrades who were residing in China then, before settling down in Thailand after the Peace Agreement. Lin Mei married her Malaysian comrade, whom she met during their underground days in Singapore. They have a daughter together, and the family finally reunited in Thailand after the Peace Agreement.

Lin Dong was educated and trained as a medical doctor in Northern Vietnam and China, and continued to play that role until the guerrillas emerged from the jungle in 1989. As a child of high-ranking party members, she had married a party leader and remained in an unfulfilled marriage until the death of her husband. She had trained many paramedics among the guerrillas but decided to reprieve her role as doctor after the Peace Agreement. She ran a small tourist business in Phuket, Thailand, for a period of time before she retired in Betong, Southern Thailand, in one of the Peace

180 *Agnes Khoo*

Villages built by the communists. She remains active today by helping to run the tour company that facilitates visits of mostly Malaysians and Singaporeans to the Peace Villages.

The third guerrilla woman included in this chapter is Cui Hong. She was born in Thailand of Chinese descent, who traces her ancestry to the Guangxi Province in mainland China. Cui Hong had basic education in Southern Thailand and continued her education in the jungle after joining the guerrillas. She was a foot soldier and a sharp shooter, and was often sent to the frontline. Cui Hong, along with her mother and siblings, joined the guerrillas as a family. Today, Cui Hong lives with her mother, husband and daughter in Betong, and is an active leader of the village. Since the Peace Agreement, she plays an important role of bridging between the Malaysians/Singaporeans among the Peace villagers and the Thai society at large.

Lin Mei: the activist and educator

Lin Mei was a student leader of Nanqiao Girls' Middle School when she joined the CPM-led student movement in 1950s Singapore. Her main role was to raise awareness about government policies that were detrimental to a colony on the cusp of independence.[35] In 1957, two years before Singapore gained self-rule but not yet full independence, she had to leave home to go underground because of severe government repression. When the Singapore underground section of the CPM retreated to nearby Indonesia for fear of complete extermination by the British-backed Lee Kuan Yew government in 1963, Lin Mei was among them.[36]

In Sukarno's newly independent Indonesia, Lin Mei saw and experienced the upsurge of communist popularity and the rising influence of the PKI (Indonesian Communist Party). On 30 September 1965, President Sukarno was overthrown by CIA-backed General Suharto in a military coup, which quickly descended into a witch-hunt for 'communists' that saw the incarceration and murders of all opposition and left-wing forces, in what has come to be known as the 'Black October' massacre.[37] Lin Mei had witnessed the widespread persecution and indiscriminate murder of the Left in Suharto's Indonesia, which had left reportedly close to a million dead or unaccounted for. She recounted her harrowing experience:

> It was a dangerous time; mobs were going around killing anyone suspected of being communists. People were implicated by guilt of association…Suharto was arresting anyone considered leftist or with connections to the Left…It was very scary, and we were very nervous. Trouble could break out anytime and anywhere.[38]

As the situation in Indonesia became increasingly dangerous, the CPM eventually sent Lin Mei to the People's Republic of China in 1977. In China, her task was to teach and care for the children of the CPM leaders and cadres who were living there as guests of the Communist Party of China (CPC). Her Indonesia-born daughter was one of them. Lin Mei's daughter studied medicine in China and worked at the CPM-run radio station in Hunan Province before the family relocated to Thailand after the Peace Agreement.

The CPM radio station in Hunan transmitted broadcasts in Malay, Chinese, Tamil and English languages directly to Malaysia and Singapore. Due to the fact that Singapore and the then Lee Kuan Yew government was not party to the Peace Agreement, Lin Mei and her daughter were stateless for many years until they were granted Thai citizenship in the mid-2000s. Her husband, Rung Fu, on the other hand, had remained stateless until he died. He was released from the Malaysian prison after the Peace Agreement, and he crossed the Malaysia-Thailand border to join his family in Yala, another Peace Village in Southern Thailand. Due to his statelessness, Rung Fu was not able to work in Thailand and could barely integrate into the Thai society, whereas Lin Mei was able to teach Chinese language in schools and at home until she retired in 2005.

Although Lin Mei's daughter is a fully trained Oriental/Chinese Medical doctor in China, her qualification is not recognised in Thailand. Hence, she could only find informal employment in the cities, among Chinese-owned companies, which relied on her bilingual skills in Mandarin and the Thai language. However, until she obtained her Thai citizenship, she was often exploited by unscrupulous employers who took advantage of her ambiguous legal status in Thailand.

Lin Dong: the medical doctor

Lin Dong is the eldest daughter of first-generation CPM Politburo members. She was born in the Malayan jungle, in the State of Selangor, during the Japanese occupation in 1944. Since both her parents were in the guerrilla army, fighting the Japanese and then the British after the Japanese were defeated, they had left Lin Dong with her grandmother and uncle. When Lin Dong turned thirteen, she was sent for by her parents who by then were living in the People's Republic of China as exiled CPM leaders.[39] She was to join them and continue her education there. She was accepted to study political economy in Jinan University in Guangzhou, China, but the CPM wanted her and her peers to study medicine. As China was not prepared to train them, Ho Chi Minh invited them to study medicine in North Vietnam instead. Hence, Lin Dong witnessed and lived through carpet-bombing by the American army in war-torn Vietnam. It was there that she developed her skills as an emergency doctor who specialised in tropical diseases and war-time injuries. Lin Dong worked as a guerrilla doctor on the Thai-Malaysian border from 1971 until the Peace Agreement in 1989, along with the other doctors who were trained in Vietnam and China (Figure 9.1).[40]

182 *Agnes Khoo*

Figure 9.1 Lin Dong (centre), the Vietnam-trained medical doctor and off-spring of two high-ranking party members, and two other women.
Source: Photo by Agnes Khoo.

Cui Hong: the guerrilla fighter

Cui Hong and her family joined the CPM guerrillas in 1967. By that time, the CPM army was already on the defensive, forced to retreat to the borders of Thailand and Malaysia for survival and self-sustenance, more or less living in isolation from the rest of the Thai and Malaysian societies. Cui Hong was a very capable guerrilla fighter, a loyal foot soldier who remained in active combat until the army laid down its arms in 1989. She lost her first husband, a Thai-Chinese national, in a battle with Malaysian troops, and has since lived with the guilt that he had sacrificed himself so that she could live.

> After some ... fierce fighting ... All of us, including him, managed to retreat safely up the hill. However, when we reached the hilltop, he told me: 'I cannot make it anymore. You go! Go!' He commanded me to go.... I was reluctant... He shouted at me in spite of his pain: 'You go!' He finally shut his eyes and repeated three times again, in a harsh tone: 'Go! Go! Go!' I obeyed him...
>
> ... (W)hen the leader and myself went back to look for him... He was still sitting there but he was motionless. He still held his rifle firmly in his hand. But he was gone. He died at the age of 28 or 30... He told me the night before that he would not live beyond 30 years old and he was

The Communist Party of Malaya's women guerrillas   183

gone the next day... He tried to protect me, to save my life, by sacrificing himself.[41]

For Cui Hong, dealing with his premature death was tough:

I felt as if I had lost something after he died. It took me a very long time to get used to his absence. I felt like I could hardly breathe... People asked me if I dream about him. I said: 'No.' I really did not dream about him. There was only once that I dreamt of him, when we were about to leave the jungle in 1989... However, by that time, I could not even remember how he looked (like) anymore. Maybe you understand how I feel... No matter how hard I try; I just cannot remember how he looked... Is this because I think of him too much? I miss him too much? ... These days I seem to remember his face again...
  ...How can I not be strong and determined? First, it was my older brother who was executed in the party's rectification campaign and then my husband. Despite all that, I remained in the ambush team.[42]

Being Thai has Cui Hong placed in good stead, especially after the 1989 Peace Agreement. She plays an active leadership role among her comrades in the Betong Peace Village. Not only is she an ex-guerrilla soldier, she is also a mother to her daughter (and son from her first husband), a daughter to her mother (who also joined the guerrillas along with all her children), leader of the women's committee of her village, a rubber tapper, a farmer and an important income-earner for her family. Even though she is Thai by nationality, she has dedicated most of her youth and adult life to an armed struggle for the independence of a country that was not her own, i.e. Malaya (Malaysia/Singapore). Had the CPM taken over state power, she would have had a choice either to remain as a Thai citizen or naturalise as a citizen of communist-ruled 'Malaya', since the CPM does not recognise the separation of Singapore from Peninsular Malaysia.

Thus, in the case of Cui Hong, the concepts of geographical-physical borders, nation-states and citizenship have to take on different meanings in practice. She speaks Thai, Mandarin and the Guangxi dialect fluently, and she lives as part of a trans-border community in which political allegiances, social and familial ties, cultural and ethnic identification and even daily economic activities transcend imposed border-markings of nation-states.

Despite her indisputable loyalty to the party and its army, Cui Hong does have very complex feelings towards them. However, the tensions and contradictions she felt towards the struggle were not articulated in ethnic terms. Her regrets and grievances stemmed from the unjust execution of her eldest brother in the party's rectification campaign to root out spies and informants working for the Malaysian state. Even though reparation was made by the party for its mistake including an official apology, Cui Hong's pain for what the family had gone through remained visible. In fact, Cui Hong

Figure 9.2 Cui Hong, the sharp shooter and loyal guerrilla fighter, then in her early fifties, thirteen years after the 1989 Peace Agreement.
Source: Photo by Agnes Khoo (2002).

herself was also accused and interrogated in the same campaign but she survived the period of paranoia. All these have left deep scars on Cui Hong and her family.[43] It is not a subject that the family talked much about, but the pain of their loss can nonetheless be felt:

> My elder brother was executed in this campaign. Later, I raised this issue with the leaders. I told them things had gone ... (too far). I told them that we were innocent; that it was unfair to treat us this way. Later, the leaders ... did apologise to us and many of us were rehabilitated including my elder brother who died.[44]

The Communist Party of Malaya's women guerrillas 185

Despite being a victim of hysteria about infiltration and spies at that time, Cui Hong was determined to clear her name and maintain her integrity. She and her first husband chose to do it by taking on one of the most dangerous and arduous tasks—infiltrating into Malaysia from Thailand on foot.

> I felt that the way we were treated in the Rectification Campaign was unfair. I thought if we went southwards to fight for the revolution, at least we could prove to the Party and the others that we were not what they thought we were. We could at least prove our loyalty. We went south in 1973.[45]

The Southwards Ambush Team, which Cui Hong was part of, would endure one of the most dangerous and difficult times in the history of the guerrilla army.

> ...We were starving most of the time; we had to live on whatever we could find in the mountain. [...] We were drenched and stayed very wet because of the rain. We would spend the whole night shivering in the cold.[46]

Cui Hong and her comrades had to overcome the harshest of both weather and different terrains. On foot, they had to cover unbelievably long distances between Thailand and Malaysia, cutting through dense and thick tropical rainforests and overcome steep and high mountains.

> We walked all the way from the southern border of Thailand to as far as the north of Malaysia, into the State of Perak...we failed twice and made it to our destination only once...[47]

Personal choice and women's agency

Although Lin Mei, Lin Dong and Cui Hong come from different socio-economic, political and cultural backgrounds, all of them have stressed that their participation in the movement has always been a result of their own conscious decisions. They were not coerced, tricked or manipulated into it. They joined out of their own political convictions, and they saw it as a path to emancipate themselves. Lin Mei's words below were echoed time and again by her comrades in different ways:

> My parents tried to persuade me to give up. They said the government had assured them that I would not be jailed if I broke away from the Party totally and stopped all my activities. I refused. I told them that this was my choice, my own decision and that I believed in our fight against colonialism, for the independence of Malaya...[48]

186 *Agnes Khoo*

For Lin Mei, the struggle between the postcolonial governments of Malaysia and Singapore and the CPM for legitimacy and hegemony was compelling for her to leave her family and join a larger political family within the army.

> Some people told me that I wasted my youth and precious time in the movement… but I really do not regret my decision. I feel that I have had some very rich and extraordinary experiences. I have no regrets. This was meaningful work even though it might not be seen by the public as such…[49]

For Lin Dong, the influences of the revolutionary fervour in 1960s–1970s Communist China, her sense of mission as an offspring of revolutionary parents and the sense of internationalism borne out of the intense conflicts during the Cold War era ultimately inspired her to become a doctor. She worked under very challenging conditions to save lives, improvising to overcome the severe limitations of the jungle and training her comrades as paramedics throughout the war years. Her political conviction was inspired in particular, by the vision of the Non-Aligned Movement that was established in 1961, six years after Indonesia's First President Sukarno had hosted the Bandung Conference.[50] She traced her strong sense of internationalism and international solidarity to the pan-Asian and pan-African movements that emerged during the Cold War. Referring to her political education in Mao's China, she explained what had inspired her internationalism:

> We saw…in China the amazing growth of power and strength of anti-imperialist countries in Latin America, Africa and Asia. We were moved by their struggles. Thousands of people were mobilised to assemble in support of these struggles…
>
> …At that time, the Third World struggles for independence …were at their height. It was the same in Indonesia, Singapore and Malaya. China was very supportive of … these … (As secondary school students)…We were taught very well about patriotism and internationalism…The spirit of internationalism was very much encouraged despite the fact that we did not know much about other countries. Our knowledge was mostly abstract but there was this commitment to work for other countries…[51]

In her interview, she also explained that her choice to return to the Malaysia-Thai Border as a CPM doctor was due to her anti-imperialist, internationalist fervour, besides her sense of allegiance to her parents, and as the 'child of the party'.

> We all had to make sacrifices in revolutionary struggles. I decided to return to the Thai-Malaysia border because I felt … that our mission was to liberate all humankind. We did not consider our self-interest at all. I chose to join the Malayan revolutionary struggle because both my

The Communist Party of Malaya's women guerrillas   187

parents were already part of it, even though I did not come just to be like them... I only thought that since the Party had groomed and trained me, I must go where the Party wanted me. It was so simple. My generation and my parents were like this. We never hesitated just because the place we wanted to go was dangerous or difficult.[52]

For Cui Hong, poverty, the lack of education and opportunities in life, and the persecution by the Thai authorities because they were communist sympathisers, were the prime motivators in joining the movement.

Even before I joined the army, the guerrillas often visited our home. I used to bring food to the hilltop for them... People like us, who were living in remote villages, tried to avoid getting caught in the crossfire. Despite that however, the situation became so polarised that we had no choice but to choose sides... Finally, my family went into the mountains to join the communist guerrillas... I learnt a lot in the army. I learnt how to read and write; how to sew, sing and dance; and also, how to dig an underground tunnel.

Why did we join the army? It was the thing to do at that time; it was common in that environment, living on the border... Even my grandmother was supportive of the revolution...[53]

In her interviews, Lin Mei does not only relate the history of repression in a newly independent Singapore, but she also includes her resistance within it. Similarly, Cui Hong does not only relate her experiences as a foot soldier but also includes her agency in her own participation. And Lin Dong does not only reminiscence about her extraordinary life in China and as a guerrilla doctor, but also talks of her experience as a married woman. For these three women, the CPM-led movement was a progressive movement that involved them in a threefold struggle: the freedom and independence of a multi-racial and multi-lingual Malaysia and Singapore, the emancipation of the poor and oppressed classes, and the liberation of women as an oppressed group in a feudalistic and male-dominated society.

The choices these women had made and the lives they chose were very much against the mainstream norms and values of their societies at that time, not only at the political and ideological level, but also at the personal level. All three of them consistently stressed that they joined the movement because they wanted a life that was different from what was expected or allowed of them. They regarded their participation in this anti-colonial/ anti-imperialist/national liberation movement, as part and parcel of their liberation as women. In Lin Mei's words:

Of course, I have changed through having joined the movement. My sisters did not join the movement, so they are completely different. I think, having been activists, we have become more broad-minded and

188 *Agnes Khoo*

open-hearted. We no longer confine ourselves to our individual problems. We also think about other people and, as and when we can, we try
our best to help others.

In the movement, you are motivated to reach out to people... You
think about changing the society, pushing the progressive movement
forward. There is a sense of mission...

Our experience in the movement also helped us to become strong; to
withstand criticism; to be humble and be ready to change ourselves for
the better.[54]

Furthermore, their awareness and identification with the poor and the oppressed plays a critical role in the way Lin Mei, Lin Dong and Cui Hong
defined their political involvement. For them, political struggles have always had a threefold objective: national liberation (from colonialism and
imperialism), class struggle and women's emancipation. To fight for their
beliefs and to live by their convictions, these women had to endure harsh
political persecution by the governments of Singapore, Malaysia, as well as
Thailand. They were ostracised and stigmatised as 'terrorists', thus making
them 'outcasts' of their communities. And yet, they managed to establish,
together with their comrades, a close-knit alternative community, which
tried to put their utopian ideals into practice.

Even though it was a community borne largely out of a necessity for survival, as the consequence of a long and drawn-out war that spanned more
than half a century (1930–1989), the CPM has profoundly and fundamentally shaped the trajectories of the three women's lives, far beyond the political movements they participated in. All the three women have lived in
different countries, and they were nourished by different cultures at different stages in their lives.

Lin Mei, Lin Dong and Cui Hong have each, in their own ways, also
touched and changed the lives of many people around them. This includes
not only the lives of those within the movement and those of their immediate families but also of the people outside the movement, whom they have
organised, mobilised and educated across nation-states. These women
have transcended numerous geographical boundaries and bridged many
socio-cultural, linguistic, ethnic and even religious divides. Their worldview has vastly expanded beyond the confines of nation-states, as well as
socio-cultural and linguistic groups. They fought for a movement that stood
for internationalism: a vision that all nations big and small, rich and poor
can exist as equals and in peace. And they continue to believe in it.

Lin Mei, for instance, has been teaching throughout her life and hence,
her intellectual influence on her students, be they within or outside the
movement, in China or in Thailand, is by no means insignificant. Lin Dong
has aptly fulfilled her role as an excellent doctor for her comrades, regardless of their nationality and ethnicity. Cui Hong has shown that by giving
her life to the liberation of a country other than her own, she is capable of
embracing internationalism and transcending nationalism.

The Communist Party of Malaya's women guerrillas 189

There is also a liberating aspect to the CPM's struggle in terms of women's empowerment, but its extent and relevance remains to be fully understood. If the CPM is to be judged in its own context, then some tangible progress has indeed been made. These women, within the limitations of their individual and collective lives, have carved out a different trajectory for themselves. As a result, they have also changed the perceptions of their husbands, parents, children and people they have come in contact with—about women, women's role in political and social transformation, and women's emancipation. The open-mindedness and the progressive mind-sets and attitudes of these political women inevitably influence the way they define and live their married lives, the way they see and deal with their families and particularly, in what they consider to be important for their daughters. They reject traditions that are oppressive to women and in their own ways fight for gender equality within the family, in the party and in the public domain. Consequently, they have become more tolerant of differences. Recollecting her experiences about gender relationships, Lin Mei had this to say:

> We tried to develop the consciousness of the women while we worked together in the kitchen and when we were feeding the chickens. We talked about all kinds of things and tried to instil some progressive ideas in them… We could feel the difference between those we tried to conscientisize and ourselves. There was more equality between us. Both male and female comrades had to work equally hard. No difference. Male comrades also helped with the housework. We did not feel that, as women, we were discriminated. The male students that went underground seemed to treat us equally.[55]

In contrast to Lin Mei, gender equality in the army is evaluated differently by Lin Dong:

> It is not true that women are better than men in the army or vice versa. Objectively speaking, I must admit that on the whole, the men were physically stronger than the women. Of course, even our ten fingers are not of the same length. There were male comrades who were weaker, as well as female comrades who were stronger. Therefore, it is not strange if individual men were less capable than individual women and vice versa.
>
> On the other hand, women were better at withstanding hunger (generally speaking). This is because women's metabolism rate is not as high as men's … However; the share of food was the same for men and women in the army. Those of us who were not doing so much physical work usually shared our food with those who needed more.[56]

For these communist women, being part of a marginalised, stigmatised, ostracised and underground political movement has been profoundly complex, painful and difficult. Nonetheless, it was a liberating experience despite their sacrifices. Thus, it is important to value these women's contribution to

190 *Agnes Khoo*

the movement without negating the challenges they had to deal with. The compromises they have made and the regrets they must live with as political activists, teachers, community organisers, guerrilla fighters, women, mothers, wives and daughters are no less significant than the gains they have achieved. As argued by Schönfeld, 'The past self still incorporates a multitude of possibilities; the present self knows of the choices that were made.'[57]

The women's question

An unexplored area of tension for the women who joined the CPM and its army has been the party's seeming lack of critical examination of its own policies and practices on the 'Women's Question', despite its professed aims for gender equality. Thus, the party may have unintentionally reproduced … 'gender ideologies and hierarchies, especially in the access to power and decision-making…'[58] in actual practice.

Women were mobilised to support the revolution, incorporating women's rights and interests in the process. However, these tend to be subsumed under the primacy of national liberation and class struggle, particularly in times of crisis and war. Thus, women were encouraged to be emancipated by leaving their traditional roles and to break out of their traditional duties to become good 'soldiers' or loyal party members. Yet, the organisational structure, culture, ethos and practices of an army—even a revolutionary one—being by and large masculine, centralised and authoritarian, continued to keep the women in their place in other ways.

Referring to Central America as an example, Chinchilla observed that even vanguard revolutionary organisations that lack an understanding of the causes of gender differences may unintentionally reproduce gender inequalities. Given that relations of comrades are presumed to be equal, especially among those with access to military training and the use of arms, '…women activists often did not raise concrete demands for greater equality or modifications of certain weaknesses in the culture or policies in vanguard organizations…' and those …who did were viewed as too radical and rebellious.[59]

This also applied to women in the CPM. Hence, Lin Dong, the most educated among the three women discussed in this chapter, said she was regarded by the male leaders as 'too outspoken' and indomitable. In fact, Lin Dong considered herself a rebel within the army. She was very animated in explaining why she would never be awarded the accolade of a 'model comrade' in the party because of her insubordination to authority and her readiness to question party policies or criticise party practices.

> Usually in the guerrilla army, we listened and obeyed our leaders, but I never did…, including to my husband, completely… My comrades tended to echo the leaders' opinions uncritically because they thought the leaders were always right… Because of my tendency to not be totally

The Communist Party of Malaya's women guerrillas   191

obedient, I was told to evaluate and criticise myself every year. My husband [who was a party cadre] even accused me of extreme individuality and heroism.[60]

Lin Dong also talked about how the hierarchy in the army based on rank and seniority did not always go with meritocracy:

> Every year, our peers and leaders assessed us on our performance. We were divided into 1st class, 2nd class, 3rd class, 4th class...On the surface, it would seem rather democratic. Everyone could evaluate the others. However, the result was the same year after year. It seems that younger comrades could never get 1st class honours, no matter how hard he or she had worked... The 1st class honours were always reserved for our senior comrades and party cadres even though these people might not have carried much food. They might not have done any essential tasks or duties, yet they would still get 1st class honours. So, no one thought much about the merit system. After all, we are here for the revolution, not to be rewarded...[61]

Factors such as the pressures of war, the party's emphasis on the collective over the individual, the clandestine nature of party work, and the compartmentalisation of roles to avoid arrests and to protect against infiltration by government agents discouraged women from sharing their problems and experiences openly among themselves and in the party or army.[62] Women's problems were regarded as 'personal' and were not expressed for fear that these would be considered as signs of 'deviation' or 'ideological weakness'.[63]

For example, Lin Mei thought that her health could have been better if she had been given better post-natal care after the birth of her daughter during her exile in Indonesia. The strict food rationing and organisational discipline had resulted in serious anaemia that continues to trouble her until this day.

> My daughter...She was a sickly and skinny child. I could not take proper care of her myself because of the kind of work I was doing. I was very sickly myself...I was for a long time very dependent on medication. I was always suffering from headaches and dizziness...with the added stress of our situation and the childbirth, my health deteriorated quickly.[64]

Lin Mei also shared about the conflict and tensions between the different roles she played in the party and family: as political activist, woman, daughter and mother. She was aware of the tensions between her loyalty to her political convictions and adherence to her party's ideology, on the one hand, and her personal needs and aspirations as a woman and mother, on the other. This became apparent in her ambivalence about how her

192 *Agnes Khoo*

revolutionary work had come between her and her daughter. This is often shared by other communist women I had interviewed or known. There was sadness whenever Lin Mei recounted how she had to send her daughter and only child, from Indonesia to China ahead of her, after the 'Black October' massacre of suspected communists on 1 October 1965 in Indonesia. Mother and daughter only met many years later. She would recall with sadness her daughter's initial reaction towards her during their first encounter in China.

> I met my daughter again after I was sent to China...She refused to call me 'mother' at our first meeting. She called me 'auntie' like everyone else. This lasted for quite a while.

Similarly, Cui Hong, who blamed herself for becoming pregnant in the jungle, given the harsh conditions in the army, felt that despite her personal circumstances, she had to work hard, if not harder, to prove herself.

> I have been through a lot in life. When I was in the assault team, despite the fact that I was already three to five months pregnant, I carried heavy loads of more than 50 kilos at a time, like all the others. I was even one of the frontline soldiers...[65]
>
> I gave birth to my first son in the army, deep in the jungle. I was in excruciating pain. My whole body was shaking so much, perhaps due to hunger, that a few people had to hold me down in order to give me injections. After my son's birth, I was dispatched southwards again, so we took him to my eldest sister-in-law so that she could take care of him... I did not think much about my son then because given the circumstances we were in, it was a curse to be pregnant. I felt more like I had contracted an illness and did not consider it as a blessing. I was also worried that my comrades would criticise me for getting pregnant.[66]

When a significant part of women's lives and subjectivities is defined as 'non-political and non-priority' even though these 'constituted part of the core fabric of the society' that the party had wanted to transform, tensions and contradictions between theory and practice inevitably arose.[67] This problem is further compounded by the fact that the CPM and its army are still being demonised, outlawed and persecuted by the Malaysian and Singaporean governments today. Hence, any public criticism of the CPM's policies of women is likely to be capitalised upon by the authorities. Therefore, the personal nuances and sensitive issues, where women's interests contradict party's interests or policies, were rarely dealt with.

Public sphere activities eclipse gendered experiences

Chinchilla's assertion that in some of the 1970s' Latin American revolutionary movements where 'the emphasis was on public-sphere activities and on working-class, peasant and poor women' resonates well with the CPM. As a result, '[p]rivate or domestic life and the subjective dimension of the gendered experience remained an enigma', including in the CPM.[68] During my seven-year long fieldwork (1998–2004) with these women, some of them would talk about their unhappy marriage with ambivalence. Some felt that the party leadership had let them down in the handling of these problems, whilst others thought their leaders had meted out justice on their behalf. For instance, a party leader who was caught having affairs with a number of other women comrades was taken to task by the party after his wife, who was also a woman cadre, complained about his infidelity to the party leadership. The party granted her request for divorce after investigation of the matter and attempts of reconciliation between the couple. Despite the years that have passed by, she was still very upset about his betrayal and she never forgave him. In this particular case, the party also meted out disciplinary measures by excluding him from promotion within the party's leadership.

This case shows that women had to, within given parameters, constantly negotiate and navigate between their private and public lives; between their private needs and desires and party-dictated ethos; and between conduct, duties and tasks. In other words, while conflict and contradictions did exist in the public domain, both within the party and the broader political movement, they were also present in the private domain, notably within their families and in their marital relationships. During one of our interviews, Lin Mei and her husband broke into an argument when he stopped her from criticising the party. This not only shed light on the tensions between the public and private domains of revolutionary life but also the tensions among revolutionary couples wherein personal relationships and party loyalties intertwined.

If women revolutionaries like Lin Dong tried to maintain their autonomy vis-à-vis the party and their husbands, they had to contend with tremendous pressure both from their peers and superiors. As politically conscious women who were very much aware of their rights and not hesitant to fight for them, these women had to nonetheless compromise from time to time within the male-dominated and male-defined structure and agenda in the party and family.

For example, while there was a genuine effort to empower women through education within the CPM, the traditional gender division of labour continued to be reproduced in daily revolutionary and guerrilla life. Like women revolutionaries who joined the movements in Central America in the 1960s, the CPM women could not completely transcend the gender division of roles and labour within the party or army.[69] The majority of them still landed with gender-based or service-oriented roles such as couriers, purveyors of supplies, cooks, tailors, teachers and nurses. Only a minority of them took on roles that are traditionally reserved for men, such as doctors, platoon leaders, camp commanders, combatants and party cadres. Having said that however, even though many CPM women guerrillas were involved in what is considered as 'traditionally feminine' activities, some of them did serve

194 *Agnes Khoo*

actively at the frontline, including the laying of mines and in ambushes. Cui Hong, for instance, was a sharp shooter and an athletic combatant. She recalled proudly how '(t)he Commander always praised me for my ability'.[70]

Based on these women's accounts, there was, to some extent, a rotation of daily tasks and responsibilities between men and women within the army. Hence, there were male cooks and tailors just as there were female sentries. However, maternal responsibilities remained with the women, and it was also the women who had to resolve dilemmas related to maternity. In order not to jeopardise the safety of the army, many new-borns were quickly brought out of the jungle to be taken care of by relatives or supporters. A much unexplored area of tension for these women would be their feelings of guilt for having 'abandoned' or 'given up' their babies. Some of the women never saw their children again. Others might have reunited later but not all the offspring chose to return to their biological parents.

The three women in this chapter tried to fulfil not only the roles and responsibilities prescribed by their societies but also those by their party and army. They constantly juggled between being 'good' mothers and daughters, caring and loving wives, militant activists, fearless operatives and brave soldiers. Negotiating these conflicting demands has stayed with them throughout their political lives, even during peace time. Arguably, the fulfilment of these different and sometimes conflicting roles implies that they have to navigate between numerous tasks and responsibilities, both public and private, on their own. This constant demand on them to be 'the superwomen' could sometimes impose considerable pressures. To be a militant, a committed party member or a combat soldier of an underground party in exile inevitably called for enormous personal sacrifices and fortitude.

Cui Hong, for instance, had remained on the frontlines as an active combatant even after having lost her first husband in action. She also had to send her first-born son away because she could not take care of him during the war, which strained their relationship. Moreover, she endured the painful memories of having lost her eldest brother in the party's rectification campaign, in which she was also accused of being a spy and nearly lost her life, yet she has remained loyal to the party until the end, which calls for tremendous strength and compassion.

Ironically, while these women were encouraged to forgo their traditional roles as mothers, wives and daughters for the sake of the revolution, many of them, including Lin Mei and Cui Hong, have reverted to these roles in their postrevolutionary, civilian lives. As much as these politicised women have educated and empowered themselves, their ambivalence between emancipation and tradition remains evident. Lin Mei, who was exiled from Singapore in her early twenties and shall remain so for the rest of her life, has often expressed regrets that she could not take care of her daughter and that she had abandoned her parents for the sake of the revolution.

> Sometimes I miss my family, I feel guilty towards them; this is something that will always be in my heart. My family did not do anything

The Communist Party of Malaya's women guerrillas   195

wrong to me, but I left them... I felt deeply that...loyalty and (filial) piety as a daughter cannot be realised at the same time because they became incompatible in a time of revolutionary struggle. To be a revolutionary automatically entailed personal sacrifice for the greater good. Nevertheless, I felt sorry for my family.[71]

Cui Hong talked about her guilt of having to see her first husband die alone in combat and, less obviously, her guilt towards their son. Lin Dong never talked about her childlessness but occasionally hinted at her ambivalence about the absence of her revolutionary parents in her life and the lack of sexual pleasure in her marriage. The occasional outbursts of Lin Mei about her poor health and the honest admission by Lin Dong that her marriage was an unfulfilling one all point to their conflicted feelings as women and revolutionaries in a centralised and hierarchical party.

Centralised party hierarchy and women's choices

Lin Mei, Lin Dong and Cui Hong had to operate within the hierarchical confines of a tightly centralised party, a clandestine movement and army, which had, as a result, fallen short in some of its handling of the 'Woman Question'. Despite the fact that the party had advocated for a balance between democracy and centralism, obedience to centralised authority still trumped internal democracy, especially during crises and war. Lin Dong recalled how she soon learnt that an invitation to 'criticise your leaders' was not to be taken literally. Thus, there was a culture of discouraging open debate and criticism of the leadership, particularly within the guerrilla army. And this lack of internal democracy might have reinforced, firstly, the traditional pattern of a top-down leadership; secondly, a hierarchy led by a small elite; and lastly, gender inequalities.[72] As 'foot soldiers' in the movement, the political influence of rank-and-file women was limited by their prescribed roles and responsibilities; as grassroots women with little say or decision-making power within the party or army, their position and experiences were different from their male and some female counterparts who held leadership roles.

The nature of clandestine work and the pressure to 'close ranks' in times of crises might have legitimised the suspension of internal debate and democracy. However, we cannot preclude that this might have also prevented the development of independent-thinking cadres even as they acted collectively.[73] Had the CPM been able to deal better with issues of internal democracy, albeit within their given circumstances, then perhaps errors committed by the party could have been minimised. It is, therefore, neither simple nor straightforward in discerning women's autonomy and agency within a revolutionary party or guerrilla army, given the many inter-related dimensions and nuances that act upon one another dialectically.

CPM revolutionaries like Lin Mei, Lin Dong, and Cui Hong did conform to certain gender roles expected of them by the party and the guerrilla

196 *Agnes Khoo*

army, albeit to varying degrees, even as they rebelled against their families and governments by becoming revolutionaries. They had consciously and actively resisted gender-based stereotypes and discrimination, which they saw as 'women's oppression', which led them to join the CPM. Hence, they have made an effort to transform mainstream gender roles and expectations through their participation in a political liberation movement, even though they could not completely free themselves from the gender roles and expectations the movement might have hitherto imposed upon them.

Having said that, however, the women revolutionaries I have interviewed were all conscious of their rights as women, even if their interpretation of these rights might differ from their party and its leaders from time to time. They did exercise their agency by deciding on when to compromise for the sake of party loyalty, group unity and cohesion, as well as family harmony. The power relations that women guerrilla and underground activists had to navigate between the party, family, comradeship and the society at large are intricate, intertwined and fluid.

All the women I have interviewed or met during the 1998–2004 period agreed that their participation in the left-wing political movement had shaped their lives profoundly. This, however, does not mean that their emancipation as women was straightforward or to be taken for granted. Their consciousness, identity and life trajectories as women and citizens in their own right have been drastically and irrevocably transformed. They recognise that the movement has made a profound and positive impact on their lives and their families. However, they also conceded that there were repercussions on themselves and their families that were not all inevitable. Hence, the pros and cons of being a woman guerrilla or a militant of a left-wing party still need to be better understood and appraised.

There were achievements, but also regrets. Here I draw the parallel with the El Salvadoran experience, highlighted by Murguialday and Vasquez as quoted by Chinchilla, with reference to how conservative frameworks regarding what women are or are not permitted to do within the party and political movement has come to be questioned through women's participation.

> The war showed them and the rest of the society that women could fight and conspire [to overthrow the established order], that they are capable of participating in the most unexpected fronts, and of efficiently carrying out tasks thought to belong to men... [it] left them with the view that if women did [not] reach the highest levels of decision-making in the military and party structures, it was not because they were not qualified but because sexist prejudices still predominated...[74]

And yet, regardless of the gain and loss for these revolutionary women, they all agreed that becoming politically conscious and empowered in the liberation movement was the most significant outcome in their lives.

Notes

1 Virginia Woolf, *Three Guineas* (New York: Harbinger Book, 1938).
2 Erzsebet Barat, 'The Discourse of Selfhood: Oral Autobiographies as Narrative Sites for Constructions of Identity', in Alison Donnell and Pauline Polkey (eds.), *Representing Lives: Women and Autobiography* (London: Macmillan Press, 2000), pp. 165–173.
3 Lois A. West, 'Introduction', in Lois A. West (ed.), *Feminist Nationalism* (New York & London: Routledge, 1997), p. xx.
4 Kumari Jayawardena, *Feminism and Nationalism in the Third World* (London: Zed Books, 1986).
5 West, 'Introduction', in *Feminist Nationalism*, p. xxxi.
6 Ibid., p. xii.
7 These names are their revolutionary names.
8 See, for example, Zhou Mei, *Elizabeth Choy—More than a War Heroine: A Biography* (Singapore: Landmark Books, 1995); Urvashi Butalia, *The Other Side of Silence: Voices from the Partition of India* (New Delhi: Viking, 1998); Alfred W. McCoy (ed.), *Lives at the Margin: Biographies of Filipinos Obscure, Ordinary, and Heroic* (Madison: University of Wisconsin Press, 2004); Suruchi Thapar-Bjorkert, *Women in the Indian National Movement: Unseen Faces and Unheard Voices, 1930–42* (New Delhi: Sage Publications India, 2006); Helen Ting and Susan Blackburn (eds.), *Women in Southeast Asian Nationalist Movements* (Singapore: NUS Press, 2013).
9 Lim Hong Bee, *Born into War* (London: Excalibur Press of London, 1994); Tan Jin Quee and Jomo KS (eds.), *Comet in Our Sky: Lim Chin Siong in History* (Kuala Lumpur: INSAN, 2001); Said Zahari, *Dark Clouds at Dawn: A Political Memoir* (Kuala Lumpur: INSAN, 2001); Chin Peng, *Alias Chin Peng: My Side of History— as Told to Ian Ward & Norma Miraflor* (Singapore: Media Masters, 2003); CC Chin and Karl Hack, *Dialogues with Chin Peng: New Light on the Malayan Communist Party* (Singapore: Singapore University Press, 2005); Fong Chong Pik, *The Memoirs of a Malayan Communist Revolutionary* (Petaling Jaya: SIRD, 2008); Abdullah CD, *The Memoirs of Abdullah C.D. (Part One): The Movement until 1948* (Petaling Jaya: SIRD, 2009); Shamsiah Fakeh, *The Memoirs of Shamsiah Fakeh: From AWAS to 10th Regiment* (Petaling Jaya: SIRD, 2009); Mahani Musa, 'Women in the Malayan Communist Party, 1942–89', *Journal of Southeast Asian Studies*, Vol. 44, No. 2 (2013); Mahani Musa, 'Malayan Women and Guerrilla Warfare, 1941–89', in *Chapters on Asia: A Selection of Papers from the Lee Kong Chian Research Fellowship*, Vol. 1, No. 1 (March 2014), p. 105. Available at: www.microsite.nl.sg/PDFsBiblioAsia/ChpaterOnAsia_v01.pdf (accessed on 21 October 2014).
10 See www.straitstimes.com/news/singapore/more-singapore-stories/story/parliament-not-acting-singapore-love-would-give-signal-v and http://therealsingapore.com/content/alfian-saat-pm-lee-you-are-just-afraid-your-truth-will-be-exposed-lies (accessed 21 October 2014).
11 Stree Shakti Sanghatana, *We Were Making History: Life Stories of Women in the Telangana People's Struggle* (New Delhi and London: Kali for Women and Zed Books, 1989); Helena Grice, 'Korean American National Identity in Theresa Hak Kyung Cha's *Dictee*', in Donnell and Polkey (eds.), *Representing Lives: Women and Autobiography, pp. 43–52*; Barat, 'The Discourse of Selfhood'; Urvashi Butalia, 'Oral History: A Feminist Methodology', in Urvashi Butalia, Melody Lu, and Jeannie Manipon (eds.), *Feminisms in Asia—Rethinking Feminist Practices: Activists as Thinkers and Practitioners—A Resource Book* (Hong Kong: ARENA, 1999); James Daniel, *Dona Maria's Story: Life History, Memory and Political Identity* (Durham, NC: Duke University Press, 2000); Lan Bo-Zhou, *The Good Women of Taiwan (Taiwan haonuren)* (Taipei: Unitas Publishing, 2001); Liz Stanley,

198 *Agnes Khoo*

The Auto/biographical I: The Theory and Practice of Feminist Auto/biography (Manchester: Manchester University Press, 1992); Thapar-Bjorkert, *Women in the Indian National Movement*.

12 Agnes Khoo, *Life as the River Flows: Women in the Malayan Anti-Colonial Struggle* (Monmouth: Merlin Press, 2007).

13 See Grice, 'Korean American National Identity in Theresa Hak Kyung Cha's *Dictee*'.

14 Ibid., p. 45.

15 Paul Thomson, *The Voice of the Past: Oral History* (Oxford: Oxford University Press, 1988).

16 Liz Stanley, *The Auto/biographical I*; Helen Nicholson, 'Promoting Herself: The Representational Strategies of Georgina Weldon', in Donnell and Polkey (eds.), *Representing Lives: Women and Auto/biography*, pp. 208–217.

17 Donnell and Polkey, *Representing Lives: Women and Auto/biography*, p. xxiv.

18 Chin Peng, *Alias Chin Peng*, p. 57.

19 Timothy N. Harper, *The End of Empire and the Making of Malaya* (Cambridge: Cambridge University Press, 2001).

20 Joseph Kennedy, *A History of Malaya* (Kuala Lumpur: Synergy Books International, 1993), pp. 255–277; Zahari, *Dark Clouds at Dawn*, pp. 1–28.

21 Abdullah CD, *The Memoirs of Abdullah C.D. (Part One)*; Chin Peng, *Alias Chin Peng*; Fakeh, *The Memoirs of Shamsiah Fakeh*; Fong Chong Pik, *The Memoirs of a Malayan Communist Revolutionary*.

22 Zhang Naihua and Wu Xu, 'Discovering the Positive within the Negative: The Women's Movement in a Changing China', in Amrita Basu (ed.), *The Challenge of Local Feminisms: Women's Movements in Global Perspective* (Boulder, CO: Westview Press, 1995), pp. 25–57.

23 Harper, *The End of Empire and the Making of Malaya*.

24 Musa, 'Malayan Women and Guerrilla Warfare, 1941–89', p. 105.

25 Khoo, *Life as the River Flows*, pp. 306, 311. Also see Musa, 'Malayan Women and Guerrilla Warfare, 1941–89'.

26 Khoo, *Life as the River Flows*; Fakeh, *The Memoirs of Shamsiah Fakeh*.

27 Tan and Jomo, *Comet in Our Sky: Lim Chin Siong in History*.

28 Khoo, *Life as the River Flows*.

29 Zahari, *Dark Clouds at Dawn*, pp. 144–147; John Roosa, *Pretext for Mass Murder: The September 30th Movement and Suharto's Coup d'état in Indonesia* (Madison: The University of Wisconsin Press, 2006), pp. 176–201.

30 The names in major capital letters are the family names, the other names are the given names.

31 See Abdullah CD, *The Memoirs of Abdullah C.D*; Chin and Hack, *Dialogues with Chin Peng*; Chin Peng, *Alias Chin Peng*; Fakeh, *The Memoirs of Shamsiah Fakeh*; Fong, *The Memoirs of a Malayan Communist Revolutionary*; Lim, *Born Into War*; Tan and Jomo, *Comet in Our Sky: Lim Chin Siong in History*; Said Zahari, *Dark Clouds at Dawn*.

32 Khoo, *Life as the River Flows*, p. 268 and p. 273.

33 Ibid., pp. 130–133.

34 Ibid., pp. 110, 118.

35 See the 'Anti-yellow culture' campaign in Musa, 'Women in the Malayan Communist Party, 1942–89', pp. 231–232.

36 Khoo, *Life as the River Flows*, pp. 253–267.

37 Roosa, *Pretext for Mass Murder*.

38 Khoo, *Life as the River Flows*, pp. 269–270.

39 Ibid., pp. 129–131.

40 Ibid., pp. 129–132.

41 Ibid., p. 117.

The Communist Party of Malaya's women guerrillas   199

42 Ibid., p. 118.
43 Chin Peng, *Alias Chin Peng*.
44 Khoo, *Life as the River Flows*, p. 111.
45 Ibid., p. 112.
46 Ibid.
47 Ibid., pp. 112, 113.
48 Ibid., p. 265.
49 Ibid., p. 279.
50 Darwis Khudori, 'Towards a Bandung Spirit-based Civil Society Movement: Reflection from Yogyakarta Commemoration of Bandung Asia-African Conference', *Inter-Asia Cultural Studies*, Vol. 7, No. 1 (2006), pp. 121–138; Kristin S. Tassin, 'Lift up Your Head, My Brother: Nationalism and the Genesis of the Non-Aligned Movement', *Journal of Third World Studies*, Vol. XXIII, No. 1 (2006), pp. 147–168; Mushakoji Kinhide, 'Bandung plus 50: A Call for a Tricontinental Dialogue on Global Hegemony', *Inter-Asia Cultural Studies*, Vol. 6, No. 4 (2005), pp. 1–14.
51 Khoo, *Life as the River Flows*, p. 130.
52 Ibid., p. 142.
53 Ibid., pp. 107–108.
54 Ibid., p. 280.
55 Ibid., p. 263.
56 Ibid., pp. 141–142.
57 Christiane Schönfeld, 'Constructing the Subject? Emmy Ball-Hennings's Autobiographical Texts', in Donnell and Polkey (eds.), *Representing Lives: Women and Autolbiography*, p. 193.
58 Norma Stoltz Chinchilla, 'Nationalism, Feminism, and Revolution in Central America', in West (ed.), *Feminist Nationalism*, pp. 201–219.
59 Ibid., p. 212.
60 Khoo, *Life as the River Flows*, p. 133.
61 Ibid., p. 147.
62 See Khoo, and Chinchilla, 'Nationalism, Feminism, and Revolution in Central America', p. 214.
63 Ibid.
64 Khoo, *Life as the River Flows*, p. 268.
65 Ibid., p. 112.
66 Ibid., p. 113.
67 Chinchilla, 'Nationalism, Feminism, and Revolution in Central America', p. 212.
68 Ibid.
69 Ibid., pp. 202–203, 206–207. These points are also echoed by Vina Lanzona in her chapter in this volume discussing the women of the Huk and Vietnamese revolutionary movements.
70 Khoo, *Life as the River Flows*, p. 112.
71 Ibid., p. 265–266.
72 Chinchilla, 'Nationalism, Feminism, and Revolution in Central America', p. 214.
73 Ibid., pp. 214–215.
74 Ibid., p. 208.

10 Love and sex in times of war and revolution

Women warriors in Vietnam and the Philippines[1]

Vina A. Lanzona

Issues of gender and sexuality have appeared relatively recently in studies and memoirs of women warriors in Southeast Asia. Greater sensitivity to gender and female experiences has added new insights and greater complexity to earlier studies on social and revolutionary movements, and these developments have facilitated more in-depth treatments of marginalised groups in Southeast Asia such as women warriors, as well as comparative studies of their experiences across the region. My own work has benefitted from such gendered perspectives as it explores issues of love, sex, romance, and intimacy experienced by the female combatants of the Huk revolutionary struggles in the Central Luzon region of the Philippines during the 1942–1956 period.[2] The highly personal narratives of former women guerrillas of the Huk movement reveal that sexual relations were very much part of revolutionary life. While the Huk organisation publicly espoused a political struggle based on concepts of independence, liberation, and communism, its male and female members pursued personal lives that included courtships, marriages, extramarital affairs, and children. Such relations were deemed so central to the workings of the movement that the leadership, mostly high-ranking members of the Communist Party of the Philippines, drew up detailed policies and resolutions that aimed precisely to regulate the private lives of its members. But how did such policies directly affect the revolutionary lives of its female guerrillas, its women warriors? And more generally, how unique or different were the Huks in terms of understanding the fragile sensitivities and complex interpersonal relationships that existed among its members?

In this chapter, I aim to place the Huks' sexual relationships and the particular ways they were regulated in the organisation into a wider regional perspective by looking across the South China Sea to Vietnam, roughly during the 1925–1975 time period. What were key relationship-related personal issues experienced by female Vietnamese revolutionaries during the nascence of a proto-communist and then communist revolutionary movement against the French from the mid-1920s, and later in Hanoi's bid to unify the divided country by conquering the South? How did the largely male leadership address such issues? I want to use this comparative approach to illustrate how universal the struggles of women warriors were in balancing their political and personal lives and their experiences as both subjects and resisters of male control. But while such experiences are indeed common to

Love/sex in war & revolution: Vietnam & the Philippines 201

women warriors, I also want to explore the specifically cultural ways that issues of sexuality are viewed and addressed in revolutionary movements.

In Southeast Asia, the experiences of women warriors in the Huk and Vietnamese revolutions cry out for a comparison. Through the scarce, yet highly personal, records provided by two female cadres from each movement, namely my interviews with the Huks' Teofista Valerio in the 1990s and the posthumously published diaries of North Vietnamese field surgeon Dr Dang Thuy Tram, but also drawing on additional case studies, I will show how revolutionary and political lives intertwined with issues of love and intimacy, and how political struggles were defined by the cadres and their organisations by taking account of the personal seriously.

Figure 10.1 The solitary sculpture of Dr Dang Thuy Tram at the clinic named after her at Duc Pho, Quang Ngai province, southcentral Vietnam, in which she was active. Medical bag slung over her left shoulder, her left sandal-clad foot appears to be stepping out from the background stone. In front of her, on the main pedestal, are two rose cactus pots centred by a three-legged incense burner. The two-storey clinic, which also features a memorial room, is diagonally to her left shoulder. The concluding chapter, by Barbara Watson Andaya, discusses such sites of memory.

Source: Photo shared by user Thai Nhi under Creative Commons Attribution 3.0 at https://vi.wikipedia.org/wiki/T%E1%BA%ADp_tin:Tuongdangthuytram.jpg (last accessed 23 Feb 2019).

202 *Vina A. Lanzona*

Background of the Huk rebellion and the Vietnamese revolution

The Huk rebellion was a result of two separate, peasant-based struggles in the Philippines. The first, which led to the formation of the *Hukbalahap* or the *Hukbo ng Bayan Laban sa Hapon* (Anti-Japanese Army) in March 1942, was initiated by leaders of peasant organisations and the *Partido Komunista ng Pilipinas* (PKP or Communist Party of the Philippines) to resist the Japanese occupation forces during World War II. Despite their eventually victorious struggles against the Japanese, the Huk organisation was delegitimised when the Philippines gained political independence from the United States in 1946. Political repression, including constant harassment and even killings, forced the Huks underground and to re-establish the *Hukbong Mapagpalaya ng Bayan* (HMB) or People's Liberation Army.[3]

Unlike the Huk rebellion, which began with resistance against the Japanese invasion and then was directed at the socially conservative leadership of the newly independent republic, the Vietnamese communist bid for national liberation and social revolution goes back to the mid-1920s. The Vietnamese Communist Party, which was soon to become the Indochinese Communist Party, was not founded until early 1930 by Nguyen Ai Quoc, the future Ho Chi Minh. Although the party was almost destroyed in ill-advised uprising events, most notably the Nghe-Tinh Soviets of 1930–1931 in northcentral Annam and the Southern Uprising in Cochinchina in late 1940, the party managed to survive. In 1941, Ho Chi Minh even established the Viet Minh, short for the 'League for the Independence of Vietnam', a broad national liberation movement, led by the Indochinese Communist Party, against the Vichy-aligned French administration and the Japanese forces in French Indochina. The Viet Minh would wait for the right moment to strike, and this came during the capitulation of Japan in August 1945. The ensuing power vacuum prompted Ho Chi Minh to proclaim the Democratic Republic of Viet Nam in early September 1945, although it would take another three decades of war and revolution to achieve Vietnam's independence as a country united under communist rule.

The first stage of struggle for the Viet Minh was launched against the returning French colonial forces, escalating into the First Indochina War in late 1946. This conflict ended in 1954, when the Viet Minh defeated the French forces in the Battle of Dien Bien Phu, eventually leading to the retreat of the French, but also the division of Vietnam at the seventeenth parallel into North and South Vietnam. As the promised referendum on Vietnam's unification did not materialise, the National Liberation Front was eventually set up in 1960 to seek the unification and independence of Vietnam under communist leadership, which was not achieved until the fall of Saigon in 1975 and formal unification in 1976.[4]

Despite differences in terms of geographical spread and history, the Huk and the Vietnamese revolutionary movements have a lot in common.

Love/sex in war & revolution: Vietnam & the Philippines 203

They both fought for independence against the Japanese in World War II and launched struggles against returning colonial forces and the governments they established in the postwar period. The anti-Japanese army of the Huks was considered as the most successful resistance army in Asia, but unlike the Viet Minh, its Communist-led rebellion after the war was defeated by the United States government-led counterinsurgency operations by 1956. Both also share a unique history—they were the first major political and military organisation in their countries to include and actively recruit women. During the 1940s and 1950s, rural women from Central Luzon in the Philippines and in North (and to some extent in South) Vietnam responded overwhelmingly to the calls of revolution and independence by leaders of the Huk movement and the Viet Minh.

The women warriors of the Huk revolution elicited a certain fascination in the public imagination through sensational news accounts of their exploits. Recruited via familial and village networks, Huk women—most of them from peasant families, poorly educated and generally perceived as traditional and passive—joined the movement. They wanted to be close to their kin, escape Japanese brutality, continue their prewar political involvement, or be part of what seemed to be a growing and strong movement for national liberation. These women studied the tenets of Marxism, trained as soldiers and spies, and learned to use weapons. Occupying the full range of military roles, some of these Filipina revolutionaries attained formidable, even fearsome reputations as aggressive fighters—hence their image as 'Amazons' within the wider culture.[5]

Incorporating women into the military and political struggle waged by the Huks confronted the male-dominated leadership of the PKP with new issues that were not originally laid out in their political and military agendas. Assigning active roles to women was one of them, although the leadership relegated most of them to 'supportive' roles, such as couriers, nurses, educators, and propaganda workers, with only a handful finding action in combat. The 'domestic' duties of cooking, washing, and housekeeping were also 'naturally' reserved for women.

From the beginning, Nguyen Ai Quoc (1890–1969), the future Ho Chi Minh, the political and spiritual leader of the Vietnamese revolution, called on women, who he remarked as comprising half of the population, to join the struggle for independence and social revolution in Vietnam. The Vietnamese Revolutionary Youth League, which he founded offered training courses in Southern China, already welcomed women. Women were also playing an active part in the underground and legal struggles of the Indochinese Communist Party. And women, mostly from North Vietnam and eventually from the South, responded overwhelmingly and enthusiastically to his call to fight against the returning French colonial forces during the First Indochina War (1946–1954) and the United States-backed South Vietnamese government during the Second Indochina War (c.1960–1975).

204 *Vina A. Lanzona*

Like the Huk women warriors, Vietnamese female revolutionaries worked in almost all branches of the revolutionary organisation—as couriers and messengers, as doctors and nurses, as spies and intelligence workers, as educators and organisers, and a few even in leadership positions. Unlike the Huk women, many women served as soldiers, who were engaged in combat zones. While Philippine society was fascinated with the Huk women because of their 'abnormal' behaviour, North Vietnamese society expected the women to join the struggle.

War was a bitter reality for Vietnamese women, occurring right within their own backyards, with bombs and enemy soldiers encroaching daily in their lives, their villages, and their homes. Thus, women had to do their share of fighting and surviving. Most of the men, including fathers, husbands, and sons, from the North especially, actively joined the war which left women tending to their fields, taking care of children, and nursing the wounded, while remaining vigilant against the actions of the enemies.

Conventional and historical accounts of the Huk and Vietnamese revolutions generally ignore issues of gender and sexuality in these movements, and particularly, the complex issues that women warriors and their presence had provoked in their revolutionary organisations. However, in recent years, several important works have highlighted the central and significant role that women have played in the revolutionary struggles in the Philippines and in Vietnam.[6] These works have shown that women challenged conventional boundaries and cultural limitations to work as couriers, nurses, propaganda workers, teachers, organisers, and even military soldiers in revolutionary movements. And yet, their personal lives, and the issues of love, sex, intimacy, and passion in the movement, still remain relatively unexplored in much of the secondary literature. Only recently was this absence addressed through intimate first-hand accounts as well as works that extensively use oral histories to unravel the actual words and experiences of these Southeast Asian female warriors.[7]

Choosing revolution: the loves of Dang Thuy Tram and Teofista Valerio

The lives and loves of two women warriors in Vietnam and the Philippines, Dr Dang Thuy Tram (26 November 1942–22 June 1970) and Teofista Valerio (20 September 1922–n.d.), best encapsulate how powerful and consuming issues of love, sex, and intimacy could be in revolutionary movements. Through the actual words that relate the experiences of these two remarkable women—Tram's posthumously published diary and my interviews with Ka[8] Teofista in the 1990s—we are able to see clearly how women warriors straddled the delicate line between the personal and the political.[9]

In July 2005, the wartime diary of Dang Thuy Tram, a North Vietnamese military doctor who worked as a battlefield surgeon in the northern part of South Vietnam during the Vietnam War, was published in Vietnam.

Lovelsex in war & revolution: Vietnam & the Philippines 205

Translated into English, her diary was published in 2007 with the title, *Last Night I Dreamed of Peace*, and instantly became popular among critics and readers. The eldest daughter of a relatively well-off family of doctors, Tram was highly educated, having attended a French elite school and then trained as a surgeon at the Hanoi University Medical School. She had great promise in the medical profession, but instead chose to serve in the war zone, volunteering for duty in a military hospital in Quang Ngai Province in Southcentral Vietnam in 1966, when she was only twenty-three years old. The diary begins there the following April, and chronicles the last three years of her life both as a field surgeon of the National Liberation Front forces working in the South and as a member of the Vietnamese Communist Party. At the age of twenty-seven, in late June 1970, Tram was killed by United States forces, while defending her hospital in the forest.[10] Saved by a U.S. military officer from being destroyed, her diaries attracted international attention following their publication and the female revolutionary instantly became a legend in Vietnam.[11]

One writer commented that what was so striking about Tram's diary was how she 'switches from the language of lovelorn teenager who desperately misses the mysterious "M" to earnest revolutionary, recalling the words of "Uncle Ho" [Vietnam communist leader Ho Chi Minh] and Lenin: "The revolutionary is a person with a heart very rich and filled with love." I am that way already.'[12] Indeed, almost every page of Tram's diary is filled with romantic longings and forlorn pleas for love. Although she never divulged the full name of 'M', he was constantly in her mind and in her writings, betraying a sense of vulnerability in Tram, as she exhibits both childishness and maturity in her relationships.[13]

On 13 April 1968, she wrote, 'So many letters come from all over...I read your letters with both joy and sadness. Why can everyone else love me so, but the man who has my faithful heart cannot? Isn't that sad, M.?' The next day, she opened up just a little bit more:

> Oh! This is the saddest part of my relationship with M. Every one blames M. and sympathizes with me. But it hurts to know they pity me! I don't care whether it is Thiet, Hao, Nghinh, or anyone else who wants to give me his sympathy, I don't want it... I can overcome my sorrows alone. I have the will to bury nine years of hope—my soul is fertile, still strong enough for a beautiful season of flowers yet... Oh, friends, please don't water this soil with tears of pity... M. has made my love for him fade with each passing day. A distance grows between us. That person doesn't deserve me, does he?[14]

But only two weeks later, Tram wrote in her diary:

> Oh, M! What can I say to you? I'm still madly, deeply in love with you, but my heart is scarred with anger and reproach... That is why I still

206 *Vina A. Lanzona*

grieve when everyone looks at me with pity. It hurts my pride. It is a deep wound impossible to heal, one I have resigned to bear all my life.

Her subsequent entries betray a constant longing for this man. 'News that you have fallen gravely ill makes me very depressed', she wrote.

If I were there by your side, I would take care of you the way a girl takes care of her lover—the way people want me to do. But the truth is not like that... Oh, M.! You are not mine, but I still want my love to lessen your pain. What can I do now? Something tells me that I will not see you again, that this past farewell will be our very last. You looked at me as I walked away without glancing back, even though I could feel your eyes following me... The seconds I spent in the arms of my beloved have become only images from the distant past.[15]

Tram's words evoke a sense of passion, revealing powerful feelings of both affection and hatred towards the man she loved and sometimes despised.

But Tram was not just a forlorn lover. Interspersed between her intimate entries were Tram's extraordinary experiences as a surgeon, including operating on soldiers without any anaesthesia or amputating their legs without them letting out a single scream or complaint. She also offers us reflections about life and death, often after losing a beloved friend and comrade in the hospital bed or in the battlefield, as well as harsh words against the 'American pirates' who had been the cause of all of her suffering. But still in the end, she always goes back to M, consumed by their past and unfinished love affair.

On 5 July 1968, she wrote, 'the truth is M. doesn't deserve my heart anymore, so why does everyone urge me to forgive him? No, I will never accept a mended love, and he is not one to beg for forgiveness. M insisted he had never wronged me, even in the slightest; that is not true.'[16] In a compelling entry, Tram equates her rejection to be an official member of the Communist Party (of Vietnam) to M's rejection of her, displaying a clear and sober understanding of how the political had fused with the personal, and how personal feelings and reactions could be interpreted as political acts. As Tram writes one day later:

I'm not a part of the Party's vanguard. My heart lacks the warming fire of the Party. I have come to the Party with a devoted and open heart, but it seems the Party has not treated me in kind. And M.—he does not deserve me, either. I have achieved none of the three pillars of life: Ideal, Career and Love. That's why I cannot avoid being sad.[17]

This entry shows how difficult it was for someone like Tram to separate her political persona from her own personal identity. The value she placed on the Party's recognition was almost as important as getting M's affection. Their rejection meant Tram's failure in what she (and perhaps the Party) considered as indispensable to life itself—ideal, career, and love—a

Lovelsex in war & revolution: Vietnam & the Philippines 207

sobering reality of how the political and personal struggles often intersect and reinforce each other in a revolutionary's life.

Unfortunately, Tram did not live through the war. While we will never know the full story between the two revolutionaries Tram and M, what we know was that at least for Tram, her passion for the revolution never diminished her passion for a certain comrade. Any news she heard about him was received with both longing and helpless frustration. Even after much attention from other men, and seemingly amorous relations with some, comrade M. continued to haunt her. And yet, in the two years of serving in different mobile hospitals, Tram never considered abandoning her duties just to be with the person she loved/hated. It was quite evident in her diaries that she was a committed revolutionary, but she was also a woman in love. Balancing the demands of the revolution and her heart was a constant struggle, one that she herself encapsulated in her last entry, dated 20 June 1970, two days before she was killed by an American platoon along a jungle trail:

> No, I am no longer a child. I have grown up. I have passed trials of peril, but somehow, at this moment, I yearn deeply for Mom's caring hand. Even the hand of a dear one or that of an acquaintance would be enough… Come to me, squeeze my hand, know my loneliness, and give me the love, the strength to prevail on the perilous road before me.[18]

Tram found solace by writing in her journal, using her words to secure a calm space where she could be herself—a child who yearns for her mother's embrace, a rebel who had thoughts of revenge, a comrade who believes in the cause, and a lover who craves for intimacy. As FitzGerald states, 'Here was a brave, idealistic young woman, but one with vulnerabilities and self-doubts: a romantic in spite of all her discipline.'[19] But it was not clear from Tram's diary whether the revolution, and the movement, to which she gave her entire life, ever knew who she was, her needs, desires, and passions. And if they did, what would they have done?

When female Huk Teofista Valerio first met Casto Alejandrino (1911–2005) in the early 1940s, she already knew who he was—a former mayor of Pampanga in Central Luzon, just north of Manila, who had given up everything for the revolution, a fearless commander, and one of the most intelligent leaders of the Political Bureau (Politburo) of the PKP. But for Teofista, Alejandrino was her first and foremost leader and comrade. They met while they were both doing revolutionary work in Nueva Ecija during World War II and worked together in the Communist Party—he in the leadership and she as part of the Provincial Committee of Central Luzon. Teofista admired Alejandrino, affectionately known as 'Gy' from afar, but she never thought of him as more than a comrade, and she herself had a romantic relationship with another Huk soldier.[20]

In October 1947, while Teofista worked at the Huk headquarters in the Sierra Madre under Alejandrino, a romantic relationship developed between them. By that time, she had already broken up with her Huk boyfriend and she felt close to Gy, who 'never used force. He talked to me intimately and

208   *Vina A. Lanzona*

I to him', she said. After six months, Teofista recalled with a smile, 'I surrendered to him'. But the relationship was complicated from the start. Alejandrino was already married to a woman in the *barrio* (village), although he stopped communicating with her after joining the Hukbalahap, the wartime guerrilla organisation. Before meeting Teofista, he had affairs with two different Huk women. But despite his reputation, Teofista was attracted to him. 'In the beginning', she thought:

> I treated him like any of our comrades. But perhaps because I was a woman and he was a man and we were constantly together...our feelings developed. We were always together, night and day, we grew close to each other and we understood each other. He then started to tell me what he felt for me. He reassured me that he was no longer with his wife. The entire period that he was in the mountains, his wife never visited him and he never visited her. And so, I believed him. And I had a problem, too. I was already in love with him.[21]

While she felt conflict at first, Teofista clearly understood what a relationship with someone like Alejandrino meant. In a simple Huk ceremony, Teofista Valerio and Casto Alejandrino were married on 26 May 1948. At that time, she later admitted, she had no thoughts for the future, never envisioning a time when she and Alejandrino would live as a 'normal' couple. And they never did. While her marriage to Gy lasted, their relationship had to withstand enormous challenges. A short time after their marriage, they were separated when Alejandrino contracted a serious illness and was forced to leave the forests of the Sierra Madre to recuperate. Teofista visited him occasionally, but stayed in the forest camps, continuing her revolutionary work. In early 1949, when Gy had recovered, he returned to the forest headquarters but a few months later, it was Teofista's turn to leave. Pregnant with their first child, Alejandrino insisted that she give birth in Manila. Teofista initially wanted to stay in the forest, but he was adamant and in August 1949, she went to Manila where she gave birth to their daughter named Baby.

During this period of separation, Gy and Teofista exchanged love letters.[22] The letters revealed the irony of their lives: they were a normal, loving couple, but their relationship was shaped by abnormal, revolutionary times. Soon after her delivery, Alejandrino wrote to Teofista approving her choice of a name for their child. 'The name you chose for baby was good', he wrote, 'I still don't know who should be her godmother. If you want someone, you can go ahead and choose.' A few days later, he wrote again asking if the baby was already 'able to go up to the mountains?'

In his letters to Teofista, Alejandrino always inquired about the health of mother and child, and talked about life in the forest. In one letter, he asked, 'By the way, to whom do you plan to leave Baby when you can already join me in the forest?' Like many couples, they addressed each other as 'love' or 'sweetheart'. Yet, there were always words of caution and despair in these letters.

Gy talked constantly about how he missed Teofista, and asked her to send him necessities such as shoes and a pair of pants. He also apologised for not providing for his family, and in one letter, sent them P20 (pesos) because she needed money. But despite the melancholy of his letters, Alejandrino remained focused on his work, excusing himself for neglecting to write because he was doing 'work for our people'.

Figure 10.2 In contrast to Dr Dang Thuy Tram and Teofista Valerio, who remained loyal to the anti-American struggle and the Huk movement, others decided to reintegrate the peacetime normative order. Looking more mature than her sixteen years, here we see Leonora Hipas, alias Kumander [Commander] Linda de Vila, with Huk uniform, straw hat, and right hand resting on her revolver, at the moment of surrender in October 1954. She and her twenty-one year old Huk husband Emilio Diesta, alias Kumander Oscar, were members of Huk Field Command 104 and confessed that their surrender was motivated by a desire to 'get married and live peacefully'.

Source: Courtesy Rizal Library, Ateneo de Manila University.

210 *Vina A. Lanzona*

Finally, after one year, Teofista felt ready to join Alejandrino in the forest camp. But on 7 September 1950, while awaiting the courier who would guide her to the Huk headquarters in the *Sierra Madre*, she was arrested by Philippine intelligence officers as part of a massive campaign against the Huks which led to the capture of Politburo leaders in Manila. When they discovered letters from Alejandrino—a wanted top Communist with a price on his head—Teofista was taken to Camp Murphy in Manila, and interrogated. When she refused to volunteer any information, they stripped Teofista and severely beat her for several days. She eventually lost the hearing in her left ear as a result of the torture, but she refused to talk. Teofista spent the next fifteen years in prison, until 1965, without receiving a single letter from her husband. Alejandrino was eventually arrested in 1960 and remained in prison after Teofista's release. Parted on 4 August 1949, they did not see one another again until 4 August 1970, exactly twenty-one years later. Even after many years, Teofista remains at a loss for words when talking about her imprisonment, the 'loneliest time of her life', when she was separated from her young daughter and yearned for Gy's companionship.

While she was in prison, Teofista learned that Alejandrino had found a new partner in the forest, another young courier named Belen.[23] When she heard about the affair, Teofista recalled,

> I was very hurt, of course. But I accepted it. After feeling my pain, I thought about it seriously. Because Gy was really sickly—he needed someone to take care of him. I also found out that Gy got married to Belen. What can I do? Gy is a man. He was far from me and I will not be able to give him what he wanted.[24]

When she got out of prison, Teofista was relieved to discover Gy had not in fact married his new partner, although Belen bore him four children. The fact that Teofista was the only woman Alejandrino married in the movement was a source of enormous pride for her. When Alejandrino was imprisoned, his romantic relationship with Belen ended. After his release, Gy and Teofista lived together briefly as husband and wife in Nueva Ecija, although he saw Belen and their children periodically. But politics always beckoned Alejandrino, and for most of his remaining years he lived with the Lavas, his old comrades, in Manila where they continued to work for the PKP. In the end, Teofista remarked poignantly, 'Gy was really married to the revolution'.

Personal memoirs of male revolutionaries, often Politburo and Communist leaders, reveal very little about emotional and personal conflicts that seemed to occupy much of the female revolutionaries' experiences and memory. Male accounts are often overtly political, written usually as justifications of their involvement, chronicling their struggles in the battlefields and in leadership meetings and offering their own reasons for the movement's success or defeat. Relying purely on men's usually written recollections would give us an incomplete picture of revolutions as occasions for

Love/sex in war & revolution: Vietnam & the Philippines 211

Figure 10.3 While Dr Dang Thuy Tram never married, Teofista Valerio's husband remained married to the revolution even after they were re-united after twenty-one years of separation. This was in stark contrast to Leonora Hipas' and Emilio Diesta's reintegration into the Philippines' traditional normative and gender order a mere day after their surrender. Their marriage in a temporary wedding hall marked a remarkable return from the topsy-turvy world of communist [atheist] insurgency and an armed woman in uniform, causing the *Philippines Free Press* to triumphantly crow about Hipas' overnight transformation: 'With the Huks she dressed like a man. Like all girls, she wanted a wedding gown for her marriage.'
Source: Courtesy Rizal Library, Ateneo de Manila University.

primarily political and military struggles. In contrast, the diaries of Tram and the oral recollections by Teofista reveal that the boundary of the political and personal was often crossed in their lives as revolutionaries. Their articulate renderings of their revolutionary lives and loves brought the war and the revolution to life, in FitzGerald's words, 'in a way that the old rhetoric

212 *Vina A. Lanzona*

of invincibility did not'.[25] While understanding that the struggles of the Viet Cong and the Huks were crucial to the lives of Tram and Teofista, the feelings and actions of their lovers seemed equally as important. But how does the movement deal with the issues of love and sexuality that consumed its (female) members while fighting a revolutionary war?

Regulating sex and passion

For the Huk revolutionary movement, relationships such as the one with Teofista and Gy—one between an older, more powerful, and usually married leader, and a young, female subordinate—constituted a serious problem. They came to be called as '*kualingking* cases', occasions when male Huk and communist cadres engaged in extramarital relations with unmarried, mostly young women in the camps while their wives and families remained in the cities and *barrios*.[26] Often the affairs were carried out through deception—the men hiding the relations from their wives and deceiving their mistresses and even their comrades. The isolation in the forest and the separation from families in the barrios led many men to seek emotional and sexual intimacy with female guerrillas in the forest camps.

These sexual and extramarital relations posed a moral and political dilemma for the Huks. Politburo members were supposed to set a moral example within the movement but their power and prominence made them particularly desirable to women. If they engaged in sexual relations they became targets of criticism while their 'mistresses' were regarded with disdain, sometimes even by the 'womanisers' themselves. The leadership's ease of access to women also aroused great resentment among rank-and-file soldiers. Because women were few, the times when Huk leaders took forest wives directly diminished opportunities available to rank-and-file male soldiers, who also resented the fact that Politburo leaders almost always went unpunished when caught in extramarital affairs. This led to a general feeling among the Huks that such relationships compromised the growth of the movement by weakening the solidarity and discipline of the guerrillas.

Kualingking cases, which were common in the Huk movement, were not only damaging to the movement but affected the morale of both its male and female members.[27] Huk women often left the movement once they got married or when they got pregnant, while male guerrillas were often reluctant to go on expansion assignments because this meant that they would be separated from their [forest] wives and families. The Huk Party leadership therefore perceived sex and family issues as urgent and necessary, incorporating them into the revolutionary agenda. For the so-called 'kualingking cases', the Communist Party leadership came up with a remarkable document, aptly titled the 'The Revolutionary Solution of the Sex Problem' in 1950.[28]

Because the sex problem was considered as a political rather than as a moral or ethical issue, the committee offered a policy to guide its comrades.[29] Acknowledging the inevitable coupling of sex and revolution, the

Love/sex in war & revolution: Vietnam & the Philippines 213

document then provides a rationale for (hetero) sexual relationships between guerrillas. 'It must be recognised that the urge to enter into abnormal sex relations', the document stated, 'is motivated by varying considerations, foremost among which are the satisfaction of biological necessity and the satisfaction of emotional hunger'.[30] Since 'biological necessity' compelled such behaviour in men—but not apparently among married women—extramarital relationships were deemed permissible by the party. According to *The Revolutionary Solution of the Sex Problem*, the party would allow a man to take a 'forest wife' only if he observed strict regulations:

> Firstly, a married man cannot take a forest wife unless he can convince the leading committee in the Reco (Regional Command) to which he belongs that either his health or his work are being adversely affected by absence from his wife.
>
> Secondly, he must write to or otherwise communicate with his wife in the lowland and inform her of his intention and need to take a forest wife. He must, at the same time, under the principle of equality, give his wife the freedom to enter into a similar relationship in the barrio or city if she, too, finds herself unable to withstand the frustration.
>
> Thirdly, the forest wife must be clearly informed that the man is already married and that their relationship will terminate when he is able to return to his regular wife. In other words, there must be no deception of the regular wife and no deception of the forest wife. If, at the end of the struggle, a man should decide that he prefers a permanent relation with the forest wife, he must completely separate from the previous wife.[31]

Although the recommendations of the Politburo committee were adopted, they generated an acrimonious debate. In order to solve other 'personal' problems related to relationships and families, the party demanded the integration of spouses (especially wives) and older children into the movement, and to insist on the distribution of younger children to friends or relatives who were not directly involved in the rebellion. Male guerrillas themselves initiated affairs because of the absence of their wives, a practice that was tolerated in the organisation. And yet, many Huk women warriors accepted these conditions and frequently recalled that relationships were consensual while admitting that 'exceptional' circumstances fomented such illicit relations. There seems to be a consensus, as one Huk woman claimed, that 'the Party addressed this issue as best as it could'.[32] In fact, many observers of the movement believed that placing the emotional and sexual lives of male and female members as part of the political agenda was in itself a revolutionary act. The legitimacy of the Party's actions can be further examined through a comparison with the leadership of the Viet Cong whose members similarly faced issues of a personal and sexual nature.

Although they are not well documented in the Vietnamese movement, it seems that guerrillas and soldiers like Tram also experienced a dilemma

214   *Vina A. Lanzona*

similar to the Huks' *kualingking* cases, of women entering into relationships with respected leaders in the Party and movement. Aside from her longing for 'M' and unlike several deeply affective relations that she sublimated as 'sister-brother relationship' and as 'that adopted-brother story again!',[33] relationships in which she usually took on the role of older sister, this was not possible with higher ranking party members. In contrast, in her affectionate relationship with Nguyen Trong Tan, the secretary of Duc Pho District, Dang Thuy Tram adopts the position of 'young sister' instead.[34] When Tan asks her in a letter whether 'you think that I deserve to be your dear big brother or not?', she notes in her diary 'I admire you, brother, and I like you very much.'[35] While she accepts him 'like a caring big brother', she also notes that his higher position renders their relation more difficult, since she '[does not] want people to think I am an easy girl, one who gives her heart readily'.[36] Moreover, Tram is concerned that her social ties with Tan could be misinterpreted as improper for 'want[ing] to have relationships with high-level officials.'[37] Roughly three months later, she describes the difficulty of properly handling her emotions and her words in public, with 'too many people around me', when she would rather 'want to run to him, to put my head on his shoulder the way I did whenever I came home to see Dad or Uncle Hien, but I stand still without uttering a word.'[38] Although Tram was obviously conflicted about how to proceed with this relationship, she hinted at times that he did not care about what others think or feel about their closeness. But she always seemed alone, at a loss, and desperately needed some guidance regarding this personal issue that clearly intersected with her political life.

Issues regarding relationships were already present in the early Vietnamese communist movement in the 1920s. Sophie Quinn-Judge's work reveals how persistent 'abnormal relationships' were in the revolutionary lives and loves of two Vietnamese women, Nguyen Tri Duc (c.1911–n.d.) and Nguyen Thi Minh Khai (1910–1941), who both joined the nascent proto-communist movement at very young ages, were educated in party schools, became militant female leaders, and who rose to the ranks in organisations that would eventually become the Indochinese Communist Party.[39] In 1927, Nguyen Tri Duc agreed to marry a senior revolutionary, Le Hong Son (1899–1933), one who commanded great respect within the Vietnamese Revolutionary Youth League, against her own desires. In reality, she was in love with another comrade, Le Quang Dat, but was rendered powerless to go against the Youth League's wishes to direct her affections to a more worthy, and certainly more important, comrade. Unsurprisingly, the marriage was not a success. In 1929, she divorced her husband and then married Le Quang Dat, her former partner, to the chagrin of the Party who accused her of having 'loose morals'.

Like Nguyen Tri Duc, Nguyen Thi Minh Khai had been subjected to similar pressures to have affairs with her comrades, but 'came through

Lovelsex in war & revolution: Vietnam & the Philippines   215

her political apprenticeship with her confidence and commitment intact'.[40] In 1931, she entered into a 'fictive marriage' with Ho Chi Minh and soon after, with another comrade. In 1933, she was pressured by the Party to pursue another liaison with an exiled revolutionary, Tran Dai Do, but this time, she vehemently refused and wrote: 'Marriage is absurd, a bore, a burden...Now everything is broken and I am no longer haunted by the idea of marriage or motherhood...My only husband is the Communist Revolution', echoing veteran patriotic leader Phan Boi Chau's advice to female revolutionaries: When asked whether you have a husband yet, you should reply, 'Yes, his surname is Viet and his family name is Nam'.[41] In all her years as a woman leader of the Indochinese Communist Party until her execution at the hands of the French in August 1941, it seemed that Minh Khai had abided by her own precept.

Relationships among comrades, while admittedly common and perceived as inevitable when men and women work closely together certainly posed organisational problems in revolutionary movements. While most relationships in the Huk movement seemed consensual, early Vietnamese female revolutionaries were often pressured to marry their male comrades for primarily political and rarely for emotional reasons in what Quinn-Judge refers to as 'fictive marriages'. Such 'fictive marriages' appeared to be tolerated by the proto-communist and then the communist movement for political and practical reasons.

'Married' couples, while doing their political work, would not be seen as suspicious, while young women would not appear as vulnerable. Extramarital relationships, however, seemed more common among the Huks, and it was these types of relationships that led the leadership to at least formulate policies regulating sex and passion.

In contrast, it seemed that there was no clear-cut policy regarding sex, relationships, or families within the Vietnamese revolutionary movement during its many different phases and periods. It was generally acknowledged that from the very beginning, Nguyen Ai Quoc, or 'Uncle Ho' [Chi Minh], a term of endearment for the nation's revered leader, called on men and women to equally participate in Vietnam's struggle for independence. Memoirs of both men and women who were involved in the revolution consistently discussed how they shared 'brotherly and sisterly love' among their fellow comrades.[42]

Even Dang Thuy Tram, several decades after the foundation of the Indochinese Communist Party, seemed at a loss when confronted with intense emotions for her comrades, especially those who were older and married. So, what did the women do? What were the options available for pioneering women such as Nguyen Tri Duc and Nguyen Thi Minh Khai? Like the Huks, these women were at their sexual and emotional prime; were separated from family and familiar support networks; and endured days and months of hardships, isolation and suffering as guerrillas, cadres or soldiers.

216 *Vina A. Lanzona*

Tram herself pondered on the relationship between love and revolution. 'Why do I deserve your great love?' she asked:

> Could this be the noble reward for a revolutionary? Now I understand why people can sacrifice their whole lives for our cause, and how they can remain absolutely faithful to the revolution. The revolution has forged a noble people and bound them into a unit firmer and more solid than anything in this life. Could anything make one prouder than to be part of this family of revolutionaries?[43]

Were the Vietnamese revolutionaries encouraged to just see each other purely as 'comrades', 'brothers' and/or 'sisters'? Were these 'comradely' and 'brotherly' relationships adequate to sustain the men and women in the movement? Was the revolution, as Dang Thuy Tram and Nguyen Thi Minh Khai reflected, the only real family of the soldiers and guerrillas? Unlike the Huks, the Vietnamese revolutionaries did not come up with concrete solutions or approaches to these personal issues. From initial observations, it seems that the responses of the two organisations varied. While the Huks came up with political solutions to personal issues, the Vietnamese leadership did not do so, often leaving their members to deal with the issues of the struggle and of the heart on their own. The Party only intervened with relationships to achieve a particular political goal, such as the case with Nguyen Thi Minh Khai. But oftentimes, it was the members' own feelings of control or restraint that guided their personal and political actions.

And yet, like the Huks, the Vietnamese communist leadership did not completely ignore the existence of these relationships, and indeed, the central role that female revolutionaries played in the movement. From the beginning, the Party was committed (at least in principle) to liberate women from the burden of tradition and to promote egalitarian relations between men and women. Since its foundation in 1930, Party doctrine had encouraged women to believe there was a place in the Party hierarchy for them, and that they would not be tied to the home and the demands of their husbands and often oppressive mothers-in-law. By the 1940s, according to Sandra Taylor, the Party was advocating 'universal suffrage, democratic liberties, equality among all ethnic groups and between men and women'. She also adds that 'Ho Chi Minh had also spoken informally of an end to arranged marriages and of the opportunities for women to learn to read, study, participate in politics and be truly men's equals'.[44]

During the early years of the Vietnamese communist movement, in the late 1920s and early 1930s, in efforts to 'proletarianise the party', all Vietnamese activists were called on to sacrifice their old lives, and abandon bourgeois attitudes all for the sake of the communist revolution and the 'working classes'. For female activists, this meant they had to renounce the right to raise their children, and sometimes had been expected to put their bodies at the service of the revolution by living as the 'wives' of male

Love/sex in war & revolution: Vietnam & the Philippines 217

activists, the already mentioned 'fictive marriages'. As Sophie Quinn-Judge states, 'There seems to have been a grey area between a real marriage and the pose of being a married couple, which the communists often adopted for the purposes of clandestine work'.[45] In the end, she adds:

> There seems to have been an overlap between those communists accused of immoral behavior towards women and those who were considered to be infected with 'petty bourgeois' tendencies... Perhaps these men were guilty of abusing the trust of young female comrades...unable to discard former notions of female virtue, according to which a woman brazen enough to leave home on her own was fair game.[46]

All these tendencies indicate that as early as in the late 1920s, conservative and patriarchal attitudes—that condoned male control over female bodies and female subservience—found their place in the nascent Vietnamese communist movement even after an initial surge of female recruitment promising liberation and individual rights.[47] In reality, according to Party member Le Quang Dat, 'liberty for women and equality between the sexes were "hollow words" [...] because [a] woman who is affiliated with the party is often forced to abandon her husband and must give herself continually to different men, because if she refuses she risks being knifed. Is this liberty of the sexes?'[48] Quinn-Judge adds that 'between 1928 and 1935, accusations of uncomradely treatment of women were a regular feature of party life'.[49] Similar to the *kualingking* cases of the Huks, she cites several cases where male Communist leaders were removed from their positions because of 'womanising'. Many others were accused of raping female comrades, while some would brutally murder their rivals over female affection. Like the Huks, the Vietnamese communists obsessed over their members' lack of discipline, especially with regard to sexual liaisons, and their lack of communist morality.

Issues of sex, marriage, and revolution in many ways also defined the life of Bao Luong (1909–1976), Vietnam's first female political prisoner, who joined Ho Chi Minh's Revolutionary Youth League (founded by Ho Chi Minh and a precursor of the Communist Party) in 1927 and later became embroiled in the infamous Barbier Street murder of late 1928.[50] Hue-Tam Ho Tai, who wrote about Bao Luong's memoirs long after her mother's oldest sister had passed away, describes female revolutionary life as constantly plagued by offers of sex and marriage:

> A Tac [a female comrade] asked whether Bao Luong had thought about the issue of sex. Bao Luong, understanding sex to mean marriage, rebelled at the idea that she had joined the revolution in order to find a husband. But A Tac explained that activists, who were mostly men, were divided in their opinions regarding the presence in their ranks of unmarried women like themselves...Women should get married as soon as possible to resolve their status, putting themselves out of reach.[51]

218   *Vina A. Lanzona*

But for both Bao Luong and A Tac, such pressures seemed contradictory to what the revolutionary movement advocated. They argued that women joined the revolution precisely because they detested oppression. 'If they were forced into marriage', they asked, 'what meaning would emancipation have for them?' A Tac continued:

> Revolution involved the transformation of individuals' mentality as well as the mentality of the society at large. Men must stop harassing women, behaving discourteously, or exploiting them emotionally. Women, for their part, must not engage in flirtatious behavior or get involved in promiscuous affairs. If men and women of goodwill could not exercise self-control, how could they hope to achieve great things?[52]

Unfortunately for Bao Luong, it was a comrade's ill behaviour and contempt for women that led to her involvement in the Barbier 'crime of passion' murder case. On 8 December 1928, she and two other comrades killed Lang, a Vietnamese Revolutionary Youth League leader accused of abusing his authority, including attempted rape and forced marriage to a young female comrade. For Bao Luong, the way the Youth League dealt with someone like Lang and her own experience of abandonment by the organisation's leadership during the crime and trial demonstrated the revolution's failure to protect the needs of women.

These early experiments on sexual relations and female experiences of neglect and abandonment did not lead to more formal deliberations on the relations between men and women in the Vietnamese communist movement. And the increased intensity of the Vietnam War further relegated such issues into the background. Throughout the second phase of the Vietnam struggle, the period of Dang Thuy Tram's involvement, there was no deliberate policy or regulation handed down by the Party that dealt specifically with interpersonal and sexual relations. At the height of the war in the 1950s and 1960s, Vietnamese women were asked to sacrifice more of their personal and sexual lives, as they became increasingly torn between their personal lives and their duties to their nation. This time, the Communist Party encouraged women to hold off on love and marriage until after the war ended, which proved too late for many. Karen Turner's work discussed how many young Vietnamese women controlled their sexual needs, and postponed marriage and pregnancy during the various stages of the Vietnamese revolution. Particularly, in North Vietnam, women had to forego romantic and sexual desires until after the conflict was over, which often resulted in unhealthy relationships with men who regarded former women guerrillas as past their reproductive prime, and possessed of scarred, unattractive, and infertile bodies.[53]

The implicit communist policy preached that men should not abandon their wives and encouraged the treatment of women as equals. But according to David Hunt, writing on Southern Vietnam, 'sexual relations outside of marriage was a fact of life in the Liberation Front'. The Front formally insisted on chastity for women while also requiring a similar restraint from men.

Love/sex in war & revolution: Vietnam & the Philippines 219

'The line on polygamy was unequivocal', and yet marriages between activists were discouraged and often prevented cadres from marrying pregnant girlfriends because the Party feared that the couple might defect to the other side to lead an easier life. 'By blocking virtually all possibilities, even conjugal, for intimacy', Hunt concludes, the Party 'left its militants no alternative to abstinence.'[54] While the struggle in North and South Vietnam was markedly different, and entailed varied political tactics and strategies, it appears that the unofficial policy regarding sex and relationships remained consistent among the communist forces operating in the two zones.

In both the Huk and Vietnamese communist movements, female revolutionaries struggled to reconcile their personal desires for intimacy and affection with the impersonal aims of the revolution and against the background of social and class values. And they did so with or without party regulation. Male cadres in both movements, however, did not seem bothered, many times abandoning their matrimonial responsibility for their revolutionary work. For the Huks, male guerrillas continued to be active in the rebellion, while practising a form of 'revolutionary polygamy' sanctioned by the leadership, when they decided to pursue Huk female guerrillas. This often led to the breakup of their marriages and confusing images or identities for the men and women in the movement. In the Vietnamese movement, Hunt observes with regard to southern Vietnam that, 'since men remained dominant in society and seized a preponderant role within the Front, a laissez faire approach left women even more exposed than they were in everyday life, where patriarchal norms offered them a limited, but not insignificant, measure of protection.'[55] Whether policies were expressly formulated, such as in the Huk movement, or remained open, unarticulated, and yet came with concomitant pressures and expectations, such as in the Vietnamese case, it is easy to see that sexist and patriarchal attitudes often shaped the attitudes of male leaders, allowing extramarital affairs to continue, pressuring women to marry solely for the purposes of the revolution, leaving male sexual offenders unpunished and their female partners vulnerable.

For Teofista Valerio, the Huks' 'Revolutionary Solution of the Sex Problem' did not offer much reprieve. When she was arrested in 1950, her high-ranking partner Casto Alejandrino immediately found another partner from within the Huk movement. The revolutionary solution not only condoned Alejandrino's new liaison, but also, in fact, further legitimised that relationship. For Dang Thuy Tram, the absence of any guidance from the Party troubled and confused her, and throughout the war, she tried to ignore such 'childish' feelings and put them aside. But as her diary reveals, this was a task that she found almost impossible to do.

Conclusion: love, sex, culture, and revolution

In many respects, the Huks, in both their acknowledgement and their regulation of personal, sexual, and familial issues in the movement, seemed more sensitive to the needs of their cadres, especially the men. At the same time,

220 *Vina A. Lanzona*

their actions acknowledged (rather than ignored) the presence of women and created a space for them to exist in this male-dominated organisation. Indeed, their approach may be interpreted as ideologically lax, an adaptation to the 'bourgeois tendencies' of romantic love and family relationships. And yet, such practices seem consistent with more tolerant cultural attitudes on gender relations and sex in Philippine society.

How did these different attitudes about personal relationships affect the internal dynamics of the Huk and the Vietnamese movements? Did the Vietnamese Communist Party's gender policies (or perhaps the lack of such policies) contribute to the success of its revolution, and the Huks' 'Revolutionary Solution of the Sex Problem' weaken the movement? If we take the example of Vietnam seriously, it seems that a stricter culture of intolerance may have contributed to the revolution's success by preventing romantic and sexual relationships from preoccupying the guerrillas. And perhaps the laxity of the Huks was a fatal weakness. But as studies on the Vietnamese revolution suggest, including the memoirs of soldiers like Tram, such strict, demonstrably patriarchal tendencies in these movements may have also alienated many of its female members.

According to Quinn-Judge, while Vietnamese women did not experience an extreme form of patriarchy that crippled the lives of Chinese women, Confucian values still shaped female roles, even under circumstances of war. This meant that women were 'expected to play a part when national sovereignty came under threat', and yet such roles should be performed 'modestly and chastely', 'without departing from their place in Confucian society', to the extent that '[t]heir courage and devotion to the nation could be seen as a form of service to their menfolk'.[56] In terms of sex and marriage in the movement, Vietnamese women were constantly reminded of their Confucian virtues, particularly by submitting themselves to male authority, such as giving in to the pressures of their male peers to sleep with them (the so-called 'fictive marriages' in the early Vietnamese communist movement), and also fulfilling the roles of the submissive wife.

All these patriarchal attitudes were however justified with the communist promise of liberation. As the Party espoused, after the revolution, women would embrace a 'new freedom' from their traditional roles, their often domineering mothers-in-law, and their pampered husbands. In contrast, the Huks did not rely on this promise of liberation. By regulating sex, passion, and relationships, they believed in the importance of personal issues in running a revolutionary organisation, and the urgency of addressing such issues of sex and passion, at the time of the revolution (and also after). For the Vietnamese leadership, such issues seemed secondary only to the larger political and military goals of national liberation and social revolution. Indeed, despite the isolation, heartbreak, and pain of many Vietnamese female revolutionaries, and their frustration about the lack of regulations on personal issues, most of them continued to devote themselves to the movement and the revolution, as any obedient daughter, sister, and wife would do in a Confucian society.

Love/sex in war & revolution: Vietnam & the Philippines 221

Could this neglect, this strict subordination of the personal to the political, explain the success of the Vietnamese revolution? Perhaps the Huks should have also relegated issues of love, sex, and passion to the side, as mere distractions to the real work at hand. Perhaps, but it remains doubtful that the Huks would have completely ignored such issues. While the Filipino Communists openly eschewed Catholic religion and Catholic virtues, their actions were still guided by the traditional norms of society. Thus, while they indeed allowed extramarital affairs, they still needed to exist within the limits of monogamy, the accepted norm in Philippine society. And yet, while many of their sexual practices were patriarchal, they did not totally discount the women and their feelings, somehow respecting their dominant role in the domestic sphere. The openness and tolerance of Philippine culture made it difficult for a revolutionary movement such as the Huks to openly exhibit disrespect for women or see them primarily as submissive wives and sexual objects. The Huks' 'Revolutionary Solution of the Sex Problem' seems like an attempt at addressing a real gender imbalance between men and women by making men accountable and acknowledging women's dominant role in marriage and the domestic sphere. And yet, it was clear that this revolutionary solution fell short in respecting the rights of women and in fact exposing them to double standards and sexual exploitation.

It is also important to note that the Vietnamese revolution existed on an entirely different plane of struggle from the Huks. Stronger and better organised militarily, it enjoyed a degree of support from the Chinese Communists that the geographically isolated Huks could only dream about. The Huks also had no Ho Chi Minh, a leader who was more intellectually attuned to Communist dogma, and exuded larger-than-life personality and right from the beginning included women in their struggle for national liberation and social revolution. Women were successfully incorporated as soldiers and workers in the Vietnamese movement, even in the absence of formal regulations of personal and sexual relations. Indeed, because they were treated as soldiers and equals, at least in the political and military sense, the party did not give them any protection in terms of their own emotional well-being. The Huks, on the other hand, seemed much more concerned with women as domestic (and sexual) partners, so it seemed logical that the resolutions they came up with dealt more with sexual and emotional issues, rather than advancing women as political and military equals.

Both the Huks and the Vietnamese revolutionaries shared similar goals and experiences, and yet they differed on their official policies and strategies, particularly with regard to issues of love, sex, and the family. But what this brief exploration demonstrates is that the personal is inextricably linked to the political in revolutionary movements. And women, in whatever roles they played, were as central to revolutions as men, but it is their very presence, their unfailing, however conflicted, commitment, and dedication to the struggle that transform revolutionary movements to consider issues of gender and sexuality as seriously as military goals and political ideology. Not only adherence to political ideology but, more importantly, cultural

222   *Vina A. Lanzona*

practices and considerations shape the varied responses of these revolution-ary movements to issues of gender and sexuality. For the Vietnamese, this meant totally incorporating women in this military struggle, although a predominant Confucian sensibility promoted female sacrifice and subser-vience and oftentimes meant subordinating their personal passions for the great revolution. For the Huks, while there were seemingly open and toler-ant attitudes towards sex, Catholic virtues ensured that such relationships would occur in a 'legitimate' and monogamous plane, and therefore strict policies were drafted to regulate sex and passion. The policies and practices, however imperfect, of both the Vietnamese and Huk movements in terms of gender and sexuality were in the end, seemed like truly genuine attempts to provide a sense of security to women who exposed themselves to love and danger at the time of revolution.

Notes

1 This essay has gone through several revisions since it was presented at the ICAS conference in 2007. My intellectual debts go to Barbara Andaya, who's given me valuable suggestions and is always a great source of support and encourage-ment, and Marcus Daniel, who is ready to share his ideas on whatever topic I choose to explore, including sex and revolution in Southeast Asia.
2 Vina A. Lanzona, *Amazons of the Huk Rebellion: Gender, Sex, and Revolution in the Philippines* (Madison: University of Wisconsin Press, 2009).
3 For major works on the Huk rebellion, see especially Benedict J. Kerkvliet, *The Huk Rebellion: A Study of Peasant Revolt in the Philippines* (Berkeley: University of California Press, 1977; Lanham, MD: Rowman & Littlefield 2002), Eduardo Lachica, *Huk: Philippine Agrarian Society in Revolt* (Manila: Solidaridad, 1971), Alfred Saulo, *Communism in the Philippines: An Introduction* (Quezon City: Ate-neo de Manila University Press, 1990), and Alvin Scaff, *The Philippine Answer to Communism* (Stanford, CA: Stanford University Press, 1955). More recent works include Teresita Maceda, *Mga Tinig Mula Sa Ibaba: Kasaysayan ng Partido Ko-munista ng Pilipinas at Partido Sosialista ng Pilipinas sa Awit, 1930–1955* [Voices From Below: A History of the Communist Party and Socialist Party Through Song, 1930–1955] (Diliman: University of the Philippines Press, 1996) and Jose Dalisay, Jr., *The Lavas: A Filipino Family* (Pasig City: Anvil Press, 1999). Mem-oirs include William Pomeroy, *The Forest: A Personal Record of the Huk Guer-rilla Struggle in the Philippines* (New York: International Publishers, 1963); Luis Taruc, *Born of the People* (Westport, CT: Greenwood, 1973) and *He Who Rides the Tiger* (New York: Praeger, 1967) and Jesus Lava, *Memoirs of a Communist* (Pasig City: Anvil, 2003).
4 There are many remarkable books, now considered as classics, which discuss Vietnam's varying struggles for independence in depth. See especially, Wil-liam J. Duiker, *The Communist Road to Power in Vietnam* (Boulder, CO: West-view Press, 1996); Frances FitzGerald, *Fire in the Lake: The Vietnamese and the Americans in Vietnam* (Boston, MA: Little, Brown, 2002 [1972]); Marilyn B. Young, *The Vietnam Wars: 1945–1990* (New York: HarperCollins, 1991); Neil Sheehan, *A Bright Shining Lie: John Paul Vann and America in Vietnam* (New York: Random House, 1988), Stanley Karnow, *Vietnam: A History* (New York: Penguin Books, 1997). Notable recent editions include David Hunt, *Vietnam's Southern Revolution: From Peasant Insurrection to Total War, 1959–1968* (Am-herst: University of Massachusetts Press, 2008), Keith Weller Taylor, *A History*

Love/sex in war & revolution: Vietnam & the Philippines   223

of the Vietnamese (Cambridge: Cambridge University Press, 2014) and Fredrik Logevall, *Embers of War: The Fall of an Empire and the Making of America's Vietnam* (New York: Random House, 2012).

5　For an in-depth treatment of the 'Huk Amazon', see Lanzona, *Amazons of the Huk Rebellion* and a related article, Vina A. Lanzona, 'Capturing the Huk Amazons: Representing Women Warriors in the Philippines, 1940s–1950s', *South East Asia Research*, Vol. 17, No. 2 (2009), pp. 133–174.

6　Several important works have discussed the role of women in the Vietnamese Revolution, including Mary Ann Tétreault (ed.), *Women and Revolution in Africa, Asia and the New World* (Columbia: University of South Carolina Press, 1994), Karen Gottschang Turner with Phan Thanh Hao, *Even the Women Must Fight: Memories of War from North Vietnam* (New York: John Wiley, 1998), Sandra Taylor, *Vietnamese Women at War* (Lawrence: University Press Kansas, 1999), and Hue-Tam Ho Tai, *Passion, Betrayal, and Revolution in Colonial Saigon: The Memoirs of Bao Luong* (Berkeley: University of California Press, 2010). For the Philippines, the most notable work so far is by Lanzona, *Amazons of the Huk Rebellion* (2009).

7　Recent works that rely on oral history accounts and interviews include Turner, *Even the Women Must Fight*, Agnes Khoo, *Life as the River Flows: Women in the Malayan Anti-Colonial Struggle* (Monmouth, Wales: Merlin Press, 2008), and Lanzona, *Amazons of the Huk Rebellion*.

8　'Ka' here meaning 'Comrade', more commonly used to address elders and more distant uncles and aunts, originally from 'kapatid', denoting a very close kinship relation, such as brother or sister.

9　All the information about the life and struggles of Teofista Valeria is based on the interviews I conducted with her in 1993 and then again in 1997 at her home in Cabiao, Nueva Ecija in Central Luzon. She was in her mid-seventies then but still very alert and spent hours talking to me about her days in the Huk movement. Information on Dang Thuy Tram is based on her bestselling, posthumously published diaries entitled *Last Night I Dreamed of Peace: The Diary of Dang Thuy Tram*, translated by Andrew X. Pham (New York: Three Rivers Press, 2007).

10　As part of the military intelligence detachment, American Army officer Frederic (Fred) Whitehurst discovered and preserved Tram's diary in 1970 while reviewing the Northern forces' documents recovered during combat operations. He held onto the diaries for thirty-five years and was finally successful in tracking down Tram's family in 2005.

11　First published in Hanoi on July 2005, the diary became an instant sensation selling 430,000 copies a year and a half later. According to Frances FitzGerald's introduction to the English translation, the book was a big hit among young readers, most of whom were born after 1975. Since the publication of the diaries, a hospital was built carrying Dang Thuy Tram's name and a memorial marks the place where she had died. According to FitzGerald, '[s]he had become a folk hero' (p. xix). See 'Introduction' by Frances FitzGerald in Dang Thuy Tram, *Last Night I Dreamed of Peace*.

12　David McNeil, 'Vietcong Doctor's Diary of War, Sacrifice,' http://english. ohmynews.com/, 10 October 2005.

13　According to FitzGerald ('Introduction', pp. ix and x), the 'M' that Tram was in love with since age 16 was Khuong The Hung, an intellectual from Hanoi, who under his pen name Do Muc, wrote poetry and composed music. He courted Tram when they were students but in 1962, he joined the guerrilla army in central Vietnam. Upon graduation, Tram followed the 'call of love and country', hoping to see M. But the romance never took off.

14　Dang Thuy Tram, *Last Night I Dreamed of Peace*, p. 8.

224 *Vina A. Lanzona*

15 Ibid., p. 17.
16 Ibid., p. 31.
17 Ibid., p. 32.
18 Ibid., p. 225.
19 FitzGerald, 'Introduction', p. xviii.
20 Teofista Valerio, interview with the author, Sta. Rita, Nueva Ecija, November 1993 and July 1997. See also Lanzona, *Amazons of the Huk Rebellion*, pp. 198–201.
21 Interview with Teofista Valerio, and Lanzona, ibid.
22 The love letters are part of the captured documents of the Politburo. Mostly written in Tagalog, they can be found in the Politburo Archives in the Special Collections of the University of the Philippines, Diliman, Main Library.
23 Like Teofista, Belen Bagul-Bagul is also of peasant background but she was still a young girl during the war. She joined the HMB in 1948 and began a relationship with Alejandrino after Teofista's arrest in 1950. Interview with Belen Bagul-Bagul, Laguna, November 1993. See also Lanzona, *Amazons of the Huk Rebellion*, pp. 201–202.
24 Teofista Valerio interview.
25 FitzGerald, 'Introduction', p. xviii.
26 Although most of the Huk men and women knew about the '*kualingking* cases', no one seems to know the origin of the term. It is not a Tagalog or Kapampangan (the language spoken in the province of Pampanga) word. But when I asked them about *kualingking* cases, everyone understood what I was referring to.
27 Interviews with Huk women indicate that these sexual liaisons were indeed numerous and commonplace in the movement as everyone I interviewed knew about these relationships. Many in fact were willing to give names, although most refused to elaborate on the 'kualingking' couples. Many women claimed that both Politburo leaders and rank and file members engaged in these relations. And yet, the sex problem was always perceived as a sensitive issue that made many reluctant to share stories.
28 Secretariat, PKP, 'Revolutionary Solution of the Sex Problem', *Politburo Exhibit no. I–15*, 12 September 1950. For an in-depth discussion of this document, see Lanzona, *Amazons of the Huk Rebellion*, pp. 212–213, 215–224.
29 The Huks themselves viewed sex and sexual relations as part of revolutionary life that should not have been suppressed because of society's own bourgeois and Catholic norms of morality.
30 'Revolutionary Solution of the Sex Problem', p. 2.
31 Ibid., and Pomeroy, *The Forest*, p. 144.
32 Celia Mariano-Pomeroy, interview with the author, Twickenham, England, October and November 1998.
33 Dang Thuy Tram, *Last Night I Dreamed of Peace*, pp. 66, 72, 74.
34 Ibid., p. 105, note 99, and p. 145, note 143.
35 Ibid., pp. 105f., entry dated 7 April 1969.
36 Ibid., p. 106.
37 Ibid.
38 Ibid., pp. 144f., 3 August 1969.
39 For more detail, see Sophie Quinn-Judge's chapter in this volume, which is based on her pioneering article 'Women in the Early Vietnamese Communist Movement: Sex, Lies and Liberation', in *South East Asia Research*, Vol. 9, No. 3 (November 2001), pp. 245–269.
40 Ibid., p. 256.
41 Ibid., p. 260, citing David Marr, *Vietnamese Tradition on Trial, 1920–1945* (Berkeley: University of California Press, 1984), p. 210.
42 See especially Nguyen Thi Dinh's moving memoir, *No Other Road to Take: Memoir of Mrs. Nguyen Thi Dinh*, translated by Mai V. Elliot (Ithaca, NY: Cornell Southeast Asia Program, 1976).

Love/sex in war & revolution: Vietnam & the Philippines 225

43 Dang Thuy Tram, *Last Night I Dreamed of Peace*, p. 61.
44 Taylor, *Vietnamese Women at War*, p. 13.
45 Quinn-Judge, 'Women in the Early Vietnamese Communist Movement', pp. 247–251.
46 Ibid., p. 255.
47 Ibid., p. 253, for a discussion on the policies regarding gender and sexuality during the early years of the Vietnamese Communist Party.
48 Ibid., p. 253, quoted from Le Quang Dat.
49 Ibid., p. 254.
50 Ho Tai, *Passion, Betrayal, and Revolution in Colonial Saigon*. Bao Lung (born as Nguyen Trung Nguyet) was Hue-Tam Ho Tai's maternal aunt, thus the memoir was both an academic and personal venture.
51 Ibid., p. 38.
52 Ibid.
53 See Turner, *Even the Women Must Fight*, and the memoirs of Nguyen Thi Dinh, *No Other Road to Take*, for treatments of the personal struggles of women from both the North and the South during the different stages of the Vietnamese revolution.
54 Hunt, *Vietnam's Southern Revolution*, p. 98.
55 Ibid.
56 Quinn-Judge, pp. 247–248.

Part IV

The United Nations, Security Sector Reform (SSR), and the gendering of Disarmament, Demobilisation and Reintegration (DDR)

11 The aftermath for women warriors

Cambodia and East Timor

Susan Blackburn

Women make many and often dangerous contributions in wartime, including spying, acting as couriers, and providing food and shelter to armed combatants. In guerrilla wars, as most wars are in Third World countries, it is notoriously hard to distinguish between combatants and non-combatants. Historically and globally, women have long been essential to military enterprises in many capacities.[1] In the aftermath of a war, however, women's contributions are readily forgotten and left unrecognised.

After armed conflict ends, countries face the tasks of Disarmament, Demobilisation and Reintegration of former combatants, a process collectively known as DDR. This chapter examines to what extent women's multiple roles in war are recognised during the DDR process, taking as examples two Southeast Asian countries, Cambodia and East Timor, which have experienced prolonged conflict. I conducted some research in these countries in 2005–2006 as part of a project examining the assistance provided by Oxfam Australia to women in post-conflict situations.[2] Examples from Southeast Asia will serve to correct the absence of studies from this region of how female ex-combatants experience the aftermath of armed conflict. Most such studies relate to Africa, probably because the level of conflict has been so high there in recent years, and women's role as combatants has become more visible precisely at a time when awareness of the gendered nature of conflict has risen.[3] Like other examples of the inadequate implementation of DDR, the case studies of Cambodia and East Timor illustrate the consequences of not considering women. Comparison of the two cases also demonstrates the importance of the particular circumstances of armed conflict for the subsequent treatment of combatants.

Since the conflicts in Cambodia and East Timor, which ended in the 1990s, the United Nations Security Council has passed Resolution 1325, dealing with women, peace and security on 31 October 2000. Containing far-reaching recommendations concerning the rights of women during and after armed conflicts, the Resolution is regarded as a turning point in international gender awareness concerning armed conflict. For the purposes of this chapter, the relevant section of Resolution 1325 is article 13, which 'Encourages all those involved in the planning for disarmament,

230 *Susan Blackburn*

demobilization and reintegration to consider the different needs of female and male ex-combatants and to take into account the needs of their dependants'. At a later point I shall discuss the difficulties of implementing article 13 in Cambodia and East Timor.

Up until recently, the way in which post-conflict[4] authorities have treated ex-combatants has been a matter of pragmatism. An obvious reason why female ex-combatants receive less attention in DDR is that they are not regarded as a threat by the new regime which is trying to establish peace and order. In contrast, stories of trouble caused by male ex-combatants are legion: they range from revolts to domestic violence. East Timor has proved a sad example of the need to treat male ex-combatants carefully: in 2006 there were revolts by discontented former fighters.[5] Historically, such trouble has been caused by men, despite very occasional references to the involvement of young women ex-fighters participating in riots after the end of a war.[6] Women who fade out of the public eye at the end of conflicts can expect little attention from hard-pressed, under-resourced and often inexperienced post-conflict governments.

The nature of armed conflict in Cambodia and women's roles in combat

Armed conflict occurred in Cambodia and East Timor roughly from the 1970s to the 1990s, in very different circumstances. In Cambodia conflict began as that country was drawn into the Second Indochina War. From the late 1960s, Vietnamese communist troops used Cambodian territory to move troops and ammunition from the north of Vietnam to the south, assisted by the Cambodian communist troops, known as the Khmer Rouge, which were attempting to overthrow the government established by Lon Nol in 1970 after his coup against Prince Sihanouk. In 1975 the Khmer Rouge defeated Lon Nol and installed the government led by Pol Pot. That regime, whose cruelty to its own people is notorious, lasted until it was ousted in 1979 by a group of Khmer Rouge defectors led by Heng Samrin, backed up by Vietnamese military invasion and occupation. Hostilities between the Vietnamese troops and Heng Samrin's forces, on the one side, and remnant Khmer Rouge, on the other, lasted until the Vietnamese withdrew in 1989 and the United Nations (UN) stepped in to resolve the dispute. According to the Paris Agreement of 1991, the United Nations Transitional Authority in Cambodia (UNTAC) was established, which lasted from early 1992 to late 1993. Even with its help, it took the Cambodian government until the mid-1990s to wipe out the remainder of the Khmer Rouge.

It is thus quite difficult to characterise the conflict in Cambodia. While it comprised elements of civil war, foreign invasion and intervention, what people mainly remember is the cruelty of the Khmer Rouge. In the 1970s and 1980s Cambodian women fought on the side of the Khmer Rouge against the government of Lon Nol (backed by the United States) and then against Heng Samrin and the Vietnamese. The Khmer Rouge recruited some women for combat roles, and many more were involved in the conflict in support roles, supplying medical and other assistance to the fighters.[7] No accurate figures are available.

In my research with Oxfam Australia in three eastern provinces of Cambodia (Takeo, Kratie and Stung Treng) in late 2005, those Cambodians who mentioned knowing female ex-combatants clearly regarded them as exceptional cases. One such account related to a woman in Takeo province who was said to have joined the army when she was twelve or thirteen years old and later married a Khmer Rouge soldier. Another Oxfam Australia staff member also recalled meeting a former Khmer Rouge woman who had become a soldier at age thirteen, and another who carried food to soldiers in the battlefield. They had joined the Khmer Rouge when Prince Norodom Sihanouk encouraged young Cambodians to resist the Americans who attacked Cambodia in an attempt to wipe out the Vietnamese communists from the late 1960s. A health worker in Kratie province related that one of her colleagues had carried food and guns to the battlefield. In Stung Treng province an Oxfam Australia staff member mentioned a married couple now living in a nearby village who had both been high ranking Khmer Rouge officers during the Pol Pot regime. Like the Takeo case already mentioned, they were reported to have joined the army because 'they loved the nation and at that time there was propaganda from the king [Sihanouk] to become a soldier in order to help the nation during the war'.[8]

The confusion in people's minds about women combatants, probably exacerbated through translation to and from English and Khmer, was seen in their description of the women they remembered as being involved in the conflict. While most identified women soldiers, others spoke of women who had taken supplies to the frontline or acted as medics. Understandably, roles were seen as diffuse. This highlights the difficulty of discussing the difference between combatants and civilians, something which has dogged the UN in its resolutions about war. UN documents refer to combatants as those who take part in hostilities yet such roles can extend far beyond the bearing of arms.

We interviewed two female ex-combatants in the country's south-eastern province of Takeo, which had witnessed heavy fighting from the late 1960s to the early 1990s. A very poor province bordering on southern Vietnam, Takeo had been a Khmer Rouge stronghold. The story of the first woman went along these lines. Born in 1960, she said her father had died 'during the war' when she was young and her mother had remarried. She did not feel that her family cared for her, and she 'was ordered to join a mobile group of young teenagers living separately from her parents', as was common under Khmer Rouge rule. She was chosen to work as a soldier and 'was sent to Vietnam to learn how to use a gun and train as a soldier' when she was around seventeen years old during the Pol Pot period. She 'learned how to shoot and use grenades on the battlefield'. After she returned from Vietnam she was sent to guard a hospital for two years (Figure 11.1).

Figure 11.1 Ex-combatant women in Takeo province, Cambodia. Often former combatant women do not want to be photographed following the conflict, in particular if they were on the losing side.
Source: Photos by Susan Blackburn (2005–2006).

Another woman we interviewed was six years older. In 1970, when she was a sixteen-year-old teenager, she 'ran away to another province as there were many Vietnamese troops arresting young women in her village'. When she was seventeen she, like the other woman, 'was made to join a mobile female group'. In 1974 she joined the army and 'was trained to fight on the battlefield', stating that she was 'forced to do this'. In 1979, she said, she 'gave up the army and returned to her own village', to learn for the first time that her relatives were killed and her parents had died.

Of their time in the Khmer Rouge army, both these women said they were forced to work very hard 'like men' and to carry heavy guns. They 'were told they had the same rights as men and could work like men'. If they were sick they were allowed only half a day of sick leave. Very often they had to stay in strongholds with men and had to wear men's clothes. They reported fighting alongside both men and women. They had women leaders also in their group 'but the women leaders had no sympathy for them and forced them to work as hard as men.'[9] The only aspect of this experience that the women reported in a positive way was that being a combatant 'made them braver than other women'. They learned to have no shyness about living together with men. On the other hand, they remembered vividly how hard they had to work, without enough food to eat – a common experience of almost all Cambodians under Pol Pot due to his regime's disastrous agricultural and economic policies.

The nature of armed conflict in East Timor and women's roles in combat

Conflict in East Timor was of a very different kind. Although fighting began in 1975 as a civil war when the Portuguese colonial rulers left, it quickly turned into a resistance struggle against the invading Indonesians who annexed the territory in 1976. Guerrilla resistance against Indonesian occupation continued until 1999 when the new Indonesian president, Dr Habibie, unexpectedly agreed to hold a referendum on the future status of the territory. This led to a new kind of conflict, as the Indonesian army backed East Timorese militias to intimidate people into voting for autonomy within Indonesia rather than independence. When East Timorese voted overwhelmingly for independence, the militias unleashed a scorched earth program, burning and looting as they forced many people to accompany them over the border into West Timor. At this point the UN, which had already established a small political mission (UNAMET or UN Mission in East Timor) in 1999 to organise the referendum, intervened to set up a UN Transitional Administration in East Timor (UNTAET) tasked with establishing law and order and helping prepare the country for independence, which it obtained in 2002.

Conflict therefore can mean different things to different generations of East Timorese. For all of them, the most vivid memories are of the terror of 1999, but older people also remember the struggle against the Indonesian military. For them, the resistance struggle is associated with winners (the victorious independence fighters, the Falintil army, backed by many ordinary East Timorese) and losers, predominantly foreign Indonesians who have since left the country. As part of the resistance against Indonesia a few women actually carried guns but far more played essential roles in supporting the guerrillas, providing them with food, medicine, shelter and intelligence. All these roles carried grave risks for women since if they were found out they could be arrested, tortured and even killed.[10] The conflict of 1999 is more complex since it had elements of civil war about it: some East Timorese backed the militias. As far as women's involvement is concerned, however, there is little evidence of their direct involvement in supporting either the Indonesians or the militias. During the Indonesian occupation, many East Timorese women were raped by Indonesian forces and subjected to sexual slavery. In 1999 some women were swept up in the militias' path and forced into marriages or to act as sex slaves for militia leaders in West Timor.

In early 2006, in the Western provinces of Covalima, Liquica and Bobonaro, we interviewed village focus groups and individuals who conveyed many accounts of women's involvement in the clandestine resistance movement. One was Maria Domingas de Santos from the women's organisation Organizacao da Mulher Timorense (OMT – Organisation of Timorese Women) in Maliana. She had been in the clandestine movement in 1994–1995, sending medicines to the forest and treating members of Falintil who were sick as

234 *Susan Blackburn*

well as hiding them in her house. In 1997 the Indonesian military arrested and tortured her and her husband.

As we shall see, the roles that women played and the nature of the conflicts in these two countries had different consequences for poor rural women. In both cases, however, this had more to do with the kind of public recognition accorded these women, rather than any material difference in their lives.

DDR arrangements in Cambodia and East Timor: consequences for women combatants

After the end of a conflict former combatants are usually dealt with through the processes known collectively as Disarmament, Demobilisation and Re-integration (DDR). Developed in UN circles, the DDR program is intended to assist countries making the transition from war to peace.[11] The first two procedures are treated very much as security issues while the last is regarded as part of the socio-economic rehabilitation of the society. It is understandable why the emphasis has historically been on disarmament and demobilisation, since men with arms are regarded as a potential threat to peace and security. Once soldiers have handed in their arms and been officially discharged from the armed forces, they are ready to be assisted to settle back into civilian life (or in some cases to be absorbed into the new regular army). Those who do not carry a gun are likely to miss out on all three stages and will never be registered as an ex-combatant. In many conflicts women fighters just disappear at the end of a war without bothering to register.[12] One of the reasons for this is their fear (shared with men) of being discriminated against once the conflict ends, particularly if they are regarded as having been 'on the wrong side'.

The case for addressing the rights and needs of female ex-combatants rests largely on the grounds of social equity. This principle is more difficult for poor governments to accept than a hard-headed view of where power lies.

What are the needs of female ex-combatants? To a large extent they are the same as those of their male counterparts. They often have serious mental and physical health problems. Having been dislocated from their homes they may need help to return, but they may not be accepted back into their old communities, or those communities may no longer exist. It is more difficult for women than for men to be reintegrated since their military way of life has alienated them from the feminine norms that are rapidly reinstated after war's end. Whereas it may be socially acceptable for men to kill on command as part of the armed forces, women who have mixed with male soldiers, carried guns and probably killed someone are subsequently regarded with suspicion and concern.[13] Studies of the fate of women soldiers in places like Eritrea make this abundantly clear.[14] Whereas Eritrean women had enjoyed gender equality in the army, they returned home to find that gender divisions were even more rigid than before. In such cases women ex-combatants may need help to settle and find employment elsewhere than in their places of origin.

Aftermath for women warriors: Cambodia & East Timor   235

In both East Timor and Cambodia the UN had played an important role in bringing armed conflict to an end, and its intervention helped shape the post-conflict arrangements in each country. Because both countries were devastated by their conflicts, international assistance was essential for their reconstruction. Aid donors have therefore had great influence. The question posed here is whether they had any impact on women's involvement in DDR.

Cambodia

In Cambodia the process of disarming and demobilising troops was messy, fragmented and prolonged. The Paris Peace Agreements of October 1991 called for the formation of a new united Cambodian army, the Royal Cambodian Armed Forces (RCAF) from the combined existing four armed forces[15] and the disarming and demobilisation of surplus forces. In February 1992, the United Nations Transitional Authority in Cambodia (UNTAC) was set up in order to implement the Paris Peace Agreements. Among other duties, it was supposed to supervise the ceasefire and arrange for the disarming and demobilising of all armed groups. However, lack of cooperation from the Cambodians meant that UNTAC was unable to carry out this task properly, and its mission ended in September 1993 with UN-monitored elections. Although about 36,000 fighters were demobilised by 1993, the Khmer Rouge continued recruiting and fighting. International funds were eventually supplied for DDR which finally began in 1997 but had to be suspended after the 1997 coup. It was not to resume until a pilot program was launched in 2000. The internationally funded program provided handouts in 2001 to soldiers who left the forces. I have not been able to find any reference to women soldiers in the documentation about the official demobilisation process, probably because the RCAF contains no or very few women.[16] It was the Khmer Rouge who was noted for their recruitment of women (and children),[17] and my own inquiries about women ex-combatants yielded references to former Khmer Rouge only.[18] Since these women were not affected by the official demobilisation process after 1997, I will not discuss that program further here.[19]

In Cambodia there is no evidence of any efforts to recognise women as ex-combatants in need of DDR assistance, and certainly not to assist Khmer Rouge ex-combatants in the immediate aftermath of the Pol Pot regime. Those who survived attempted to remake their lives in any way they could. In this respect the aftermath of fighting in Cambodia probably resembled that of most poor countries throughout history. That women were neglected did not differentiate them from most men.

Nowadays, no glory attaches to the Cambodian conflict. The whole period from the 1970s to the 1990s is a bleak one in Cambodian history, and there has been no celebration of victors and very little punishment of losers. Pol Pot and Ieng Sary were tried in absentia in 1979 in Phnom Penh and sentenced to death,[20] and international criminal trials of the dwindling

236 *Susan Blackburn*

number of remaining Khmer Rouge leaders, long postponed, finally passed life sentences against two of them in 2010 and 2014. To judge from our interviews, it is socially and politically acceptable to have fought against the Lon Nol regime, since members of the current government were involved in that struggle, but it is better to avoid talking about any participation in the Pol Pot regime, in which some current government personnel were also involved. On the other hand, with the passage of time Cambodians avoid blaming most people who served the Pol Pot government. Unlike the hatred directed at Khmer Rouge leaders, ordinary Cambodians who implemented their commands are generally absolved from guilt by most of their fellow-citizens who consider they were forced to obey, although they may suffer or fear discrimination.

In 2005, when I asked the Cambodian staff of Oxfam Australia and their provincial government counterparts about the existence of women ex-combatants in the rural areas where they worked, most denied knowing of any.[21] One counterpart in Takeo province agreed that there probably were female ex-combatants in the area where he worked, 'but they do not want to let us know. They prefer to keep it secret as it may affect their status because people discriminate against former Khmer Rouge soldiers.' Those who mentioned knowing of such women clearly regarded them as exceptional cases. The fact that only Khmer Rouge ex-combatants were mentioned may mean that people were not aware of any women who fought for other parties in the Cambodian conflict.[22]

While there was reluctance at higher levels to identify female ex-combatants, at the village level in Takeo province people readily acknowledged to us that there were women ex-combatants living in their midst. They did not hold any grudges against them, probably because any violence in which they had been involved had been committed elsewhere, but also because of the widespread view that people were forced to commit such acts by the Khmer Rouge: 'They had no choice' was the frequent refrain.

Our inquiries revealed no particular difficulties facing women ex-combatants in settling back into the community. Some now participated in community development projects. Two female ex-combatants we interviewed in Takeo province said they suffered no discrimination although one mentioned 'there are rumours that some people think we are not good women'.

In the aftermath of any war, the health problems of ex-combatants may be quite serious, particularly if they were injured during duty, or if they suffer conflict-induced trauma. The female ex-combatants we heard about or interviewed in Cambodia were in poor health. Many who were recruited as teenagers during the conflict had no opportunity to gain an education. Ill health and lack of education are, however, experienced by most who survived that period, and it is difficult to warrant singling out Cambodian ex-combatants for special treatment. The fact that many of their problems are shared by non-combatants is in some ways an advantage since it means

Aftermath for women warriors: Cambodia & East Timor   237

there is likely to be more sympathy and support, which is particularly important in such matters as post-conflict trauma. In this respect the situation is very similar to that in East Timor.

East Timor

Compared with Cambodia, although East Timor also suffered great poverty and destruction, more attention was paid to women in that country after 1999. In part this is accounted for by the different nature of the armed conflict there: the struggle for independence is heroic. Also, by the time of UN intervention in East Timor in 1999, international thinking on women combatants had developed further than during the Cambodian intervention, and there was more international support for women. But progress has been slight, and the problems of identifying combatants in a guerrilla war remain.

In East Timor, not only prestige but more tangible rewards are available for some former fighters, including women. The initiative and altruism they displayed during the conflict have allowed some of them to take leadership roles in the new nation's democratic processes. Such women have been elected to national and local councils and have prominent roles in NGOs. However, women have been unable to share in the assistance given to some of their male colleagues who bore arms. As part of the DDR program, some former Falintil fighters have been incorporated into the new national security forces and others have received cash and training to help them settle back into society. Women have not enjoyed these privileges.[23]

Unlike in Cambodia, in East Timor people were generally prepared to talk to us about women's role in armed conflict. The exceptions were villages in Covalima province which had been dominated by the pro-Indonesian militias: there some people resented discussing involvement in the conflict. It was a reminder that women might also have assisted the militias, for which they could expect no favourable recognition at all. Women who had been involved with the losing side prefer to keep quiet about it, at least in public.[24] In that respect, the situation did resemble Cambodia.

In early 2006 we spoke with a number of East Timorese about what had happened to former female fighters. They were very conscious that there was controversy about the recognition and reward of combatants. In Covalima province we were told that 'The condition of women who were active in the independence movement has not changed. There has been almost no attention from the government or any organisation to help them.' In Liquica province a village leader said that 'Until now we don't know what to do about them [women involved in the clandestine movement] because the government has not yet spoken about how to support them.' A village chief in Covalima said of the many people in his area who were active in the movement for independence, 'Now they don't have jobs and they haven't received any recognition from the government.' This was echoed by an NGO

238 *Susan Blackburn*

member in the same province: 'Suai was a conflict area where there were many women involved in the independence movement. They have become victims and some of them haven't got work yet. Some of them carried guns against the enemy but they still haven't received any compensation.'

Maria Domingas de Santos, from the Organisation of Timorese Women (OMT), said when we interviewed her that she thought it very important that women's work in the clandestine movement should be recognised: 'They should get support for their projects or activities but not in terms of actual reward. Rewards cause discrimination because there are a lot of other factors involved such as political parties and this would cause jealousies.' After all, she added, 'We won the war not because we shot each other but more through our referendum.' Thus, she emphasised how diverse were the roles of those who supported the independence struggle. In 1999 for many men and women voting proved as dangerous, and as important for independence, as bearing arms.

As a leader of the OMT, Maria Domingas de Santos illustrates how female ex-combatants may enjoy some advantages over non-combatants, albeit fewer than those enjoyed by their male counterparts. They may have learned some skills that will assist them in future life, most notably resilience, confidence, contacts and leadership. In Cambodia, as I have noted, the ex-combatants I interviewed remembered only their own bravery and resilience with any degree of positive sentiment when they recollected the war years. In the case of East Timor there is leadership value in having been an ex-combatant: they are generally highly regarded and stand a good chance of being elected to the many positions opening up in East Timor's new democratic society. Even for those who fought for independence, however, as Maria Domingas de Santos observed, bickering between political parties has affected how ex-combatants are treated.

The UN mission in Cambodia and the first two in East Timor (UNAMET and UNTAET) pre-dated Resolution 1325, but already in the East Timorese case a greater gender awareness marked the international intervention. This was obvious in the support UNTAET supplied to women to allow them to participate in the new political arrangements being made for the country's independence. It was a sign of changing times. A Commission for Reception, Truth and Reconciliation was established then. The fact that it took testimonies from many women affected by the conflict also shows willingness in East Timor to acknowledge what women suffered and what they contributed to the winning of independence.[25] On the other hand, there is little sign of gender awareness in the DDR process in either East Timor or Cambodia.

International policy on women and DDR

Concern about the fate of women ex-combatants is a fairly recent phenomenon. In part this is a reflection of the growing role of girls and women as

Most international acknowledgment of women ex-combatants has come only since the late 1990s.[26] The watershed was Security Council Resolution 1325 on Women, Peace and Security, passed on 31 October 2000.[27] Subsequently in 2002 the UN Secretary General made a report to the Security Council on Resolution 1325 which included a chapter on DDR.[28]

fighters, but it has also been a result of the growth of global feminism, reflected in the policy of gender mainstreaming in the United Nations. Seen most obviously in international conferences, the women's movement has led to pressure to extend policies concerning DDR to include women. The importance of this international pressure lies in the fact that international intervention, particularly that of the UN, is a dominant force in reaching peace settlements in most wars. In this respect Cambodia and East Timor are perhaps the initial examples of a world-wide trend.

Most international acknowledgment of women ex-combatants has come only since the late 1990s.[26] The watershed was Security Council Resolution 1325 on Women, Peace and Security, passed on 31 October 2000.[27] Subsequently in 2002 the UN Secretary General made a report to the Security Council on Resolution 1325 which included a chapter on DDR.[28]

A spate of reports on women and DDR followed Resolution 1325.[29] Five years after the 2000 resolution, an NGO working group reported on progress.[30] It found that 'only a small fraction of people around the world know about SCR 1325' and the obligations it entails for the UN and member states (p. ix). It acknowledged that the Resolution 'is ground breaking because of the depth of change in the approach to international peace and security that is necessary for its implementation' (p. 2). The report focussed on UN operations, and it recommended that a Security Council Monitoring Mechanism be established to monitor implementation of the Resolution. However, the UN as an organisation does not have full control over all the important aspects of the Resolution, particularly as it relates to DDR. Clearly, a major reason for the neglect of women in DDR processes is that they are unrepresented or under-represented in peace negotiations. Thus the issue of DDR is intertwined with wider issues of gender representation in decision-making, as is fully recognised by Resolution 1325. This conclusion is reinforced by research conducted by Vanessa Farr on DDR in 2003: she too found 'a significant gap between broad policy commitments to the inclusion of gender perspectives and specific actions on the ground' because of 'the ongoing exclusion of women from leadership positions in arenas of political influence'.[31]

At this point it is worth considering Anton Baaré's argument that taking a strictly rights approach to women in DDR is 'not necessarily in the best interests of the women and girls affected'. He asks who can realistically implement the demand for more women in reintegration programs and whether it would not be more practical to give far more attention to 'the development of solid parallel programs and targeted programs for women affected by war *concurrently* implemented with a DDR program'.[32] Unfortunately, if donors are unwilling to provide funds for women in reintegration programmes they are equally unlikely to do so outside those programmes. Baaré's proposal also avoids the issue of gender discrimination within DDR programs.

Implementing DDR in accordance with Resolution 1325 would be an extremely demanding matter for countries like Cambodia and East Timor. For

240 *Susan Blackburn*

a start, it would seem to require that women were leaders in armed conflicts (not just subordinates), since only leaders get a place at the peace table. The inclusion of a few token low-ranking women would be unlikely to achieve much. The terms of the resolution also assume that resources are available to care for the demobilisation and reintegration requirements of all those in need as a result of armed conflict, not just the winners or armed combatants. As it is, only the victorious male troops are assisted because they can otherwise cause trouble, and expenditure on reintegration is low, even for them. To provide resources to cover all ex-combatants, broadly defined, would necessitate a large international fund and would have to extend over several years to be effective.[33] Providing such assistance would also require a new approach to justice and reconciliation, recognising that most wars are internal conflicts where the victors and the vanquished are all fellow-citizens who, it is hoped, will live peacefully together in a post-conflict society. Many victims will ask why the perpetrators of violence should be rewarded with assistance in reintegration.[34] What does reward and punishment mean in this situation? What does justice mean for those who suffered in the conflict? Who is an innocent victim (children forced to fight, sex slaves…)? These unresolved and intractable questions already plague many men and women in the wake of conflicts in Cambodia and East Timor.

Although the push for gender-sensitive DDR originates at the UN, the importance of the international dimension should not be overstated. Without the backing of a local women's movement, international organisations can do little to promote women's rights. In this respect there are important differences between post-conflict Cambodia and East Timor. In the former country since 1979 there had been a mass organisation of women (the Women's Association of Cambodia) but it was controlled by the Cambodian Communist Party and did not have the freedom to pursue its own agenda.[35] Consequently it did not take up the cause of female ex-combatants. From the early 1990s, supported by foreign aid, a number of independent local women's organisations emerged.[36] Although they addressed wide-ranging issues concerning women, none took up the politically unpopular cause of the needs of women who had fought for the Khmer Rouge. Such women received assistance merely on the same basis as other needy women, and indeed there is a case to be made that they should not be singled out as ex-combatants so long as stigma is attached to that identity. In East Timor, however, an independent women's movement had been growing since the late 1990s, and although it suffered a severe setback with the devastation of 1999, it regrouped and joined with the international community in pushing strongly for women's rights including in relation to DDR.[37]

Without a strong domestic constituency lobbying for the rights of women in DDR, international pressure is likely to be ineffective.[38] International donors can, of course, do much to build the capacity of local women's organisations, as they have done in East Timor, but this usually occurs after peace negotiations which have made the arrangements for DDR. The proposal to bring women into DDR is fraught with dilemmas, not surprisingly since it shakes the whole foundation of the male-dominated war machine. Nevertheless, progress has been made in the last twenty years or so, as examples such as El Salvador show. At the settlement of the twelve-year war in El Salvador in 1992, women did participate in reintegration negotiations and succeeded in ensuring that both male and female combatants received integration packages.[39] Significantly, UN involvement was critical in the peace process.

Conclusion

Change in international thinking on treatment of women ex-combatants is gradually having effect in conflicts where international intervention occurs. But ambivalent attitudes towards women fighters, particularly in 'unpopular' conflicts, will continue to mean that they are hard to incorporate in DDR arrangements. As argued above, local conditions also account for unevenness in the application of UN resolutions on the matter.

If DDR were seriously to incorporate gender, which would require recognition of the multiple roles of women in prosecuting wars and of the need to apply DDR in a non-discriminatory way to all those caught up in warfare, regardless of sex or side, attitudes to armed conflict would be transformed. It would have to be recognised that DDR should not relate to reward and punishment, but that it must be part of a wider process of reconciliation and healing. Conflict sweeps up both men and women in many capacities. Helping them to settle back into a peaceful society involves recognition of their varying experiences and needs. It would also require far greater resources than are currently devoted to DDR.

Thus, thinking about gender transforms thinking about war, combat, peace, reconciliation – an excellent example of how 'gender mainstreaming', properly pursued, subverts male-dominated concepts and structures. But how realistic is it for the future? A non-discriminatory approach to DDR is slow in coming, as is amply illustrated by the examples of Cambodia and East Timor.

Notes

1 See Cynthia Enloe, *Does Khaki Become You?: The Militarization of Women's Lives* (London: Pandora Press, 1983), Cynthia Enloe, *Maneuvers: The International Politics of Militarizing Women's Lives* (Berkeley: University of California Press, 2000).
2 This project also covered Sri Lanka. I gratefully acknowledge the assistance of the Australian Research Council, and also the outstanding cooperation of Oxfam Australia staff, and that of their partners, in conducting the research. Research coordinators in Cambodia and East Timor were Prak Sokhany and Celine Massa, and I wish to thank them, and the local interviewers they trained, for their indispensable assistance. Finally, of course, our informants must be thanked.

242 *Susan Blackburn*

3 Examples of such research on Africa include Elise Fredrikke Barth, 'Peace as Disappointment: The Reintegration of Female Soldiers in Post-Conflict Societies: A Comparative Study from Africa', in *PRIO Report 3* (Oslo: International Peace Research Institute, 2002); Meredeth Turshen and Clotilde Twagiramariya (eds.), *What Women Do in Wartime: Gender and Conflict in Africa* (New York: Zed Books, 1998); Susan McKay, 'Reconstructing Fragile Lives: Girls' Social Reintegration in Northern Uganda and Sierra Leone', *Gender and Development*, Vol. 12, No. 3 (2004), pp. 19–30; Angela Veale, *From Child Soldier to Ex-Fighter: Female Fighters, Demobilisation and Reintegration in Ethiopia* (Pretoria: Institute for Development Studies, 2003); Emily Schroeder, 'A Window of Opportunity in the Democratic Republic of the Congo: Incorporating a Gender Perspective in the Disarmament, Demobilization and Reintegration Process' (The Hague: International Institute for Social Studies, 2005); Tanya Lyons, *Guns and Guerilla Girls: Women in the Zimbabwean National Liberation Struggle* (PhD thesis, University of Adelaide, 1999); Dyan Mazurana and K. Carlson, 'From Combat to Community: Women and Girls of Sierra Leone' (Hunt Alternatives Fund, 2004); Chris Coulter, *The Postwar Moment: Female Fighters in Sierra Leone* (Migration Studies Working Paper Series No. 22, University of Witwatersrand, 2005); Sally Baden, 'Post-Conflict Mozambique: Women's Special Situation, Population Issues and Gender Perspectives to Be Integrated into Skills Training and Employment Promotion' (Brighton: ISS, University of Sussex, 1997); Christina Binder, Karin Lukas and Romana Schweiger, 'Empty Words or Real Achievement? The Impact of Security Council Resolution 1325 on Women in Armed Conflicts', *Radical History Review*, Vol. 101 (2008), pp. 22–41. I have also come across a useful study from Latin America by Camille Pampell Conaway and Salome Martinez, 'Adding Value: Women's Contribution to Reintegration and Reconstruction in El Salvador' (Hunt Alternatives Fund, 2004).

4 I am aware that to many observers it sounds naive to speak of 'women in post-conflict situations', since conflict of many kinds, including domestic violence, is ongoing. However, the phrase 'post-conflict' is currently used in international circles such as World Bank studies to refer to the situation after armed conflict has officially ended.

5 See Damien Kingsbury and Michael Leach (eds.), *East Timor: Beyond Independence* (Clayton: Monash Asia Institute, 2007), pp. 5–9 and 21–22.

6 In the case of Sierra Leone in 2002, see Mazurana and Carlson, 'From Combat to Community: Women and Girls of Sierra Leone', pp. 4, 26. Perhaps this is a harbinger of the future in cases where there are large numbers of female fighters.

7 Kate G. Frieson, *In the Shadows: Women, Power and Politics in Cambodia*, Occasional Paper No. 26 (Victoria, BC: Centre for Asia-Pacific Initiatives University of Victoria, 2001) describes the importance of the roles played by women to the Khmer Rouge fighting the Lon Nol regime. Two women were allocated to the support of each soldier, providing food and medical care. They also disseminated propaganda for the Khmer Rouge (pp. 8–10). Huy Vannak, *The Khmer Rouge Division 703: From Victory to Self-destruction* (Phnom Penh: Documentation Centre of Cambodia, 2003), gives examples of women in combat and support roles in the Khmer Rouge army (pp. 6, 11, 18–19, 22, 39, 72).

8 Huy supports the picture of young people being keen to volunteer for the Khmer Rouge army when its fighting was directed against the Americans between 1970 and 1973, but having to be forced to join from late 1973. See Huy Vannak, *The Khmer Rouge Division 703*, pp. 11, 18–20.

Aftermath for women warriors: Cambodia & East Timor   243

9 This view of the Khmer Rouge regime as proclaiming a rhetoric of gender equality but in fact just requiring women to work like men is supported by Zal Karkaria's study of the Khmer Rouge's policies on women, entitled 'Failure through Neglect: The Women's Policies of the Khmer Rouge' (MA thesis, Concordia University, 2003) and also by Frieson, *In the Shadows*, p. 10.

10 Irena Cristalis and Catherine Scott, *Independent Women: The Story of Women's Activism in East Timor* (London: Catholic Institute for International Relations, 2005).

11 DDR is a contested term, because it is seen by many as conceived in narrow security terms. A critical analysis is contained in Nicole Ball, *Disarmament, Demobilisation and Reintegration: Mapping Issues, Dilemmas and Guiding Principles* (The Hague: Netherlands Institute of International Relations, August 2006).

12 Tsjeard Bouta, Georg Frerks, and Ian Bannon, *Gender, Conflict, and Development* (Washington, DC: The World Bank, 2005).

13 Ibid., pp. 10–17.

14 Sondra Hale, 'Liberated but Not Free: Women in Post-War Eritrea', in Sheila Meintjes, Anu Pillay, and Meredeth Turshen (eds.), *The Aftermath: Women in Post-Conflict Transformation* (London: Zed Books, 2001), pp. 125–126.

15 These belonged to the Government of Prime Minister Hun Sen in Phnom Penh and the opposing forces of the Khmer People's National Liberation Front, the Sihanouk National Army and the Khmer Rouge.

16 Lack of reference to gender in the DDR process seems all the stranger in Cambodia when one considers the Ministry of Women's Affairs also is in charge of Veterans' Affairs.

17 Licadho, 'Child Soldiers in Cambodia Briefing Paper' (Phnom Penh: Cambodian League for the Promotion and Defence of Human Rights [Licadho], 1998), p. 3.

18 The provinces where we conducted interviews were not those where demobilisation had occurred (*People's Daily*, 17 April 2001).

19 A description of DDR in Cambodia can be found in Albert Carames, Vicenc Fisas and Eneko Sanz, *Cambodia* (Agencia Cataluna de Cooperacio al Desenvolupament, 2007). In 2000, Cambodia had an estimated 160,000 personnel in its armed forces (in a population of about eleven million) and spent 30–40% of its annual budget on the military sector (Garth Shelton et al., *Demobilisation and Its Aftermath: A Profile of South Africa's Demobilised Military Personnel* (Cape Town: Institute of Security Studies, 2001), pp. 54–55). The DDR process has been highly controversial and plagued with allegations of corruption in Cambodia. Hence, the World Bank, one of the main funders of the DDR in Cambodia, in 2003 reduced its $18 million loan for the demobilisation program and called for $2.8 million to be paid back because of corruption; see Human Rights Watch, *Cambodia* (2005). A conference on military reform, demobilisation and reintegration was held in Cambodia in 2002 and reported in guarded terms that contained no reference to gender; see Kao Kim Hourn, 'Military Reform, Demobilisation and Reintegration: Measures for Improving Military Reform and Demobilisation in Cambodia' (Cambodian Institute for Cooperation and Peace, 2002).

20 Evan Gottesman, *Cambodia after the Khmer Rouge: Inside the Politics of Nation Building* (New Haven, CT: Yale University Press, 2003), pp. 60–66.

21 We asked twenty-three individuals about their knowledge of former female combatants in the areas where they were working in Takeo, Kratie and Stung Treng provinces. Fourteen staff said they were not aware of any such women as against nine who had heard of some but not necessarily met them.

22 See Trude Jacobsen's chapter in this volume on Cambodian views of armed women.

244   *Susan Blackburn*

23 Elisabeth Rehn and Ellen Johnson, *Women, War, Peace: The Independent Experts' Assessment on the Impact of Armed Conflict on Women and Women's Role in Peace Building* (New York: UNIFEM, 2002), Chapter 2; and Vijaya Joshi, 'UN Transitional Authority in East Timor: Ally or Adversary for Women?' (Medford, MA: Fletcher School of Law and Diplomacy, Tufts University, 2005), pp. 18–19. On the post-conflict experience of East Timorese women combatants see also the chapter by Jacqueline Siapno in this volume and Sara Niner, 'Bisoi: A Veteran of Timor-Leste's Independence Movement', in Susan Blackburn and Helen Ting (eds.), *Women in Southeast Asian Nationalist Movements: A Biographical Approach* (Singapore: National University of Singapore Press, 2013), pp. 226–249.

24 This situation may, of course, change with time. People who were on the losing side in wars against colonial rulers later often became national heroes and heroines. History involves constant reassessment of the past.

25 Commission for Reception, Truth, and Reconciliation (CAVR), 'Chega! Final Report' (Dili: CAVR, 2005).

26 The International Labour Organisation was one of the first UN agencies to move on this issue: its 1997 report has a chapter on training requirements for women ex-combatants. See International Labour Organisation, *Manual on Training and Employment Options for Ex-Combatants* (Geneva: ILO, 1997).

27 United Nations Security Council, 'Resolution 1325' (New York: United Nations Security Council, 2000).

28 United Nations, *Women, Peace and Security* (New York: United Nations, 2002).

29 In Africa the World Bank has become increasingly conscious of the involvement of girls and women in armed conflicts. In 2002, it commissioned Nathalie de Watteville to produce a report entitled, 'Addressing Gender Issues in Demobilisation and Reintegration Programs', in its *Africa Region Working Papers Series No. 33* (New York: The World Bank, 2002). Bouta, Frerks and Bannon, *Gender, Conflict, and Development*, discuss World Bank policy on demobilisation and reintegration, including women combatants. Vanessa Farr produced for UNIFEM a checklist on gender-aware DDR 'Gender-Aware Disarmament, Demobilization and Reintegration (DDR): A Checklist' (UNIFEM, 2003), followed by UNIFEM's own analysis of DDR, 'Getting It Right, Doing It Right: Gender and Disarmament, Demobilization and Reintegration' (Washington: United Nations Development Fund for Women, 2004). In 2004 the UN Department of Peacekeeping Operations also produced a gender resource package containing a chapter on gender and DDR; see United Nations, 'Gender Resource Package for Peacekeeping Operations' (Washington: Department of Peacekeeping Operations, United Nations, 2004), p. 24.

30 Peace and Security NGO Working Group on Women, 'From Local to Global: Making Peace Work for Women' (n.pl.: 2005).

31 Vanessa Farr, 'The Importance of a Gender Perspective to Successful Disarmament, Demobilization and Reintegration Processes', *Disarmament Forum*, Vol. 4 (2003), p. 30. In 2008, Anne Marie Goetz, UNIFEM's adviser on Governance, Peace and Security, stated that 'Disarmament, demobilisation and reintegration processes still rarely addressed the needs of women associated with fighting forces...' (quoted in Tahlif Deen, 'Rights: Women Out in the Cold at Peace Talks', *Global Information Network* (New York, March 4, 2008), p. 1).

32 Anton Baaré, 'An Analysis of Transitional Economic Reintegration' (Stockholm: Swedish Initiative for Disarmament, Demobilisation and Reintegration, 2005), p. 11.

33 Joanna Spear, 'From Political Economies of War to Political Economies of Peace: The Contribution of DDR after Wars of Predation', *Contemporary Security Policy*, Vol. 27, No. 1 (2006), p. 177.

34 Ibid, p. 178.
35 Frieson, *In the Shadows*, pp. 12–13.
36 Krishna Kumar and Hannah Baldwin, 'Women's Organizations in Postconflict Cambodia', in Krishna Kumar (ed.), *Women and Civil War: Impact, Organizations, and Action* (Boulder, CO: Lynne Rienner, 2001), pp. 129–148.
37 Cristalis and Scott, *Independent Women: The Story of Women's Activism in East Timor*.
38 This point was recently emphasised by the then Executive Director of UN Women, Michelle Bachelet, 'Women, War and Peace', 3 March 2011.
39 Conaway and Martinez, 'Adding Value: Women's Contribution to Reintegration and Reconstruction in El Salvador'. Nevertheless, another study notes that whereas women fighters held 30% of combat roles during the civil war in El Salvador, 70–80% of them 'received no benefits under the government's land transfer program'; see Binder, Lukas and Schweiger, 'Empty Words or Real Achievement?', p. 25.

12 Brave warriors, unfinished revolutions

Political subjectivities of women combatants in East Timor

Jacqueline A. Siapno

This chapter is a research study of the roles, lived experiences, and thoughts of women warriors (ex-Falintil combatants) in the revolutionary anti-colonial resistance movement in East Timor against Indonesian occupation and subsequently, the place of women in the Falintil-FDTL (*Forcas Defesas de Timor Leste* or the military) and the Police or PNTL (*Policia Nacional de Timor Leste*) in post-independence East Timor after 1999.[1] Some of the research is taken from a study commissioned by the Timor Leste's National Commission on Planning, in cooperation with the Ministry of Defense, in 2008, focusing on engendering the security sector. The study was commissioned by Ms Milena Pires and her team at the National Commission on Planning, with the author as Principal Investigator. Upon embarking on the research, the author was first warned by the former Director of the National Commission on Planning that they had previously commissioned approximately 800+ research reports, most of which have hardly ever been read by any state, government, and public sector officials. The intention and idea of the state-sponsored research was to open up the discussion on civilian oversight of the military; uncover the dynamics of civilian-military-police relations, in order to link research and policy; and transform Timorese society from a zone of militarised masculinities prone to do 'commando style' to one of more open, inclusive, egalitarian, democratic, pluralistic dialogue. The findings were presented in a public seminar entitled 'Security Sector Reform: Gendered Perspectives' in Delta Nova, Dili, attended by representatives from the military, police (including commanders from the rural districts), the former Minister of Defense and former Minister of Interior during the Fretilin government, international security forces (including UN (United Nations) and ISF), the former UN SRSG Atul Khare and his wife Vandna Khare, and former UN Police Commissioner, Rodolfo Tor.

It is an observation and reflection on the unfinished, and perhaps even 'betrayed' revolution in East Timor, from an anti-colonial revolutionary resistance movement which many had idealised would 'liberate Timorese society from conservative established social and gender relations and enable the newly independent country to become economically self-sufficient and

East Timor: brave women warriors, unfinished revolutions 247

politically and culturally de-colonised. What happened to women warriors after the revolution, in post-independence East Timor? What happens to women after winning the revolution? How do they get involved in the transition to revolutionary government? Why were women ignored and neglected after the revolution? Why is their input (and especially their health and well-being) not given any priority? Why are they betrayed by the very revolution for which they gave up their lives (and loves) for?

Despite considerable institutional support and very capable research assistance, capturing the voices of women in the security forces was not an easy process. Part of our challenge was to understand and read beyond the 'silence' manifested in the interviews. In some instances, women were unable to speak and express their opinions because their male military Commanders were sitting right there and refused to leave. In these cases, the women asked us to re-schedule a meeting, somewhere else (away from listening range of their male Commander), where they were then able to speak more freely about problems and challenges in their institutions. In other cases, they seem to have been given instructions not to speak (i.e. to give us 'access', but not provide information), or to provide the 'correct, official answers'. In some occasions, a male Commander pulled them aside for briefing, just before the interview.

For us, this offered an interesting insight into civil-military relations, and how female civilians are perceived. If the reader listens to the recorded tapes directly (in Tetum), one will sense that on certain questions, such as on 'discrimination' and whether or not the institution had 'non-discrimination policies', there are protective silences. Women spoke on sensitive issues, such as discrimination, corruption, and sexual harassment, only in whispered confidences. Some interviewees refused to be recorded, so we had to take very good notes...including on the silences on specific questions. In several cases, we were unable to interview high-ranking male policy makers and security sector personnel, who told us that they were 'too busy' to meet. It is likely that they see the issue of women and gender as 'trivial', or wanted to avoid questions, and consequently did not make time for us to meet. On a more positive note, however, several of the women, especially in PNTL, spoke articulately and openly on their conditions of work, strategically identifying this research as an opportunity to express their views, and to initiate 'reform' within their institutions. These interviews are crucial in these essays; they provide the spaces for the women to articulate their aspirations and visions on engendering security sector reform (SSR).[2]

I began learning about East Timor in 1989, when I worked as a volunteer for Amnesty International and few of us in the international solidarity movement imagined then that it would someday be possible for this little country to gain independence from Indonesia—a sprawling archipelagic state with the financial and manpower resources to brutalise and eliminate the resistance movement, and the support by countries like the United States, Australia, and basically all the major powers.

248   *Jacqueline A. Siapno*

Prior to the arrival of Western European powers in the sixteenth century in search of sandalwood and spices, and the peak of high colonialism in the early nineteenth century, Timor used to be a unified island composed of multiple linguistic groupings (up to thirty-two languages, including Mambai, Fataluku, Kemak, Baikeno, and others), organised into small kingdoms ruled by local *liurai*. The Dutch and the Portuguese divided the island into two, with West Timor being occupied by the Dutch and later on by Indonesia, and East Timor occupied by the Portuguese. In 1975, Portugal withdrew from its colonies, and East Timorese leaders declared independence. Shortly thereafter, Indonesia invaded, killing thousands of Timorese and driving the rest of the population into malnourishment and death. The UN made several resolutions condemning the invasion and acknowledging Timor Leste's right to self-determination and sovereignty, but it was only in 1998, one year after the fall of strongman Suharto that his successor, B. J. Habibie, offered a referendum for the East Timorese to choose independence or integration with Indonesia. The UN-sponsored referendum was held on 30 August 1999, with the majority of the Timorese choosing independence.

But eleven years later reflecting on the dynamics and consequences of this unfinished revolution, I realise (based on the research fieldwork with ex-Falintil women warriors and Falintil-FDTL in the military) that for many women, a revolution for national independence is not enough.[3] In some ways, I have come to 'identify' with the struggle of the Timorese women. I am not Timorese, I am a malae/foreigner, although I have lived in Timor Leste for more than fifteen years, building a home there, raising a family, and have become a Timorese citizen. I did not come here to work for the UN or the World Bank, or any other international organisation, which is how many foreigners come to be here in East Timor. Instead, I always chose to work in the local universities (including Universidade Nacional Timor Leste, Universidade da Paz, and Universidade Dili). For years, I struggled not to be Timorese, as I could not stand other foreigners who embraced ultra-nationalist Timorese identity without critically reflecting on their own colonial identities. But after my son was born, and realising that he is half-Timorese, half-Filipino, I began reading more historical accounts about polyglot populations and flexible identities.

One of the books that influenced me a great deal is James Scott's *The Art of Not Being Governed*, especially on the concept of inclusion and absorption of polyglot populations in the 'manpower state'. A state that is in need of manpower sees ethnic identity as a social and political invention, an alloy, an amalgam that bears traces from many diverse sources, of culture as 'a provisional work in progress', rather than rigidifying itself into homogeneity. Scott writes: 'If this explicitly political perspective has any merit, its effect is to radically decenter any essentialist understanding of "Burmanness" or "Siameseness" or, for that matter, "Hanness."'[4]

East Timor: brave women warriors, unfinished revolutions

The struggles that I have joined hands with Timorese women deal with 'democratisation' and 'gender equality'... a revolution from within...and our homes are the first spaces where it started. For example, when the Domestic Violence Law was intensively discussed and then passed in Parliament in 2010, it engendered public debate on how much it transform established gender and family social relations. We were learning that celebrating Independence Day and building a nation is not about the crises and conflicts that sometimes break our hearts, but our capacity to heal that which has been broken, our capacity for genuine cosmopolitan solidarity, and our common humanity. In some sense it was easy to support the 'revolution' for East Timor's national independence, but it is now, after that independence, that our true revolution from within begins. I can only hope and pray that for my son's generation, there will be no more violence and no more impoverishment, and that this relatively young nation will someday find some peace, tranquillity, equilibrium, and continue as a work-in-progress towards the revolutionary project for which so many idealistic people have given their lives.

Figure 12.1 Mana Bilesa, then a Falintil fighter, in uniform and with assault rifle in Viqueque district, East Timor, in 1995. Independence has brought new opportunities but also challenges for women serving in Timor Leste's police and armed forces.

Source: Photo in the collection of Jacqueline Siapno.

250 *Jacqueline A. Siapno*

Women as 'fragments' in the unfinished revolution

> In terms of the numbers of women Falintil combatants in the eastern sector, I [Mana Bisoy] don't know the details as the eastern sector was quite far, but for the western sector when the resistance movement started around 1983, there were approximately more than 60 women... but during the war most of them either surrendered, were captured, or killed...for some of those who surrendered, they managed to continue to work in the clandestine movement...but after 24 years of war only nine of us women are left alive.[5]

In 2006, as the security situation in East Timor continued to disintegrate, I critically reflected on the problem that those involved in 'security sector reform' and 'peacekeeping' are predominantly male: the government leaders in 2006 who played on the fears of people, the political parties, but also the PNTL (National Police), F-FDTL (Military), the UN Peacekeeping forces, UN Police, International Stabilisation Forces (ISF, Australian Defense Force), church leaders, and gang leaders. I began to wonder: has it always been this way? Is there, was there no alternate history of women's participation in the politics of security and nation-building? When people talk about 'security sector reform' in East Timor, especially the UN, the F-FDTL, PNTL, and the government, are women ex-combatants (e.g. Falintil veterans) who played such an important role during the struggle for independence, included or excluded? Following Cynthia Enloe's questions in *The Curious Feminist*, 'in times of crisis, are those who are feminised portrayed and/or are constituted as needing to be benevolently protected by militarised masculinities?' Are the dominant males really providing security or are they just putting on a spectacle of 'performing security'? Do female ex-combatants in Falintil accept that the men in Falintil-Forcas Defesas de Timor Leste are the sole decision-makers and representatives of 'national security' and nation-state-building? It makes one pause to meditate on the processes of transformation that transpired in the country: women were transformed from courageous, proud warriors to becoming dis-empowered 'Internally Displaced Persons' and refugees in their own country, and huge gaps existed between the official nationalist narratives on 'self-sacrificing revolutionary women' to paradoxical personal narratives of betrayal, failure, and discrimination (not only within the F-FDTL military, but also in the PNTL police, and by Members of Parliament).

In the interviews with ex-Falintil guerrillas, we learned that women ex-combatants/warriors had not only been captains and adjutants in the military, but also political advisors for strategic defence, many of them performing multiple functions as surveillance, intelligence agents, combatants, temporarily visiting mothers, but at the same time were still required to do the labour of cooking and washing for the combatant men in the battlefield.

East Timor: brave women warriors, unfinished revolutions 251

In the interviews with women ex-combatants, such as the one below with 'Mana Bisoy', they told us that they were 'commanded' (by 'the Commando') to leave their babies and little children behind. They had no choice—being a warrior was a full-time commitment, and motherhood, breast-feeding, and raising a child did not fit into that picture. Either they had to leave their babies behind with the nuns in a convent, or with other relatives, surrender, or be killed. But no woman was allowed to be with her child, or bring her child along in combat, in the mountains.

> I am now [in 2007] 44 years old and my child is now 13 years old. She has been in the care of a nun in the Carmelite order, because at that time the situation was so horrible and as guerrillas who participated in the resistance struggle we were told to leave our children behind—to 'get rid of them'. So we asked some young people to help us take the children to the villages, near the town, and they were the ones who delievered the children to the Carmelite nuns. A Latin American nun named Hidalia Taverra took care of my child, to this day my child is still with her.
>
> After the war, we came down and returned to the city. But my child's father who is now with the Falintil-FDTL and I have separated because he has another wife, he has two other wives, so I wanted to separate from him. I too have a new husband. I have re-married. When the war was over and I had come down to the city, my child did not know who I was...she called me 'auntie'. Now she knows who I am. At the time I gave her away she was only two years old going to three years old. We were in the mountains, she was in the city. I only saw her again when she was already six years old.
>
> Not all of us have been re-united with our children by our side...like Bimali and her child, Bijou-Mali and her child, same thing with Bi-Leta and her child, Bi-Hanik and her child...all of us just separated from our children...we were told to 'get rid of them' (*soe tiha*)...Falintil's children. Some have been re-united with their mother and father, some have not. And even if we have them by our side, the child has no trust in us, because since s/he was little s/he has been taken away from us, and now that s/he is big, s/he cannot trust us like a child ought to be able to trust her mother. When I became a refugee in Motael, she began to get to know me. The nun told her: 'this is your mother, go and sleep together with her'. But when she had night terror during sleep, she didn't want me, she said: 'I want to sleep with my mother Hidalia'. She wanted to sleep together with the nun who raised her, she refused to sleep with me. Sometimes she even makes a mistake always calling me 'mana' (older sister), or 'tia' (auntie), up to this day. Even today, when I called her on the telephone, she called me 'tia' (auntie): 'oh, auntie won't be able to come?' She still doesn't understand.
>
> We veterans do not have the conditions to raise a family, we do not have the right conditions...there is no home, no food to give the children,

252   Jacqueline A. Siapno

and it simply was not sustainable to raise or even be with our children, by our side, in the battlefield. A child has to have clothes, to have food and drink, and a place to sleep...but we had no home. After the war was over, I returned to the city and lived in the Taibessi public market. After that, I had actually built a simple house on government land, but during the recent crisis last year, it was burnt to the ground. So I lived in Taibessi market again. It's not appropriate for my child to live with me in the market. She does not seem to trust her mother who lives in a public market, so she continues to live with the nun who raised her. She is now in junior high school (SMP). These are some of the dificulties we face with our children when we have come down from the mountains.

...There is no space, no conditions for us to be able to bring our own child to live together with us, as a mother and child. This is the situation we women ex-veterans face to this very day...In 2005, we conducted a debate in the National Parliament, me, Biloumaili, Bilesa, and Aurora Ximanes, the four of us...about the rights of children. Since we came down to the city, our eyes have been opened, and we have been able to see what may be better for us, because when we were in the mountains we had no idea, we thought we would never have a home. Just moving day and night, walking during the whole day and night, with no home to sleep in peacefully, there is no peace, there is no good food, it is rare for us to even have rice, there is no way we could get rice in our hiding places in the mountains, it was difficult to get rice everyday, we only ate the leaves of plants and trees, or deer meat that we hunted ourselves, sometimes sagu or kumbili (yams)...Now that the war is over, you'd think we'd at least have a home to live in, a simple place to sleep, but sadly, that is not the case...It seems that the war this time is heavier...as we continue to be separated from our children to this day, we still cannot pick them up to return to our side. We do not have the right conditions to raise a child. State officials refuse to open their eyes to help us, to help us find our children whom some of us have lost, some have found them, others not, but there seems to be no possibility as the Parliament doesn't pay attention to our situation.

In the oral histories and personal narratives of the women ex-combatants in Falintil, this heavy self-sacrifice of being 'commanded' to separate from, literally, to 'get rid of' (*soe tiha*) their babies and little children came up several times in lengthy three-hour interviews with several informants. It was not just the intensity of their emotions when they were narrating these particular moments in their lives that gave me pause, but also the number of times it was repeated during the interviews, which indicated to me that this was something extremely poignant in their embodied experience/s as warriors, surveillance/intelligence agents, and combatants. Despite no longer being in a traditional 'battlefield', the wounds of separation had still not healed. In a new, perhaps even more complex 'arena' one of their peacetime struggles

East Timor: brave women warriors, unfinished revolutions 253

is to convince Members of Parliament that ex-Falintil veterans, especially women, need financial support, educational, and health resources.

These interviews reveal a very strong sense of regret and betrayal: a sense of betrayal of having followed orders (from 'the Commander') to make self-sacrifices—of personal happiness (as the war killed most of their romances and marriages), the joys of motherhood, the possibilities for educational growth—in the name of the national struggle for independence, and now nation-state-building as one of the world's newest member states of the UN. Even after thirteen years, or twenty years later, they are still asking: 'is it...was it worth it?' For some of them, like Mana 'Bisoy', their bodies still hold the remnants of that past life as combatants, with bullets still lodged in their stomachs and thighs, paralysing some of their muscles. They have appealed to the then President of Parliament, Francisco Guterres Lu Olo, to support them with funds so that they can have an operation, but to no avail.

They embody a profound knowledge and wisdom about the impact and aftermath of war on women's bodies and on their communities—of the pain of losing your child that may never heal, of bullets that may never leave your body, and of scars that will never go away even with time. And yet in post-independence East Timor, they are being told by predominantly male political leaders that this kind of survivor-visionary wisdom counts for nothing, as everyone else has suffered. In the hierarchy of suffering and self-sacrifice, somehow the males in the Falintil seem to be regarded as more 'worthy' of having 'made history'; of being idolised in the National Museum of Resistance (in central Dili, located next to the National University); and of being rewarded more medals, salaried positions and high ranks in the F-FDTL, if not material wealth and benefits.[6] In contrast, most of the ex-combatant women I interviewed then either live in simple huts or in camps for internally displaced persons (IDP) in Hera, Metinaro, while several of their former male comrades have comfortable homes and drive Mitsubishi's four-wheel drive Pajeros. In the 'post-conflict' new 'battlefield' of humanitarian aid, re-integration, reconstruction, peacekeeping under the rubric of nation-state-building, one of their former Falintil comrades, Francisco Guterres Lu Olo, told them that they had to acquire computer skills, learn English, and gain a university diploma, making them feel unworthy of employment and full participation as citizens in building this newly independent nation. Worse still, according to the ex-combatant women, he directly humiliated them in public, calling them *beik tein* (in Tetum, it could mean illiterate, uneducated, infantile, also 'stupid').

Engendering security sector reform (SSR)

How do women define 'national security' and 'security sector reform'? Are women and their needs included or ignored in matters pertaining to 'national security'? How do they interpret their marginalisation in security issues? How would national security operate when women and women's issues were put at the center instead? Is there an over-emphasis and prioritisation of 'militarised security' and militarism as an ideology rather than other aspects of security, such as 'food security' and human security? Can we learn from the examples of other countries where food security and women's contribution is significant, and where 'community policing' rather than militarisation is the top priority?

In our research in the School of Democratic Economics (SDE), this realm of 'family resilience' from food security to supporting and maintaining the survival, healing, and financial security of the family continue to rest heavily on mothers and women. This includes ensuring access to clean water, making sure there is food everyday, taking care of the children and elderly when they are sick, being the glue that keeps the family and the community together. Men tend to continue to rely on their formerly clandestine and ex-guerrilla roles, where they meet up with their old resistance networks to plan community or political activities in the public sphere, leaving everything in the household management to the realm of the female. Most of this work continues to be undervalued and unacknowledged. However, with the opening up of possibilities and opportunities for Timorese women to either work or go abroad to study and/or work, one sees the extraordinary phenomenon of Timorese men adapting to being primarily responsible for childcare and some housework (although some will still manage to subcontract this work to other women in the extended family).

The example below of how women soldiers and police define 'national security' is based on interviews with women in the current Falintil-FDTL (military) and PNTL (police). Sociological and anthropological research is always useful in un-packing terms, such as 'discrimination', which in the Timor Leste context, has become loaded with meanings. What do the women Petisionarios-F-FDTL mean when they use the word 'discrimination'? And what do the women in F-FDTL mean when they say 'there is no discrimination'? There is a gap between official rhetoric on 'discrimination' and un-official perspectives based on the experiences of women in the PNTL (police forces), F-FDTL (military), and Petisionarios-F-FDTL (women military who left their barracks in 2006). The example below illuminates these paradoxes:

During interviews with women F-FDTL in the Metinaro headquarters, they mentioned that during the distribution of uniforms, everyone (including the women) was given male uniforms and male underwear. Given the context that 'everyone is treated as a male, with a male body', they paradoxically did not consider this 'discrimination'. When we cross-checked with a male Lieutenant in the F-FDTL, he confirmed that these were 'donations' from China and that if there is anyone to blame for 'discrimination', it should be the Chinese donors. This problem with uniforms specifically designed with male bodies in mind emerged again when PNTL women in the districts raised the issue of lack of uniforms for pregnant police officers. In other countries (e.g. New Zealand), there are flexible options for women police to

East Timor: brave women warriors, unfinished revolutions   255

continue to work during pregnancy. Comparative positive examples from other countries for retaining talented women (who are also mothers) in the police force needs to be studied seriously and implemented in Timor Leste (including the example of childcare facilities within the security institutions in the Philippine Police and Armed Forces, an example given by the former UN Police Commissioner Rodolfo Tor).

Embodying/Engendering SSR

Ms Z is a police officer in the elite Rapid Intervention Unit (UIR, *Unidade Intervencao Rapida*) in the PNTL, who is committed and determined to being and becoming a 'professional warrior'. She is exemplary in many respects, being the only woman in UIR who had undergone all of the most challenging physical and weapons training in that unit. She was also involved in the *Operasaun Conjunta* in Ermera in 2008. When we asked her about women's possibilities for promotion within the PNTL, she responded that it was based on 'komportamentu diak' (*good behaviour*). When we asked her further what she meant by 'komportamentu diak', she identified several characteristics, including not complaining about terrible weather and sleeping conditions during Operasaun Conjunta, and not giving the impression that women in the police forces just get pregnant all the time. It is necessary to un-pack this 'komportamentu diak', as we identified that most of it refers to a male body. In using a male body as the model of the 'ideal combatant or professional warrior', women's bodies then become 'transgressors' to the fixed model. We identified three strategies of women in the security forces to survive:

1   Assimilation. Thus Ines, one of the police officers in UIR, is proud to be more masculine than feminine and appears to be determined not to break the 'male codes'. When we asked her if she had plans of getting married one day, getting pregnant, and having a child, she laughed—as if this was a question that should not be directed to her, but to the other women. If this model is the dominant bloc, then there is no hope for the other women who already have children and who are struggling to balance work and family within these institutions;
2   Separation. Several of the pregnant women, married women, and women with children we met in these institutions insisted on their 'femininity' within these predominantly male institutions. They continue to keep their hair long, wear skirts, and enjoy coming to work with their pregnant bodies. Separate but equal. They want institutional reforms to benefit women, as they plan to stay—but only if there is genuine reform to improve their chances for promotion, longer maternity leave, better family-friendly policies;
3   Hostility. Some of the women we met, including higher-ranking women, and especially women in the districts, expressed outright hostility to

256 *Jacqueline A. Siapno*

the patriarchal and paternalistic institutional security structure and towards the government. Their strategy is to eloquently articulate critical analysis of their subordination, to the point of hostility, with no sense of institutional loyalty or implication in the processes of disempowerment. They explicitly identify discrimination, patriarchy, and impoverishment of women as the root causes of their oppression within these security structures.

Where to begin in terms of engendering security sector reform in Timor Leste? Since the attempted assassinations on the President and Prime Minister on 11 February 2008, and even before that during the 2006 political crisis, and if we are to take a *longue durée* approach, since 1999, 'national security', and in particular the problem of 'reforming the security sector', has been a serious challenge in Timor Leste. During the crisis in 2006 and up to the present, 'security' has relied heavily upon the support of international security forces and external influences (i.e. UNPOL, ISF) working together with the F-FDTL and PNTL. Some of the general problems and challenges go back to the failed processes of Demobilisation, Disarmament, and Reintegration (DDR, in the transition from non-statutory guerrilla forces to the established state army). These are not necessarily unique only to Timor Leste but have also been identified in other 'post-conflict', newly independent, Third World countries in Southeast Asia, Africa, and Latin America.[7] However, there are serious obstacles to SSR that are specific to the formation of the security forces in Timor Leste. Through our interviews with women in the PNTL and F-FDTL, we were able to illuminate the following challenges:

1   The continuing resilience of corrupt, untouchable, 'commando-style' mentalities, behaviours, and practices going back to the clandestine and commando practices entrenched from the Indonesian occupation period and the ex-Falintil resistance (only a process of 'decolonising the mind', Ngugi wa Thiongo's phrase would engender reform). Women, because of their very low and marginalised status in the security institutions, are more astute in observing these 'abnormalities', which amongst the men have become 'normalised corruption' and 'normalised marginalisation of ethics'.
2   Weak, if not absent, institutional policies and mechanisms to implement non-discriminatory and representative politics ('discrimination' was a very sensitive issue, in the F-FDTL in particular). But instead of being discussed, it is repressed or its existence is denied.
3   The broader historical-socio-political-economic divisions that split the security forces internally: the previous politicisation of the security forces as an 'apparatus' not for the state and the people, but for one political party; the Petisionarios-F-FDTL (primarily from Loromonu) and the F-FDTL and subsequently claims of 'regional discrimination'

East Timor: brave women warriors, unfinished revolutions 257

and dominance of ex-Falintil veterans from Lorosae), but also externally, causing serious lack of trust between civilians and the military due to the violence in 2006 which until today remains un-investigated (the recommendations of the UN Independent Commission on Investigation have been pushed aside), and between the local security forces and the external/international forces who were requested to come and 'stabilised the country'. Women widows of PNTL and F-FDTL killed in May 2006, and women PNTL officers seriously wounded on 25 May 2006, to this day articulate that there has been neither political justice nor emotional healing (the basic conditions for sustainable peace) on the grave issues that initiated the political violence in 2006.

Here are some ideas about engendering democratic spaces for the formulation of the 'National Security Policy' and within that 'Defence Reform' and 'Police Reform', which emerged from interviews with women in the police and military forces. These women point out the benefits of being more consultative, inclusive, and participatory, rather than keeping it to a few 'dominant blocs of powerful men'. The women asked these questions: has there been consultation to ensure that the defense and police reform agenda reflects the concerns of women and marginalised men? Have community-based organisations been included in the defence and police reform process? In order for any 'National Security Policy' or SSR programme to have any legitimacy, and to be sustainable, it must be consultative, people must have a sense of local ownership of it, and it must take into account the different security and political justice needs of women, men, girls, and boys in this society. It must also take into account their own community assessments of their security risks, threats to their lives, vulnerabilities, in-securities, and resilience. Another challenge we identified from the very beginning of the research is that due to the historical context of tensions between civil-military relations, security institutions may see civilian oversight bodies including critical women's groups, Parliament, and human rights organisations as political opponents and critics, rather than as potential partners, and therefore may be unwilling to work with them. Are women's organisations included as potential partners? Or are they seen as threats and hostile enemies?

A similar question, inverted, may be asked of women's groups and community-based organisations: instead of continually meeting amongst the converted, do they include police and military amongst their list of potential partners for sustainable peace? Improving civil-military relations, through joint discussions, through women in the PNTL and F-FDTL (who are less rigid and more flexible in terms of creative approaches to peace building) may reduce 'paranoia'; may (or may not) engender 'emotional healing' of trauma between PNTL and F-FDTL, between civilian and military relationships; and may re-build a sense of trust on security institutions, and renewed faith in national institutions more generally. There are some organisations now conducting civilian oversight of the military in police, including

258   *Jacqueline A. Siapno*

Fundasaun Mahein, one of Commissions in Parliament, and other groups, but these continue to be quite weak. Yet these are the steps necessary to build sustainable peace in Timor Leste, which not only incorporates but also prioritises human security (including the elimination of violence in the home against women, children, and vulnerable groups). Without emotional healing, political justice and economic empowerment, and institutions, systems, mechanisms, and processes being set-up and strengthened to enable and foster all of these to happen, we can never have sustained peace and sustained healing from post-traumatic stress disorders and ongoing conflict and violence.

Between the rhetoric of political ideals and everyday practice

Revolutionary movements always recruit female labour and commitment to enable their success. But once the revolution is won, women are sent back to their traditional roles in the low ranks of the hierarchy, not in the political discourses in the public sphere but in the actual everyday politics. The current government can no longer continue with the current politics where women are 'left to pick-up the pieces, wash the dirty dishes, and the victims' of male aggression in the country. There are ex-Falintil women who continue to have health problems, including bullet wounds still lodged in their bodies, and police women in PNTL who suffered from serious post-traumatic stress disorders as a result of the shootings in 2006, are in serious need of health services to enable them to begin the process of 'emotional and physical healing'.

As one example of the gaps between rhetoric and reality, in spite of all the rhetoric on implementing the Convention on the Elimination of Discrimination against Women (CEDAW), the problem of sexual harassment in several institutions, including the police, is prevalent. In our research, we uncovered several serious cases, including a previous PNTL Commander in Ainaro investigated for serious misconduct towards six female PNTL colleagues in 2003. According to the PNTL officer (Agent Lurdes, who became an Instructor in the Academia Policia) who investigated the case, the PNTL Commander told his female colleagues: 'If you want to be promoted, you'd have to sleep with me'. In spite of the serious charges of misconduct, he was not punished, but transferred to Liquica instead where he apparently repeated the same pattern of sexual harassment. The weakness of implementing Disciplinary Measures and Professional Standards has created a culture of impunity, whereby unethical conduct such as sexual harassment, gun-toting (and other inappropriate use of force and abuse of power) continues. When we interviewed and had a discussion with the Secretary of State for Security, he informed us that 'these (i.e. sexual harassment and the other problems) are more widespread than we think'.

Another example is on women's health issues: un-treated physical wounds and psychosocial trauma from 1999 to 2006, and the absence of any medical

East Timor: brave women warriors, unfinished revolutions   259

and/or counseling support. PNTL Human Resources personnel informed us then that there were approximately 121 PNTL 'victims' of the 2006 crisis, and 29 PNTL wounded. Some PNTL women interviewed, in NID (National Intelligence Department), pointed to the bullet wounds still lodged in their bodies that needed to be operated on. They almost refused to speak to us, as they said they had already told the government about this problem, but have not heard any response. One of them said: 'I have no faith in the government. Why waste my time talking to you?' Other PNTL women we interviewed told us that they individually took the initiative to seek mental medical treatment at the hospital, because, as one of them, a sub-inspector, poignantly recounted: 'I was afraid I would go insane'. When asked if PNTL as an institution has ever offered any psycho-social counseling or support for them, she replied: 'None. I had to take my own personal initiative. If I waited for the institution, I may have gone insane.' This seems to be a serious problem which the PNTL as an institution needs to address. Being 'in denial' about the impact of the 2006 crisis on the police and military, and not providing the support and space on 'political justice and emotional healing issues' caused further serious problems in the long term.

The most serious problem in terms of the huge gaps between rhetoric and reality has to do with the mentality and attitudes of high-ranking leaders who have been recorded and cited (in our own interviews, but also in the media) of making public statements denigrating women's participation, reducing their role to a reproductive one (i.e. 'we would like to reduce the number of women in the police as all they do is get pregnant'; 'we would like to introduce a new regulation in the military whereby if women do join, they should be single, and if married, should not be allowed to have children until after 2 to3 years in the military'). To be fair, there is a lot of political goodwill to pass all kinds of laws, including the Domestic Violence Law in Parliament that benefits and protects women's rights, and state-organised public seminars including one recent conference on 'Gender, Family Planning, and Reproductive Health' organised by Parliament. The Ministry for Gender and Equality, for a relatively young country, has made more gains than some very old countries, including placing Timor Leste's first-ever representative in the UN CEDAW Committee, Ms Milena Pires. However, a huge gap remains between political idealism and rhetorical speeches and everyday reality, where women continue to experience domestic violence and institutional violence (in various forms). There seems to be commitment from the current sixth Constitutional Government, under Prime Minister Rui Araujo, to address gender injustice and inequality, but the public sector and its mostly misogynist mentalities, attitudes, mechanisms, practices, and processes do not help in effective implementation of institutional changes.

One senior security adviser in the Office of the President even used the term 'systematically pregnant'. While it is understandable that patriarchal and discriminatory mentality and attitudes are a product of socio-cultural-historical formations, it devalues women PNTL and F-FDTL's contributions

260   *Jacqueline A. Siapno*

to nation-building. Democratic spaces valuing women's sacrifices, commitment, and contributions to the security institutions should be engendered, so as not to repeat the history of the marginalisation of ex-Falintil women and discrimination against the women Petisionarios-F-FDTL. Abusive language that puts down and humiliates women within these institutions should not to be tolerated. High-level commanders should set exemplary behavior and models, rather than the opposite.

There is also the gap between urban and rural police women, and more generally, the impoverished condition of women in the armed forces. Women PNTL in the rural districts (i.e. Baucau, Los Palos, Ainaro, and Maliana) lamented the poor quality of uniforms and boots given to them. They had to save from their own personal salaries in order to be able to purchase their own uniforms. Because of their love for their country and their high ethical values, some of them sew patches on the uniforms so that they can continue to use them. When women PNTL from the districts come to Dili, they commented that they feel embarrassed because compared to their Dili counterparts, their uniforms are all worn-out. When we presented this problem to the Secretary of State for Security then, he confirmed that the problem with the uniforms and boots is due to corruption and a greedy company who won the tender, but who then procured very low-quality uniforms. When we asked him how he felt about the extreme contradiction that there are very dedicated women police officers in the districts who are sewing their uniforms and buying their own boots and uniforms, while unethical businessmen corrupt the state's funds (an explanation that the women police are not yet aware of), he replied: 'Yes, I completely understand your question. I empathise with the women. And we have to do something to stop these corrupt practices amongst companies who have the tenders for procurement'.

These impoverished women suffered from lack of access to uniforms, facilities, training, or transportation; and having no computer, toner, filing/archival system, transportation, radio, and other facilities (especially in the districts). Female PNTL in the districts were not able to do their investigation of criminal cases properly because they did not have an appropriate filing/archival system in place. Their investigation was mostly done with pen and paper, and did not seem to be archived systematically. This was a recurring complaint by respondents in the districts. So, even if someone else wanted to follow up on criminal investigations, it would have been challenging, as there was no proper archival/filing system in place, computerised or otherwise. In addition, there was a serious lack of coordination between the police and the judicial sector. We were asked to make the recommendation then that a Unit be created, within the Prosecutor-General's Office, to ensure 'accountability' of the PNTL and investigate their practices.

Concluding remarks

There are many levels in the systems of silence and cultures of silence in Timor Leste that inhibit the state and society more generally from acknowledging

East Timor: brave women warriors, unfinished revolutions 261

the contributions, self-sacrifices, and dreams of women warriors—from ex-Falintil to women in the current F-FDTL and PNTL. These systems of silences begin from the silence on Domestic Violence (e.g. 'Do not talk to the "malaes" (foreigners): they already think the Timorese are violent anyway; and that Timorese men are bad children who refuse to reform'), a legacy of double colonialism. Many of the women we interviewed summarised their feelings in this way: 'My state does not represent my interest', in spite of the huge sacrifices they made to struggle for independence. Others lamented: 'This is a difficult dialogue they are not ready to have'.

Years later, as I critically reflect on these questions, I began to understand that the future of Timor Leste depends on what kinds of illuminations we adopt, what kind of ethical politics we pursue, and what kinds of policies we struggle for in acknowledging the enormous contributions of the ex-combatant women, and poor women generally, who were interviewed for this paper. From the oral histories of ex-Falintil and F-FDTL women we learn about power and extraordinary resilience, quiet confidence, and inspiring faith in the agency of individuals to engender social transformation and revolutionary change, in spite of state institutions that continue to disillusion and fail them. Contrary to the dearth of 'gender and development' research focusing on East Timorese women, they remained to be seen as 'dependent' women needing to be 'saved' by international gender experts (from ADB, UNIFEM, WB, UNDP, OXFAM) who want to make them 'happy', even if they don't want to be made happy (by all these over-confident interveners); or represented in different categories of victimhood: as 'victims' (not only of war, conflict, and political violence, but also domestic violence); and as victims of sexual exploitation and abuse. As demonstrated here, what is missing are accounts of the resilience, power, courage, and pride of these women as warriors and survivors, and of their roles as military strategists, political thinkers/advisers, reconstructors, and peace-builders. Why? Who benefits from the continued and repetitive politics of representation of Timorese women as weak, dependent, helpless, vulnerable, insecure, and in need of benevolent protectors (whether by security men, or gender and development experts from the First World who can 'empower' them)?

We need to continually articulate and write a different history of Timorese women that is much more inclusive, especially from the rural mountain regions, and which takes a *longue duree* perspective of 42,000 years of Timorese history, in which women did have agency, did play very powerful and inspiring roles, including as traditional chiefs (liurai feto) and queens in traditional kingdoms, as leaders and strategists in resistance and rebel movements, and as survivor-visionaries of post-independence societies providing an alternative 'ethical politics' and the 'checks-and-balances' to a state and government that can and may betray its own 'revolutionary' ideals.

Why the concepts of 'unfinished' and 'betrayed revolution'? There's a general public opinion transcending party lines that the state and government have failed in education, anti-corruption, alleviation of poverty, inequality, and injustice, and democratisation in the continuing nation-building process

262   *Jacqueline A. Siapno*

of Timor Leste. Perhaps the expectations were too high in the first place and unrealistic for a newly independent nation-state to meet, given the complex post-war, post-conflict environment where so much wastage of financial resources has happened (on the part of the international organisations and the local elite leadership). Are there positive examples of DDR and SSR that Timor Leste can share with other post-war countries to avoid the same mistakes? Some of the notes and observations in this chapter can be 'lessons learned' for other communities struggling with the same conflict and post-conflict issues, especially on the importance of prioritising human security, food security, and openness to and inclusion of women's and children's perspectives above and beyond militarised security. In a country led predominantly by former guerrillas, clandestine revolutionary heroes, and the persistence of the ideologies of masculinist-nationalism and its imaginary, it will be these male elites and their appendage of female elites who will be in the mainstream history books, regardless of whether or not they were ethical human beings who lived a life of integrity and dignity, according to former revolutionary ideals. Poor women and children continue to be just 'fragments', if not 'excess luggage' to be discarded in the entire nation-building process. In conclusion, these kinds of schemes to 'improve the human condition', through revolutionary war and national independence, are unfortunately, and paradoxically, also just plain hostile to inclusive, egalitarian, democratic, participatory, and pluralistic processes—in practice (but in rhetoric, in the realm of hopeful imaginaries, it all sounds very ideal).

Notes

1 I wish to thank my East Timorese colleagues Joaninha de Araujo Quintao, Carlos Godinho, Flotilda da Costa, Joanna Amaral, Mica Barreto Soreas, Therese Tam Nguyen, Ivete de Oliveira, and most specially Milena Pires, for providing invaluable research support and critical discussions in conducting interviews in East Timor. Writing in a time of conflict and violence in East Timor, with minimal infrastructural facilities, security, and space, is extremely difficult. I would not have been able to conduct the interviews without their utter determination, rigorous logistical support in mapping and preparing for interviews in sensitive zones (i.e. IDP camps in Hera, Metinaro), and in their own moving personal examples of hopefulness and resilience, inspiring me to not give up on writing in a time of political violence in Dili.

2 Another important resource used in this essay was the workshop we organised on 3 May 2008 on 'Security Sector Reform: Gendered Perspectives' in Delta Nova, Dili, Timor Leste. F-FDTL and PNTL women spoke up in the public forum, identifying key problems within their institutions (e.g. the PNTL from Maliana who spoke up about discrimination and corruption in the Border Patrol Unit).

3 FFDTL stands for Falintil-FDTL: Forcas Defensas de Timor Leste, Armed Forces of East Timor.

4 James Scott, *The Art of Not Being Governed: An Anarchist History of Upland Southeast Asia* (New Haven, CT: Yale University Press, 2009), p. 80.

5 Interview conducted in Tetun with then fourty-three-year-old 'Mana Bisoy', Maria Rosa da Camara, ex-Falintil veteran/combatant, 2 July 2007, Taibessi,

Dili, East Timor. She became a Member of Parliament, CNRT (Conselho Nacional da Resistencia Timorense) party. 'Mana' is an honorific term used in several ways: as a term of respect, even for women younger than one's self, or has a higher position in the structural hierarchy; or as a term of endearment to be inclusive of someone who is usually regarded as an 'outsider'. It can also be used to mean 'sister', but has a different meaning from other words signifying sister, e.g. 'alin feto'—which is a position marker: a young female who is of 'lower rank' and 'status'. Often times 'mana' is also used in patron-client relationships in the entrenched patronage-system, especially when the lower-ranking person using the address wants something from the 'mana boot' (literally: big sister; or, donor).

6 See also my analysis of the displays, and the politics of representation in this National Resistance Museum, in Jacqueline Siapno, 'Timor Leste: On a Path of Authoritarianism?', in Daljit Singh and Lorraine C. Salazar (eds.), *Southeast Asian Affairs* (Singapore: ISEAS, 2006), No. (1) (2006), pp. 325–342.

7 See also Susan Blackburn's chapter included in this volume.

Part V
Conclusion

13 Rethinking the historical place of 'warrior women' in Southeast Asia

Barbara Watson Andaya

Reaching from the sixth century into modern times, this book has viewed conflict in Southeast Asia from a perspective that is simultaneously gendered, regional and comparative. At the most basic level, all the authors have demonstrated that although women's experience of warfare can take many forms, 'her-stories' are consistently different from those of men. In the process, they have identified lines of research that resonate with findings in other world areas where armed combat has been central to the assertion of ethnic or national identity. In Southeast Asia, as elsewhere, the assumption that warfare is primarily a male domain has far-reaching implications for popular evaluations of women's contribution to the evolution of the modern state. Even when 'women warriors' have been identified and lauded in the nationalist epic, their perceived exceptionalism has encouraged stereotyped portrayals and has ignored the involvement of their less prominent sisters. While encouraging a more nuanced view of women in warfare, the contributors to this volume thus direct our attention towards previously marginalised participants. In simultaneously presenting new sources and posing new questions, they have also provided welcome evidence of the expansion of women's studies in Southeast Asia over the last generation. Yet the fact that so much remains unanswered is a reminder that the sources impose very real limits on any investigation of the ways in which understandings of gender have shaped both the history and the historiography of Southeast Asia.

Lauding 'women warriors' in the early twentieth century

Visitors to any Southeast Asian country will be struck by the public space allotted to the individuals who have played a significant role in the nation's narrative, and the innumerable 'sites of memory'—statues, streets, airports, buildings—by which their names have become fixed in popular histories.[1] In a region where every country except Thailand came under colonial control, it is hardly surprising that such individuals are commonly those who resisted foreign control, especially through leadership in combat.

268   *Barbara Watson Andaya*

Because such leadership is typically male, and because masculinity is inextricably embedded in the discourse of nationalism and revolution, the persistent reminders of heroism in warfare would seem to suggest that affirming a female 'martial tradition' is necessary in order for women to be brought into the state iconography.[2]

Although not all feminists would agree with this viewpoint, it would probably have been accepted by authors of the locally produced 'national' histories that began to appear in the 1920s and 1930s. In some cases it was not difficult to locate heroines whose prominence in warfare had already established their place in communal memories. In Vietnam, great 'women warriors' like the Trung sisters and Lady Trieu, renowned for their resistance against the Chinese close to two millennia ago, had long been extolled in literati writings.[3] The character of Srikandi, the warrior wife of Arjuna in the Indian epic, the *Mahabharata*, had figured in Javanese shadow plays for hundreds of years, and her name had long been associated with a seventh-century candi on the Dieng plateau.[4] Similarly, most Thais were familiar with the story of Queen Suriyothai, whose death in battle against the Burmese in 1548 had been celebrated in chronicles from at least the eighteenth century.[5] Yet in Southeast Asia more generally accounts of 'women warriors' and stories of female heroism on the field of battle survived primarily not in written documents but in oral accounts and local memory. Sometimes, it is true, elite historians did try to tap existing material and incorporate women into their accounts of a patriotic past. For example, in 1907 the Confucian-educated nationalist scholar Phan Boi Chau (1867–1940) was obviously concerned that the 'female generals of our country' were rarely mentioned in existing histories. He therefore drew attention to Bui Thi Xuan, a military commander during the short-lived Tay Son regime (1788–1802) who, he said, was 'good at leading armies'. Many of his readers would have recalled that Bui Thi Xuan was renowned for her martial skills and ability to train elephants for warfare against the opposing Nguyen forces. She and her husband won several battles, but were both executed following their capture in 1802 when the Nguyen came to power, with Bui Thi Xuan reputedly trampled to death by an elephant.[6] Yet although Phan was willing to admit that 'wearers of hairpins and dresses' could lead armies and even slay 'those with whiskers', his greatest praise was still reserved not for women as military leaders but for the virtuous mothers and wives who supported their sons and husbands and assisted them to gain distinction.[7] Similar preferences are evident in the 1906 introductory issue of Siam's first magazine for women, *Kunlasatri* (Ladies of Good Birth and Breeding). Certainly, the (male) author of this article referred to Queen Suriyothai and her heroism against the Burmese; he also made favourable mention of two sisters from the island of Thalang (now Phuket), Thao Thepkasattri and Thao Srisunthorn, who had been awarded noble titles by Rama I (1782–1809) in recognition of their leadership in resisting Burmese armies.[8] Nonetheless, *Kunlasatri* left readers in no doubt that the ideal woman was represented by the talented yet

Rethinking the historical place of 'warrior women' in SEA   269

deferential Lady Nophamat, a fictional figure popularly believed to have lived in the Sukhothai period.[9]

Beneath the surface, however, such attitudes were already undergoing change as global influences pressing for women's rights intersected with the elevation of patriotism as a core element of indigenous nationalism. Phan Boi Chau himself spoke of heroism 'burgeoning on the five continents' and hoped that Vietnam could produce a modern-day heroine who could be a female counterpart to legendary Chinese generals.[10] The female editor of a new Thai magazine for women, *Satri Niphon* (Women's Writing), first published in 1914 at the outbreak of the First World War, reported the martial exploits of European women, including the willingness of students to volunteer as soldiers. Invoking examples like Suriyothai and the two sisters from Thalang, the editor had no doubt that, if necessary, women in Siam 'would compare well with these foreigners and do exactly the same'.[11] Royal endorsement helped strengthen public familiarity with such figures, while continuing to emphasise their ability to maintain their wifely and maternal obligations. In 1917 Prince Damrong, regarded as the founder of Thailand's nationalist narrative, published the first popular history book, *Thai Fought Burma* (*Thai Rop Phama*). His second chapter described how Queen Suriyothai, disguised as the Crown Prince and riding on an elephant at the head of the Siamese army, was killed while saving her husband the king from certain death.[12] Contributing to these accolades was Damrong's half-brother, Prince Narathip Praphan Phong (1861–1931), who composed a poem entitled 'In Joyful Praise of Thai Women Warriors', extolling the two Thalang sisters who could both 'rock the cradle and wield the sword', while never failing to delight their husbands.[13]

Nationalism and women warriors in the 1930s

In the years after the First World War the growing involvement of Southeast Asian women in nationalist issues encouraged male historians and political leaders to hold up 'female warriors' of the past as exemplars for the present. In 1929, attempting to rally Indonesian women to the nationalist cause, the young Sukarno (later Indonesia's first President) invoked the mythical figure of Srikandi, the warrior wife of Arjuna, as a model for emulation.[14] It is worth noting, however, that Sukarno made no mention of female leaders in more recent resistance movements, most notably Aceh, where Cut Nyak Dien (1850–1908) was among several women whose reputation was already well established in local traditions (Chapter 6). In Siam, by contrast, the leaders of the 1932 coup that brought about a constitutional monarchy saw positive advantages in recognising the achievements of a heroine from the northeastern region. Known as 'Lady Mo', she is popularly believed to have repulsed a Lao attack in the 1827 and to have been rewarded with the royal title Thao Suranari (Dame Gallant Lady). In 1935, after the suppression of a royalist rebellion in the northeast, the new Bangkok government and

270   Barbara Watson Andaya

local leaders collaborated in erecting a statue of Thao Suranari in the regional capital of Khorat (Figure 13.1) as a reminder of past loyalties.[15] Prince Damrong and other court historians had previously acknowledged that Thao Suranari was 'clever', but did not refer to her military leadership, which was not mentioned in the documents they had used.[16] In elevating a woman who was now a national heroine, the Khorat monument symbolises a time of growing interest in female patriotism, especially as exemplified in warfare. Newspaper editors, novelists, theatre producers and film makers all recognised the popular appeal of 'warrior women' and of the theme of female sacrifice in battle and their willingness to die defending Thai honour, typically against Burmese invasion. *The Blood of Suphan*, a popular dance-drama produced by Luang Wichit Wathakan (now considered the primary architect of Thai nationalism), celebrated the valour and tragic death of a young village woman as she fought Burmese armies and abuse of local populations. It was subsequently published in serial form and was widely distributed among Thai schools, with a film produced in 1937.[17]

A similar process is evident in the Philippines, although the trajectory had been slow moving. A generation earlier, in his private correspondence, José Rizal referred to the 'Princess Urduja' described by the fourteenth-century traveller, Ibn Battuta, arguing that her domain, 'Tawalisi', was in the northern Philippines. However, this 'woman warrior' did not enter the public sphere until the American academic Austin Craig included Rizal's letter in his 1916 pamphlet, 'Particulars of the Philippines Pre-Spanish Past', locating her kingdom in Pangasinan.[18] A few years later Craig published a textbook that attributed Urduja with an 'outstanding utterance' entirely lacking in the Ibn Battuta account. 'You know that I am governor of this port in place of my brother because, with my army of free women, slave girls and female captives, all of whom fought just as well as men could, I won a big battle.'[19] Popularised in books such as *Stories of Great Filipinos*, intended 'to acquaint the young Filipinos with the achievements of their ancestors' and endorsed by scholars such as Encarnacion Alzona (the first Filipina to obtain a Ph.D.) and the respected historian Gregorio Zaide (1907–1988), Urduja was absorbed into the school curriculum as 'the Amazonic ruler-warrior of ancient Pangasinan'.[20]

In a climate where calls for increased female participation in the political process were becoming more vocal, the attention given to Urduja reflected demands for a greater inclusion of women in Philippine history. Zaide himself explicitly stated that 'a true history' of the nation's political emancipation should give attention 'to the role played by women', the 'unsung heroines' who had proved ready to stand forth 'in the country's hour of need'.[21] On this occasion Zaide was referring to the 1896 Revolution, but he found earlier examples of female courage in the eighteenth-century heroine Gabriela Silang (1731–1763). Following her husband's death, Gabriela had assumed leadership of the 1762 Ilokano uprising against the Spanish. Although her courage and sagacity 'as valiant as that of her husband' had been praised

Figure 13.1 Statue of Thao Suranari, local heroine of Nakhon Ratchasima, Thailand. Originally erected in 1935 and restored in 1967.

Source: Adapted, under Creative Commons Attribution 4.0 International, from Supanut Arunoprayote's early 2019 photo at https://en.wikipedia.org/wiki/Thao_Suranari (last accessed 23 Feb 2019).

in the classic 1890 *Historia de Ilocos* by the nationalist Isabelo de los Reyes, it was through Zaide's writings that she became 'Ilocandia's Joan of Arc'.[22] Yet it has also been argued that the exercise of recovering heroines from the pre-American past unwittingly served the colonial system by juxtaposing accounts of Spanish tyranny with the implied benign nature of American rule.[23] For instance, elite endorsement of American democracy appears in a major novel of the period, *The Filipino Rebel*. Maximo Kalaw (alternatively regarded as a supporter of independence and a 'model colonial') initially depicts his heroine Josefa as a fervent *barrio* revolutionary, prepared to kill 'the cruel Americans'. However, after receiving a modern education

272 *Barbara Watson Andaya*

under colonial tutelage, she goes to the United States and returns to the Philippines as an advocate for women's rights.[24] Against this background there was no reason for the American regime to see the representations of the lives of Filipino heroes and heroines as a threat to the established order.

Elsewhere, the attitude of colonial governments towards 'female warriors' of the past was more ambiguous, especially as nationalism gathered force. In French Indochina, for instance, colonial officials were initially quite amenable to the lauding of Vietnamese heroines who had fought against some 'other' foreign rulers, usually the Chinese. Their incorporation into officially sanctioned school textbooks meant, as a modern author recalls, that 'Every little girl born in Vietnam (even a product of French elementary education like me), knew the legend of Lady Trieu, who pledged she would ride the wind to save her people from drowning in slavery.'[25] By contrast, French authorities were quick to censor eulogies of women warriors they considered could potentially inspire rebellion. In the 1920s this led to the banning of seven of the thirteen books focusing on Vietnamese and non-Vietnamese women who had taken a leading role in opposing foreign rule and unjust regimes.[26] Similarly, while Dutch admirers praised the young noblewoman Raden Kartini as representative of 'the benefits of colonial rule', the 'aggressive' (*strijdlustig*) women prominent in Aceh's anti-colonial resistance could hardly be presented as exemplars of Indonesian womanhood.[27] By 1945, when Dutch antagonism towards Indonesian nationalism was far greater, the Dutch author, Madelon Székely-Lulofs, was unable to find a publisher for her semi-factual but sympathetic biography of Cut Nyak Dien, whom she called 'an Acehnese queen'.[28] At a time when the Dutch were intent on re-imposing their control of Indonesia, the celebration of a resistance heroine was clearly controversial, and the manuscript was only accepted for publication in 1948 after several years of rejection.[29]

Women warriors as national heroines

Throughout Southeast Asia developments following the Second World War, most notably the demise of colonialism, raised new questions about the rights of women and their place in the national story. While Székely-Lulofs' historical novel of 'an Acehnese queen' had met a cool response in the Netherlands, it was soon translated into Indonesian, where it became a primary source for later biographies.[30] This publicity undoubtedly aided in President Sukarno's 1964 installation of Cut Nyak Dien (together with her compatriot Cut Meutia, 1870–1910) as a 'national heroine'. Aceh continued to figure prominently when there was any call to demonstrate the female contribution to Indonesia's evolution, and from the 1950s local historians drew on various sources to develop detailed accounts of several women warriors, including a shadowy sixteenth-century 'female admiral'. Given the name Keumalahayati, she was said to have attacked Portuguese Melaka, leading an army of widows whose husbands had died in combat against European infidels.[31]

Rethinking the historical place of 'warrior women' in SEA 273

When the Indonesian government proclaimed 1994 as the Year of Women, the three (male) historians recruited to produce a commemorative volume predictably concentrated on Aceh because here the myth that 'the military is only accessible to men' could be disproven.[32]

In this rising tide of hagiography, the visuality of the public image has been among the more effective ways of registering a female presence in the national epic. Erected in 1971, the Gabriela Silang Monument in Manila's Makati district represents her on horseback with her upraised hand holding a *bolo* or sword, her long hair flying in the air and one breast partially uncovered—the epitome of the warrior woman. In Thailand the original statue of Thai Suranari was replaced by a new representation in 1967, with the addition of an inscription emphasising her courage and hand-to-hand combat with the Lao troops.[33] At a time when the left-wing movement was gathering strength, it was probably no coincidence that the previous year a monument commemorating the allegiance of 'The Heroines of Thalang' had been constructed in Phuket. With replicas scattered all over the province, these two women have become central to constructions of local identity. As one might expect, Phuket's National Museum, inaugurated in 1989, devotes considerable space to their achievements, and every March a festival is held in their honour.[34] The public space devoted to women whose patriotism had been demonstrated against the enemy continued to expand, in some cases with direct royal support. The late King Bhumibol named a park near Ayutthaya after Queen Suriyothai, and in 1995 a massive statue that in which she was depicted her riding her elephant into battle was inaugurated by Queen Sirikit.[35]

Predictably, 'women warriors' received the greatest attention in Vietnam, where gender equality was a basic platform in communist ideology and where women like Nguyen Thi Minh Khai, executed by a French firing squad in 1941, had been prominent in anti-French resistance (Chapters 7 and 10). During the 1950s the communist government of northern Vietnam designated a cohort of 'new heroes' that included Nguyen Thi Chien (b. 1930), a guerrilla fighter who led a platoon of female soldiers, survived French torture and gained national recognition as a Heroine of the People's Armed Forces.[36] The same title was awarded to Mac Thi Buoi (1927–1951), a young peasant woman who died at French hands without ever divulging her knowledge of resistance activities.[37] After the de facto division of Vietnam in 1954 and the escalation of the conflict between the communist north and the southern regime, various forms of visual representations extolled the courageous female fighter, like the stamp that reproduced the 1967 print of a tall American captured by a petite peasant woman.[38] Urged on by the state, individual districts established 'houses of memory' and other commemorative sites to recognise the deeds of local heroes, men and women, a process that continued after unification in 1975. Local communities have been eager to display their ties to exemplary figures who have contributed to the nation's development, and even recent additions to the heroic assemblage have

274   *Barbara Watson Andaya*

gained their own cult following. By 1973, for instance, visitors to the tomb of the young heroine Mac Thi Buoi were so numerous that it was necessary to construct additional buildings in which to pay tribute to both her and her family. Ten years later an imposing statue was erected, and in 1995, a house of memory with its own cultural space was built to accommodate the rituals in her honour.[39] In other places connections to iconic figures of the distant past have also been revitalised. A statue of Le Chan, the virgin warrior said to have fought beside the Trung sisters, was erected in the port city of Hai Phong in 2000, and in 2008 a temple dedicated to the Tay Son general Bui Thi Xuan was inaugurated in her home district.[40]

In sum, then, a traveller through the Southeast Asian region will see that despite male dominance in all areas of political life, the names of emblematic women, attached to organisations, streets, buildings, and public spaces (and in some cases even battleships), attest their inclusion in the nation's heroic pantheon. The trend has become particularly marked over the last twenty years or so, when a plethora of films, television dramas, celebratory publications, school textbooks and monumental statuary have helped to implant images of 'women warriors' in the collective consciousness, reinforcing the idealised standards by which female patriotic commitment can be measured.

Stereotypes and sources

This cumulative attention to female leadership, especially in battle, is undeniably welcome, if only because it counters stereotypes of women as either timid, inexperienced and in need of male protection, or alternatively, as scheming and jealous manipulators. At the same time, however, written and visual representations, often hagiographic, have themselves contributed to other formulaic depictions. To some extent, this can be explained by the lack of detail in court chronicles and other written sources, which have allowed free reign to the multiple processes by which legends are created. In consequence, the typical picture is of a young, beautiful and committed wife who fights courageously beside her husband and either dies with him or assumes his mantle after he is killed. Physical attributes that distinguished cultural giants in the past but appear bizarre in contemporary eyes have been quietly laid aside. Vietnamese now remember Lady Trieu for her golden armour, her ivory shoes and her patriotic suicide, but there is rarely any mention of other details recorded in older sources—her giant height, her yard-long breasts, her booming voice and her voracious appetite.[41] Even in modern times, historians have felt no compunction in presenting heroines in a manner that complies with audience expectation. Although there is no surviving description of Gabriela Silang, Zaide did not hesitate to describe her as 'pretty', and her contemporary statues and portraits adhere faithfully to the prescribed model.[42] Indeed, if one reads through the Philippine newspaper coverage, it would appear that virtually every captured female member of the left-wing Hukbalahap was 'attractive' or even 'beautiful',

Rethinking the historical place of 'warrior women' in SEA   275

and that despite their ruthlessness and skill with weapons they remained at heart truly 'feminine'.[43] By the same token, websites for Cut Nyak Dien are more inclined to display modern portraits of a commanding, handsome and healthy woman than of the feeble and semi-blind captive depicted in Dutch photographs following her arrest in 1905 (compare Figures 6.1 and 1.1).[44]

Several contributions to this book have emphasised the contexts in which such stereotypes have developed. We are reminded that the complex inter-action between cultural memories, popular history, and the demands of the state exercises a far-reaching influence on the ways in which historical sources are deployed by later generations. Early nationalist historians were themselves unaware of their own influence on these processes, since they rarely discussed the historiography by which legendary representations arose. Because these narratives may be centuries old, challenges to heroic portrayals that are inextricably connected with local or national identity can elicit passionate and sometimes violent opposition. After intense de-bate, academic arguments that there was no historical basis for Urduja eventually led to her elimination from Philippine history books, although the release of an animated film in 2008 may reinstate her position, at least in Pangasinan.[45] For most people in northeast Thailand, the Khorat statue of Thao Suranari symbolises the courage of their ancestors and their loyalty to Bangkok. As the focus of a significant cult, the spirit of 'Grandmother Mo' is also credited with the power to assist her devotees in attaining var-ious goals such as improved health success and success in business or ro-mance. The community was therefore incensed when academics, arguing that surviving documents provide no evidence of a battle in which a local woman was involved, questioned her historicity.[46] The release of the Thai movie, *The Legend of Suriyothai*, in 2001, with an English version two years later, also aroused some controversy. Though endorsed by none other than Prince Damrong, the story of the queen who disguised herself as a man but died defending her husband from a Burmese attack was based on a chroni-cle compiled some 200 years after the event.[47] Nonetheless, the enthusiastic reception of this film, with its historical outline embellished by details of romantic intrigue and palace conspiracy, prompted one scholar to wonder whether the academic study of the past is now irrelevant in the creation of popular history.[48] Films recounting the lives of other warrior women, such as Gabriela Silang and Cut Nyak Dien, provoke a similar reaction.[49] In short, myth-making is alive and well in the twenty-first century, and future historians will need to gauge the extent to which eyewitness accounts, pho-tographs, documentaries, and personal memoirs have impeded this creative process of imagination and idealisation.[50]

Non-combatants in warfare

Questions about historical sources and their use open up other avenues for investigation. Although most of the contributions to this book con-centrate on the twentieth and twenty-first centuries, the earlier chapters

276   *Barbara Watson Andaya*

encourage us to think of the wider context of warfare, especially in terms of the involvement of non-combatants. This approach also encourages cross-cultural comparisons, not only within Southeast Asia but further afield, both in space and in time. In Western society, for instance, the offering of prayers in times of war was traditionally women's work, and during the Second World War American women were instructed to 'pray often—this is the most important part you have as a Christian woman on the home front'.[51] In traditional Southeast Asian cultures a man's female kin were also spiritually engaged in the conflict, even though they were not physically fighting. Describing the Manila region in the late sixteenth century, for instance, Miguel de Loarca noted that women refrained from work while their men were at war, and later ethnographic evidence from other societies shows a range of taboos and rituals that mothers, wives and daughters were required to observe in order that warriors would return safely.[52] In Europe another non-combatant category, 'camp followers' came to be associated with prostitutes, but until the nineteenth century a secondary 'army', both male and female, was characteristic of any campaign. Women were not merely sexual partners, but assumed a variety of necessary tasks—as cooks, laundresses, housekeepers, porters, nurses, at times even removing the dead from the battlefield.[53] And while barracks concubinage certainly developed in colonial armies, and although villagers were forced to provide 'services' (including sexual access) for armies on the march, it appears that in earlier times 'camp-follower' could also be a soldier's own kinfolk. A bas-relief on Angkor's Bayon depicting a family following the royal army reflects the reality of much indigenous warfare, since a fifteenth-century Thai poem refers to 'men who brought their families' to the battle. The Bugis and Makassarese from southwest Sulawesi were renowned for their fighting ability, but again their armies were not composed simply of men. A Bugis contingent assisting the Dutch against a Chinese rebellion in 1742 consisted of 500 warriors as well as their wives, and over time the motley collection of 'followers' came to substantially outnumber the actual fighting force.[54] Although the women involved fulfilled typical 'female' roles, they could also take on key responsibilities in the battle itself by preparing defences, mixing gunpowder, preparing weaponry and tending the wounded. The chronicler of the first Spanish expedition to the Philippines thus described how women and children joined men in throwing lances, stones and mud at advancing forces.[55] The belief that women had privileged access to ingredients used in magical potions could even provide the guarantee of a particularly formidable weapon, their own body fluids. In the seventeenth century, for instance, it was claimed that the blowpipes of Makassar warriors were so deadly because their women, in charge of concocting the ingredients smeared on arrowheads, mixed the poisonous sap of the *upas* tree (*Antiaris toxicaria*) with their own menstrual blood.[56] In northern Thailand a statue of the legendary Queen Camadevi, erected in 1982, commemorates her victory over a forest king who, according to popular accounts, is rendered powerless when he inadvertently accepts a turban made out of her menstrually bloodstained undergarments.[57]

Female access to supernatural influences

Thinking about the ways in which 'her-story' has been constructed also raises questions about our interpretations of the position of 'women warriors' in times past. If we approach earlier sources on their own terms, rather than simply seeking evidence that women could and did replicate male roles, different paths of inquiry may be opened up. For example, the idea that supernatural influence could determine the outcome of any conflict was deeply embedded in societies where a person's entire life was thought to be governed by factors outside his or her personal control. Regardless of its size or the nature of its equipment, any armed force was subject to decimating sickness, malfunctioning weaponry, inadequate supplies, adverse weather, and other unforeseen events. From this perspective, success was not primarily a function of technological skills, military strategy or even leadership. Ultimately, victory in battle depended on supernatural support, and this required not merely the rituals of those at home but the actual presence of individuals thought to possess the ability to act as a conduit to non-human powers.

Historical sources from pre-modern Southeast Asia indicate that many of these individuals were female, and it is significant that Lady Sinn (Chapter 2) is called 'sacred mother' (*sheng-mu*), a title that the Chinese often bestowed on deified women. The belief that supernatural assistance was considered necessary for victory may also explain why certain women were prominent at the head of armies as they set forth to meet the enemy. A fifteenth-century Thai text from Chiang Mai, for instance, describes how the king despatched a force under the leadership of the queen-mother to attack a neighbouring kingdom. She was responsible for making the requisite offerings to the spirits ('an albino buffalo, thirteen albino chickens, 13,000 ducks, and a cushion and mats, betel nut tray, water ewer, new pots, new bowls and new mats'), which ensured that the cannon could be effectively fired and victory attained.[58] With this description in mind, it may be easier to understand the significance of a princess, accompanied by her women, who is depicted in a battle scene in a Thai temple mural.[59]

Another representation of spiritually powerful individuals comes from a Bugis manuscript recounting events in seventeenth-century Sulawesi. The text relates that the small Bugis kingdom of Lamatti, threatened by an invading army, sent out a party of female *bissu*, or transgender spirit practitioners, to meet the advancing force. Their leader, an old woman, was borne on a palanquin followed by about a hundred others who chanted as they swung their 'swords' or weaving beaters. Unharmed by the bullets fired from the enemy guns, their invulnerability provided Lamatti with 'a spiritual shield' that protected them from attack.[60] As Carolyn Brewer has

278 *Barbara Watson Andaya*

shown, accounts of the often hostile encounters between Spanish missionaries and religious leaders in the Philippines attest the prominent role played by female 'priestesses' (*babaylan*) who often emerged as 'male-like' instigators of resistance. Although the audacious manner in which one such *anitera* (shaman, spirit medium) confronted Spanish priests in 1595 is particularly striking, other such figures were highly effective in rallying peasants in anti-Spanish uprisings.[61] Similarly, a noblewoman who commanded a troop of 500 people in Prince Dipanagara's war against the Dutch in 1820–1825 was revered because of her reputation as a religious authority, acquired through meditation in caves along Java's south coast. Her renown was such that even after hostilities ceased the protective amulets inscribed with sacred texts that she distributed were especially valued because they were associated with a person superior in spiritual knowledge and practice.[62]

These examples suggest that although the stereotypes of women warriors in modern accounts have focused on youth and beauty, older women had a special role to play, particularly as mediators between contending parties. Post-menopausal women, notably those of high birth, were culturally effective because they were no longer fertile and therefore occupied a liminal position between male and female.[63] In addition, they commanded respect as 'grandmother' figures, and an Ifugao epic from the Philippines describes a situation in which a woman intercedes in the fighting of two heroes, gaining their attention because she is 'motherly'.[64] Southwest Sulawesi provides another example. In 1683, after a battle between the Bugis and the Toraja in which many lives were lost, an old blind woman, whom the Toraja called their 'queen', was led down to the Bugis camp to plead for peace on behalf of her own people. So accepted was the practice of using senior women in this capacity that even the Dutch East India Company was known to use them to liaise with enemy forces.[65]

The supernatural forces that resided in all charismatic individuals also meant that the women who occasionally emerged as leaders in warfare could themselves be regarded as living amulets, their mere presence on the battlefield ensuring invulnerability and victory for their followers. In the late seventeenth century, when the British sea-captain William Dampier visited Mindanao in what is now the southern Philippines, he commented that the Muslim regent's consort, 'the War Queen, we called her', always accompanied her husband 'whenever he was called out to engage his Enemies, but the rest [of his wives] did not'.[66] It is surely significant that in Java a former commander of the female guards, the devout Ratu Ageng Tegalraja (c. 1734–1803), a secondary wife of Hamengkubuwono I (r. 1749–1792), followed all her husband's campaigns, and even gave birth during an encampment.[67] In many cases the ritualised singing, dancing, chanting and exhortations of such women were considered necessary to ready soldiers for the attack.[68] In the early nineteenth century, John Crawfurd's account of a Bugis queen wielding a spear and urging her warriors on to battle through high oratorical language is by no means an isolated incident.[69]

Rethinking the historical place of 'warrior women' in SEA   279

Indeed, another Scotsman in Burma, describing Shan troops massing for an attack on the British in 1825, specifically remarked on

> three young and handsome women of high rank who were believed by their superstitious countrymen to be endowed not only with the gift of prophecy and foreknowledge, but to possess the miraculous power of turning aside the balls of the English, rendering them wholly innocent and harmless. These Amazons, dressed in warlike costume, rode constantly among the troops, inspiring them with courage and ardent wishes for an early meeting with their foe. . . . [70]

These descriptions suggest that we should also look more closely at the armed guardswomen present in a number of Southeast Asian courts (Chapters 4 and 5). Praised by Europeans for their beauty, their horsemanship and their skill with weaponry, the parades, tourneys and royal audiences in which these 'Amazons' participated were an essential part of the theatrical staging of royal power. As guards, they were also a necessary addition to palaces where men were forbidden to enter the women's quarters. On the other hand, such weapon-carrying women also embodied deep-seated beliefs that the mingling of male and female elements generated a special kind of energy that could be reinforced by links with mainstream religiosity. In Siam, for instance, female guards escorted the monks officiating at palace rituals held during the Buddhist 'rain retreat' (*Phansa*), a time of special spiritual renewal.[71] In this connection, it is relevant to note that the diary of a guardswoman in the Jogjakarta court devotes much attention to religious observances and that the female bodyguard as a whole was charged with reciting prayers and incantations during the British attack on the palace in 1815.[72] As noted earlier, one of Dipanagara's commanders was known as a religious adept, and another, a senior cavalry leader, demonstrated her dedication to the holy war by shaving off her hair. The 'dread' with which she was regarded was not merely the result of her reputation as a ruthless fighter who gave her opponents no quarter, but to her unequivocal commitment to the Muslim cause.[73]

In re-focusing on these intangible attributes, we may come closer to appreciating why certain women have assumed a particular role in the *imaginaire* of Southeast Asian societies and why they have been distinguished from others who may have been equally brave and equally skilled. Modernity's discomfort with anything that smacks of 'magic' and the nature of academic research have combined to discourage serious investigation of belief in the paranormal as a quality of leadership. However, though mocked by a Manila newspaper in 1935, peasant conviction that a seventeen-year-old girl could miraculously produce guns from the bark of certain trees is a telling comment on the role of trans-human forces in attracting followers and legitimising leadership.[74] Exploration of this topic naturally requires connections with local populations that take time to develop, and information is typically anecdotal and incomplete. A colleague, for example, was told about a

280   *Barbara Watson Andaya*

famous woman who fought on the side of rebel guerrillas in the jungles of northern Sulawesi during the Permesta Rebellion (1957–1961) against Indonesia's central government. Although this woman was involved in numerous gun battles, she was always able to elude bullets because she could interpret the calls of owls and thus knew when the enemy was near.[75] Indeed, the idea that women possess particular access to magic is deeply rooted in Indonesian society, and claims that sorcery was commonly practised by the communist-affiliated Gerwani (Movement of Indonesian Women) circulated widely after the alleged communist coup in 1965. It is not surprising, then, to read that in Bali a prominent communist leader, a woman of great height and supernatural strength, was believed to have extraordinary *sakti* (supernatural power). According to one informant, if an ordinary man shouldered a load that she had been carrying he would get flaming welts on his shoulder where her bamboo pole bore down on his body.[76]

Memories of the past, anticipations of the future

The elevation of certain women as 'warriors' raises other intriguing questions, especially regarding the ways in which memories of their achievements are negotiated, contested and sustained. In all Southeast Asian societies (as elsewhere) the landscape itself functioned as a cultural encyclopaedia, for rivers, trees, mountains, and caves provided the mnemonic anchors that fixed legends in a heroic and largely oral past. A rock shaped like a woman's body on a mountain east of Hanoi, for instance, recalls a peasant said to have met her death during ancient wars against the Chinese.[77] But maintenance of an individual's place in the select company of heroines demands more purposeful human recognition—monuments, statues, buildings, streets, place names. In the eighteenth century, one Vietnamese scholar commented specifically that the temple erected to honour the Trung sisters 'is majestic and well cared for', and that on festival days 'the local people perform in battle array with elephants and horses'.[78] Yet there is no firm guarantee that buildings will remain permanent or that ceremonies will be perpetuated. Composed in the fifteenth century, the Chiang Mai chronicle records that a group of women, taken during a battle, successfully seized the swords of their sleeping captors during the night, and after killing several, were able to escape and join their menfolk. In their honour, the local community constructed a temple, 'which came to be called the Temple of the Brave Women'.[79] Today, however, this monument survives only in the written word and we are left to speculate where such a shrine might have stood. Even the grave of the Acehnese icon, Cut Nyak Dien, located in west Java where she was exiled by the Dutch, was not discovered until 1959 and has only recently been renovated.[80]

While physical structures honouring the female contribution to military success may survive, they are not necessarily a guarantee that the individuals thus commemorated will be incorporated into popular imagination.

Rethinking the historical place of 'warrior women' in SEA 281

In 1989, Mrs. Siti Hartinah, wife of Indonesia's president Suharto, officiated at the opening of a monument to the short-lived (1945–1946) Surakarta branch of the Laskar Puteri Indonesia (LPI, Indonesian Women's Guerrilla Forces). Consisting of about 200 young women, including Siti Hartinah, the LPI provided medical and field support to pro-independence guerrillas.[81] However, notwithstanding the sponsorship of Indonesia's First Lady and her desire to show that women played an important role in the revolutionary struggle, the memories which the Surakarta monument was intended to invoke have largely died away.

Precisely because their intentions were so purposeful, what Pierre Nora has termed 'sites of memory' (*lieux de mémoire*) can complicate historiography because they have the capacity to be interpreted on many levels and because their creation and survival reflects a particular investment in the past.[82] Miss Bunluang, said to be Thao Suranari's chief aide, is unrecognised in Thailand's national historiography, but the situation may change in the future, since local villagers have built her a shrine and ritually honour her spirit.[83] By contrast, devotees of Le Chan, one of several women who fought beside the Trung sisters, have been more successful in gaining public acknowledgement. Her temple, once quite modest, was rebuilt in 1919 and is now a much frequented place of veneration, while her statue in Hai Phong is touted as a major tourist attraction.[84] With far greater resources than local authorities, a prime investor in the past is always the state itself, and many sites of memory typically reflect ongoing efforts to shape history in terms of official memories. One panel of the reliefs around the base of the monument dedicated to Indonesia's 'Heroes of the Revolution' depicts the 'traitorous' Gerwani women (who had actively promoted themselves as 'women warriors' in the tradition of Srikandi) dancing in trance-induced triumph around the bodies of Indonesian generals.[85] But other unofficial 'memory-sites'—jails, torture chambers, execution sites, destroyed homes—may serve to perpetuate a past that can be subversive and that some would wish to forget. Like its modern counterparts, the Vietnamese state rejects the notion that war ghosts, wandering souls who have no memorial and no resting place, still populate the landscape. However, as Heonik Kwon's remarkable study indicates, even a modest suburban house once used as an interrogation centre by the South Vietnamese can be haunted by the spirit of a female revolutionary who died during questioning.[86]

It is ironic that the brutality of warfare has simultaneously provided the opportunity for 'warrior women' to become the focus of popular cults, honoured because of their empathy with ordinary people. A fifteenth-century scholar remarked that the Trung sisters had endeared themselves to the general populace not only because they had 'the virtue of scholars and the temperament of warriors', but because prayers addressed to their spirits 'have never gone unanswered'.[87] In Buddhist Southeast Asia, Preah Neang Dharani, the Earth Goddess who defeated the armies of Mara, is intimately associated with the life-giving properties of water (Chapter 3). Cult figures

282 *Barbara Watson Andaya*

like Khorat's Grandmother Mo, whose status originated in their role as warriors, have similarly been detached from their martial background to become caring spirits ever ready to listen to the requests of their devotees. A collection of *neak ta* (spirit) stories from Cambodia tells of one old woman, known for her virtue and powers of prophecy, who promised that after her death she would always come to the assistance of her 'children'. True to her word, she returned to rally the people against a Vietnamese attack. The grateful villagers then established annual rituals for a *neak ta* now conceptualised as a benevolent and personalised grandmother whose displeasure is only aroused when she is venerated without true sincerity.[88]

Gender relationships in times of conflict

These and other stories of female courage, leadership and compassion may survive through oral transmission, but because memories, like ghosts, 'come and go like swallows' there is always some seepage from the cultural depository.[89] On the other hand, technical advances mean that modern historians have unprecedented opportunities to record conflict-related thoughts and opinions of women, both combatants and non-combatants. What then will they remember? Will they recall a time when they were physically and emotionally tested, and yet did not fail? Do they remember opportunities for women to gain new status as nationalists and defenders of liberty, like the women of the Rani of Jhansi Regiment (Chapter 8)?[90] Or will they speak of hardship and frustration, when female bodies were seen as an impediment to victory in a masculinised combat? As our contributors have shown, women's experiences of conflict are invariably different from those of men, and for those directly involved, the relinquishment of motherhood was often cited as the greatest hardship. The contributions dealing with guerrilla warfare show very clearly that the inclusion of women willing to take on male-like roles did not allow for families, pregnancy or the rearing of children (Chapter 10). Some women chose to remain single, but for those who had borne children the separation of mother and child, sometimes forever, presented a unique sacrifice. Death in conflict and from disease took their toll, but the female body was vulnerable in other ways. Communist guerrillas in Malaya, for example, reported that although women fighters used both contraceptives and abortifacients, pregnancy did occur and cases of maternal mortality were not uncommon.[91]

Another sensitive subject concerns sexual assault, especially since ancient ideas about rape as the 'right' of marauding armies has survived into modern times.[92] In some cases the loss of virginity is presented as an acceptable sacrifice that women can offer in a great cause. Miss Bunluang, Thai Suranari's lieutenant, is thus said to have given herself to the enemy Lao commander, allowing her fellow-soldiers to steal the arms of the drunken enemy troops.[93] The use of rape as a form of punishment and as a means

Rethinking the historical place of 'warrior women' in SEA 283

of humiliating men is well documented in Indonesian military treatment of Gerwani and Timorese women, and in recent disclosures concerning the Khmer Rouge (Chapters 11 and 12). Discussing this subject can be especially painful because so much fighting in Southeast Asia has taken the form of a civil war, so that the perpetrators could be one's own countrymen, or worse, one's comrades in arms. Female soldiers in the Indonesian National Revolution (1945–1950) soon discovered that protests were pointless if male leaders demanded their sexual services, and the adoption of a military uniform did not eliminate male perceptions of female combatants as sexually available.[94] The invisibility of Indonesian women as fighters is graphically evident in the commemorative dioramas displayed in the Satriamandala Armed Forces Museum, where women might be depicted holding weapons but the reality of their participation in combat is never acknowledged.[95]

In this context, the concept of the 'cross-dressing' that typifies women warriors deserves some attention, for connotations may differ according to the cultural context. In 2002, Phuket residents thus expressed concern that South Korean tourists were interpreting the 'masculine' appearance (short hair and traditional dhoti-like *chongkraben*) of the Thalang heroine statues as indicative of a 'tomboy' (lesbian) orientation.[96] At a deeper level, although the practicalities of combat argued for the adoption of men's clothing— some guardswomen in Dipanagara's army wore full male Javanese battle dress[97]—the public display of male weapons and dress registered the transition from 'woman' to 'warrior'. Lady Trieu is remembered for her golden armour; Queen Suriyothai disguised herself as the Crown Prince; women in a Makassarese chronicle put on trousers and shirts before proceeding to the battlefield to join their menfolk.[98] Another traditional epic from Mindanao describes how the aristocratic heroine fights against an evil spirit who has sought to seduce her lover. First, however, her skirt turns to trousers and her small dagger, used by females, the *tinangke*, turns to a sword, a *kampilan*.[99]

These examples suggest that although women disguising themselves as men may have been a favourite literary or performative theme, it signalled a reallocation of gender expectations that encoded physical courage as a male rather than a female attribute. A Javanese text praising a brave woman because she acted 'like a man' simply reiterates a recurring refrain that is also heard from women themselves.[100] As the wife of the Katipunan leader Andrés Bonifacio, Gregoria de Jesus (1875–1943) joined the revolutionary forces against Spain and proudly recorded that her male companions regarded her as a soldier. To reach this standard 'I learned to ride, to shoot a rifle, and to manipulate other weapons which I actually used on many occasions'.[101] At the same time, the expectation that male performance in combat sets the standard for all fighters can itself be a source of female discontent. Women veterans were often resentful of the demands placed on them (at times by their own commanders), and a refusal to recognise the physical limitations that were simply part of being female.

284 *Barbara Watson Andaya*

Even more insidious are the cultural stereotypes presented to any woman who takes up arms against an enemy. Ideally, even if her forces are victorious, she herself often meets a noble death in battle; in the case of defeat she should avoid capture and sexual dishonour by committing suicide, for surrender is not easily incorporated into the heroic myth. Those who survive the conflict should lay aside their warrior persona and take up their true vocations as wife and mother. For many ex-combatants it is this stereotype that represents the reality of post-conflict social expectations. Despite the publicity accorded Vietnam's 'long-haired army', for instance, the post-war acceptance of female veterans was often dependent on their display of 'feminine qualities, prime among which was the ability to attract a husband and successfully bear children'.[102] Indeed, even at the height of the conflict with the Americans, Vietnam's propaganda posters frequently presented images of the patriotic woman as simultaneously a soldier and a mother.[103] And while gender roles are still fundamental to indigenous understandings of womanhood, the post-conflict problems faced by female veterans in Southeast Asia are compounded in cases where they fought on a losing side, like the *yuthaneary krahom* (red female combatant) of the Khmer Rouge (Chapter 11). Indeed, testimonies in Khmer Rouge trials—one *neary krahom* said she killed at least 300 people—provide shocking evidence of the little-discussed cruelty of which women themselves are capable.[104]

These accounts, the more disquieting because they are so opposed to approved female roles, demonstrate yet again that women's involvement in warfare, even when celebrated, has not fundamentally challenged traditional gender constructs, and that the possibilities for renegotiating established gender lines appear limited at best.[105] In 1961, for example, a young Indonesian woman named 'Herlina' was parachuted into western New Guinea (Irian Barat), having volunteered for inclusion in the campaign intended to 'liberate' this last bastion of Dutch colonialism.[106] A widely circulated photograph of the attractive twenty-year-old—'our Srikandi'—surrounded by white United Nations soldiers provided welcome publicity for President Sukarno's claims that the prominence of soldier-like women was proof of Indonesia's gender equality.[107] Although the 1985 version of Herlina's memoirs included a chapter on her parachute experience, 'jumping down into the Irian jungle', her unique participation in the nationalist epic has been virtually forgotten.[108]

Conclusion

In December 2015 the United States joined a number of other countries in opening all combat roles to women, re-kindling old debates in an ongoing controversy.[109] On the one hand, a strong body of opinion arguing for inherent gender differences contends that women's increased military participation undermines the traditional family structure while impairing military efficiency. On the other hand, feminists have been divided. Some believe that full acceptance in the military is necessary for liberating and defending women from patriarchy and providing new opportunities for leadership. In their view, such policy shifts represent a recognition of gender equality and acceptance of women's ability to assume roles traditionally assigned only to men. A second group warns of the dangers of the 'warrior mystique', which promotes martial and masculine values rather than redefining gender-based social values and hierarchical power structures. From this perspective the expanded military participation of women points to an unwelcome militarisation of society, not evidence of women's achievement of 'equality'.[110]

Although these issues are certainly globally relevant, one could also argue that the debates in Southeast Asia are cast rather differently. In societies where armed resistance against foreign rule acted as a crucible for the forging of the 'true' nationalist, the display of physical courage and a willingness to risk death or imprisonment for the sake of the nation became the *sine qua non* for the 'real' patriot. This conceptualisation of warfare as a pre-eminent but male-dominated stage for the display of national loyalties has had significant implications for the place of women in regional historiography. Certainly, historical records show that in many Southeast Asian societies women traditionally joined with their menfolk in defence of their community and that the special contribution they could make to success in combat was recognised. Nonetheless, there is no denying the fact that the direct involvement of women as fighters was uncommon. They were certainly expected to offer assistance when their community was at war, but this was viewed as primarily supportive of male action—carrying messages, preparing weapons, cooking, building defences, caring for the wounded. In some cases the problem of the relative absence of 'women warriors' in the sources has been circumvented by broadening the category of conflict to include the 'socio-cultural war'. This allows for the inclusion of educationalists, journalists, activists, figures in literature and the wives or daughters of prominent leaders.[111] Yet the tendency to select emblematic women as national heroines also emphasises the anonymity of the many others whose memories survive only at the local level, if at all.

Within Southeast Asia the call to give greater space to women's history has been only moderately successful, and the obligatory genuflection to selected and well-known figures is generally deemed sufficient. In allowing us to hear previously silenced voices, this book is therefore an important contribution to our understanding of Southeast Asia's past. Equally, it may also help promote greater interest in Southeast Asia outside the region. Admittedly published well over a decade ago, the global coverage of women warriors by David Jones includes a section on Asia, but Southeast Asian countries are not mentioned, apart from a brief reference to Siam and a discussion of Vietnam's female martial tradition. By contrast, 'women warriors' in the rest of Southeast Asia have not captured Western attention, even when by any standards their exploits appear exceptional.

286   *Barbara Watson Andaya*

The material provided in this volume thus serves as a reminder that women's history in Southeast Asia is still a very new field and that research is capable of yielding surprising results. We may bemoan the lack of evidence for female involvement in warfare in earlier times, but in 2007 a Japanese team working in northwestern Cambodia uncovered a pre-Angkorian burial site containing five female skeletons that had been buried with steel or bronze swords and helmet-shaped objects. The possibility of comparing such finds with other archaeological discoveries—for instance, in the Kazakh area of central Asia—may open up fresh ways of thinking about gender roles in early Southeast Asia.[112] Future historians will also benefit from other investigations mounted by contemporary researchers, notably visual testimony and the compilation of oral accounts. While many questions will remain unanswered, we now have the technological capacity to record the complexity of the female experience in ways never before possible. As a result, the primary sources available for coming generations will not just talk *about* women, but will allow women to speak for themselves. Yet despite its corrective contribution, *Women Warriors in Southeast Asia* also shows that the history of this region has been shaped by men who have generally seen the activities of women as irrelevant to the national narrative. In Southeast Asia, as in the much of the world, this issue remains both unresolved and persistently relevant.

Notes

1 The phrase 'sites of memory' is taken from Pierre Nora, 'Between Memory and History: *Les Lieux de Mémoire*', *Representations*, 26, Special Issue: Memory and Counter-Memory (Spring, 1989), pp. 7–24.

2 David E. Jones, *Women Warriors: A History* (Washington, DC: Brasseys, 1997), p. xii.

3 Keith Weller Taylor, *The Birth of Vietnam* (Berkeley, CA: University of California Press, 1983), pp. 90, 334–339; K.W. Taylor, *A History of the Vietnamese* (Cambridge: Cambridge University Press, 2013), pp. 21–2, 29; David G. Marr, *Vietnamese Tradition on Trial, 1920–1945* (Berkeley, CA: University of California Press, 1981), pp. 198–199.

4 Claire Holt Art in *Indonesia Continuities and Change* (Ithaca, NY: Cornell University Press, 1967), p. 53.

5 David K. Wyatt, ed. and Richard D. Cushman, trans. *The Royal Chronicles of Ayutthya* (Bangkok: The Siam Society, 2000), pp. 32, 34.

6 Marr, *Vietnamese Tradition on Trial*, pp. 211–212; Le Thi Nham Tuyet, *Images of the Vietnamese Woman in the New Millennium* (Hanoi: The Gioi, 2002), pp. 14–15.

7 George E. Dutton, Jayne S. Werner, and John K. Whitmore (eds.), *Sources of Vietnamese Tradition* (New York: Columbia University Press, 2012), p. 365.

8 E.H.S. Simmonds, 'Francis Light and the Ladies of Thalang', *Journal of the Malayan Branch of the Royal Asiatic Society*, Vol. 38, No. 2 (December 1965), pp. 217–222.

9 Scot Barmé, *Woman, Man, Bangkok: Love, Sex, and Popular Culture in Thailand* (New York: Rowman and Littlefield, 2002), pp. 26–29.

10 Dutton et al., *Sources of Vietnamese Tradition*, p. 365.

11 Barmé, *Woman, Man, Bangkok: Love, Sex, and Popular Culture in Thailand*, p. 35.

Rethinking the historical place of 'warrior women' in SEA 287

12 For an English version, see Prince Damrong Rajanubhab, *The Chronicle of our Wars with the Burmese*, Phra Phraison Salarak and Thein Subindu (trans.); Chris Baker (ed.) (Bangkok: White Lotus, 2001), pp. 18–19.

13 Simmonds, 'Francis Light and the Ladies of Thalang', p. 217; Suvanna Kriengkraipetch, 'Woman-Warriors: Dual Images in Modern Thai Literature', in William E. Burgwinkle, Glenn Man, and Valerie Wayne (eds.), *Significant Others: Gender and Culture in Film and Literature, East and West* (Honolulu, HI: University of Hawai'i Press and East-West Center, 1993), pp. 31, 33, 43 n.1. I am most grateful to Dr. Kennon Breazeale and Mrs. Vilaileka Thavornthanasarn for assistance in tracking down this poem, which was apparently first published in 1955, more than twenty years after Prince Narathip's death.

14 Kathryn Robinson, *Gender, Islam and Democracy in Indonesia* (London: Routledge, 2008), p. 48; Colin Brown, 'Sukarno on the Role of Women in the Nationalist Movement', *Review of Indonesian and Malayan Affairs*, Vol. 15, No. 1 (1981), p. 74.

15 The statue was designed by the Italian-born sculptor Corrado Feroci (1892–1962), who was awarded the Thai name of Silpa Bhirasri. He trained Thai artists in Siam's Fine Arts Department, which was headed by the nationalist Luang Wichit Wathakan. See Chris Baker and Pasuk Phongpaichit, *A History of Thailand* (Cambridge: Cambridge University Press, 2009), pp. 127, 297.

16 Charles Keyes, 'Opening Reflections: Northeast Thai Ethnoregionalism Updated', in Philip Hirsch and Nicholas Tapp (eds.), *Tracks and Traces: Thailand and the Work of Andrew Turton* (Amsterdam: Amsterdam University Press, 2010), p. 20; Keyes, 'National Heroine or Local Spirit?', p. 118; Barmé, *Woman, Man, Bangkok*, pp. 236–238.

17 Barmé, *Woman, Man, Bangkok*, pp. 218, 238–241.

18 José Rizal, Letter to A.B. Meyer, 7 January 1889 in *José Rizal, Escritos políticos e históricos* [José Rizal, Political and Historical Writings], Vol. VII (Manila: National Commission for the Centenary of José Rizal, 1961), pp. 49–54; Rosa Maria Magno, *Urduja Beleaguered and other Essays on Pangasinan Language, Literature and Culture* (Manila: Kalikasan Press, 1992), pp. 42–46.

19 Austin Craig, *Gems of Philippine Oratory* (Manila: University of Manila Press, 1924), pp. 7, 11.

20 Francisco Benitez and Conrado Benitez, *Stories of Great Filipinos* (Manila: National Book Company, 1932), pp. 13–14. See further Encarnacion Alzona, *The Filipino Woman: Her Social, Economic, and Political Status, 1565–1933* (Manila: University of the Philippines Press, 1934), p. 17; Gregorio Zaide, *Philippine History and Civilization* (Manila: Philippine Associated Publishers, 1939), p. 82; Gregorio Zaide, *Philippine Political and Cultural History*, Vol. I (Manila: Philippine Education Company, 1949), p. 54.

21 Gregorio Zaide, 'The Women of the Katipunan', *Philippines Free Press* (26 November 1932), pp. 26–27.

22 Isabelo de los Reyes y Florentino, *Historia de Ilocos* [History of Ilocos] (Manila: Establecimiento tipográfico la Opinión, 1890), p. 189; Zaide, *Philippine History and Civilization*, p. 254.

23 Tera Maxwell, 'Urduja through the Looking-Glass: A Response to Colonial Trauma', in Kum-Kum Bhavnani, John Foran, Priya Kurian, and Debashish Munshi (eds.), *On the Edges of Development: Cultural Interventions* (New York: Routledge, 2009), pp. 199–200.

24 Maximo Manguiat Kalaw, *The Filipino Rebel: A Romance of American Occupation in the Philippines* (Manila: Filipiniana Book Guild, 1964; reprint of 1927 edition), pp. 59, 62–66, 208; Denise Cruz, *Transpacific Femininities: The Making of the Modern Filipina* (Durham, NC: Duke University Press, 2012), p. 117.

25 Uyen Nicole Duong, *Daughters of the River Huong* (Washington, DC: Ravensyard, 2005), pp. 121–122.

288 *Barbara Watson Andaya*

26 Marr, *Vietnamese Tradition on Trial*, p. 211.
27 Danilyn Rutherford, 'Unpacking a National Heroine: Two Kartinis and their People', *Indonesia*, Vol. 55, No. 1 (1993), pp. 23–40; H. C. Zentgraaff, *Atjeh* (Batavia: De Unie, 1938), pp. 88, 90; J. C. Witte, 'Tropenjournalist H.C. Zentgraaff' ['The Tropical Journalist H. C. Zentgraaff'], *Spiegel Historiael*, Vol. 15, No. 3 (1980), pp. 157–164.
28 M. H. Székely-Lulofs, *Tjoet Nja Din: de geschiedenis van een Atjehse vorstin* [Cut Nyak Din: The History of an Acehnese Queen] (Amsterdam: Moussault, 1948).
29 Frank Okker, *Tumult: Het levensverhaal van Madelon Székely-Lulofs* [The Biography of Madelon Székely-Lulofs] (Antwerpen/Amsterdam Atlas, 2008); Marijn van Wieringen, '"Enfin – ik hoop nog eens beroemd (!) te worden": De brieven van M. H. Székely-Lulofs' ['"Anyway – I still hope to be famous (!)"; The Letters of M. H. Székely-Lulofs'] MA Thesis, University of Groningen, 2010. http://arts.studenttheses.ub.rug.nl/10327/1/Ma-s1513893-M.L.A.vanWieringen. pdf. Accessed 15 November 2018, used with permission.
30 Abdoel Muis (trans.), *Tjoet Nja Din: riwajat hidup seorang Atjeh* [*Cut Nya Din: The Life of an Acehnese*] (Djakarta: Chailan Sjamsce, 1954).
31 Elsa Clavé-Çelik, 'Images of the Past, Realities of the Present: Aceh's Inong Balee', *IIAS Newsletter*, Vol. 48 (2008), pp. 10–11 points to the problematic sources used for accounts of Keumalahayati's exploits, including the novel *Oude Glorie*, set in Aceh in the early seventeenth century and published in 1935 by a Dutchwoman, Marie van Zeggelen (Amsterdam: Nederlandsche Keurboekerij, 1935). In numerous Indonesian reprintings her name has been given as 'Marie van Zuchtelen' and the title of her book as 'Vrouwlijke Admiral Malahayati'. See, for example, Teuku H. Ainal and Mardhiah Aly, 'Pergerakan wanita di Aceh masa lampau sampai kini' ['The Women's Movement in Aceh from the Past until the Present'], in Ismail Suny (ed.), *Bunga rampai tentang Aceh* [Anthology on Aceh] (Jakarta: Bhratara Karya Aksara Press, 1980), p. 286.
32 T. Ibrahim Alfian, Ismail Sofyan, and M. Hasran Basry (eds.), *Wanita utama Nusantara dalam lintasan sejarah* [Prominent Indonesian Women in the Course of History] (Jakarta: Jayakarta Agung, 1994), p. xix.
33 Charles F. Keyes, 'National Heroine or Local Spirit? The Struggle over Memory in the Case of Thao Suranari of Nakhon Ratchasma', in Shigeharu Tanabe and Charles F. Keyes (eds.), *Cultural Crisis and Social Memory: Modernity and Identity in Thailand and Laos* (Honolulu, HI: University of Hawai'i Press, 2002), pp. 117–118.
34 Kriengkraidpetch, 'Woman-Warriors: Dual Images in Modern Thailand Literature', p. 33; www.phuket.com/phuket-magazine/phuket-heroines.htm. Accessed 15 November 2018; Jones, *Women Warriors*, pp. 31–35.
35 Paul M. Handley, *The King Never Smiles: A Biography of Thailand's Bhumibol Adulyadej* (New Haven, CT and London: Yale University Press, 2006), p. 385.
36 Louise Williams, *Wives, Mistresses, and Matriarchs: Asian Women Today* (New York: Rowman & Littlefield, 1999), pp. 95–108.
37 Benoît de Tréglodé, 'Sur la formation d'une nouvelle géographie culturelle patriotique au Vietnam: Essai sur le culte de Mac thi Buoi' ['On the Formation of a New Patriotic Cultural Geography in Vietnam: An Essay on the Cult of Mac thi Buoi'], in John Kleinen (ed.), *Vietnamese Society in Transition: The Daily Politics of Reform and Change* (Amsterdam: Het Spinhuis, 2001), pp. 202–220.
38 See Sandra C. Taylor, *Vietnamese Women at War* (Lawrence, KS: University of Kansas Press, 1999), p. 110; Michael J. Allen, *Until the Last Man Comes Home: POWs, MIAs, and the Unending Vietnam War* (Chapel Hill, NC: University of North Carolina Press, 2009), p. 23.

Rethinking the historical place of 'warrior women' in SEA 289

39 Benoît de Tréglodé, *Héros et Révolution au Viêt Nam, 1948–1964* (Paris: L'Harmattan, 2001), pp. 325–353. This has been translated into English as *Heroes and Revolution in Vietnam* (Singapore: NUS Press, 2012). See also de Tréglodé, 'Sur la formation d'une nouvelle géographie culturelle', pp. 202–220.
40 'Who was the warrior, Le Chan?' www.phespirit.info/places/2007_03_vietnam_1.htm. Accessed 15 November 2018; 'Bui Thi Xuan Temple Inaugurated'. www.baobinhdinh.com.vn/news/2008/7/62580/. Accessed 15 November 2018.
41 Le, *Images of the Vietnamese Woman*, p. 13; Marr, *Vietnamese Tradition on Trial*, pp. 198–199.
42 David Routledge, *Diego Silang and the Origins of Philippine Nationalism* (Quezon City: Philippine Center for Advanced Studies, 1979), plate 8; Zaide, *Philippine Political and Cultural History*, p. 359.
43 See, for instance, Vina Lanzona, *Amazons of the Huk Rebellion: Gender, Sex and Revolution in the Philippines* (Madison, WI: University of Wisconsin Press, 2009), pp. 132–136, 151, 155, 173, 181–182, 190.
44 See the portraits of Cut Nyak Dien by Dede Edi Supria (b. 1956) in Clavé-Çelik, 'Images of the Past and Realities of the Present', p. 11.
45 Magno, *Urduja Beleaguered*, pp. 42–51. For an impassioned refutation of academic arguments, see Antonio del Castillo Y. Tuazon, *Princess Urduja Before and After her Time: A Pre-Hispanic History of the Philippines* (Lingayen, Pangasinan: A. del. Castillo y Tuazon, 1986).
46 Keyes, 'National Heroine or Local Spirit?', pp. 113–120; Mayoury Ngaosyvathn and Pheuiphanh Ngaosyvathn, *Paths to Conflagration: Fifty Years of Diplomacy and Warfare in Laos, Thailand, and Vietnam* (Ithaca, NY: Cornell University Southeast Asia Program, 1998), pp. 28–29.
47 Maurizio Peleggi, *Thailand: The Worldly Kingdom* (London: Reaktion, 2007); Richard Cushman (trans.) and David K. Wyatt (ed.), *The Royal Chronicles of Ayutthaya* (Bangkok: The Siam Society, 2000), pp. 32–34, 50, 51; Adam Knee, 'Suriyothai becomes Legend', in Leon Hunt and Leung Wing-Fai (eds.), *East Asian Cinemas: Exploring Transnational Connections on Film* (London: I.B. Tauris, 2008), pp. 123–137.
48 Lysa Hong, 'Does Popular History Need Historians?', *Warasan Thaikhadiseuksa*, Vol. 1, No. 2 (April–September 2004), pp. 31–66.
49 In 1989, *Tjoet Nja' Dhien* was judged the best international film at the Cannes Film Festival. A Tagalog Indie film, *Gabriela*, was produced by Jun Aristorenas in 1971; Mario O'Hara's *Henerala* was not completed because of his death in 2012, but according to one observer it 'could have been a masterpiece', painting Gabriella as 'a sensual human being'. Francis Joseph A. Cruz, 'The Great O'Hara', *Philippine Star*, June 12, 2012 www.philstar.com/supreme/2012/06/30/822786/great-ohara. Accessed August 7, 2014. Another film on Gabriella's life, directed by Carlo Maceda, appeared in 2013, and seeks to make history 'more relevant' to the younger generation. See www.pep.ph/guide/indie/12610/movie-review-christine-patrimonio-projects-deadly-determination-as-gabriela-silang. Accessed August 7, 2014.
50 Lanzona, *Amazons of the Huk Rebellion*, pp. 130–144.
51 Gerald L. Sittser, *A Cautious Patriotism: The American Churches and the Second World War* (Chapel Hill, NC: University of North Carolina Press, 2010), p. 196.
52 Emma Blair and James Alexander Robertson (eds. and trans.), *The Philippine Islands, 1493–1898* (Cleveland, OH: Arthur H. Clark, 1903–1909) 5, p. 163; see further Barbara Watson Andaya, 'History, Headhunting and Gender in Monsoon Asia: Comparative and Longitudinal Views', *South East Asia Research*, Vol. 12, No. 1 (March 2004), p. 42.

290   *Barbara Watson Andaya*

53 Holly A. Mayer, *Belonging to the Army: Camp Followers and Community during the American Revolution* (Chapel Hill, NC: University of North Carolina Press, 1999).

54 Georges Groslier, 'La femme dans la sculpture Khmère ancienne', *Revue des Arts Asiatiques*, Vol. 11, No. 1 (March 1925), p. 37; A. B. Griswold and Prasert Na Nagara, 'A Siamese Historical Poem', in C. D. Cowan and O. W. Wolters (eds.), *Southeast Asian History and Historiography: Essays Presented to D.G.E. Hall* (Ithaca, NY: Cornell University Press, 1976), p. 149; Leonard Y. Andaya, 'Nature of War and Peace among the Bugis-Makassar People', *South East Asia Research*, Vol. 12, No. 1 (March 2004), pp. 74–76.

55 Felice Noelle Rodriguez, 'Juan de Salcedo Joins the Native Form of Warfare', *Journal of the Economic and Social History of the Orient*, Vol. 46, No. 2 (2003), p. 154.

56 E. M. Beeckman (ed. and trans.), *The Poison Tree: Selected Writings of Rumphius on the Natural History of the Indies* (Kuala Lumpur: Oxford University Press, 1993), p. 131.

57 Donald K. Swearer and Sommai Premchit, *The Legend of Queen Cama: Bodhiramsi's Camadevivamsa, a Translation and Commentary* (Albany, NY: State University of New York Press, 1998), p. 24.

58 A.B. Griswold and Prasert na Nagara, 'A Declaration of Independence and its Consequences: Epigraphic and Historical Inscriptions Number 1', *Journal of the Siam Society*, Vol. 56, No. 2 (July 1968), p. 26, fn. 39; David K. Wyatt and Aroonrut Wichienko (trans.), *The Chiang Mai Chronicle* (Chiang Mai: Silkworm Books, 1995), pp. 80–81.

59 David K. Wyatt, *Reading Thai Murals* (Chiang Mai: Silkworm Books, 2004), pp. 54–55.

60 L. Andaya, 'Nature of War and Peace', pp. 75–76.

61 Carolyn Brewer, *Holy Confrontation: Religion, Gender and Sexuality in the Philippines, 1521–1685* (Manila: Institute of Women's Studies, St. Scholastica's College, 2001), Chapter 5, esp. pp. 167–168; Eric Anderson, 'Traditions in Conflict: Filipino Responses to Spanish Colonialism, 1565–1665', Ph.D. Dissertation, University of Sydney, 1977, pp. 69, 100, 218.

62 Peter Carey, *The Power of Prophecy: Prince Dipanagara and the End of an Old Order in Java, 1785–1855* (Leiden: KITLV Press, 2007), p. 614.

63 Anthony Reid, *Southeast Asia in the Age of Commerce, 1450–1680. Vol. 1. The Lands below the Winds* (New Haven, CT: Yale University Press, 1988), p. 166; Barbara Watson Andaya, *To Live as Brothers: Southeast Sumatra in the Seventeenth and Eighteenth Centuries* (Honolulu, HI: University of Hawai'i Press, 1993), pp. 58–59.

64 Jovita Ventura Castro et al., *Anthology of ASEAN Literatures: Epics of the Philippines* (Quezon City: ASEAN Committee on Culture and Information, 1983), p. 30.

65 L. Andaya, 'Nature of War and Peace', p. 76; Els M. Jacobs, *Koopman in Azië: De Handel van de Verenigde Oost-Indische Compagnie tijdens de 18de Eeuw* [Merchant in Asia: The United East India Company's Trade during the 18th Century] (Zutphen: Walberg Pers, 2000), p. 65.

66 William Dampier, *A New Voyage around the World*, ed. Albert Gray (London: Argonaut Press, 1927; reprint, New York: Dover Publications, 1968; originally published in 1697), p. 250. See further Barbara Watson Andaya, *The Flaming Womb: Repositioning Women in Early Modern Southeast Asia* (Honolulu: University of Hawai'i Press, 2006), p. 170; B. Andaya, 'History, Headhunting and Gender', pp. 13–52.

67 Peter Carey (ed.), *The Archive of Yogyakarta, Vol. I. Documents Relating to Politics and Internal Court Affairs, 1782–1810* (London: Oxford University Press for the British Academy, 1980), pp. 190–191; Carey, *The Power of Prophecy*, pp. 765–768.

Rethinking the historical place of 'warrior women' in SEA   291

68 Comparisons could be drawn with the *Mociuaquetzque* (valiant women) in pre-Hispanic Mexico, who accompanied warriors into battle. Elizabeth Salas, *Soldaderas in the Mexican Military: Myth and History* (Austin: University of Texas Press, 1990), p. 7.

69 John Crawfurd, *History of the Indian Archipelago, containing an Account of the Manners, Arts, Languages, Religions, Institutions, and Commerce of its Inhabitants* (Edinburgh: Archibald Constable, and Co., 1820), p. 74.

70 Major Snodgrass, *Narrative of the Burmese War* (London: John Murray, 1827), p. 231.

71 Anna Harriette Leonowens, *The English Governess at the Siamese Court, Being Recollections of Six Years in the Royal Palace at Bangkok* (London: Trübner and Co, 1870), p. 106.

72 Ann Kumar, *Java and Modern Europe: Ambiguous Encounters* (London: Curzon Press, 1997), pp. 57–67: Carey, *The Power of Prophecy*, p. 337.

73 Carey, *The Power of Prophecy*, p. 615.

74 David R. Sturtevant, *Popular Uprisings in the Philippines 1840–1940* (Ithaca, NY: Cornell University Press, 1976), p. 246. For a contemporary researcher's insistence of taking the supernatural seriously, see Mikael Gravers, 'Cosmology, Prophets, and Rebellion among the Buddhist Karen in Burma and Thailand', *Moussons*, Vol. 4 (December 2001), pp. 3–32.

75 Personal communication, Kirsten Brown, November 2001.

76 Lyn Parker, *From Subject to Citizens: Balinese Villagers in the Indonesian Nation State* (Copenhagen: NIAS, 2003), p. 77.

77 Ann Helen and Walter Unger, *Pagodas, Gods and Spirits of Vietnam* (London: Thames and Hudson, 1997), p. 14.

78 Cited in Patricia M. Pelley, *Post-Colonial Vietnam: New Histories of the National Past* (Durham, NC: Duke University Press, 2002), p. 180.

79 Wyatt and Wichienkoo, *The Chiang Mai Chronicle*, p. 65.

80 Imas Kurniasih, *Perempuan Pemicu Perang* [Women as the Catalyst for War] (Jogjakarta: Pinus, 2008), p. 161.

81 Abdul Gafur, *Siti Hartinah Soeharto: First Lady of Indonesia* (Jakarta: Citra Lamtoro Gung Persada, 1992), pp. 109–115, 242.

82 Nora, 'Between Memory and History', pp. 7–24.

83 Keyes, 'National Heroine or Local Spirit?', pp. 124–126.

84 Philip Taylor, *Goddess on the Rise: Pilgrimage and Popular Religion in Vietnam* (Honolulu: University of Hawai'i Press, 2004), p. 42; 'Who was the warrior, Le Chan?' www.phespirit.info/places/2007_03_vietnam_1.htm. Accessed 15 November 2018. Another general, Thieu Hoa, and her parents are honoured every year by a festival held in the district of Vinh Tuong, which is also listed on the tourist calendar. Do Phuong Quynh, *Traditional Festivals in Vietnam* (Hanoi: The Gioi, 1995), pp. 61–5; Le, *Images of the Vietnamese Woman*, p. 13.

85 Steven Drakeley, 'Lubang Buaya: Myth, Misogyny and Massacre', *Nebula: A Journal of Multidisciplinary Scholarship*, Vol. 4, No. 4 (December 2007), pp. 11–35, www.nobleworld.biz/nebulaarchive/nebula44.html. Accessed 15 November 2018; Saskia Wieringa, *Sexual Politics in Indonesia* (London: Palgrave Macmillan, 2002), p. 192.

86 Heonik Kwon, *Ghosts of War in Vietnam* (Cambridge: Cambridge University Press, 2008), pp. 72, 87–88, 114.

87 Taylor, *The Birth of Vietnam*, p. 336.

88 Keyes, 'National Heroine or Local Spirit?, p. 128; Alain Forest, *Le culte des génies protecteurs au Cambodge: Analyse et traduction d'un corpus de textes sur les neak ta* (Paris: L'Harmattan, 1992), pp. 203–208.

89 Kwon, *Ghosts of War in Vietnam*, p. 26.

292 *Barbara Watson Andaya*

90 See further the personal experiences of women recorded in Irna H. N. Hadi Soewito, *Seribu wajah wanita pejuang dalam kancah Revolusi '45* [A Thousand Faces of Women Fighters in the 1945 Revolutionary Struggle] (Jakarta: Gramedia Widiasarana Indonesia, 1995–1998), 3 volumes; Mary Margaret Steedly, *Rifle Reports: A Story of Indonesian Independence* (Berkeley: University of California Press, 2013), pp. 52, 172.

91 Xiulan, *I want to Live!* (Selangor, Malaysia: Star Publications,1983), p. 103.

92 Soemarsaid Moertono, *State and Statecraft in Old Java: A Study of the Later Mataram Period, 16th to 19th Century* (Ithaca, NY: Cornell Southeast Asia Program, 1963), p. 86; Geoffrey Robinson, 'Colonial Militias in East Timor from the Portuguese Period to Independence', in Karl Hack and Tobias Rettig (eds.), *Colonial Armies in Southeast Asia* (London: Routledge, 2006), p. 259.

93 Keyes, 'National Heroine or Local Spirit?', pp. 133, n.23.

94 Wieringa, *Sexual Politics in Indonesia*, p. 84.

95 Katherine E. McGregor, *History in Uniform: Military Ideology and the Construction of Indonesia's Past* (Singapore: NUS Press, 2007), p. 149.

96 Peter Jackson, 'Performative Genders, Perverse Desires: A Bio-History of Thailand's Same-Sex and Transgender Cultures', *Intersections*, Vol. 9 (2003), http://intersections.anu.edu.au/issue9/jackson.html.

97 Carey, *The Power of Prophecy*, p. 629; Saraswati Sunindyo, 'When the Earth is Female and the Nation is Mother: Gender, the Armed Forces and Nationalism in Indonesia', *Feminist Review*, Vol. 58 (Spring, 1998), p. 12.

98 L. Andaya, 'Nature of War and Peace', p. 74.

99 Castro et al., *Anthology of ASEAN Literatures*, p. 449.

100 Peter Carey (ed.), *The British in Java, 1811–1816: A Javanese Account* (London: Oxford University Press for the British Academy, 1991), pp. 30, 186.

101 Cited in 'Gregoria de Jesus', in Rafaelita Hilario Soriano (ed.), *Women in the Philippine Revolution* (Quezon City: Printon Press, 1995), p. 61.

102 Karen Gottschang Turner (with Phan Thanh Hao), *Even the Women Must Fight: Memories of War from North Vietnam* (New York: John Wiley and Sons, 1998), p. 182.

103 See the Dogma Collection online: http://dogmacollection.com/gallery/women-under-arms.html. Accessed 15 November 2018. More combat-oriented paintings are in Jessica Harrison-Hall, with contributions by Sherry Buchanan, Katharine Lockett, and Thu Stern, *Vietnam Behind the Lines: Images from the War, 1965–1975* (London: British Museum, 2002), pp. 40, 62–64. In a similar vein, Le, *Images of the Vietnamese Woman*, p. 17 emphasises that while Vietnamese mothers 'bravely confronted the enemy' they were nonetheless devoted to 'a sacred cause: bringing up children'.

104 Huy Vannack, *The Khmer Rouge Division 703: From Victory to Self-Destruction* (Phnom Penh: Documentation Center of Cambodia, 2003), pp. 6, 12–14.

105 Francine D'Amico, 'Feminist Perspectives on Women Warriors', *Peace Review: A Journal of Social Justice*, Vol. 8, No. 1 (1996), pp. 379–384.

106 Herlina published her memoirs soon after, entitled *Pending Emas* (Jakarta, Indonesia: PT Gunung, 1965). A revised version that appeared in 1985 was translated as *The Golden Buckle* (Yogyakarta, Indonesia: Gadjah Mada University Press, 1990).

107 Sunindyo, 'When the Earth is Female', p. 9; Robinson, *Gender, Islam and Democracy*, pp. 50–51.

108 Naning Pranoto, *Her Story: sejarah perjalanan payudara* [Her Story: A History of the Feminist Journey] (Jakarta: Kanisius, 2010), p. 202.

109 Matthew Rosenberg and Dave Philipps, 'All Combat Roles Open to Women', *The New York Times*, 3 December 2015. www.nytimes.com/2015/12/04/us/politics/combat-military-women-ash-carter.html. Accessed 29 October 2018;

David E. Burrelli, 'Women in Combat: Issues for Congress', https://fas.org/sgp/crs/.../R42075. pdf. Accessed 3 May 2015; Kathleen Parker, 'Women in Combat will put Men at Greater Risk', *The Washington Post*, 11 December 2015. www.washingtonpost.com/. Accessed 26 November 2018; Meghann Myers, 'Has Combat Arms Gender Integration Been Successful? The Army Will Let You Know in 2020', *Army Times*, 11 October 2018. www.armytimes.com/news/your-army/2018/10/11/has-combat-arms-gender-integration-been-successful-the-army-will-let-you-know-in-2020/. Accessed 26 November 2018.

110 D'Amico, 'Feminist Perspectives on Women Warriors'.

111 For instance, Andri Rahman Alwi et al., *7 Ibu Bangsa [Seven Mothers of the Nation]: Cut Nyak Dien, Inggit Garnasih, Kartini, Megawati Soekarno, Roehana Koeddoes, Tien Soeharto, We Tenriolle* (Jakarta: RahZenBook, 2008); Krienkrapetch, 'Women-Warriors', pp. 35–43.

112 'Warrior Women unearthed in Cambodia', www.southeastasianarchaeology.com/2007/11/15/warrior-women-unearthed-in-cambodia/. Accessed 15 November 2018; Jeannine Davis-Kimball with Mona Behan, *Warrior Women: An Archaeologist's Search for History's Hidden Heroines* (New York: Warner Books, 2002), pp. 55–61.

Index

Note: *Italic* page numbers refer to figures and page numbers followed by "n" denote endnotes.

Acehnese anti-Dutch resistance fighters 113; Acehnese language 115; Advisor for Native Affairs 118; anti-Dutch resistance 119, 120, 129; archival evidence 117; Dutch authority 114; female body guards 111; GAM 109, 128, 129, 134n67 (*see also* Gerakan Aceh Merdeka (GAM)); Groote Dames 120; Helsinki Peace Agreements 110, 128; Indonesian language Facebook 109; Indonesian national heroines 111–13; Indonesian War of Independence 118; MoU 128; post-conflict period 129; post-independence developments 119; socio-political elite 130; territorial aristocracy 110; *Teuntra Neugara Aceh* 110; *ulèëbalang* families 116

Acehnese heroines 12, 121

Aceh, Anti-Dutch resistance: Advisor for Native Affairs 118, 132n25

Aceh, post-independence relations with Jakarta: Abdurrahman Wahid 129

Acehnese women (including leaders and warriors) 11, 12, 15, 109, 117–21, 123, 129

Alejandrino, Casto 207–10, 219, 224n23; *see also* Valerio, Teofista

Amazon xix, 9, 24n4, 64, 65, 67–9, 72, *73*, 75, 76, 77, 78, 80, 82n20, 203, 270, 279

Andaya, Barbara Watson 3–7, 22, 65, 80

anti-colonialism/anti-colonial war/ anti-imperialism 11; anti-colonial liberation movement 5, 7, 176; anti-colonial revolutionary resistance movement 246; anti-colonial struggles 173; anti-Dutch rebellion 91; anti-Dutch resistance 119, 120, 129; anti-Dutch War(s) of Independence 12; anti-French resistance 138; anti-Jakarta resistance 13; and anti-imperialist movements 176; anti-Japanese army 203 (*see also* MPAJA); Rani Lakshmibai's exploits 160

anti-colonial armies and resistance: left-wing political movement 196 (*see also* communism); *see also* anti-colonialism

anti-British: Army of Liberation 161; *Azad Hind* (Free India) 161, 169n8; Bengali Volunteers 159, 167; Bengali women revolutionaries 159; Lakshmibai (Rani/Queen) 159–61

anti-Chinese: Trung sisters xiv, *xiv*, xvin6, 9, 14, 138, 268, 274; Ba (Lady) Trieu 14, 268; Le Chan 274; also in Lady Sinn paper; (also Chinese-dominated Communist movements)

anti-Dutch 13, 91, 113, 115, 119

anti-French: 273; anti-French resistance 26n23, 138, 200, 202

anti-Jakarta / Indonesian: 1950s; GAM; TNA; East Timor 233

anti-Japanese: anti-Japanese sentiment 176; *see also* Huk; MPAJA

anti-Japanese forces (Huk, CPM, MPAJA) 203

anti-Spanish: Bonifacio, Andrés 283 and Gregoria de Jesus 283; Katipunan 283; Silang, Gabriela 270, 273, 274, 275, 278

296 *Index*

armed conflict 19–21, 94, 229–34, 240 (*see also* anti-colonial armies)
Austroasiatic society 32
autonomy thesis 4

Baen 54, 55, 62n42
Bai Yue 26n30, 33, 35, 3
Bao Luong (Precious Honesty; Nguyen Trung Nguyet) 216, 217, 218; *see also*: rue Barbier murder
Bei shi (History of the Northern Dynasties) 32, 34, 35, 43, 46n12
Betong Peace Village 18, 179, 180, 183; (*see also* Malaya Communist Party)
Bhumibol, King 273
Bhupalan, Rasammah Naomi (née Navarednam) 168, 170n11
Blackburn, Susan 20, 244n23
The Blood of Suphan (Wathakan) 270
Bonifacio, Andrés 283
Bose, Subhas Chandra *16*, 16–17, 158–61; Army of Liberation 161; Bengali Volunteers (women's section of) 159, 167; boycott foreign cloths 159; Calcutta Congress (1928) 167; conception of regiment 159–61; Gandhian non-violence 158; Indian Congress (1938–1939) 158; Indian National Army 158, 161; Lakshmi Swaminadhan 158, 159, 165–7; in Malaya 159; Rani of Jhansi Regiment 159; speech 164; 'total mobilisation' 159
bourgeois tendencies (Vietnam) 217, 220
Brave warriors: embodying/engendering SSR 255–8; political ideals, rhetoric of 258–60; security sector reform 253–5; unfinished revolution, women as 'fragments' in 250–3
Brewer, Carolyn 277–8, 290n61; on the babaylan 278
British colonialism 161, 176, British Raj 158; *see also* colonialism)
Bui Trung Luong (female activist with NGTMK) 145

Calcutta Congress 1928 167
Camadevi (Queen) 276
Cambodia: article 13 230; case studies of 235–7; Cambodian Communist Party 240; Cambodian communist troops 230; collective consciousness 8; DDR arrangements 234–8; East Timor, armed conflict in 233–4; Royal Cambodian Armed Forces (RCAF) 235; women warriors, armed conflict in 230–2
Cambodia, cultural memory 49; Dhammayut Buddhism 57; Funan 48; goddess representation 48; Khmer Rouge regime 51; *khsae/omnaich* 48; querulous queens (*see* querulous queens); 'spirit of the fire-chamber' 50; *Srei Khmau* 50; Thai hegemony 57; visual representation 52
Cambodian court politics; Ang Duong (King) 53–4, 57, Ang Chan 54
Cambodian perspectives, female agency: *brai krala plerng* 50; *brai kramom* 50–1; Buddhism 51; Cambodian civil war 58; *Cbpab Srei* 58, 61n34; correct behaviour 59; cultural autonomy 57
Cambodian spirits: Bellicose behaviour 9; querulous 53; bellicose *brai see* querulous queens
Camp followers/Domestic Duties xix, 5, 276; cooking 23; Aceh: 123, 125; CPM, male 193, 194; East Timor: 250; 285; East Timor 250, 258; Huk: 203; Housekeepers, housekeeping, xix, 23, 203, 276; laundresses xix, 276; tailors, CPM 193, 194; washing, VN 203
Cangwu Commandery 36
Catholicism/Christianity 19; Abbé 75; Bishop 70; Catholic countryside (Philippines), Spanish missionaries 79; 221–2 (Catholic religion and virtues), Spanish priests, missionaries, religious leaders 278
Cbpab Srei 58, 61n34
CCP *see* Chinese Communist Party (CCP)
Charney, Michael W. 3
Children *see* family/intimate relations
China: Guomindang-Communist 139; non-Chinese communities 176; non-Chinese elements 31
China, *Sui shu* account 43; Chen dynasty 33; descendants 34; Sui dynasty 32
Chinese: cultural matrixes 32; electrical factory 141; national mythology 8; polities 31; state formation and expansion 8; women 177; pre-Chinese language 31
Chinese Communist Party (CCP)/ Communist Party of China (CPC) 136, 137, 141, 147, 221; Chen Duxiu (Leader of the CCP) 136

Index   297

Commanderies, Chinese: Cangwu 36; Gaoliang Commandery 34–5, 37–8; Nanhai 36; Yulin 36; Zhuguan 36
celestial beings *see* spirits
Clandestine movement 233, 250
Cochinchina Regional Committee 142, 151, 154n2; *see also* Vietnam
Cold War 175, 177, 186
colonialism: direct colonial power 10; *see also* imperialism
communism/Communist Parties and movements: communist-affiliated Gerwani (Movement of Indonesian Women) 280; community development projects 236; communist-led rebellion 203; Communist Party of China (CPC) 18, 181; Communist Party of Malaya (CPM/MCP) 176–7 (*see also* CPM-led movement; 'model comrade'; MPAJA; women guerrillas; Southwards Ambush Team; women guerrillas) Communist Party of the Philippines 200; communist revolutionary movement 147, 200
communist women: generation of 178; role of 175
compilers/chronicler (of travel accounts): Guyon, Abbé Claude Marie 75–6; Hakluyt, Richard 74; Samuel Purchas 66, 70, 74; Valentijn, François 76–7, 87 (*see also* travelers)
'conspiracy of silence' (Communist Party of Malaya) 175
conscription *see* recruitment
Convention on the Elimination of Discrimination against Women (CEDAW) 258, 259; *see also* United Nations; United Nations Convention on the Elimination of Discrimination against Women (1979)
court women: Acehnese politics and society 75; Buddhism 71; Dutch East India Company (1602) 72–3; Dutch traders 73, *73*; English East India Company (1600) 72; Hinduism 71; *India Orientalis* 74; indirect political influence 71; Java War 77; *Orientalische Reise* 76; role and status 72; court politics
CPC *see* Communist Party of China (CPC)
CPM-led movement 187
CPM/MCP (Communist Party of Malaya) *see under* communism

Cui Hong 17, 182–5, 187, 188, 194
Cut Nyak Dien 269, 272, 275, 280; *see also* Tjut Nyak Dhien
cultural autonomy 57

Damrong, Prince 268, 269, 270
Dang Thuy Tram, Dr 19, 20, 201, *201, 204–12, 209*, 211, 215, 216, 218, 219; killed by an American platoon 207; letters 205–6; political and personal struggles 206–7; as surgeon 206
Darul Islam 19, 121, 133n62, 134n66; Darul Islam rebellion 12, 26n33
Davies, John 74, 75
decolonisation 11, 23; *see also* anti-colonialism
deification: *see* Lady Sinn; Trung Sisters
de Jesus, Gregoria (Philippines) 283
Deng Yingchao 140
Dien Bien Phu 203; *see also* Vietnam
Disarmament, Demobilisation and Reintegration (DDR): description of 243n19; failed processes of 256; female ex-combatants 230; inadequate implementation of 229; international policy 238–41; women warriors 234–8
Disciplinary Measures and Professional Standards 258
Domestic Violence Law 248, 261; *see also* sexual violence
Dutch: antagonism 272; archival records 89; colonialism 176; expeditions 66, 67; traders 73, *73*
Dutch Colonialism: Dutch East India Company (1602) 72–3; *see also* VOC (Dutch East India Company)
Dutch East India Company (1602) 72–3; *see also* VOC (Dutch East India Company)

East Timor: article 13 230; 'betrayed' revolution in 246; case studies of 237–8; civil war, elements of 233; conflict in 233; DDR arrangements 234–8; Human Resources personnel 259; against Indonesian occupation 246; non-discrimination policies 247; *Operasaun Conjunta* 255; treat male ex-combatants 230; women warriors, armed conflict in 233–4
early Vietnam/under Chinese occupation: Trung Sisters xiv, *xiv*, xvin6, 9, 14, 138, 268, 274; Ba (Lady) Trieu 14, 268; Le Chan 274

298 *Index*

Edmondson, John 154n1
English colonialism 176
English East India Company (1600) 72;
  see also English Colonialism
Enloe, Cynthia (*The Curious
  Feminist*) 250
ethnic Chinese 176
executions: Bui Thi Xuan 268; Gabriela
  Silang 270, 274; Nguyen Thi Minh
  Khai 144, 150, 151

Falintil-FDTL (Forcas Defesas de Timor
  Leste or the military) 246, 250, 251,
  253–7, 260; ex-Falintil guerrillas 250
Family Welfare Guidance
  (Indonesia) 121
Far Eastern Bureau (Vietnam) 146
family/intimate relations 120, 220
Fatimah, Aceh (women in men's
  clothing) 117; Rani Lakshmibai 160);
  (Dr Dang Thuy Tram) 205
female combat roles, Aceh: 12, 13, 112,
  129; Tjut Nyak Dhien, 114; Potjut
  Meurah Intan, 114; female combat
  roles (and commanders): capturing/
  guarding enemy (VN) 273; combat
  (throwing lances, stones, mud) 276;
  foot soldiers and sharp shooter (CPM,
  Cui Hong) 180, *184*, 194
female combat role, theft: stealing rifles,
  VN 138; Miss Bunluang 282
female commander, being killed in
  action: Dahomey 85n80; Tjut Meutia
  113; Teungku Tjutpo 113, 117
female commander, being wounded
  in action: 115 (Potjut Meurah /
  Aceh); 257, 258, 259 (Timor Leste);
  Being wounded through enemy
  contact (e.g. torture, etc): 210
  (Teofista Valerio); 233 (East Timor);
  234 (Maria Domingas de Santos
  and her husband); 273 (Nguyen
  Thi Chien)
female commander, killed through
  enemy contact, execution,
  assassination, torture: Nguyen
  Thi Minh Khai 153, 273; Princess
  Baen 62n42
female combat roles, being captured /
  arrested: Vietnam: (Nguyen Thi
  Thanh, aka Bach Lien) 138 (Nguyen
  Thi Minh Khai) 15, 146, 150, 152;
  (Nguyen Tri Duc) 14, 141, 157n57;
  (Bui Thi Xuan) 268

female combat roles, Potjut Baren, 123;
  Tjut Nur Asyikin–GAM, 123
female combat roles, Timor Leste:
  234 (Maria Domingas de Santos),
  250, 251
female combat roles, Huk: 210 (Teofista
  Valerio), 274
female combat roles, Cambodia: Neang
  Teav 50; mahakshatri 56
female combat roles, surrendering: 48
  (Liu Ye); *209, 211* (Leonora Hipas and
  Emilio Diesta); 250 (East Timor)
female guerrillas: ex-Falintil guerrillas
  250; female ex-combatants 230–1,
  234, 236; female grassroots guerrillas
  175; female violence 9 (*see also* sexual
  violence); female warriors (*see* women
  warriors)
female heroines 111–13, 272–4; *see also*
  heroines
female leadership: Female
  revolutionaries: struggling, personal
  desires 219; Vietnamese 200
feminism: feminist theory 79, 174; global
  feminism, growth of 239; Western
  feminism 137
Filipina revolutionaries 203 (*see also*
  women warriors)
Filipino Communists 221; (*see also* PKP
  or Philippine Communist Party)
Filipino heroes and heroines 272
First Indian War of Independence 160
First Indochina War 203
FitzGerald, Frances 207, *211*, 223n11,
  223n13
forest wife 213; (*see also* sexual relations)
French Indochina: Annam 11, 138, 144,
  154n2, 202; Cochinchina 11, 142, 143,
  151, 154n2, 202; Tonkin 11; *see also*
  Vietnam
French militarism 14
French Revolution 9
frontline, ambush team 17; infiltrating
  another country: 185 (CPM); killing
  and killers 280, 284, 300; women
  fighting (Aceh) 117, 118
Funan 8, 38, 48

GAM *see* Gerakan Aceh
  Merdeka (GAM)
Gandhian non-violence 158 (*see also*
  India)
geishas *see prajurit estri,*
  Mangkunegara I

Index 299

gender: based stereotypes and discrimination 196; differences 6, 190, 284; equality 3; relationships 280–4

gender policies, Vietnamese Communist Party 220; Huk movement 212

Gerakan Aceh Merdeka (GAM) 12; anti-personnel mines 121–2; *ceramah* 125, 126; *Darul Islam* 121; Family Welfare Guidance 121; guru penerangan 125; immortalisation 121; Indonesian governmental programmes 120; information teacher 125; *inong balèë* 122–3 (*see also inong balèë*); international media 122; military training 124–5; motivation and roles 123–4; *Reformasi* (reform) period 121; politics and society 75; West Coast 78, 112

Goldstein, Joshua 5, 6, 24

Grant De Pauw, Linda 5

Greeve, Jan 96–101

Grice, Helena 175

Guangdong cultures 45

guerrillas 177, 213, 215; male 212, 213, 218, 219; sexual relationships between 213; women 200, 212, 219; *see also* female guerrillas; women warriors

Guo Ren Luan aka Lin Mei 17, 18

Guterres Lu Olo, Francisco (East Timor) 253

Habibie, B. J. 124, 233, 248

Ha Huy Tap 143, 149, 150, 151

Hainan connection 41–2

Hamengkubuwono I 279

Helsinki Peace Agreement 110, 122, 126, 127, 128; *see also* Aceh)

heroines (national), Indonesia: Herlina 284; Tjut Nyak Dhien 111; Tjut Meutia 113; *see also* Acehnese heroines

heroines (national), Philippines: Princess Urduja 270; Ilocandia's Joan of Arc (Zaide) 271; Silang, Gabriela 270, 273, 274, 275; Gregoria de Jesus 283

heroines (national), Siam/Thailand: Lady Mo / Thao Suranari (Dame Gallant Lady) 269; Ladies of Thalang, Thao Thepkasattri and Thao Srisunthorn (Phuket) 268, 269, 283; Queen Suriyothai 268, 269, 273, 275, 283; *see also* Miss Bunluan 281

heroines (national), Vietnam: Bui Thi Xuan 26n23, 268, 274 (*see also*

sculpture/statue/monuments/museum); Dang Thuy Tram 19, 20, 201; Lady Trieu 14, 268, 272, 274, 283; Mac Thi Buoi 273–4; Nguyen Thi Chien 273; Nguyen Thi Minh Khai 144, 150, 151; Trung Sisters xiv, xvi, 9, 14, 45, 268, 274, 280, 281; *see also* Le Chan; Nguyen Tri Duc; Tran Dai Do

He Xiangning 140

Ho Chi Minh 136, 138, 139, 143, 146, 152, 154n8, 202, 203, 205, 214, 215, 216, 217 (Also Nguyen Ai Quoc)

Homo Floresiensis 78

Hue-Tam Ho Tai 136, 142

Huk Rebellion/Huk revolutionary movement 5; guerrilla movement 19; *Hukbalahap* (*Hukbo ng Bayan Laban sa Hapon* or Anti-Japanese Army) 202; *Hukbong Mapagpalaya ng Bayan* (HMB or People's Liberation Army) 202; rebellion, background of 202–4; revolutionary struggles 200; sex and passion 212–19; sexual relationships 200; women warriors 204; *see also* sexual relations

imperialism, American: 11 (also Spanish-American War), 20, American army 181, 223n10; 203; *see also* anti-colonialism; colonialism

imperialism, British: 10 (expedition); 11, 15 (British India), 67, 69, 72 (English East India Company), 75, 77, 146, 158, 160, 161, 164, 173, 176, 177, 178, 180, 181, 278, 279

imperialism, Chinese: (Lady Sinn, commanderies, Bai Yue, etc, Vietnam) 272; Chen dynasty 33, 40; Hundien (Funan) 48; Sui dynasty 32; *Sui shu* 43; Wang Sengru 38; Wan Zhen 35; *see also* Lady Sinn and Vietnamese anti-colonialism

imperialism, Chinese commanderies: Cangwu 36; Feng Ang 35, 37, 42; Feng Bao 33, 35, 37, 39; Gaoliang Commandery 34–5, 37–8; Nanhai 36; Yulin 36; Zhuguan 36

imperialism, Dutch: 10, 11, 12, 64, 67; East Timor xxi, xxvi, 72–3, 76, 91–6, 99–103, 131n15, 248, 278; *see also* Dutch East India Company (1602)

imperialism, French: 11, 14, 15, 57, 58, 85n80, 136–57, 202, 203, 215, 272, 273; (*see also* French Indochina)

300   Index

imperialism, Japanese: French
Indochina 202; Southeast Asia 4,
11, 176; Singapore 164, *166*, 169n4,
171n38; anti-Japanese sentiment 176;
Japanese occupation 181, 202; *see also*
Anti-Japanese forces (Huk, CPM,
MPAJA)
imperialism, Indonesian (East Timor)
248; transmigration 126, 135n85
imperialism, Portuguese (East Timor):
10, 11, 54, 70, 73, 77, 233, 248, 272
imperialism, Spanish: 10, 11, 79;
missionaries, 271, 278
independence: independent Malaya 177;
independence, national movement for
176; *see also* anti-colonialism
India:'Colonel Latika' 159; Indian
Congress (1938–1939) 158, 159;
Indian Independence League (IIL)
16, 158, 160, 161, 162, 164; Indian
independence struggle 160; Indian
Legion 158; Indian migrants in
Singapore 161; Indian Mutiny 4,
160; Indian National Army (INA)
15, 158–61, 163, 169n4; Indian
nationalism 158; Indian Rebellion
160; Mohan Singh 169n4; non-
communal India 168; Rash Behari
Bose 161; Second War of Indian
Independence 160
Indian National Army (INA) 15,
158–61, 163, 169n4
Indochinese Communist Party (ICP)
14, 137, 144, 149, 151–3, 202,
203, 214, 216; Associations for
Women's Liberation 137; *see also*
communism
Indonesia: pre-modern Javanese
diaries 88; pro-Indonesian militias
236; *Reformasi* (reform) period 121;
Tentara Nasional Indonesia (TNI)
123; Yogyakarta 87, 91, 97, 99
Indonesia, early modern: Dutch
expeditions 66, 67; Mataram
10, 76, 95
Indonesia, *inong balèè* 130n3; anti-GAM
militias 126; *ceramah* 126; Helsinki
Peace Agreement 126; jungle-based
roles 127; *Malahayati Darah Juang*
128; moral and physical protection
127; *wilayah* 126
Indonesia, post-independence: armed
forces 4; governmental programmes
120; 'Black October' massacre 180,
192; Ahmed Sukarno 111, 284;

Abdurrahman Wahid 129; Megawati
Sukarnoputri 126; Bacharuddin Jusuf
Habibie 124, 233, 248; *also see*: Aceh;
East Timor
Indonesia, Under Dutch rule *see* Dutch
Colonialism
Indonesia, War for independence:
Indonesian National Revolution
(1945–1950) 283; Indonesian War of
Independence 12, 118
Internally Displaced Persons (IDP)
250, 253
'internationalism' 177, 178
International Labour Organisation
244n26
inter-state diplomacy 4
intimate (sexual) relations: *kualingking*
cases 212, 214, 217, 224n26, 224n27;
fictive marriages 214, 215; *see also*
sexual relations

Janaki Davar 159, 164, 165, *166*,
167, 168
Javanese literature 89
Java War 77
Jayawardena, Kumari 173–4
Jones, David E. 5, 285

Kartini, Raden 272; *see also* female
heroines
Khoo, Agnes 17, 18
Khmer Rouge: regime 51, 230–1, 284;
leaders: Pol Pot 230, 231, 235, 236;
Heng Samrin 230–1; Ieng Sary 235;
Lon Nol 230, 236
killing 38, 180, 202, 248, 280
Kinship: Bao Luong (Nguyen Trung
Nguyet) and Hue-Tam Ho Tai
155n16; Bhupalan, Rasammah Naomi
(née Navarednam) 168, 170n11; as
conceptual category 111, 132n26;
Feng Ang (grandson) 35, 37, 42;
Janaki and Papathi Davar, father
is 168; Lady Sinn and Feng Bao
(husband) 33, 35, 37, 39; Trung Sisters
xiv, xvi n6, 268, 274, 280, 281
Kollontai, Alexandra 140
kualingking cases 212, 214, 217, 224n26,
224n27; *see also* Huk Rebellion/
Huk revolutionary movement; sexual
relations)

Lady Sinn 7–8, *32*; birth and death
dates 34; Chinese states 39–40;
cultural blending 37; deification of

Index 301

40–1; Gaoliang Commandery 34–5; Guangdong cultures 45; Hainan connection 41–2; historical process 34; Lingnan, socio-economic conditions 37–9, 44–5; rediscovery 42–3; Sinn clan 35–7; *Sui shu* account (*see* China, *Sui shu* account)

Lakshmibai (Rani/Queen) 159–61; *see also* Rani of Jhansi Regiment

Lakshmi Swaminadhan, Dr 158, 159, 165–7 (*see also* RJR; INA); 2nd husband (Lakshminadhan) 160

Lanzona, Vina A. 19, 20

Lam Duc Thu 139, 141, 146

Laskar Puteri Indonesia (LPI, Indonesian Women's Guerrilla Forces) 281; *see also* Indonesia; monuments

Last Night I Dreamed of Peace (diary of Dang Thuy Tram) 205, 223n9

Latin American revolutionary movements 192

League of Oppressed Peoples 139

Lebra, Joyce 3

Le Chan 281

Ledgerwood, Judy 53

Left-wing politics 196; *see also* Anti-colonialism and Communism

Lee Kuan Yew 180, 181

Lenin xx, *145*, 149, 205

Liao Zhongkai 140

liberation movements: liberation of India 159, 163; liberation of nation-states 177; *see also* anti-colonial armies and resistance

Lin Dong 17, 18, 174, 178, 179, 181–2, *182*, 185, 186, 187, 188; gender equality; physical differences

Lingnan, socio-economic conditions 37–9, 44–5

Lin Mei (Guo Ren Luan) 18, *18,* 180–1, 186–8, 191

Liu Ye 48

logistics, logistical support: Aceh 12; 23, 120, 124, 126, 127; Cambodia and East Timor 58, 229; East Timor 233; feeding, VN 138; Iban headhunters xiii; Khmer Rouge 242n7; moral support, Aceh 120; Porters: xix, 23, 276; purveyors of supplies, CPM 193; spiritual support, Bugis 276, 277; spiritual support, Java 278

Mahabharata xxii, 268; warrior wife Srikandi (of Arjuna) 268, 269, 281

Malaya: Malayan Emergency 17; Malayan People's Anti-Japanese Army (MPAJA) 177; *see also* Colonialism, Anti-colonialism and Communism

Mana Bilesa (Timor Leste) *249*

Mana Bisoy (Timor Leste) 21, 250, 251

Maoist-style rectification campaign 18, 183

Maria Domingas de Santos (Timor Leste) 233, 238

Marr, David 136, 137

marriage 217; arranged marriages 216; fictive marriages 215, 217, 220; forced marriage 218; real marriage 217; sexual relations outside of 218; fictive marriages 214, 215; *see also* sexual relations

Marx, Karl *145*

Marxism 153, 203

masculinity 4, 268; male military commanders 247; male guerrillas 212, 213, 218, 219

May 30th strike movement 140

Megawati Sukarnoputri 126,

mental health: paranoia (CPM) 184, paranoia (Timor Leste) 257; insane (Timor Leste) 259; emotional healing (Timor Leste) 257, 258, 259

military-civil society 3

military/ideological training 124–5 (Aceh), 164 (RJR), 190 (Central America)

Minh Mai 53, 57, 61n34

Miss Bunluan 281

mobilization/motivation 278, 279; Dr. Lakshmi, 162; mobiliser/mobilisers/ mobilizing, Aceh xiii, 23; 124, 125; NTMK 144, 150, 151; 'total mobilisation' (INA/RJR) 159; *see also* revolutionary movements

model comrade 190

Molotov-Ribbentrop Pact 151

MPAJA *see* Malayan People's Anti-Japanese Army (MPAJA)

multi-culturalism 176, 177

monuments (Representations of female warriors): Gabriela Silang Monument 273; *see also* sites of memory, sculptures

museums: Gaozhou Municipal Museum 35; Phuket's National Museum 273; Satriamandala Armed Forces Museum 283, National Museum of Resistance in Dili 253

302 *Index*

National Commission on Planning
(Timor Leste) 246
nationalism, definitions of 173;
national histories of Malaysia
and Singapore 175; Third World
nationalist movements 173–4; *see also*
anti-colonialism
neo-colonialism 173; *see also* colonialism
and anti-colonialism
New Culture Movement 136
New People's Army (Philippines) 5
Nguyen Tri Duc 214, 216
non-Aligned Movement 177, 186
Nora, Pierre 281; *see also* sites of
memory
North Vietnamese society 204; *see also*
Vietnam
non-governmental Organizations
(NGOs): Amnesty International
247; International Committee of
the Red Cross 122; Organisation of
Timorese Women (OMT, Organizacao
da Mulher Timorense) 233, 238;
Oxfam Australia 231, 236; Red Aid
International 146

Oral history/interviews: voices of
revolutionaries 174–5; voices
of women 247; *see also* Khoo;
Blackburn; Siapno; Lanzona
Orientalische Reise 76

Pakubuwana III 96
palace guards: Aceh 23, 88;
archaeological and archival record 7;
armed guardswoman/women 66, 76,
77, 79, 279, 283; as battlefield troops
(Yogyakarta, Java) 91; bodyguards: 4,
10, 64, 66; European representations
9–10; geo-cultural contours 7–9; 23;
74; geo-cultural contours, Aceh 88;
geo-cultural contours, Dahomey 78;
guardswomen (Siam) 77, 279; Java 10;
palace guards as dragoons 91; sentries,
CPM 194; Yogyakarta 91
pan-Asian and pan-African
movements 186
Partido Komunista ng Pilipinas (PKP or
Communist Party of the Philippines)
202, 203; *see also* Communism
patriarchy 136, 138, 153, 220, 285
Peace Agreements: Paris Peace
Agreements of October 1991 230,
235; Paris Peace Conference 1919 138;

Tripartite Peace Agreement December
1989 (Malaysia and Thailand) 18, 122,
178–9, 183; UN peacekeeping 250; *see
also* Helsinki Peace Agreement
Pearl River Delta 35
People's Republic of China in 1977
179, 180
Phan Boi Chau 136, 215, 268, 269
Philippines: Filipino Communists 221;
Filipina revolutionaries 203 (*see
also* women warriors); Philippine
Communist Party/*Partido Komunista
ng Pilipinas* (PKP) xxiii, 202, 203, 207,
210; Philippine Military Academy 4;
Philippine Revolution 5; *see also* Huk
rebellion/movement
Pires, Milena (East Timor) 246, 259
PKI (Indonesian Communist Party) 180;
see also Indonesia; Communism
PNTL (Policia Nacional de Timor Leste)
246, 250, 254, 255, 258, 260
Political Bureau (Politburo) 213;
Politburo (CPM) 181; Political Bureau
(Politburo) of the PKP 207, 210, 212
politics: political involvement 178;
political leadership 4–5; political
loyalties 8; political warfare 5; *see also
individual countries*
Popular Front government 150
Portuguese colonial rulers 233; *see also*
colonialism
post-conflict politics and society: post-
conflict arrangements 235; post-
conflict East Timor 21; post-conflict
situations 229; post-conflict societies
3, 20, 23; post-independence armed
forces 3; post-war decision-making 22;
post-war reconstruction 178; socio-
economic rehabilitation 234; solid
parallel programs 239
Potjut Baren 113, 114
Potjut Meuligo 113, 115–16
Potjut Meurah Intan 113, 115
prajurit estri, Mangkunegara I: anti-
Dutch rebellion 91; Chinese war
91; Contract of Reconciliation 98;
diary passage 89–91; Dutch archival
records 89; *gajihing (wulan) Siyam*
93; Javanese literature 89; *kraton*
accounts 93; Mangkubumi 92; middle-
eastern Muslim traders 98; military
conflict 94–6; Pakubuwana III 96;
political developments 103; pre-
modern Javanese diaries 88; Surakarta

Resident 101; VOC resources 100;
Yogyakarta 87, 91, 97, 99
pregnancy 141; 148; 152; *see* intimate,
sexual relations
Preah Neang Dharani 51, *52,* 56
"The Progress of Feminine Youth" 148
proto-communist revolutionary
movement 137, 200; *see also*
communism
Purchas, Samuel 66, 70

querulous queens: agency 53; *Cbpab
Preah Rajasambhir* 53; *Cbpab Srei*
53; Code of conduct for women
53; condemnation and punishment
model 54; elite-authored texts 54;
mahakshatri 56; 'natural' timidity
52–3; Ramadhipati I 55

Rabotnitsa (Soviet paper) 136
Raffles, Stamford 72, 80
Raleigh, Walter (Sir) 67
Rama I 268
Ramusio, Giovanni Battista 70
Rangoon 17, 158, 169n8
Rani of Jhansi Regiment (RJR)
282; Lakshmi harvests volunteers
165–7; multiplying 163–5; nucleus
of regiment 161–3; suitable role
model 159–61; Mrs Satyavati Thevar
165, *166*; Recruits: Mrs Blanche
Thevar 166; Mrs Das 166; *see
also* Bose, Subhas Chandra; Rani
Lakshmibai
recruitment 12, 16, 123; *see also*
conscription
Rapid Intervention Unit/UIR (East
Timor) 255
Rebellion, Permesta 280
Rectification Campaign 185; *see also*
Communism
Rehabilitation *see* post-conflict politics
and society
Regio Femarum: court women (*see*
court women); Dutch expeditions
66, 67; 'ethnography of difference'
65; European publications 70–1;
European reports 64; eyewitness
reports 78; feminist theory 79; *Homo
Floresiensis* 78; medieval warrior
queens 67–9; region-wide economic
change 66; 'scientific' knowledge 65;
temporary marriages 66
Reid, Anthony 4, 24, 64

religion: Abbé 75; anitera (shaman, spirit
medium) 278; Bishop 70; *bismillah*
xxiii, 132; Buddhism xxi, 51, 57; Bugis:
bissu (transgender spirit practitioners)
277; Catholicism/Christianity (*see*
Catholicism/Christianity); Chiang
Mai, supernatural assistance 277;
Confucianism: 136 (hierarchy), 138
(society), 220 (values); conversion to
Islam 55; Darul Islam rebellion 12,
26n33, 119, 121, 133n62, 134n66;
dayah 117; Dhammayut Buddhism 57,
61n31, 71; grandmother figures 278;
hajiah xxi; hajj 117; *Hikayat Iskandar*
(Alexander Romance) 68; hinduisation
121; Hinduism 71; Hindu-Javanese
104n12; Hindu-Javanese 104n12;
Islam/Muslim *kaphé*: xxi, 115, 116,
118, 132n38; Islamic-Javanese martial
arts 104n12; Java, religious authority
278; Javanese-Islamic calendar
104n10, 104n11; *jilbab* (Islamic
headscarf in Indonesia) 109; *mahram*
xxii, 127, 124; Menak Epic 89, 92,
99; Muslim cause 279; Philippines,
babaylan (female 'priestesses') 278;
praying 121; pre-Islamic 11, 55, 168;
pre-Islamic 78, 79; Quranic readings;
sharia law 129; *Seuramoe Mekkah*
xxiv, 109; Srikandi (Mahabharata)
xxii, 79, 121, 129, 268, 269, 284; *ulama*
(Islamic religious scholars) 117
Republic of South Vietnam ('South
Vietnam'): Ngo Dinh Diem xvin6;
Madam Nhu *xiv*, xvin6; Trung Sisters
Monument xiv
revolutionaries: Acehnese women 11,
12; Annam 11; anti-colonialism 11;
anti-Dutch War(s) of Independence
12; anti-Jakarta resistance 13;
careers 14; Cochinchina 11; CPC 18;
Darul Islam rebellion 12; dynamic
historical process 22; elite-driven
attempts 22; female combatants 20–1;
French militarism 14; GAM 12;
ICP 14; IIL 16; INA 15; Indonesian
War of Independence 12; Maoist-
style rectification campaign 18; in
Philippines and Vietnam 19–20;
post-conflict East Timor 21; post-
conflict societies 20, 23; post-war
decision-making 22; proto-communist
and communist movements 13;
Rani of Jhansi Regiment project 17;

304 *Index*

semi-colonial independence 11; social integration 21; Tonkin 11; Tripartite Peace Agreement of December 1989 18; Western powers 10–1; revolutionary women 178–80; *see also* female/women warriors

revolutionary movements 200, 201, 204, 215, 221–2, 258; Revolutionary Party 144; *see also individual countries*

revolutionary women: Vietnamese 204; heroines 272; and Huk rebellion 202–4; proto-communist movement 136; sex, relationships, or families 215; women, role of 223n6; women warriors 201; *see also* revolutionaries

revolutionary polygamy 219; *see also* Huk movement

The Revolutionary Solution of the Sex Problem 212, 213; *see also* Huk Rebellion/Huk revolutionary movement; Intimate relations

rights of working people 137

Rosenberg, Matthew 292n109

Rue Barbier murder 142

Sahgal, Lakshmi 159, 168n2, 169n10; *see also* India

sakti (supernatural power) 280; *see also* spirits

Satri Niphon (Women's Writing) 269

Satyavati Thevar *166*

School of Democratic Economics (SDE) (East Timor) 254

Scott, James 248, 262n3; 'manpower state' 248

sculptures *32, 201*; Paul Van Thê; 287n15; Corrado Feroci aka Silpa Bhirasri 287n15; *see also* monuments

Security Council: monitoring mechanism 239; Security Council Resolution 1325 on women 239

security sector reform (SSR) 246, 250, 262n2; aspirations and visions 247; disarmament, demobilisation and reintegration 262; embodying/engendering 253–8; gendered perspectives 246, 262n2; police reform process 257; security forces in Timor Leste 256

Sehgal, Lakshmi *16*, 16–17

sex and sexuality: attempted rape 142, 218, 233, 282; Le Duy Diem 141; Le Van Phat 142; Nguyen Huu Can 142;

Nguyen Van Son 142; Nguyen Van Tram 142; rape 142, 218, 233, 282; Rue Barbier murder 142, 155; sex slaves 233; sexual licence 138, 141; sexual misconduct (alleged or real) and womanizing, 141, 142, 258; sexual relations (*see* intimate relations); sexual services 283

Shan troops 279

Siam: Nophamat, Lady (Ideal of a Siamese Lady) 269; *see also* Thailand

Siapno, Jacqueline 20, 21

Sihanouk, Norodom 230, 231; *see also* Cambodia

Silang, Gabriela (Philippines) 270, 273, 274, 275

Sinn, Lady 35–7, 277

'sites of memory' *(lieux de mémoire)* 267, 273, 281, 286n1; shrine (Miss Bunluang 281, 282; temple, Bui Thi 274; temple and statue, Le Chan, 274; tomb, Mac Thi Buoi 274; statue, Thao Suranari 270, *271,* 275; *see also* monuments

Sixth Congress 1928 137

'socialisation of women' 138

Southeast Asian (un-)exceptionalism 23–4

Southwards Ambush Team 185

Spear, Joanna 244n32

spirits/ghosts/celestial beings, Cambodia: *apsara* (celestial) xix, 8, 49; *araks brai* (wild spirits) 49; *brai krala plerng* ('spirit of the fire-chamber') 50; *brai kramom* (unmarried female spirit) 50–1; human-created spirits / black magic 50; human sacrifice 51; Lady Mau 49; and life cycles of women 50; *me sa* (white lady) 49; *neak ta* (ancestor spirits) 49; *srei khmau* (black lady) 49, 50; *see also* Cambodian spirits

statue 8, 51, 267, 270, 273, 274

strategies of women security forces: assimilation 255; hostility 255–6; separation 255; *see also* post-conflict politics and society

Sukarno 120–1, 180, 186, 284; *see also* Indonesia

Sun Kui 39

Tai, Hue-Tam Ho 217

Taylor, Philip 290n84

Taylor, Sandra 216

Tegalraja, Ratu Ageng (Indonesia) 278

Teungku Fakinah 113

Index 305

Teungku Tjutpo Fatimah 113, 117
Teuntra Neugara Aceh 110
Thailand: *The Legend of Suriyothai*
(movie) 275; Nophamat, Lady (Ideal
of a Siamese Lady) 269; Quang Thai
152; Suranari, Thao (Dame Gallant
Lady) 269, 270, *271*; Suriyothai,
Queen 268, 269, 283; *Thai Fought
Burma* (*Thai Rop Phama;* Damrong,
Prince) 269; Thai hegemony 57; *see
also* Siam
Third World liberation 178
Third World nationalist movements
173–4; *see also* nationalism
Thompson, Ashley 49
Tran Dai Do 214, 215
Tran Ngoc Danh 147
Tran Phu 144, 147
Transnational revolutionary careers:
Nguyen Tri Duc 13, 14, 136–44, 153,
214, 215; Nguyen Thi Minh Khai 13,
14, *15*, 136, 137, 143–53, 214–16, 273;
see also Revolutionaries
travelers 64
Timor Leste: civilian-military-police
relations 246, 247; CNRT (Conselho
Nacional da Resistencia Timorense)
party 262–3n3; National Commission
on Planning 246; *see also* East Timor
Tjut Meutia 12, 113–14, 120
Tjut Nyak Dhien 12, *13,* 109, *110,*
111–14, 120, 134n65, 289n49; *see also*
Cut Nyak Dhien
Tonkin 11; *see also* Vietnam
torture: Aceh 123; East Timor 233;
French Indochina 143; Maria
Domingas de Santos, 234; Nguyen
Thi Chien 273; Princess Baen 61n42;
Teofista Valerio 210; torture chambers
281; *see also* Tran Ngoc Danh;
Tran Phu
'traditionally feminine' activities 193–4
transmigration (Indonesia), Dutch
origins 126, 135n85
travellers, observers, and authors/
chroniclers (European and Arab):
Andersen, Jürgen 76, 84n66; Nicolo
Conti 69; Barbosa, Duarte 72, 78,
83n48; Beaulieu, Augustin de 75,
84n61, 88; Cavendish, Thomas
72; Crawfurd, John 278; Dampier,
William 278; Pigafetta, Antonio 69,
78; Prester John 68; Pires, Tomé 69,
72, 79; Peter Mundy 76, 88; Lancaster,
James 80; Ibn Battuta 68, 270; Marco

Polo 69; Marsden, William 69;
Beinecke manuscript 83n36; *see also*
Compilers/Chroniclers

United Nations (UN) 230; United
Nations Security Council 229,
244n27; United Nations Transitional
Authority in Cambodia (UNTAC)
230, 235; UN Peacekeeping forces 250;
UN Resolution 1325 229, 238; UN
Transitional Administration in East
Timor (UNTAET) 233
United Nations Convention on the
Elimination of Discrimination against
Women (1979) 258, 259
unsung heroines 270; *see also* women
warriors

Valerio, Teofista 201, 207, 208, 209, 211,
212; arrested 210; interview 224n20;
letters 208; struggles of 223n9; *see also*
Casto Alejandrino
VCP *see* Vietnamese Communist
Party (VCP)
Vichy-aligned French administration
202; *see also* Vietnam, French
Indochina
Viet Minh 202, 203
Vietnam 4–6; Bui Thi Xuan, Tay Son
268, 274; Democratic Republic of
Vietnam ('North Vietnam'): 5, 18,
156n36, 202; Nguyen forces 268; post-
unification Vietnam: 273; Tay Son
regime 268; Third Indochina War 230;
Vietnamese Communist Party (VCP)
136, 146, 202; Vietnamese movement
213; Vietnamese Nationalist Party
145; Vietnamese Overseas Bureau
143; Vietnamese Revolutionary Youth
League 203, 214, 218; Vietnam War
204, 218
Vietnam, French Indochina: Annam 11,
138, 144, 154n2, 202; Cochinchina
11, 142, 143, 151, 154n2, 202; Popular
Front in France 150; Tonkin 11;
Vichy-aligned administration and
Japanese occupation 202
Vietnam, early resistance against the
French: Phan Dinh Phung 139,
155n19; Phan Boi Chau 136; Nguyen
Thi Ba 26n23; Vietnamese émigré
community in southern China (137)
and Siam (139); Nguyen Thi Thanh
aka Bach Lien (White Lotus) 138,
155n15

306   *Index*

Vietnam, First Indochina War ('French War'): 202; Dien Bien Phu 202; Nguyen Thi Chien 273, Mac Thi Buoi 273, 274

Vietnam, National Liberation Front 202, 205 Revolutionary Youth League, Minh, Ho Chi 217

Vietnam, Second Indochina War ('American War'): Cambodia 203, 218–19, 230; Dang Thuy Tram: 204–7; 213–14; Lin Dong, CPM 18, 24, 179, 181

Vietnamese communist movement 216; in 1925 139; Nguyen Thi Minh Khai 143–53; Nguyen Tri Duc 139–42; radicalism 136; rejecting tradition 138; rights of working people 137; in 1920s 137, 138; woman trap 142–3

Vietnamese female revolutionaries 204; heroines 272; *see also* revolutionaries

VOC (Dutch East India Company) 72–3; Dutch traders 73; van Goens, Rijklof 10, 76, 87; van Neck, Jacob Corneliszoon 66; van Noort, Olivier 70–2; van Warwijk, Wybrandt (Warwick) 73, 74, 88; *see also* Dutch colonialism

voices of revolutionaries 174–5; voices of women 247; *see also* oral history)

Vo Nguyen Giap 152

weapons, non-fire: *bolo* 273; dagger 77; *grasmes* (grass-cutting knife) (Dutch) 118; *kelewang* (knife) 118; kris 72, 77, 89; lance 88; pike 87; *rencong* (Acehnese dagger / knife) 12, 27n35, 112, 119, 132n22; sabre 77; sword *xiv*, *32*, 50, 69, 71, 72, *73*, 73, 74, 88, 160, 269, 273, 277, 283, 286; shield 70, 88, 160; *tinangke* (small dagger) 283

weapons, fire: arquebus *73*, 74; artillery 91; assault rifle 125; assault rifle, (AK-47, M16), *249*; cannon 277; firearms 77; grenade, Aceh 125; hand weapon 91; handgun: 125; musket 77; revolver *209*; rifle 64, 74, 138, 161, 162, 182, 283

weapons to be projected: blow pipe 73, 76, 87, 88, 276; venomed darts 70; bow 9, 48, 67, 70, 71, 73, 74, 76, 78, 83n36, 88, 89; arrow 48, 67, 70, 76, 78, 83n36, 88, 89; javelin 70

Western European powers 248; *see also* colonialism

women: of CPM and guerrillas 177–8; ex-combatants 236, 238, 239, 241; health issues 258–9; liberation movement in China 176; oppression 196; question 190–2; societies 159; *Women and Labour* (journal) 136; working-class women 137; *see also* female warriors

women guerrillas: Communist Party of Malaya 176–7; Cui Hong 182–5; gendered experiences 192–5; internationalist revolutionaries voices 174–5; Lin Dong 181–2; Lin Mei 180–1; nationalism and nationalist struggles 173–4; party hierarchy and women's choices 195–6; personal choice and women's agency 185–90; revolutionary women 178–80; women of CPM and guerrillas 177–8; women's question 190–2

women's roles in combat: Cambodia, armed conflict in 230–2; East Timor, armed conflict in 233–4

women warriors 200, 201, 203, 204, 213, 267; Cambodia, armed conflict in 230–2; DDR arrangements 234–8; in early twentieth century 267–9; East Timor, armed conflict in 233–4, 246; guerrilla wars 229; international policy 238–41; as national heroines 272–4; nationalism and 269–72; in the 1930s 269–72; supernatural influences 277–80; women combatants 234–8

women as propaganda workers: Cambodia 231, 242n7; Huk / VN 203, 204

women leaders: Trung Sisters *xiv*, xiv, 9, 14, 138, 268, 280; Liu Ye 48 (Funan); Lady Trieu 14, 268, 272, 274, 283; Lady Sinn 7, 8, 9; Military commander: Bui Thi Xuan 274, 268; Thao Suranari (Lady Mo) 269, *271*; Miss Bunluang 281, 282; Gabriela Silang 270 (Philippines)

World War I 269

World War II 173, 176, 177, 202, 207, 276

Zheng He 41

Zhou Enlai 140

Printed in the United States
by Baker & Taylor Publisher Services